The Rise of the Israeli Right

The Israeli Right first came to power nearly four decades ago. Its election was described then as 'an earthquake', and its reverberations are still with us. How then did the Right rise to power? What are its origins? Colin Shindler traces this development from the birth of Zionism in cosmopolitan Odessa in the nineteenth century to today's Hebron, a centre of radical Jewish nationalism. He looks at central figures such as Vladimir Jabotinsky, an intellectual and founder of the Revisionist movement, and Menahem Begin, the single-minded politician who brought the Right to power in 1977. Both accessible and comprehensive, this book explains the political ideas and philosophies that were the Right's ideological bedrock, as well as the compromises that were made on its journey to government.

Colin Shindler is Emeritus Professor at the University of London's School of Oriental and African Studies and the founding chairman of the European Association of Israel Studies. He is the author of eight books on Israel, including the best-selling *History of Modern Israel* (Cambridge University Press, 2008, 2013), which has been translated into Italian, Polish and Estonian.

In memory of
Derek Pollock
(1919–2014)

The Rise of the Israeli Right

From Odessa to Hebron

COLIN SHINDLER

University of London

CAMBRIDGE UNIVERSITY PRESS

CAMBRIDGE
UNIVERSITY PRESS

32 Avenue of the Americas, New York, NY 10013-2473, USA

Cambridge University Press is part of the University of Cambridge.

It furthers the University's mission by disseminating knowledge in the pursuit of education, learning and research at the highest international levels of excellence.

www.cambridge.org
Information on this title: www.cambridge.org/9780521151665

First published 2015

A catalog record for this publication is available from the British Library.

Library of Congress Cataloging in Publication Data
Shindler, Colin, 1946– author.
The rise of the Israeli right : from Odessa to Hebron / Colin Shindler.
pages   cm
Includes bibliographical references and index.
ISBN 978-0-521-19378-8 (hardback)
1. Revisionist Zionism – History – 20th century.   2. Jabotinsky, Vladimir, 1880–1940.   3. Jews – Palestine – Politics and government – 20th century. 4. Jews – Israel – Politics and government – 20th century.   5. Israel – Politics and government – 20th century.   I. Title.
DS150.R5S55   2015
956.94'04–dc23   2015008288

ISBN 978-0-521-19378-8 Hardback
ISBN 978-0-521-15166-5 Paperback

Contents

Illustrations

Maps

Acknowledgements

This book is intended for interested readers – for those who are perplexed by the rise of the Israeli Right to a dominant position in political life and wish to make sense of it.

It would be easy, of course, to write a polemic which is coloured either by a blameless romanticism or alternatively by an all-pervading criticism. Hopefully I have not done this. The struggle of any historian is to separate the striving for objectivity from personal views, no matter how strongly held.

This book builds on my previous works about the Israeli Right. Since the researching and writing of *Israel, Likud and the Zionist Dream* (1995) and *The Triumph of Military Zionism* (2006), there has been a renewed interest in the Israeli Right, particularly in the figure of Vladimir Jabotinsky. Many younger writers have uncovered new perspectives on his ideas and actions and are effectively reclaiming him from those in the political arena who wish to use him merely to meet the political exigencies of the day.

Indeed, Jabotinsky's writings were quoted by many who were opposed to Netanyahu's controversial intention to develop the 'Israel as a Jewish State' bill as an addition to the Basic Law in late 2014. It seems that the gap between intelligent historical analysis and reductionist political expediency is becoming more visible.

The rounded figure of Jabotinsky that comes down to us as a fin-de-siècle writer and activist is in no small measure due to Leonid Katsis in Moscow, who has published several volumes of Jabotinsky's writings in Russian – and in particular from his pre-Zionist period.

I have drawn upon this and also on Jabotinsky's early contributions to the Italian and Russian press. Moreover, I have attempted to utilise unpublished articles in order not to simply repeat what I and other writers have written in the past. There is always the illusion and the delusion that you know everything about a specific historical character. This is always superseded by the joy and anguish on reading new research and the realisation that in fact you know little about your subject of choice. So my hope is that this book should not be the last word but merely a stepping-stone.

The works of colleagues in Israel, Arye Naor and Yehiam Weitz, have certainly aided my understanding of the life and times of Menahem Begin – particularly during his sojourn in the political wilderness between 1949 and 1977. The book hopefully underlines Begin's shrewd climb to power and the fine balance that he maintained between ideology and ambition.

I am in the debt of several people who have helped me in a variety of tasks. I should like to thank Haya Lewi, Ned Temko, Shmuel Salinger, Naomi Yalin, Yossi Ahimeir, Peter Bergamin, Avi Shilon, Yoram Shamir, Yossi Kister, Becky Kook, Barry Davis and Howard Spier.

I would also like to thank Amira Stern at the Jabotinsky Institute, Anat Banin at the Central Zionist Archives, Assaf Gamzou and Hila Zahavi of the Israel Cartoon Museum and Ori Rub of the Menahem Begin Heritage Center – all in Israel. The staff of the Dorot Division of the New York Public Library were always – as usual – extremely helpful. In London I was always astonished to find unusual works when accessing the tremendous collection of Hebraica which has been put together by Shmuel Salinger over many years at my own institute, the School of Oriental and African Studies, University of London.

Shmuel Salinger further helped me to maintain a consistency in transliterating Hebrew titles into English, utilising the Library of Congress system.

I would also like to thank Will Hammell and Kate Gavino of Cambridge University Press for their guidance and expertise.

This book is dedicated to the memory of my late father-in-law, Derek Pollock, who passed away in April 2014. He was a self-educated man who read widely and came of political age during service in the British army in the Middle East in the 1940s. He therefore lived through most of the events described in this book. He read everything that I wrote and was not shy in criticising some of it. It is a pity that he is not with us in order to read this book. Moreover, he understood my odyssey in life.

I thank him for the years of informal chat and unexpected insights, his generosity of spirit, inspiration and interest.

My wife, Jean, has once again put up with the solitude of research and writing. Her love and support are always central to everything I do.

I have tried to use a transliteration of other languages which is consistent. However, where familiarity occasionally trumps convention, I have utilised the former. Of course, any errors of fact and interpretation are entirely my own.

Glossaries

POLITICAL PARTIES AND GROUPS

Agudat Yisrael
: ultra-orthodox party, founded in 1912 to oppose the Zionist movement

Ahdut Ha'avodah
: socialist Zionist party, founded in 1919 by Ben-Gurion and Tabenkin

Amlanim
: opposition group within Hapoel Hatzair in Palestine in the 1920s

Berit Ha-Biryonim
: nationalist group in Palestine led by Abba Ahimeir in the early 1930s

Berit Shalom
: Jewish-Arab reconciliation group in Palestine in the 1920s

Betar
: nationalist Zionist youth group, founded by Jabotinsky in Riga in 1923

Biluim
: settlers of the first Zionist immigration to Palestine in 1882

Bnei Akiva
: mainstream religious Zionist youth movement which embraced the Right after 1967

Degel ha-Torah
: established through split in Agudat Yisrael by Eliezer Schach in 1988

Democratic Movement for Change
: established in 1977 as centre party by Yigael Yadin

Free Centre
: established in 1967 through a split in Herut

Gahal
: established through an alignment between Herut and the Liberals in 1965

Gahelet
: religious youth group which propounded redemptionist Zionism

General Zionists	promoted the views of small businessmen and private enterprise
Gesher	political group formed by David Levy for the 1996 election
HaBayit Hayehudi	religious Zionist party established by a merger of the National Religion Pary (NRP) and the Far Right in 2008
Hadash	left-wing alliance of Jews and Arabs established in 1977
Haganah	the defence arm of the Yishuv and forerunner of the Israel Defence Forces
Hapoel Hatzair	non-Marxist, Tolstoyan pioneering party, established in 1906
Hashomer Hatzair	dovish pioneering Marxist Zionist group, established in 1913
Hebrew Committee for National Liberation	established in the United States by Hillel Kook in 1944
Herut	the Irgun as a political movement, established by Begin in 1948
Histadrut	General Federation of Workers in the Land of Israel, established in 1920
Im Tirzu	nationalist extra-parliamentary group established in 2006
Irgun Zvai Leumi	nationalist military group, led by Menahem Begin from 1943
Kach	Meir Kahane's Far Right party banned from participating in Knesset elections
Kadima	Centre-Right party established by Sharon in November 2005
La'am	Likud component, composed of former Labour party and Free Centre members
Labour	established in 1968 from Mapai, Ahdut Ha'avodah and Rafi
Land of Israel Movement	established after the Six-Day War to retain conquered territories
Lehi	Fighters for the Freedom of Israel, established by Avraham Stern in 1940
Liberals	formerly the General Zionists, established in 1961
Likud	the main right-wing Israeli party, established by Sharon and Begin in 1973
Ma'arakh	alignment established by Labour and Mapam in 1969

Maki	Eurocommunist section of the Communist party, led by Moshe Sneh after 1965
Mapai	leading labour Zionist party, 1930–1968, during the state-building years
Mapam	Marxist Zionist party, founded in 1948, second-largest party in first Knesset
Matzpen	anti-Zionist split from the Israeli Communist party, close to European New Left
Maximalists	radical right wing of the Revisionist party in the 1930s
Meimad	dovish religious Zionist group formed for the 1999 election
Meretz	leftist Zionist party established in 1992 by Ratz, Mapam and Shinui
Mizrahi	first religious Zionist party, established in 1902
Moked	Far Left group established for the 1973 election
Moledet	transfer party of the Far Right, established by Rehavam Ze'evi in 1988
National Union	coalition of Far Right parties formed for the 1999 election
Palmah	elite fighting force, allied to Ahdut Ha'avodah, led by Yigal Allon in the 1940s
Poalei Agudat Yisrael	pioneering ultra-orthodox party, established in 1922
Poale Zion	main socialist Zionist party in Palestine, founded by Jewish workers in 1906
Progressives	founded in 1948 by German immigrants and liberal General Zionists
Rafi	established in 1965 after a split from Mapai, led by Ben-Gurion, Dayan and Peres
Rakah	pro-Soviet wing of Communist party, after a split in 1965
Ratz	civil rights and peace party, led by Shulamit Aloni in the 1980s
Redemptionist Zionists	religious Zionist settlers who followed Zvi Yehudah Kook
Revisionist Zionism	founded by Jabotinsky in 1925 to return to Herzlian Zionism
Shas	Sephardi ultra-orthodox party established by Ovadiah Yosef in 1984
Sheli	dovish party, established in 1977 from Moked
Shlomzion	short-lived party formed by Ariel Sharon for the 1977 election

Siah	Israeli New Left, established following the 1967 war
State List	Rafi faction that did not join Labour party in 1968, led by Ben-Gurion
Tami	Mizrahi breakaway from the NRP, established in 1981
Tehiyah	Far Right party, established in 1979 in opposition to Camp David agreement
Tekumah	Far Right group formed in the late 1990s, component of the National Union
Telem	party formed to support Moshe Dayan in the 1981 election
Tserei Tsion	non-Marxist pioneering Zionist group in Tsarist Russia
Tsomet	Far Right party with Labour roots, established in 1983 through a split in Tehiyah
United Torah Judaism	main ultra-orthodox party established in 1992
Yesh Atid	centrist party established by Yair Lapid for the 2013 election
Yishuv	Jewish settlement in Palestine before 1948
Yisrael Beiteinu	party of the Far Right and Russians, established by Avigdor Lieberman for the 1999 election

GENERAL GLOSSARY

Al Hamishmar	Mapam's daily newspaper
aliyah	Jewish immigration to Israel from the Diaspora
aliyah bet	illegal immigration to Palestine (1934–1948) during the British Mandate
Altalena	Irgun arms ship, shelled and sunk on Ben-Gurion's orders in 1948
Ashkenazim	Jews generally originating from Eastern Europe
Balfour Declaration	British declaration in 1917 promising a Jewish national home in Palestine
Bar Kokhba rebellion	uprising in Judea against Roman rule, 132–135
Canaanism	endorsing the evolution of a Hebrew nation rather than a Jewish one
Davar	the Histadrut's Hebrew daily newspaper
Deir Yassin	village in which many Arab civilians were killed in an Irgun and Lehi attack

Doar Hayom	Revisionist daily newspaper in the 1920s
Fatah	leading Palestinian Arab nationalist organization, founded by Arafat
Futurism	intellectual and cultural movement in Italy and Russia
Green Line	1949 armistice boundary between Israel and the West Bank
Gush Etzion	Jewish settlements in pre-state era, now in West Bank
Ha'aretz	leading liberal Israeli daily newspaper
Halakhah	Jewish religious law
Hamas	leading Palestinian Islamist organization founded in 1988
Hamashkif	Revisionist daily newspaper, 1938–1949
Haolam Hazeh	investigative, irreverent journal, edited by Uri Avneri
Hapoel Hamizrahi	pioneering religious Zionist party
Haskalah	Jewish Enlightenment
havlagah	military self-restraint in responding to Arab attacks
Hayarden	Revisionist periodical in Palestine in the 1930s
Haynt	leading Yiddish newspaper in Poland before 1939
Hazit Ha'am	newspaper established by the Maximalist Revisionists in 1932
Ma'ariv	Israeli daily newspaper
Metzudah	journal established by members of the Irgun in 1932
Moment	Warsaw Yiddish daily newspaper, 1910–1939
Shoah	the Nazi Holocaust, 1939–1945
Unzer Welt	Warsaw Yiddish journal of the New Zionist Organisation, 1935–1939
Wissenschaft des Judentums	the Science of Judaism
Yediot Aharanot	Israeli daily newspaper
yeshivah	men's religious seminary

NAME GLOSSARY

Abba Ahimeir (1898–1962)	intellectual mentor of the Zionist Maximalists
Yigal Allon (1918–1980)	founder and commander of the Palmah and foreign minister

Shulamit Aloni (1928–2014)	leader of Meretz and minister of education
Natan Alterman (1910–1970)	Hebrew poet and translator
Arieh Altman (1902–1982)	head of Revisionist movement after 1945 and Herut member of Knesset
Moshe Arens (1925–)	Likud leader, foreign minister and defence minister
Haim Arlosoroff (1899–1933)	Hapoel Hatzair activist and Mapai leader, assassinated in 1933
Yohanan Bader (1901–1994)	Herut ideologist, editor and member of Knesset
Ehud Barak (1942–)	military leader, minister of defence and prime minister of Israel, 1999–2001
Menahem Begin (1913–1992)	prime minister of Israel, 1977–1983
Yossi Beilin (1948–)	architect of the Oslo Accord, 1993 and leader of Meretz
David Ben-Gurion (1886–1973)	founding father of Israel; first prime minister of Israel, 1949–1954; 1955–1963
Naftali Bennett (1972–)	Israeli entrepreneur and leader of HaBayit Hayehudi
Norman Bentwich (1883–1971)	English Zionist and attorney general in Mandatory Palestine
Shlomo Ben-Yosef (1913–1938)	Betar member hanged by the British
Yitzhak Ben-Zvi (1884–1963)	labour Zionist leader and second president of Israel, 1952–1963
Folke Bernadotte (1895–1948)	UN Middle East mediator, assassinated by Lehi
Haim Nahman Bialik (1873–1934)	Hebrew national poet
Yosef Haim Brenner (1881–1921)	Hebrew writer, killed in 1921 disturbances
Yosef Burg (1909–1999)	NRP leader and Israeli minister
Richard Crossman (1907–1974)	British minister, 1964–1970, and editor of *New Statesman*
Gabriele D'Annunzio (1863–1938)	writer, poet and Italian nationalist
Moshe Dayan (1915–1981)	Israeli Defence Forces chief of staff; minister of defence and of foreign affairs

Abba Eban (1915–2002)	Labour leader, writer, diplomat and minister of foreign affairs
Rafael Eitan (1929–2004)	Israeli Defence Forces chief of staff and founder of Tsomet
Levi Eshkol (1895–1969)	Mapai politician and prime minister of Israel, 1963–1969
Israel Galili (1911–1986)	Haganah chief of staff and Ahdut Ha'avodah politician
Nahum Goldmann (1895–1982)	leading Diaspora Zionist diplomat with dovish views
Eliahu Golomb (1893–1945)	Haganah founder and labour Zionist
A. D. Gordon (1856–1922)	Zionist pioneer and Tolstoyan mentor of labour Zionism
Yehudah Leib Gordon (1831–1892)	Hebrew poet and writer
Shlomo Goren (1917–1994)	Ashkenazi chief rabbi and leading religious Zionist
Maxim Gorky (1868–1936)	progressive Russian writer
Uri Zvi Greenberg (1894–1981)	Zionist Maximalist and Hebrew poet
Meir Grossman (1888–1964)	leading Revisionist, editor and journalist
Ahad Ha'am (1856–1927)	Zionist intellectual and writer
Theodor Herzl (1860–1904)	father of the modern Zionist movement
Chaim Herzog (1917–1998)	lawyer, writer, diplomat, president of Israel, 1983–1993
Moses Hess (1812–1875)	socialist theoretician and early progenitor of socialist Zionism
Vladimir Jabotinsky (1880–1940)	liberal nationalist, Revisionist Zionist and head of Betar
Meir Kahane (1932–1990)	Far Right politician and founder of Jewish Defence League
Zvi Hirsch Kalischer (1795–1874)	early progenitor of religious Zionism
Rudolf Kastner (1906–1957)	subject of controversial trial, assassinated by Far Right
Karl Kautsky (1854–1938)	leading Marxist thinker who opposed October Revolution

Teddy Kollek (1911–2007)	Mapai politician and mayor of Jerusalem, 1965–1993
Avraham Yitzhak Kook (1865–1935)	first Ashkenazi chief rabbi in Mandatory Palestine
Hillel Kook (1915–2001)	Revisionist thinker and leader of the Bergson group in the United States
Zvi Yehudah Kook (1891–1982)	spiritual mentor of Gush Emunim and religious settlers
Vladimir Korolenko (1853–1921)	leading Russian writer and journalist
Antonio Labriola (1843–1904)	leading Italian Marxist thinker
Ferdinand Lassalle (1825–1864)	founding father of German Socialism
David Levy (1937–)	Likud Mizrahi politician and Israeli minister
Avigdor Lieberman (1957–)	founder of Yisrael Beiteinu and foreign affairs minister
Rosa Luxemburg (1871–1919)	Polish-German revolutionary and Marxist thinker
Judah Magnes (1877–1948)	chancellor of Hebrew University and binational state advocate
Julius Martov (1873–1923)	leading Menshevik who opposed the October Revolution
Golda Meir (1898–1980)	Mapai politician and prime minister of Israel, 1969–1974
Robert Michels (1876–1936)	German political thinker
Adam Mickiewicz (1798–1855)	Polish national poet and fighter for Polish independence
Binyamin Netanyahu (1949–)	prime minister of Israel, 1996–1999, 2009–
Max Nordau (1849–1923)	founder of the modern Zionist movement, writer and philosopher
Ehud Olmert (1945–)	founder of the Free Centre, prime minister of Israel, 2006–2009
Amihai 'Gidi' Paglin (1922–1978)	chief operations officer of the Irgun after 1946
Józef Pilsudski (1867–1935)	founder of the modern Polish state in 1918
Leon Pinsker (1821–1891)	Zionist leader, writer and publicist
Aharon Propes (1904–1978)	founder and first member of Betar

Yitzhak Rabin (1922–1995)	prime minister of Israel, 1974–1977, 1992–1995
Yonatan Ratosh (1908–1981)	Revisionist, Canaanite, poet and writer
David Raziel (1910–1941)	head of the Irgun, 1937–1940
Duc de Richelieu (1766–1822)	first governor of Odessa and prime minister of France
Herbert Samuel (1870–1963)	first British high commissioner of Palestine
Pinhas Sapir (1906–1975)	Labour politician and leading economist
Eliezer Menahem Schach (1898/9?–2001)	spiritual mentor of Degel ha-Torah
Menahem Mendel Schneersohn (1902–1994)	*rebbe* of Lubavitcher Hassidim
Mendele Mocher Sefarim (1836–1917)	Yiddish and Hebrew writer and editor
Yitzhak Shamir (1915–2012)	Lehi leader and prime minister of Israel, 1983–1984, 1986–1992
Moshe Sharett (1894–1965)	minister of foreign affairs and prime minister of Israel, 1954–1955
Ariel Sharon (1925–2014)	military leader and prime minister of Israel, 2001–2006
Nahum Sokolov (1859–1936)	writer, journalist, editor and Zionist leader
Georges Sorel (1847–1922)	political thinker and writer on revolutionary syndicalism
Oswald Spengler (1880–1936)	political philosopher on the structure of history
Baruch Spinoza (1632–1677)	Dutch philosopher and exponent of biblical criticism
Avraham Stern (1907–1942)	poet and theoretician of Lehi
Yitzhak Tabenkin (1887–1971)	maximalist labour Zionist and kibbutz movement ideologue
Shmuel Tamir (1923–1987)	lawyer, politician and Israeli minister
Yosef Trumpeldor (1880–1920)	military figure and founder of the Zion Mule Corps

Wolfgang von Weisl (1896–1974)	journalist, writer and early Revisionist
Chaim Weizmann (1874–1952)	founding father and first president of Israel, 1949–1952
Ezer Weizmann (1924–2005)	minister of defence and president of Israel, 1993–2000
Yigael Yadin (1917–1984)	archaeologist, military leader, politician and minister
Yehoshua Hirsh Yeivin (1891–1970)	writer, journalist and Maximalist Revisionist
Natan Yellin-Mor (1913–1980)	editor, Maximalist Revisionist, founder of Lehi
Ovadiah Yosef (1920–2013)	Talmudic scholar, founder and spiritual mentor of Shas
Rehavam Ze'evi (1926–2001)	military figure, minister and founder of Moledet

Chronology

1931   Irgun Zvai Leumi formed
1933   Murder of Haim Arlosoroff
1933   Revisionist movement splits at Katowice conference
1935   Establishment of the New Zionist Organisation
1936   The Arab Revolt breaks out in Palestine
1937   Peel Commission advocates a two-state solution
1938   Shlomo Ben-Yosef hanged by the British
1938   Third World Conference of Betar in Warsaw
1938   David Raziel orders Irgun attacks on Arab targets on
        Black Sunday
1940   Jabotinsky dies in New York
1940   The Irgun splits over allying itself with Britain to fight Nazi
        Germany
1940   Avraham Stern establishes the Irgun B'Yisrael, later Lehi
1942   The systematic mass extermination of Jews commences in
        occupied Europe
1942   Avraham Stern killed
1942   Menahem Begin arrives in Palestine
1943   Yellin-Mor, Shamir and Eldad take over the leadership of Lehi
1944   Menahem Begin, commander of the Irgun Zvai Leumi,
        proclaims the Revolt
1945   Liberation of the concentration camps – 6 million Jews
        exterminated
1947   Partition of Western Palestine into a Jewish and an Arab state
1948   The State of Israel proclaimed by the Jews during the War of
        Independence
1948   Menahem Begin transforms the Irgun into a political
        movement, Herut
1949   Mapai wins the first Israeli elections
1956   Suez campaign in collusion with Britain and France ends in a
        military victory over Nasser
1965   Ben-Gurion breaks away from Mapai to form Rafi
1965   Herut and the Liberals form Gahal under Menahem Begin
1967   A national unity government established which includes
        Menahem Begin
1967   Israel's victory over Egypt, Jordan and Syria in the
        Six-Day War
1968   The beginning of Jewish settlements on the West Bank
1968   The formation of the Israeli Labour party
1973   Gahal and remnants of the Labour party form Likud under
        Begin
1973   Yom Kippur War ends in a muted victory for Israel at the cost
        of thousands of lives

1974	The establishment of Gush Emunim, the religious settlers group
1974	Yitzhak Rabin becomes prime minister for the first time
1977	Menahem Begin elected prime minister
1977	Anwar Sadat visits Jerusalem and speaks to the Knesset
1979	Begin and Sadat sign the Camp David Accord
1980	Basic Law proclaims Jerusalem the capital of Israel
1981	Golan Heights annexed by Israel
1981	Israel bombs the Osirak nuclear reactor in Iraq
1982	The Sinai settlement of Yamit evacuated and destroyed
1982	Sharon's invasion of Lebanon brings out 400,000 demonstrators for Peace Now
1984	Labour's Peres and Likud's Shamir form a rotational government
1987	The First Intifada breaks out
1988	Hamas emerges from the Muslim Brotherhood
1988	Hussein separates the West Bank from Jordan
1988	Yitzhak Shamir wins the election for the Likud
1990	Several Far Right parties enter government
1991	Iraqi missiles hit Tel Aviv during the first Gulf War
1992	Yitzhak Rabin elected prime minister
1993	Rabin and Arafat sign the Oslo Accord in Washington
1994	Hamas's first spate of suicide bombings
1995	Yitzhak Rabin assassinated by an opponent of the peace process after a peace rally
1996	Peres loses the election to Likud's Netanyahu
1997	Netanyahu and Arafat sign an agreement on Hebron
1998	Clinton oversees the Wye Plantation agreement between Israel and the Palestinians
2000	The breakdown of the Camp David negotiations and the outbreak of al-Aqsa Intifada
2001	Ariel Sharon defeats Ehud Barak and becomes prime minister at seventy-two
2002	Bush's Rose Garden speech
2003	Sharon advocates disengagement from part of the territories
2004	President Bush's letter recognizes Israel's right to annex some settlements
2005	Mahmoud Abbas elected president of the Palestinian Authority after Arafat's death
2005	The Gaza settlements evacuated without violence
2005	Likud and Labour split and realign to form the Kadima party under Sharon
2006	Hamas defeats Fatah in elections for the Legislative Council

Introduction

Between Fidelity and Heresy

In the twenty-first century, the Likud appeared to be the dominant party of government. Under successive Netanyahu administrations, the party garnered 20–30 seats out of 120 in elections. Although this was a poor showing in comparison with 48 seats in its heyday in 1981, the twenty-first-century Likud relied on the fact that smaller parties preferred it to any alternative from the Centre Left. Indeed, in the 2009 election, the Likud was the second-largest party. Yet the smaller Far Right, religious and ethno-nationalist parties projected a greater affinity for Netanyahu than for Tsipi Livni and her Kadima party. Therefore, what mattered was not which party emerged as the largest in any election, but whether it could forge a coalition with other parties – often on the political margins – to create a blocking majority of at least 61 seats.

It had been the Left and socialist Zionism which had built the state and led it to victory in the war of Israel's independence in 1948. Their political hegemony and machismo seemed all-pervading, and the position of their leading party, Ben-Gurion's Mapai, seemed impregnable. Indeed, after Menahem Begin had turned the Irgun Zvai Leumi into the Herut movement for the first Israel election in January 1949, it won a paltry 14 seats out of 120 and emerged as the fourth-largest party. In the subsequent election in 1951, Herut lost half its seats and was on the precipice of oblivion. Despite widespread dissension within Herut and the dropping away of many of its stalwarts, Menahem Begin persevered to build a cluster party of the Right which finally displaced Labour in 1977. Herut became Gahal in 1965, which in turn became the Likud in 1973. Begin succeeded because as the Left fragmented, the Right coalesced.

From 1977, the year of 'the earthquake', until 1996, both the Likud and Labour led coalition governments. The dual election for premier as well as for party in 1996 caused a dramatic fragmentation such that the Likud shrank in size. The Likud became dependent on smaller parties on the Far Right to form a government.

Ariel Sharon's decisive leadership in combatting the al-Aqsa Intifada between 2001 and 2004 was instrumental in bucking this trend. Following Operations Defensive Shield and Determined Path and the building of the security barrier, Sharon's standing in the opinion polls rose dramatically. By 2003 he had restored the Likud to thirty-eight seats plus another two from the collapsing Russian party, Yisrael B'Aliyah.

Sharon's incapacitation due to a stroke and the debacle of the second Lebanon War in 2006 eventually led to the unexpected return of the Likud to power and a restoration of Netanyahu to the premiership. Netanyahu managed to reverse the move towards the centre in the wake of electoral disillusionment with the peace process and an ongoing conflict with Palestinian Islamism. Yet it was the smaller parties which propelled him back into the prime minister's chair. Moreover, while the Likud's standing had remained relatively static under the aegis of an unadmired Netanyahu, the Far Right – both nationalist and religious – stepped into the political vacuum created by the inability of the Centre Left to present either coherent policies or credible leaders. The pattern of a shrunken Likud leading the smaller parties of the Right became the template for Israel's government. All this represented a move away from the broad philosophy of the credited founder of the Zionist Right, Vladimir Jabotinsky.

Despite the Israeli Right's embrace of the historical figure of Jabotinsky as a political tool in ongoing campaigns, the real Jabotinsky was far more complex in his political thought – someone whose legacy has been lost in the mist of time. As with Lenin or the Baal Shem Tov, the ideas and persona of the founder of a dynamic movement have been mythologised to meet the political exigencies of the present.

Jabotinsky was immersed in the political whirlpool of fin-de-siècle, pre–World War I Europe when a student in Rome. He explored syndicalism, anarchism and later Futurism, but he was also affected by Italian liberalism – to which he often referred in his writings.[1] In the 1930s he bemoaned the political seduction of the young in an age of totalitarianism and authoritarianism. The promotion of Betar as 'obedient rebels'

[1] Vladimir Jabotinsky, 'Zeyde Liberalizm', *Haynt*, 14 October 1932.

provided Jabotinsky with a political instrument to utilise against his internal opponents.[2]

He instead espoused the increasingly unpopular belief in parliamentary democracy and the rule of law.

This reaction to the often accepted ideological wisdom of the day was related to his questioning of the role of Judaism in Jewish political life. While he certainly utilised religious imagery to attract followers,[3] Jabotinsky never warmed to the idea of organised religion and deference to rabbis. He believed that it was the people's sense of nationhood, rather than religion per se, that had allowed the Jews to survive two millennia of persecution and exile. This inversion of the reason for Jewish survival down the centuries – the nation now at the centre with religion on the outside – was the dividing line between Jabotinsky and religious Zionism. For Jabotinsky, nationalism rather than religion was the holy Torah.[4]

Judaism was a national commodity, belonging to all Jews. Jabotinsky argued, however, that there was no connection between this national possession and 'the religious obligations ascribed to it'.[5]

Jabotinsky identified not only with Garibaldi, but also with the biblical Gideon ben Yoash, the military saviour of the Jews.[6] He rejected the monarchism of the religious for the republicanism of Gideon – who like Cromwell refused to wear the crown. Belief in God was transformed into belief in the nation.

Yet he also opposed the maximalism of intellectuals such as Abba Ahimeir and youthful political activists such as Menahem Begin. Although he was head of the Irgun, Jabotinsky was ambivalent and often conflicted about the need for retaliatory violence. This often placed him at odds with military figures such as David Raziel and Avraham Stern. While he attempted to navigate the choppy waters of Revisionist Maximalism – sometimes compromising, sometime opposing[7] – the worsening situation in Europe in the 1930s and static situation in Palestine mitigated against any success.

---

[2] Daniel Kupfert Heller, 'Obedient Children and Reckless Rebels: Jabotinsky's Youth Politics and the Case for Authoritarian Leadership 1931–1933', *Journal of Israeli History* vol. 34, no. 1 (March 2015), pp. 1–24.

[3] Arye Naor, 'Jabotinsky's New Jew: Concept and Models', *Journal of Israeli History*, vol. 30, no. 2 (September 2011), pp. 141–59.

[4] Vladimir Jabotinsky, 'Shir Ha-Degel', *Rassviet*, 15, 16 and 17 April 1927.

[5] Arye Naor, 'The Leader as a Poet: The Political and Ideological Poetry of Ze'ev Jabotinsky', *Israel Affairs*, vol. 20, no. 2 2014 pp. 161–81.

[6] Vladimir Jabotinsky, 'Ha-Neder', 17 August 1934, Jabotinsky Institute Archives, Tel Aviv.

[7] Vladimir Jabotinsky, 'Maximalism', *Moment*, 1 February 1935.

Yet Jabotinsky did provide the Zionist Right with an anti-socialist veneer. In part this was due to the Bolshevisation of Russia following the October Revolution. While always an opponent of Tsarist autocracy, he gradually came to hate Lenin's suppression of Russian culture and freedom of thought and speech – particularly the closing of the non-Bolshevik press, such as his own newspaper, *Russkie Vedomosti*.[8] Russia was no workers' state. Like his hero, the poet, Dante Alighieri, condemned in absentia, Jabotinsky could not return to his native city. By 1930 he was in exile twice over – from Odessa and from Palestine.

Jabotinsky moved from a non-socialist position to an anti-socialist one. In the wake of the emigration of the Polish Jewish middle class to Palestine in the mid-1920s, he began to passionately espouse private enterprise and the cause of the individual against the collective.[9]

Jabotinsky was in fact not entrapped by ideology, but exhibited a flexibility in dealing with opponents such as Ben-Gurion. Indeed, it can be argued that the ideologists – Tabenkin on the left and Begin on the right – prevented an agreement between Jabotinsky and Ben-Gurion in 1934 which would have changed the course of Zionist history.[10] In 1915 Jabotinsky proclaimed that a settlement was not the be-all and end-all of the Zionist enterprise.[11] In his speech to the New Zionist Organisation conference in Prague at the beginning of 1938, he attacked Ben-Gurion's arguments for partition in the belief that the state would expand in the future. Jabotinsky condemned 'small-scale Zionism' and argued that if a smaller partitioned state proved to be acceptable, then there would never be an opportunity to later expand. If Arab land was conquered in the future, it would lead to unforeseen problems. As he put it, 'Only an idiot would believe that a military occupation would be a possibility.'[12]

Jabotinsky died in New York in 1940. Therefore, unlike his successors, he was not hampered by the burden of state and the difficult choices that had to be made. The three Likud prime ministers, Begin, Shamir and Netanyahu – as well as the two Kadima premiers, Sharon and Olmert – all had to recognise the limits of ideology and power. Being in government was fundamentally different from the freedom of opposition. All

[8] Vladimir Jabotinsky, Letter to Anya, 11 June 1919, *Igrot, 1918–1922* (Jerusalem, 1997).
[9] Vladimir Jabotinsky, 'The Shopkeeper', *Rassviet*, 29 May 1927.
[10] Menahem Begin, 'Address to the Second World Conference of Betar', 6 January 1935, Jabotinsky Institute Archives, Tel Aviv.
[11] Vladimir Jabotinsky, 'Activism', *Di Tribune*, 15 October 1915.
[12] Vladimir Jabotinsky, Opening Address at the New Zionist Organisation conference, Prague, September 1938, in *Neumim, 1927–1940*, Ketavim 5, ed. Eri Jabotinsky (Jerusalem, 1958), p. 298.

these prime ministers, regardless of their loyalty to ideology, had to recognise the world of realpolitik and the political pressure of the United States.

Throughout his life, Menahem Begin proclaimed a fidelity to Jabotinsky's teachings. Yet there were fundamental philosophical differences between the two men. A central one was that Begin believed in military Zionism and a revolt against Britain. Jabotinsky was less enamoured of the prospect of violence and preferred diplomacy.

Jabotinsky was acutely aware, very early on, of the British attempt to row back from the Balfour Declaration.[13] Even so Jabotinsky regarded the pro-British orientation as both central and important. At one time, he worked with the Labour MP Josiah Wedgwood on the idea of Palestine as a seventh dominion of the British Empire, and there was even talk about Palestine becoming a crown colony. The watershed of the pro-British orientation was the killing of Jews by Palestinian Arabs during the disturbances of 1929. Many Zionists, including Jabotinsky, were highly critical of British conduct during this period.[14]

During the Revisionist conference in Prague in August 1930, there were vociferous attacks on British policy – particularly in the wake of the Shaw Commission and the general British approach of blaming the Jews for the situation. The Revisionists were annoyed at the British perception that while pogroms in European Russia were reprehensible and should be condemned, in the Middle East murder, mayhem and massacre were quietly acknowledged as a traditional way of solving problems.[15]

Yet the tide of history flowed in Begin's direction. For many small nations Albion was seen as indeed perfidious and two-faced. Jan Masaryk, the Czechoslovak foreign minister, felt betrayed by Britain. Promises made became promises broken in the late 1930s. Masaryk sarcastically proposed to Chaim Weizmann that they purchase a fine three-storey house in London. The bottom floor would be reserved for Haile Selassie, the exiled emperor of Ethiopia. The middle floor would house Masaryk and his countrymen. The top floor would be inhabited by Weizmann and his Zionist colleagues. All harboured a sense of betrayal by the British despite the genteel explanations as to why a course of action was necessary.[16]

[13] Vladimir Jabotinsky, Letter to Richard Lichtheim, 1 March 1922, *Igrot*, 1918–1922 (Jerusalem, 1997).
[14] Vladimir Jabotinsky, 'Address to a meeting of Revisionists in Paris,' 29 August 1929, *Rassviet*, 9 September 1929.
[15] *Rassviet*, 27 April 1930.
[16] Anita Shapira, *Ben-Gurion: Father of Modern Israel* (London, 2014), p. 112.

Following Jabotinsky's death, his movement fragmented into three main factions: the Revisionists themselves, the Irgun Zvai Leumi and Lehi. The latter two took up arms. While Begin's Irgun considered itself an underground army which was fighting the British occupier, Shamir's Lehi conducted individual acts of terror, including the assassination of British officials and Jews who worked for the British.

Menahem Begin, however, led a charmed political life. In 1948 he emerged as the undisputed leader of the Zionist Right – not only because he had courageously led the Irgun but also because many of his potential rivals were dead and buried. The deceased Jabotinsky was proclaimed 'the Father of the Revolt' against the British, while the very much alive Abba Ahimeir – who had an equal claim to that title – was marginalised. In the years between the first election in 1949 until 1977, when Begin became prime minister, he astutely widened his political support in building a cluster party, the Likud. As a traditional Jew, he promoted 'Jewishness' rather than 'Israeliness' and appealed to religious Zionists.[17] To the General Zionists, he upheld the rule of law and democratic norms. To the labour Zionists, he reflected Ben-Gurion's sense of reality and willingness to take hard decisions.

While Begin adhered selectively to some of Jabotinsky's ideas, he concurred with Jabotinsky's assessment of the passing of liberalism – albeit in the aftermath of the Shoah. In February 1950 he commented:

When liberal thought flourished it was said of the state's authority that it ought to be limited to the role of 'night watchman'. That period is past and every free man prays that we will not be forced to admit that it has gone forever.[18]

Ben-Gurion, however, depicted Begin and his party, Herut, as poisonous weeds accidently planted in the golden garden of Zionism. They were seen as fascists who happened to escape such labelling purely because they were Jewish. Herut was viewed as a party of gunmen and gangsters, far removed from the struggle for an independent Israel.

The promotion of a more conciliatory, less outspoken, older Begin after 1967 led to a wider public acceptance. By the end of the 1960s, even Ben-Gurion – and certainly after the death of his wife – seemed to drop his long-time antagonism towards Begin.[19] His State List, which he

[17] Naor, 'Jabotinsky's New Jew'.
[18] Menahem Begin, Speech in the Knesset, 1 February 1950, in Itamar Rabinovitch and Jehuda Reinharz, eds., *Israel in the Middle East: Documents and Readings on Society, Politics and Foreign Relations, 1948–Present* (Oxford, 1984), p. 45.
[19] David Ben-Gurion, Letter to Menahem Begin, 6 February 1969, Jabotinsky Institute Archives, Tel Aviv.

FIGURE 1. Mapai election poster (late 1948) indicating a Herut gunman shooting a worker-pioneer in the back. The words 'rak kak' (Only Thus!), the Revisionist and Irgun slogan plus the map of an Israel incorporating both banks of the Jordan are inscribed on the gunman's cuff. The caption reads 'the key of Herut' which is probably an answer to a contemporary Herut poster showing Ben-Gurion with the key to the future – as long as you were a member of and voted for Mapai.
Courtesy of the Central Zionist Archives.

headed in the 1969 election, became one of the founding components of the Likud four years later.

In his drive for power, Begin dispensed, one after another, with the services of veteran Revisionists, former comrades from the Irgun, youthful upstarts and charismatic military men who wished to displace him. His toughness, exemplified by his long sojourn in the political wilderness, was also defined by his understanding of the non-negotiable ideological boundaries of the state.

Yet Begin in government realised that power offers possibilities for change – and change might mean adjusting the principles of a lifetime for what might be viewed as the greater good. After all, his party had joined the Histadrut in the 1960s after decades of refusal while the claim to the East Bank was gradually downgraded. It was therefore Menahem Begin who made peace with the largest Arab state, Egypt, and returned territory which many on the right ideologically regarded as part of the Land of Israel.

The Camp David Accord, signed by Begin and Sadat in 1979, led to a fragmentation of the Israeli Right. Those who could not stomach the agreement accused Begin of betrayal and left the Likud to form Far Right parties. The umbrella which Begin had erected to shelter the Right was now in tatters.

Begin's successor, Yitzhak Shamir, who opposed the Camp David Accord, similarly believed that no part of the historic homeland should be given up and no settlements evacuated. Yet he accepted the first partition of Palestine in 1920 while rejecting the second one in 1947. He did not oppose the accord with Jordan in 1994. On the other hand, his views on the Palestinians had not changed. He argued that the Oslo Accord in 1993 would lead to the destruction of Israel. While he later berated Netanyahu for relegating ideology to a lower rung, he could not avoid the reality of the Madrid conference in 1991, which he reluctantly attended. Unlike Jabotinsky, both Begin and Shamir bore witness to the Shoah and this affected them to the core. Unlike the cosmopolitan Jabotinsky, both men exhibited a deep suspicion of outsiders.

The Right was aided by the emergence of redemptionist Zionism from traditional religious Zionism after 1967. The desire to colonise the West Bank – and beyond – to recapture and re-establish locations of biblical remembrance particularly moved the religious Zionists from left to right. Their political religiosity transformed religious Zionism into Zionist religion. The original mission of religious Zionism was simply to safeguard the place of religion in the new state and to ensure that any government understood the needs of the religious public. The national religious camp therefore supported the British proposal for Jewish settlement in Uganda in 1902 and endorsed the UN partition of Mandatory Palestine in 1947. The dormant messianism within religious Zionism was awoken chiefly through the teachings of Zvi Yehudah Kook, who unlike his father, the revered Avraham Yitzhak Kook, had also lived through the Shoah and witnessed the establishment of Israel.

The 1970s also gave rise to an awareness in religious circles that conventional Zionism had brought neither normalisation of the Jewish condition nor an end to anti-Semitism. The conclusion was that the task of Zionism was not to achieve normalisation and assimilate into the nations of the world, but to transform the Jews into a holy people as part of the messianic process.

In the early 1980s the desire to colonise the West Bank and to integrate it into a Greater Israel found its political inspiration in the IRA hunger strikers and the struggle of the Viet Cong in Vietnam. They too had resisted partition long after the formal division of their countries.[20]

With the passing of the generation of Begin and Shamir – and the reality of the Oslo Accord with Arafat – the relegation of ideology seemingly took place within the Likud. The inflexibility of ideology was often substituted by banging the drum of security. Yet even Begin had argued that the retention of territory prevented not only another war but also the occurrence of another holocaust. Begin highlighted the security question for the Right when he resigned from Golda Meir's government in August 1970 during the War of Attrition.[21] The retention of the territories, he believed, would ensure peace, whereas the 'land for peace' formula would have the very opposite effect. The status quo of remaining in the West Bank was therefore preferable to leaving it. During the Camp David negotiations in 1978, Sharon advised Begin that the evacuation of Yamit in Sinai did not impair Israel's security. Sharon further suggested that the security argument did not displace the case of historic right, but instead overlaid it with today's reality.

Following the Oslo Accord, Netanyahu completed the transformation of the Likud from a party based on an outworn ideological faith to one based on an ever-present need for security. Netanyahu maintained a precarious balance between the pragmatists and the ideologists of the Far Right. While the ongoing planning and implementation of the expansion of West Bank settlements proceeded apace, he was willing to return 13 percent of the West Bank territory at the Wye Plantation negotiations in 1998. Unlike Begin and Shamir, Netanyahu did not

[20] Ehud Sprinzak, *The Ascendance of Israel's Radical Right* (Oxford, 1991), p. 183.
[21] Arye Naor, 'The Security Argument in the Territorial Debate in Israel: Rhetoric and 150–77.

promise to retain 'the Land of Israel' in its entirety. His prevarication in resigning from the Sharon government over the proposed withdrawal from Gaza suggested a lingering indecision over the merits of ideological commitment.

Yet this displacement of the primacy of ideology was not shared by either the Far Right or the religious Right. In addition to fidelity to restoring the entire Land of Israel, Menahem Begin's advocacy of regime change – from ousting Abdullah from Jordan in 1950 to forging an alliance with the Christian Maronites in Lebanon in 1982 – seemed to be placed on the shelf following the Lebanon debacle. Instead the Far Right stepped into the breach in advocating this approach. Avigdor Lieberman during Operation Cast Lead in 2009 and Naftali Bennett during Operation Protective Edge in 2014 both urged Netanyahu to allow the Israel Defence Forces (IDF) 'to finish the job' in eradicating Hamas from Gaza. Netanyahu, wary of the potential number of casualties and the political cost of re-occupation, refrained from taking any action. The task of Likud prime ministers therefore appeared to be primarily to defend Israel strongly when it was assaulted, but to defer and to stonewall politically while expanding the West Bank settlements.

Up until the election of 2015, Lieberman tried to project his party as 'the real Likud', in opposition first to Sharon and then to Netanyahu. Yisrael Beiteinu significantly described itself as 'a national movement with the clear vision to follow in the brave path of Ze'ev Jabotinsky'.

Lieberman differed from the Likud and its traditional adherence to the Land of Israel in suggesting that the solution to the demographic problem lay in a two-state solution with more ethnically homogeneous populations. He argued, therefore, that Israel should annex major settlement blocs near the Green Line while transferring the area around Umm al-Fahm and Tayibe in Israel where Israeli Arabs were concentrated to Palestinian sovereignty.

While the religious Right continued to occasionally challenge the authority of the state, the aura of figures such as Naftali Bennett – young, bright and professionally successful – persuaded many non-religious Jews to vote for HaBayit Hayehudi in 2013. Even so, many in the religious camp saw an Israel characterised by licentiousness and permissiveness – a corroding influence which could bring about the spiritual withering of the state.

In one sense little had altered since the formation in the early 1950s of the small group of religious Zionists, Gahelet, which first followed Zvi Yehudah Kook, then grew into Gush Emunim and finally cascaded as a plethora of Far Right religious parties. The founding charter of Gahelet stated:

We must kindle the flame of the future generations, to look forward to the day in which every man in Israel will sit under his vine and fig tree in full observance of the Torah of Israel.[22]

In addition, the authority of rabbis was elevated in decision-making in parties such as the National Religious Party which originally tended to reflect the inner workings of the secular parties. This accentuated the dilemma as to what to obey – the ruling of the rabbis or the law of the land. During the evacuation of the Gaza settlements in 2005, some rabbis ruled that it was right for religious soldiers to refuse to obey orders.

The activism of the religious Right also accentuated exclusionism in Israeli society. Ethno-nationalist parties often presented platforms based on both a mixture of legitimate rights and an elevation of victimhood. While such exclusionism was always practised by leaders of orthodoxy towards Reform Judaism and homosexuals,[23] its secular equivalent on the far right extended to those on the political spectrum whose views were considered unsavoury.

The Far Right's presence in government during the 2009 Knesset bore witness to several attempts to curtail civil liberties in line with its belief in a more limited democracy in Israel, manifested as assaults on academia and the judiciary. While this was reminiscent of some of the radical approaches of the Maximalists in the Revisionist movement in the 1930s and indeed Herut's beliefs in the 1950s, it was not tempered in the twenty-first century by Begin's respect for democratic procedure and the rule of law.

Indeed, in his address to the second conference of Herut in February 1951, Begin quoted Montesquieu regarding the separation of powers into the legislative, the executive and the judiciary. In a lengthy discourse, he argued strongly for 'the supremacy of law', which should accompany 'the independence of the judiciary'.[24]

---

[22] Gideon Aran, 'From Religious Zionism to Zionist Religion: The Roots of Gush Emunim', in Peter Medding, ed., *Studies in Contemporary Jewry*, vol. 11 (London, 1986), p. 130.

[23] Shai Bermanis, Daphna Canetti-Nisim and Ami Pedahzur, 'Religious Fundamentalism and the Extreme Right-Wing Camp in Israel', *Patterns of Prejudice*, vol. 38, no.2 (2004), pp. 159–76.

[24] Menahem Begin, Speech to the second conference of the Herut movement, 26 February 1951, Menahem Begin Heritage Center, Jerusalem.

This was not an approach taken by ethno-nationalist parties such as Shas and Yisrael Beiteinu.[25] The sense of victimhood allowed both parties to castigate the judiciary prior to the 1999 election. Ovadiah Yosef accused the Supreme Court judges of being intrinsically evil and responsible for all that was bad in the world.[26]

Ironically the secularist Yisrael Beiteinu has been at odds with the religious parties – Shas in particular – over questions of status and identity which the mass emigration from the former USSR brought with it in the 1990s.

A repeating theme in Netanyahu's 2013 government had been his demand that the Palestinian Authority – and others – recognise Israel as a Jewish state, even though it was a point of Zionist principle neither when Begin negotiated with Sadat in 1977 nor when Rabin signed a peace agreement with King Hussein in 1994. Netanyahu did not mention it during his first tenure as prime minister, and it was not a precondition for signing either the Hebron agreement in 1997 or the Wye Plantation agreement the following year. In 2014 Netanyahu gave notice that he would 'legally anchor' Israel as a Jewish state as an addition to the Basic Law. One implication, it was argued, was that it would upset the undefined balance between Jewishness and democracy. Another was a potential eroding of the status of Israeli Arabs. While the Far Right in government and coalition rallied to Netanyahu, he was opposed by traditional members of Likud – the president, Reuven Rivlin; Moshe Arens; Dan Meridor – who argued that it went contrary to Jabotinsky's approach and Begin would never have allowed it. When Netanyahu quoted Ben-Gurion in support of his proposal, Peres, who served in Ben-Gurion's governments, castigated him. This led directly to the dissolution of the Netanyahu administration and new elections in 2015.

All this was a long way from Jabotinsky's day, when Russian intellectuals established the Revisionist movement to counterbalance socialist Zionism. After all, Jabotinsky spoke ten languages fluently – and could converse in several more. During the past ninety years, there has been a dilution of intellectual thought on the right. In its place there has been a rise of an anti-intellectualism, coloured by a crude populism – political wisdom has drained away. As one writer puts it:

The capacity to grasp and manipulate complex ideas is enough to define intellect but not enough to encompass intelligence, which involves combining intellect

---

[25] Ami Pedahzur, 'The Transformation of Israel's Extreme Right', *Studies in Conflict and Terrorism*, vol. 24, no. 1 (2001), pp. 25–42.

[26] *Ha'aretz*, 11 February 1999.

with judgment ... Intelligence minus judgment equals intellect. Wisdom is the rarest quality of all – the ability to combine intellect, knowledge, experience, and judgment in a way to produce a coherent understanding.[27]

Few politicians are declared to be 'wise' in Israel today.

On the other hand, perhaps it is simply unfair to compare figures from Zionism's heroic period one hundred years ago with today's party managers and spin doctors. Perhaps the dream was always easier than the reality.

Despite this, it is significant that in the twenty-first century, Jabotinsky has been rediscovered by many young people. No longer a one-dimensional figure quoted during a political campaign to bolster a political stand, his writings provoke interest, debate and discussion. This is his intellectual legacy down the century and the hope for a regeneration of political life in Israel.

---

[27] Thomas Sowell, *Intellectuals and Society* (New York: Basic Books, 2010), pp. 2–5, quoted in Asaf Sinaver, 'Abba Eban and Anti-intellectualism' (unpublished).

Birth and Rebirth

THE CITY OF DREAMS

When Vladimir Jabotinsky arrived in Rome in the autumn of 1898, it is highly likely that he was totally oblivious to the Roman triumphalism, displayed on the Arch of Titus, which depicted the defeat of the Jews in the Land of Israel in the year 70. The inscription 'Judea Capta' had no real meaning for Jabotinsky.

He had attended school in multi-ethnic Odessa and eventually persuaded his mother that he should be allowed to escape the city's provincialism and Russia's authoritarianism – and study abroad. He was a thoroughly Russified Jew, yet unlike other Jewish intellectuals who had willingly relegated their Jewishness, he had no inkling of the historical legacy of his forefathers and no knowledge of the inner lives of the impoverished Jews of the Moldavanka district of his own city. According to the 1892 census, around 112,000 Jews were living in Odessa and constituted a third of the port city's population. While approximately 90 percent of Odessa's Jews spoke Yiddish, a small minority, fewer than 15,000, stated that Russian was their first language.[1] This was the young Jabotinsky's cultural milieu; he was a speaker of Russian and Italian rather than of Hebrew and Yiddish.

He was a child of Novorossiya – New Russia – and its beacon city of Odessa. The city proved to be a powerful magnet for Jews seeking a creative space where they could reinvent themselves and their understanding of Jewishness. Odessa was deemed to be an integral part of Russia, yet

---

[1] Robert Weinberg, *The Revolution of 1905 in Odessa* (Bloomington, IN, 1993) p. 13.

FIGURE 2. The young Jabotinsky (Odessa, 1899).
Courtesy of the Israel Government Press Office.

more than fifty different languages were spoken in this most unusual and independent of cities. Significantly the *rebbes* of the Tsarist Empire, the men of great Talmudic learning, had no great desire to move to Odessa to encounter such openness. The city was seen as home to the Berlinchiki, the exponents of the Berlin Enlightenment, and those who wished to tinker with Jewish tradition. This tendency was reinforced numerically by the expulsion of Jews from Russian cities in the 1880s and the 1890s, as well as the famine of 1891–1892. Many Jewish revolutionaries were drawn to Odessa in order to escape police surveillance.

As Jabotinsky noted later in life, Odessa did not possess any real traditions – only a desire to challenge the status quo. Indeed, in defiance of the rabbis, a majority of Jewish-owned shops were reputed to be open on the Jewish Sabbath. While 97 percent of Russia's Jews spoke Yiddish, only 89.5 percent of Odessa's did. Young people defiantly held parties on

Yom Kippur, the holiest day in the Jewish calendar.[2] Despite such a revolt against Judaism, accompanied by an ongoing acculturation, the Tsarist authorities did not differentiate between their Jews. They regarded them as a whole as a nationality and stamped 'Jew' in their passports. Odessa was cultured and irreverent, rebellious and innovative. Many Jews felt entirely at home.

The founding of Odessa in 1794 followed Catherine the Great's wars against the Ottomans. It was seen as repeating the founding of St. Petersburg in the north as an outlet for Russian ambition and trade and as a means of encouraging ties with Europe. For the city's founders, the prime exemplar was Naples.

At the end of the nineteenth century, less than 50 percent of the population was Russian. Odessa was home to a plethora of ethnic minorities. The city was founded by José Pacual Domingo de Ribas y Boyons, the son of the Spanish consul in Naples and his Irish wife. The city's first governor was the French nobleman Arman Emmanuel Sophie de Vignerot Septimanie du Plessis, the fifth duc de Richelieu. He had been part of the French court and served with the monarchist forces of Prince de Condé. With the victory of the Revolution, he escaped to Russia and served in its armies during Catherine's second war against the Ottomans.

In Odessa, he built a theatre, public schools and a library. He established a printing press and founded a gymnasium for merchants' sons. And to provide an Italianate veneer, he planted trees everywhere. By 1812, the city boasted a population of 32,000. Its broad tolerance was indicated by the fact that the Jews were not blamed for the plague of 1813. The lingua franca was Italian. It was used in business transactions and in everyday life as well. The street signs were in both Russian and Italian. There was an 800-seat opera house in which visiting Italian companies would play. A French language biweekly swiftly followed when the *Journal d'Odessa* was launched. Richelieu returned to France after the fall of Napoleon and twice became prime minister.

His successor was yet another French nobleman, Louis Alexandre Andrault, comte de Langéron. He was then succeeded by Mikhail Semyonovich Vorontsov, the son of the Russian ambassador to the United Kingdom. The anglophile Vorontsov was actually brought up in London and graduated from the University of Cambridge. He eventually became the commander of the Russian occupation forces in Paris.[3]

---

[2] Ibid., p. 12.
[3] Charles King, *Odessa: Genius and Death in a City of Dreams* (New York, 2011), p. 94.

Odessa's cosmopolitanism and broad dissidence were therefore in-built from the beginning. The city became a centre of political activity after 1814 to liberate the Greek lands from the Ottomans and to free the Italian states from the grip of the Hapsburgs. Garibaldi was reputed to have awakened to the cause of Italian unity at a meeting with a *carbonari* in Odessa. Indeed, after the Decembrist uprising in 1825, Tsar Nicholas I became very wary of the city. This prefigured a deepening suspicion in the 1870s, when the authorities regarded Odessa as a breeding ground of revolutionary subversion. The Poles too utilised Odessa to plot their failed uprising of 1863.

Jabotinsky recalled that there was a Bulgarian Street, a Gypsy Street, a Polish Climb, an Armenian Alley, Turkish and Tartar settlements, a Karaite 'Kenassiah' and a Persian Bazaar:

> The native Ukrainians who called themselves 'South Russians' manned the sailing boats, loaded and unloaded, laid stones for houses and sidewalks, and walked behind the oxen, dragging the heavy wheat wagon from the rapids of the Dneiper to the Quarantoine – a matter, sometimes of a thousand miles over crooked, muddy roads.[4]

Odessa boasted a free port status and a deep harbour which did not easily freeze over. It attracted Jews generally because of the prospect of economic betterment. The opening of the Suez Canal in 1869 further helped the development of Odessa. Jews were dominant in numerous industrial enterprises and trading companies. The city was close to the grain-producing regions of southern Russia, and Jews became involved in the city's trade in that commodity. Jews accounted for two-thirds of the city's registered merchants and traders and nearly three-quarters of its innkeepers and proprietors of public houses.[5]

Despite a sense of being founding fathers and a real sense of belonging, there were serious anti-Jewish riots in 1821, 1859, 1871, 1881 and 1900. In 1821 the Greeks attacked Jews they believed had aided the Turks in killing the Greek patriarch of Constantinople. There was also commercial rivalry between Greeks and Jews.

In addition, there was a deep-seated Russian fear of Jews in Odessa. This resulted in an unofficial boycott of Jewish workers in many Russian-owned factories. Although there were no residential restrictions on Odessa's Jews, the reality was that there was a distinct separation between the lives of the Russians and the Jews.

---

[4] Vladimir Jabotinsky, 'Ida Kremer's City', *Jewish Tribune*, 14 May 1926.
[5] King, *Odessa*, p. 153.

Odessa was, of course, famous for its plethora of Zionist thinkers –
Ahad Ha'am, Haim Nahman Bialik, Leon Pinsker and many others. But
Jabotinsky was not one of them. He remained completely untouched
by the Haskalah (Jewish Enlightenment) and had no concept of the traditional Jewish world of Eastern Europe which the early Zionists desperately wanted to change. His youthful rebellion was more focused on
the values of the Richelieu Gymnasium. The adolescent Jabotinsky saw
himself as primarily a Russian literary figure who was opposed to the
Tsarist authorities. At this point in his life, he was more interested in
translating Verlaine and Poe into Russian. Indeed, one of his first literary
efforts, 'Gorod Mira', was published in *Voskhod*, a periodical opposed to
Zionism, in November 1898.[6]

Jabotinsky felt at home in Rome, not only because of the prolifera-
tion of Italian culture in Odessa but also because many of its Jews were
acculturated, assimilated and occasional converts to Roman Catholicism.
It was also a liberal society where Jews such as Sidney Sonnino and
Luigi Luzzati could become prime minister and General Giuseppe
Ottolenghi could be appointed the minister of war. Moreover, the struggle for national liberation in Italy and the demand for the emancipation
of Italian Jews were 'virtually synonymous'.[7] The forces ranged against
the Italians in their struggle were not exactly progressive. In the north
was the Austro-Hungarian Empire, in the centre the Vatican and in the
south the Spanish monarchy. The liberally minded Jews, by and large,
were therefore highly appreciative of the Risorgimento and integrated
into fin-de-siècle Italy.

In Rome, Jabotinsky in addition to his studies at the university worked
as a correspondent for the daily *Odesskii Listok*, a paper which catered
to a large readership of Russified Jews. His articles were in the main
centred on the theatre and the opera house, with occasional forays into
contemporary Italian politics.

He wrote reviews of a performance of Edmond Rostand's *Cyrano de
Bergerac* at Rome's Valle Theatre[8] and Pietro Mascagni's new opera, *Le
Maschere*, at the Costanzi.[9] He interested himself in the plight of Sicilian

---

[6] Michael Stanislawski, *Zionism and the Fin de Siècle: Cosmopolitanism and Nationalism
from Nordau to Jabotinsky* (Berkeley, CA: 2001), p. 128.

[7] Alexander Stille, 'The Double Bind of Italian Jews', in Joshua D. Zimmerman, ed., *Jews in
Italy under Fascist and Nazi Rule, 1922–1945* (Cambridge, 2009), p. 25.

[8] Vladimir Jabotinsky, 'Cyrano de Bergerac on the Roman Stage', *Odesskii Novosti*, 14
May 1900.

[9] Vladimir Jabotinsky, 'The New Opera, Le Maschere', *Odesskii Novosti*, 3 January 1901.

workers in the sulphur mines in a review of Giuseppe Sinopoli Giusti's play *La Zolfara*.[10] He also went to see an early work of the feminist Amelia Rosselli, *L'Anima*, at the Dramatico Nazionale Theatre.[11] She was quite typical of many Italian Jews during that period. Indeed, her family had been deeply involved in the Risorgimento and she was close to the Socialist party. In a later memoir, she remarked:

> We are Jews, but first and foremost Italians. I, too, born and raised in that profoundly Italian and liberal atmosphere, preserved only the purest essence of my religion in my heart.[12]

The exploits of Garibaldi, Mazzini and Cavour – and the saga of the reunification of Italy – enthused Jabotinsky. The Italian language, prose and poetry captivated him, and he often quoted Italian writers in his early writings. The Italian struggle in particular became an example to be emulated later in his Zionist period. The patriotic poetry of Giuseppe Giusti, particularly on the eve of the 1848 revolutions, was enticing.[13]

All this provided a cultural window on the world for Jabotinsky's readership in faraway Odessa and especially for aspiring, acculturated Russian Jews.

THE PROGRESSIVE RUSSIAN

Jabotinsky also wrote about Italian politics and was strongly opposed to Prime Minister Francesco Crispi's imperialist adventures in Ethiopia. Crispi, a *garibaldino* who had fought for Italian independence, now seemingly relegated the ideas of Mazzini and Cavour to a lower rung. Empire now also became an Italian aspiration. In response, Jabotinsky wrote an anti-war play, *Krov*, ostensibly characterising the Boer War but in reality an attack on Crispi's policies and the calamity of the Italian defeat at the hands of Ethiopian Emperor Menelik at the Battle of Adua in 1896. Jabotinsky's heroes were 'anti-monarchist, anti-papist, anti-colonial republicans'.[14] In March 1899 he paid tribute to the left-wing socialist Felice Cavolloti, who was killed in a duel.[15] He was enthusiastic when

[10] Vladimir Jabotinsky, 'Letters from Naples', *Odesskii Novosti*, 15 August 1901.
[11] Vladimir Jabotinsky, 'Spirit and Body', *Odesskii Listok*, 17 March 1899.
[12] Stanislao G. Pugliese, 'Contesting Restraints: Amelia Pincherle Rosselli: Jewish Writer in Pre-Fascist Italy', *Women in Judaism*, vol. 1, no. 2 (1998).
[13] Vladimir Jabotinsky, 'Mrakobes', *Feuilletons* (St. Petersburg, 1913); 'Reactionary' (1912), Jabotinsky Institute Archives, Tel Aviv.
[14] Stanislawski, *Zionism and the Fin de Siècle*, p. 137.
[15] Vladimir Jabotinsky, 'Rome', *Odesskii Listok*, 13 March 1899.

Giuseppe Zanardelli, supported by liberals and radicals, was appointed prime minister[16] and condemnatory of the hitherto admired Gabriele D'Annunzio for seemingly abandoning progressive causes.[17] His worldview therefore was not untypical of many Russian intellectuals at the time – one framed by symbolism, decadence, art nouveau and nihilism. It was also a period when established classical writers such as Tolstoy were being superseded by Chekhov and Gorky,[18] exponents of an avant-garde Russian culture. The succeeding generation appreciated contemporary writers and enjoyed the work of Verlaine, Poe, Ibsen, Rimbaud and Maeterlinck.

In addition to D'Annunzio and Cavolloti, Jabotinsky admired numerous left-wing journalists such as Salvatore Barzilai and would associate with them at the well-known haunt of writers and intellectuals, Rome's Café Aragno.[19] Jabotinsky heard lectures at the university by luminaries such as Antonio Labriola and Enrico Ferri, whose names he would recall in his autobiography in the 1930s. In early articles for the Odessa press, he mentioned Labriola's *Essais sur la conception materialiste de l'histoire* – written in the form of letters to Georges Sorel – and Ferri's personality and powers of oration.[20]

Jabotinsky attended two lecture series on philosophy by Labriola, 'the father of Italian Marxism', who had translated the Communist Manifesto into Italian and written three works on historical materialism in the 1890s. A disciple of the Hegelian 'idealist realism' philosopher Bertrando Spaventa, Labriola was often involved in debates with the proponents of positivism. Significantly Labriola developed his theories when the reunification of Italy had already been accomplished – according to the Hegelian thesis of the nation creating the state. Labriola was deeply attracted to the writings of Spinoza, which he knew 'by heart and with loving understanding'[21] and which influenced his views on rationalism:

Until the heroism of Baruch Spinoza shall become the matter-of-fact virtue of everyday life in the higher developed humanity of the future, and until myths, poetry, metaphysics and religion shall no longer overshadow the field of

---

[16] Vladimir Jabotinsky, 'Rome', *Odesskie Novosti*, 1 May 1901.

[17] Vladimir Jabotinsky, 'Rome: Gabriele', *Odesskii Novosti*, 25 April 1901.

[18] Stanislawski, *Zionism and the Fin de Siècle*, p. 134.

[19] Vladimir Jabotinsky, 'Café Aragno', *Odesskie Novosti*, 4 May 1900.

[20] Vladimir Jabotinsky, 'The Year 1898', *Odesskii Listok*, 1 January 1899; 'Rome', 8 February 1899.

[21] Antonio Labriola, *Socialism and Philosophy*, trans. Ernest Untermann (Chicago, 1934), p. 319.

consciousness, let us be content that up to now, and for the present, philosophy in its differentiated and its improved sense has served, and serves, as a critical instrument and helps science to keep its formal methods and logical processes clear: that it helps us in our lives to reduce the obstacles which the fantastic projections of the emotions, passions, fears and hopes pile in the way of free thought; that it helps and serves, as Spinoza himself would say, to vanquish "imaginationem et ignorantiam".[22]

Despite his orthodox Marxism, Labriola was a critic of determinist theories and argued that there were no 'immanent laws of historical development'.[23] Jabotinsky was impressed by Labriola's intellectual openness and opposition to a cut-and-dried, preordained scientific template. Jabotinsky's secretary and first biographer later commented:

Historical materialism implied a monistic outlook, because he regarded it as a unified entity of theory and practice, rising above the theoretical abstractions of all-explaining historical factors. To Labriola, there was no predetermination in human life; progress is not fated. Men themselves must produce the future and in progress there are always regressions, deviations and errors.[24]

Jabotinsky's arrival in Italy coincided with a profound reconsideration of Marxist theory in Western Europe. It initiated a gradual move of part of the Left to the right – a transition replicated in Palestine in the 1920s when former socialist Zionists emerged as the Maximalist wing of Jabotinsky's Revisionist movement. The catastrophic defeat of the French by the Prussians in 1870 had created a deep questioning of the political system. The first mass movement of the Right, Boulangism, attracted anti-liberal Marxists in the 1880s. A decade later, the perceived failure of Marxist determinism, the advent of a social democratic revisionism and the political symbolism of the Dreyfus affair laid the theoretical basis for fascism. Indeed, for some, the proletariat, which had not lived up to its revolutionary expectations, was proving to be a disappointment. The nation therefore came to be regarded as 'the only historical force which could still serve as an agent of moral regeneration and social transformation'.[25] The writings of Gustav Le Bon, Georges Sorel and Robert Michels influenced many Italian socialists. The Italian school of political sociology, which adapted Sorel's ideas, rejected parliamentarianism,

---

[22] Ibid., pp. 90–91.
[23] Ibid., p. 67.
[24] Joseph Schechtman, *Rebel and Statesman: The Jabotinsky Story – The Early Years, 1880–1923* (New York, 1956), p. 51.
[25] Ze'ev Sternhall, *Neither Right Nor Left: Fascist Ideology in France* (Princeton, NJ, 1986), pp. 17–18.

individualism, liberalism and democracy. Sorel himself broke with social-ism in 1901 and viewed the syndicalist movement in France as the real reflection of the revolutionary proletariat – a movement which carried the seeds of early Christianity. He wrote:

> The truth of Marxism lay not in its pretended 'science of society', but in providing the rules for revolutionary conduct. The specific goal of syndicalism was to inure men to those rules, to create the new men for the new society.[26]

Yet Sorel passed through many ideological phases, including a flirtation with proto-fascism.

Earlier in his life Sorel, like Jabotinsky, had been influenced by Antonio Labriola and regarded his *Essais sur la conception materialiste de l'histoire* as 'a landmark in the history of socialism'. Sorel looked for heroes, which he believed was the link to a productive life. In particu-lar, the works of Renan and Proudhon were influential in this regard. He entertained the possibility of socialist institutions which were free from state interference and straightjacketed Marxism. Like Labriola he disliked any ideological rigidity which prevented intellectual exploration. He opposed any notions of born-again Jacobinism.

If Antonio Labriola defended Marxism within a flexible interpretation, his virtual namesake, Arturo Labriola, Sorel's leading disciple and editor of *Avanguardia Socialista*, not only promoted revolutionary syndicalism but was able to fuse it theoretically with nationalism. In 1909, Giuseppe Prezzolini published *La teoria sindacalista*, which explained the need for the transition from revolutionary syndicalism to national syndicalism. World War I moved this stream of political thought into a proto-fascist mode, and it was Mussolini, the former socialist activist and editor, who imbued it with totalitarianism. Mussolini never had any qualms about dispensing with the profound anti-nationalism of the socialist tradition. Indeed, he later claimed that some Communists were his 'spiritual sons'.[27]

This fragmentation and evolution of Marxist orthodoxy was often accompanied by a latent anti-Semitism. Both Sorel at one point in his career and Michels argued that the presence of Jews in European socialist parties was both disruptive and disproportionate.[28]

---

[26] James Gregor, *Young Mussolini and the Intellectual Origins of Fascism* (Berkeley, CA, 1979), p. 39.

[27] Domenico Settembrini, 'Mussolini and the Legacy of Revolutionary Socialism', *Journal of Contemporary History*, no. 11 (1976), pp. 239–268.

[28] Roberto Michels, *La sociologia del partito politico nella democrazia moderna* (Turin, 1912), pp. 274–80.

World War I offered figures such as Mussolini and D'Annunzio a unique opportunity to embrace nationalism with an unprecedented fervour in an attempt to reclaim Italian-speaking areas of the Austro-Hungarian Empire – *Italia irredenta* – and to mobilise the masses in the nationalist cause.

Although many acculturated Italian Jews supported Mussolini during the early days of Fascism – and even during his previous phase as a socialist writer and activist – he had not been averse to making derogatory remarks about Jews.[29] Moreover, in Mussolini's eyes, the October Revolution had solidified the relationship between Jews and Bolsheviks. He therefore penned articles bearing titles such as 'I complici' (The accomplices) and 'Ebrei, Bolscevismo e Sionismo italiano' (Jews, Bolshevism and Italian Zionism).[30] Despite this, the first Fascist government included a former chairman of Pro Israele, Giovanni Colonna di Cesarò, but Mussolini was unpredictable in his views and initially cool towards Zionism.

Several of Jabotinsky's respected teachers were part and parcel of this ideological upheaval and transformation. The criminologist and socialist parliamentarian Enrico Ferri eventually supported Mussolini's Fascist regime. Vittorio Scialoja, who taught Roman law to Jabotinsky, became a minister in Mussolini's government in the 1920s.

Another of Jabotinsky's lecturers, a laissez-faire economist and profound opponent of Marxism, Maffeo Pantaleoni,[31] urged the ascending Fascist party to adopt an anti-Semitic tone. Periodicals such as *La Vita Italiana* and dailies such as *Il Populo* painted the Jews in conspiratorial colours. Indeed, Pantaleoni had introduced the *Protocols of the Elders of Zion* to the editor of *La Vita Italiana*.[32] He viewed Jewish financiers as 'the greatest evil of all'. *Il Populo* argued that 'Jewish Bolshevik leaders were financed by Jewish US bankers'.[33] Even Mussolini was criticised – for submitting to 'the blandishments of Italian Jews'.[34]

[29] Giorgio Fabre, 'Mussolini and the Jews on the Eve of the March on Rome', in Joshua D. Zimmerman, ed., *Jews in Italy under Fascist and Nazi Rule, 1922–1945* (Cambridge, 2009), pp. 56–57.

[30] Vincenzo Pinto, 'Between Imago and Res: The Revisionist Zionist Movement's Relationship with Fascist Italy, 1922–1938', *Israel Affairs*, vol. 10, no. 3 (2004), pp. 90–109.

[31] Vladimir Jabotinsky, 'Crisis of the Proletariat', *Poslednie Novosti (Paris)*, 19 April 1932; *Reshimot*, Ketavim 16, ed. Eri Jabotinsky (Jerusalem, 1958), pp. 275–83.

[32] Renzo de Felice, *The Jews in Fascist Italy: A History* (New York, 2001). p. 39.

[33] *Il Populo*, 4 June 1919.

[34] Maffeo Pantaleoni, 'Lutocrazia e bolshevismo giudaicos gretolano il fascismo', *La Vita Italiana*, July 1921.

Jabotinsky remained aware of the evolving Italian experience – even though he never espoused Mussolini's path and was increasingly wary of Italian Fascism later on in life. In 1930 he castigated Jews who were captivated by the age of ideology. 'It may signify Marx, Lenin, Gandhi, perhaps tomorrow Mussolini'.[35]

Yet there were parallels. Mussolini similarly wanted to create a nation out of disparate ethnic fragments. He looked back to ancient Rome and utilised it as a template for the present in order to enthuse and excite. He promoted *romanità* (Romaness) and demanded that Italians refuse to conform to their stereotypical image – that they embrace machismo and become less 'Italian'.

Jabotinsky entered this ideological fin-de-siècle maelstrom at its inception as a wide-eyed teenager, escaping the dead hand of Tsarism. The decline and fragmentation of Marxist theory in Italy were symbolised by the death of Antonio Labriola, his much-respected teacher, in 1904. Jabotinsky, therefore, was confronted not only by traditional Italian liberalism but also by the myth-making and the mobilisation of the revolutionary syndicalists who subsequently embraced nationalism. Moreover, his roommate and friend in Rome, Roberto Lombardo, was becoming active in the anarcho-syndicalist movement. Indeed, Lombardo had originally written the basis for the anti-war *Krov*, which was reworked by Jabotinsky. Back in Odessa, Jabotinsky read widely on anarchism and was arrested in April 1902.[36] During a talk at the Writers' Club, he had repeated the social anarchist Mikhail Bakunin's warning about a future 'dictatorship of the proletariat'. Shortly after this, Jabotinsky wrote a paean to Charlotte Corday, the assassin of the Jacobin Jean-Paul Marat. Police also questioned him about his relationship with Vsevolod Lebedentsev, a member of the Left Social Revolutionaries. The police suspected that Jabotinsky was similarly a member of the Left SRs.

This was the ideological turbulent river that Jabotinsky and many other young Russian intellectuals dipped into. It consisted of many tributaries and testified to this period of political transition. Jabotinsky was therefore typical of his time.

To the writer Arthur Koestler, Jabotinsky was 'a National Liberal in the great nineteenth century tradition, a revolutionary of the 1848 brand,

---

[35] Vladimir Jabotinsky, 'His Children and Ours: On Herzl's Children', *Haynt*, 26 September 1930; *Hadar*, no. 1–3, February 1940.
[36] Hillel Halkin, *Jabotinsky: A Life* (New Haven, CT, 2014), pp. 32–33.

successor to Garibaldi and Mazzini'.[37] To the historian Walter Laqueur, he was 'a Sorelian who had never read Sorel'.[38]

Not all Sorelians ended up as worshippers at Mussolini's altar; however, it is clear that he was highly influential in stirring the ideological brew at a time when many young people looked for a political path.

THE WINDS OF CHANGE

While Jabotinsky occasionally transmitted these winds of change to his Odessa readers, he, like many a troubled Russian youth, found great difficulty keeping afloat intellectually under the Tsar's rule. Yet he seemed to have taken great care to avoid negative commentary about the political scene in Russia in his writings. However, he did contribute several short reports to *Avanti*, the periodical of the Italian Socialist party in 1901.[39] This was probably more out of anger at the correspondent in Russia of *Tribuna*, whose fawning tributes to the Tsarist authorities clearly irritated him. His first article reflected his support for a huge student demonstration in Kazan Square in St. Petersburg on 4 March 1901 – and his outrage at a mounted Cossack charge at the peaceful crowd, utilising the *nagaika*, a whip with an embedded piece of metal.[40] Hundreds were arrested, imprisoned and exiled. Following his return to Russia, he wrote several articles about the plight of students in the Odessa press.[41] Jabotinsky's sense of solidarity with his fellow students in the many protests in numerous Russian cities eventually earned him a six-week detention in an Odessa prison in the spring of 1902.[42]

In one article in *Avanti*, Jabotinsky attacked the notion of a *Tribuna* correspondent that the students were opposed by the Russian masses. He pointed to a demonstration in Odessa in April 1899 when ordinary Russians had spontaneously chanted 'Long live the students' and that the

---

[37] Memorial meeting booklet for Ze'ev Jabotinsky at St Johns Wood Synagogue, London, 9 July 1964.

[38] Walter Laqueur, *The History of Zionism* (London, 2003), p. 360.

[39] Vladimiro Giabotinski, *Avanti* 10 April 1901 and 16 April 1901.

[40] Samuel D. Krassow, *Students, Professors and the State in Tsarist Russia* (Berkeley, CA, 1989), pp. 119–40.

[41] Vladimir Jabotinsky, 'Causerie: To Mr. A. R. in Dresden', 8 November 1901 *Odesskie Novosti*; 'Causerie' 27 November 1901; 'Causerie' 13 December 1901.

[42] Vladimir Jabotinsky, *Avtobiyografyah: Sipur Yamai*, Ketavim 1, ed. Eri Jabotinsky (Jerusalem, 1947), pp. 40–42. Jabotinsky did not write any articles between 23 April and 9 June 1902. See Vladimir (Ze'ev) Zhabotinskii, *Polnoe sobranie sochinenii v 9 tomakh*, Kniga 1 ed. Leonid Katsis (Minsk, 2008).

bosiaki ,[43] Russian sansculottes , had protected the young demonstrators from the police. Significantly he pointed out that normally the Russian masses were just too preoccupied with their own everyday burdens and a fatalistic acceptance of suffering to become involved politically. Liberals and socialists, he said, truly loved the indifferent masses, but they oper-ated without consulting them. Only when democracy had been achieved, they argued, would the masses truly appreciate what had been done in their name. Jabotinsky unabashedly described the ignorance of the Russian masses in unflattering terms. He labelled them in a derogatory fashion as 'il populino' rather than as 'il populo'. Jabotinsky rational-ised that the term 'the Russian people' applied solely to the intelligentsia. And unlike the masses, the intelligentsia were politically active. 'They will not be crushed underfoot by the horses,' he wrote. Moreover, he pointed out that approximately 80 percent of the Russian press was liberal and that Marxism had recently made great strides amongst young Russian men and women.[44] Youth, he recorded, were 'the compass of the ship, "Russia"'. New ideas would move Russia forward, but this could arise only through an unfettered freedom of expression. Russia was desper-ately in need of 'the air of freedom'.[45]

Even at this early stage of his career, it is self-evident that Jabotinsky had little faith in an unquestioning belief in the masses in Russia. This dovetailed with the views of Robert Michels, who argued that only dur-ing a crisis would the masses ditch their hallowed apathy and dramati-cally move towards political action. During such times a leadership would emerge from the bourgeois intelligentsia which would articulate the aspi-rations of the masses.[46] Such a precondition, it was argued, existed in pre–World War I Italy in the movement of revolutionary syndicalism – a movement which preached virtue over compromise.

In 1908, in *Reflections on Violence*, Sorel argued that only in struggle could self-sacrifice be truly understood. Sorel spoke about 'an energising myth' which could move multitudes. Such views were swirling about in the intellectual atmosphere when Jabotinsky was in his formative years in Italy.

---

[43] *Bosiaki* is an abbreviation of *bez opredelennykh zaniatii* (the barefoot ones). See Robert Weinberg, *The Revolution of 1905 in Odessa: Blood on the Steps* (Bloomington, IN, 1993), p. 135.

[44] Vladimiro Giabotinski, *Avanti*, 10 April 1901.

[45] Vladimiro Giabotinski, *Avanti*, 16 April 1901.

[46] Gregor, *Young Mussolini*, pp. 64–65.

The young Jabotinsky of fin-de-siècle Rome was thus far removed from the Jabotinsky of the 1930s, the oracle of nationalist Zionism. Indeed, he contributed literary articles to the Russian Marxist periodical *Zhizn'* and unequivocally proclaimed that 'my country [Russia] needs freedom' in his articles in *Avanti*.[47] He admiringly stated that St. Petersburg was far 'redder' than Odessa, and he seemingly believed as 'a self-evident truth' that socialism would bring about social justice. In later life, he famously proclaimed that fin-de-siècle Italy was far more his spiritual homeland than holy Russia.[48] He never fully abandoned this dimension of his personality. Moreover, the cultural influence of the great Russian writers was ever present.[49] The Russian writer and rootless cosmopolitan always coexisted precariously with the passionate rhetorician of Zionism. Jabotinsky took great care to compartmentalise these different reflections of his identity.

When Jabotinsky returned from Italy to Odessa in 1901, he continued to write for *Odesskii Novosti*, which had a national readership, under the well-known byline 'Altalena', as well as other publications under a variety of pseudonyms.[50] He reviewed Ibsen's *The Wild Duck*,[51] commemorated the fiftieth anniversary of Gogol's death[52] and discussed reflections on both Russian opera, Glinka's *Ruslan and Lyudmilla*,[53] and Italian opera, *Tosca*'[54]

Yet even before leaving Rome, Jabotinsky – and many like him – were entering into a period of intellectual bewilderment due to the profound challenges to previous certainties in both Italy and Russia. He had written an abiding criticism of the new direction taken by D'Annunzio at the same time as he attacked the suppression of student demonstrations in Russia.[55] All this occurred as aestheticism, symbolism and decadence were becoming yesterday's philosophies. Many began to gravitate towards politics or religion or nationalist movements as vessels of containment. In addition, the Russian Social Democratic Labour Party was

[47] Vladimiro Giabotinski, *Avanti*, 16 April 1901.

[48] Jabotinsky, *Avtobiyografyah*, p. 28.

[49] Hamutal Bar-Yosef, 'The Reception of Leonid Andreev in Hebrew and Yiddish Literature', *Symposium*, vol. 58, no. 3 (2004), pp. 139–51.

[50] Leonid Katsis, *Vladimir (Ze'ev) Jabotinsky and His Recently Discovered Works: Problems of Attribution and Analysis* (Leiden, 2012), pp. 417–37.

[51] Vladimir Jabotinsky, 'Causerie', *Odesskie Novosti*, 1 November 1902.

[52] Vladimir Jabotinsky, 'Causerie', *Odesskie Novosti*, 19 February 1902.

[53] Vladimir Jabotinsky, 'City Theatre', *Odesskie Novosti*, 18 April 1902.

[54] Vladimir Jabotinsky, 'Marie D'Arneiro', *Odesskie Novosti*, 7 February 1902.

[55] Vladimir Jabotinsky, 'From the Shores of the Tiber', *Odesskie Novosti*, 7 March; 25 March 1901.

fraying around the edges due to the repeated assaults of Lenin and the Iskra group. Despite Lenin's best efforts, there was also a movement in the opposite direction. As in Italy, the official face of Marxism was sporting ideological fractures. In July 1903, former Marxists, liberals and social democrats who rejected the determinist view of history formed the Union of Liberation, which evolved into the Constitutional Democrats, the Kadets. During this period Jabotinsky had taken to writing about anarcho-libertarian topics, from the right of prostitutes to ply their trade[56] to the right of journalists to be free of the slant of their paper.[57] All this was accentuated by the increasing ideological and religious exclusivity of the Russian intelligentsia. The automatic adherence of Jews to its ranks was now questioned.[58] Dostoyevsky was preferred ideologically to the philosemites Gorky and Korolenko.[59]

THE SALVATION OF ZION

Jabotinsky's writings about students – both Italian and Russian – led to an invitation to address the Literary Artistic Club of Odessa, which boasted a mainly student audience, on the subject 'Individualism and Collectivism'. Here again, he showed that he had little faith in the Russian masses and stressed the role of the individual in making and changing history. Much to the irritation of his audience, he quoted Bakunin's defence of the individual when disputing Marx and Marxism in idealising the masses. He further addressed the issue in a play, *Ladno*.

Such an espousal of individualism led to questions about the situation of Jews in Russia and beyond. Following his return from Italy, there were references in his articles, albeit indirectly, to the Jewish question. At the end of 1901, Jabotinsky addressed the question of anti-Semitism and tolerance in an article entitled 'Mr A. R. in Dresden'.[60] A few weeks later, Jabotinsky wrote 'On Zionism'[61] in response to an article by an advocate of Russification, Iosif Bikerman, in the liberal yet anti-Marxist *Russkoe Bogatsvo*.[62] Bikerman argued that Zionism was utterly utopian

[56] Vladimir Jabotinsky, 'Causerie', *Odesskie Novosti*, 5 March 1902.
[57] *Odesskie Novosti*, 24 October 1902.
[58] Brian Horowitz, 'Russian-Zionist Cultural Cooperation, 1916–18: Leib Jaffe and the Russian Intelligentsia', *Jewish Social Studies*, vol. 13, no. 1 (Autumn 2006), pp. 87–109.
[59] Maurice Friedberg, 'The Jewish Search in Russian Literature', *Prooftexts*, vol. 4, no. 1 (January 1984), pp. 93–105.
[60] *Odesskie Novosti*, 27 November 1901.
[61] *Odesskie Novosti*, 8 September 1902.
[62] Iosif Bikerman, 'O sionizme i po povodu sionizme', *Russkoe Bogatsvo*, no. 7, July 1902.

and would detach the Jews from the spirit of universalism. He argued, therefore, for an alliance with the progressive Russian intelligentsia. In response Jabotinsky denounced him for his scientific view of history in believing that everything followed a natural pathway.

A week later, Jabotinsky published a homage to Émile Zola, the day after his death, in which he invoked the Dreyfus affair.[63] While this article was a broad tribute to Zola's literary achievements and intellectual courage, it was clear that there was a subtle change towards a liberal understanding of nationalism. Indeed, Jabotinsky remarkably commented with reference to Zionism that 'such a nationalism is the highest form of progress'.[64]

In another article, 'On Nationalism', in 1903 he argued that class differences would eventually disappear, but not national modes of thinking and behaving.[65] Yet no mention was made of Jews.

Jabotinsky's views were changing. On a personal level, he asked himself where he was heading as a young Russian writer – and there were no clear answers. While he had written profusely for both the press and the theatre, there had been no dramatic public recognition of his talents. His status was still confined to the shadows. He was searching for new pathways to make sense of himself and his country, Russia.

In a plaintive letter to Maxim Gorky, he hinted at his sense of disillusionment and the dead-end street which he felt he had come to inhabit.[66] In contrast, Gorky had emerged from the provincial press into the glaring lights of literary acclaim. A meeting with the writer Vladimir Korolenko had propelled him on his path. Yet Gorky believed that art simply for art's sake betrayed the shallowness of the Russian intelligentsia in the midst of widespread misery. He therefore combined a Tolstoyan sense of social realism with a romantic notion of revolution. In a political sense, he had become aware of the plight of the Jews when he witnessed a pogrom in Nizhni-Novgorod in 1884. He commented later that the Jewish community had 'fought for political freedom in Russia with much more honesty and energy than many Russians'.[67] Like Jabotinsky he had been outraged by the suppression of the student protests in

[63] Vladimir Jabotinsky, *Odesskie Novosti*, 'Causaries: His Achievements', 18 September 1902.

[64] Stanislawski, *Zionism and the Fin de Siècle*, p. 155.

[65] *Odesskie Novosti*, 30 January 1903.

[66] Vladimir Jabotinsky, Letter to Maxim Gorky, 10 August 1903, *Igrot, 1898–1914* (Tel Aviv, 1992).

[67] Solomon M. Schwartz, *The Jews in the Soviet Union* (Syracuse, NY, 1951), p. 276.

St. Petersburg in March 1901[68] and was imprisoned for his views. There were indeed many parallels in the journeys of Gorky and Jabotinsky, but only the former had succeeded in gaining acknowledgement as a man of letters.

As in the case of many an Italian socialist, Jabotinsky eventually embraced nationalism as a means of repairing the world and providing himself with an identity and a direction. Any entry into the world of Russian nationalism was barred by the fortifying forces of reaction. In addition, while he expressed sympathy for Ukrainian nationalism, his enthusiasm for it was probably less than intense. So when he was invited to attend the Sixth Zionist Congress in Basel in the summer of 1903, the effect was revelatory, rapid and dramatic. He returned to Odessa as both a Zionist and a Jew. Literally overnight, he had become a true believer. Yet for all his newly found passion in the Zionist arena, he remained the archetypal outsider. It was convenient to classify the Jews as a tri-lingual people – and the Russian Diaspora, which embraced Russian, Yiddish and Hebrew, was no exception. They spoke Russian, the language of the country in which they lived, Yiddish between themselves and Hebrew, the holy language, reserved for prayer and its commentators. Yet Jabotinsky, the Russified Jew, did not fit into such a neat categorisation. In parallel with his fervent embrace of Jewish nationalism, he paradoxically remained a rootless cosmopolitan and a Russian writer. Despite his fluency in a multitude of languages, he was a son of the Russian literary tradition. Jabotinsky spoke and wrote 'an impeccable, rich and expressive Russian which was both polished and colloquial, felicitous in phrasing, high-spirited and pithy'.[69]

When he was already defined as a committed expounder of Zionism, Jabotinsky wrote a subsequently little-known article in 1910, entitled 'Three Arts'. In this, he contrasted the poet, the orator and the politician – and deconstructed them and their techniques. It was perhaps a deprecatory yet lucid self-analysis, or rather a dissection of the imagery with which outsiders perceived him – for example, his caricature of the poet:

I would pass my days in silence and darkness, listening in to the birth music of my rhymes. Think of the unbearable ecstasy and torment of witnessing how – almost without your conscious will – like-sounding words gather in your head; how first

[68] Tova Yedlin, *Maxim Gorky: A Biography* (Westport, CT, 1999), pp. 30–31.
[69] Schechtman, *Rebel and Statesman*, pp. 65–66.

they are flung about in chaotic disorder, then slowly settle down and arrange themselves in harmonious order.[70]

Jabotinsky depicted each of the three practitioners as being in conflict with the others. Perhaps this was the inner conflict that was taking place within himself, a conflict he was unable to resolve and did not wish to resolve.

[70] Jabotinsky Institute Archives, Tel Aviv.

2

Fully Fledged Zionism

READING AND WRITING

The figure of Theodor Herzl, the founder of modern Zionism, entranced Jabotinsky – although it is likely that he never met him.[1] The early death of Herzl in 1904 profoundly shocked Jabotinsky. It propelled him to look at Herzl as if he were a combination of national deliverer and holy man:

Sometimes from the midst of a nation's gifted individuals there arises a personality who is endowed with an exceptional sensitivity which other mortals lack. Everything sacred that is scattered in fragments in the souls of millions is collected in the soul of this man, is welded into one piece – and then the God of the nation speaks through the lips of this man and creates with his hands, and he becomes the chosen leader of the masses with the right to achieve their elementary will. Happy are those nations to which destiny grants such a leader.[2]

So wrote the twenty-four-year-old Jabotinsky. He quoted from the poetry of the Italian poetess Ada Negri about the legend of the living water – water that makes you immortal. Yet it is clear that the trauma of finding Herzl and then losing him almost immediately was tantamount to a heavenly sign for the anti-religious, anti-mystical Jabotinsky that his destiny was somehow bound up with Herzl's legacy. In an article eulogising Herzl, he effectively wrote about himself:

We were sitting at the time in the gutter, at the end of the great highway of life and on this road we watched the majestic procession of nations on their way to their

[1] Michael Stanislawski, *Zionism and the Fin de Siècle: Cosmopolitanism and Nationalism from Nordau to Jabotinsky* (Berkeley, CA, 2001), pp. 168–77.
[2] Vladimir Jabotinsky, 'Shiva: On the Death of Herzl', *Evreiskaya zhizn'*, no. 6, June 1904; *Hadar*, November 1940.

historic destinies. And we were sitting aside, like beggars with outstretched hands, begging for alms and swearing in different languages that we merited the charitable offering. Sometimes it was given to us, and then it appeared that we were pleased and contented because the master was in a good mood and had thrown us a gnawed bone. So it only appeared, for deep in our souls was growing a repulsive disgust for the beggar's spot in the gutter and for the outstretched hand, and we felt a confused attraction for the great highway, a desire to walk upon it like others, not to beg but to build our own happiness.

We changed; we were brought to life by touching the earth upon which he moved. It is only recently that I felt that earth and it is only from that moment that I understood what it meant to live and breathe – and if on the morrow I should have awakened to learn that this was merely a dream, that I am what I had been, and that ground is not and cannot be under my feet, I would have killed myself, for it is impossible for one who has breathed the mountain air to return and be reconciled to sprawl once more in the gutter.

I feel that it is in the word 'work' that we find the purpose and the reward of life. Are we striving for the significance of life? Do we want happiness? Do we want salvation?[3]

Herzl was seen as a figure who had awoken the slumbering Jewish masses. 'His will was like an iron fist'.[4] The figure of Garibaldi was invoked and the slogan *Italia fara de se* – 'Italy will help itself' – applied to the Jewish situation.[5] Herzl was characterised as leading his people forward towards redemption in Israel. Jabotinsky described him as 'our eagle, our sacred, kindly tribune'. According to Jabotinsky, Herzl had appealed to something deep in the Jewish soul – and urged the Jews to create their own history, 'step out on the arena and see to it that from now on your destiny shall be created by you only'.[6] Jabotinsky had found his calling. In 1906, he defined it in neo-religious terms:

My work is that of a mason, building a new temple for the one and only deity. The name of that deity is the Jewish people.[7]

This epitomised his understanding of the Jewish question at the beginning of the twentieth century.

Like several other early Zionists, he did not accept that the Jews had survived down the long centuries of persecution and harassment solely

---

[3] Vladimir Jabotinsky, 'Hesped', *Evreiskaya zhizn*, no. 6, June 1904; *Jewish Herald*, 22 July 1949.

[4] Ibid.

[5] Vladimir Jabotinsky, 'Nashi Kritiki', *Evreiskaya zhizn*, no. 3, March 1904; 'The Critics of Zionism', *The Maccabean*, vol. 12, no. 5 (May 1907); vol. 12, no. 6 (June 1907); vol. 13, no. 1 (July 1907).

[6] Vladimir Jabotinsky, 'Sidya na Polu', *Evreiskaya zhizn*, no.6, June 1904; 'Shiva: On the Death of Herzl'.

[7] Vladimir Jabotinsky, 'I Have Faith', *Jewish Standard*, 18 December 1942.

FIGURE 3. Lithograph of Theodor Herzl, Basel (November 1901).
Copyright B. Auskrin; courtesy of the Jabotinsky Institute, Tel Aviv.

because of their faith. Rather, Judaism had been a supportive cloaking device for the real reason. National consciousness, it was argued, had developed fully and deeply – to an unmatched extent. This allowed the Jews to survive the loss of land and national sovereignty. A later adherent of Jabotinsky wrote about 'the religious sanctification of the national elements of the Jews':

While in ancient times Jewish religion was but one of the national elements, all the national elements now became part of religion. In any case Jewish nationalism became so entwined with Jewish religion that the two seemed identical.[8]

---

[8] Ben-Zion Netanyahu, Introduction to Leon Pinsker, *Road to Freedom: Writings and Addresses* (New York, 1944), p. 11.

It was further argued that the advent of the French Revolution and the European Enlightenment began to pierce this protective shield of Judaism. Many Jews began to assimilate, acculturate or even convert to Christianity. The challenge to Judaism in Western Europe led to new religious forms – modern orthodox, reform, conservative. The challenge in the East coalesced with a rejection of rabbinic authority and often the embrace of liberalism or an embryonic socialism. However, this often meant a renunciation of Jewishness or at least the national elements within it. Indeed, the French revolutionaries granted emancipation to the Jews on the basis that they belonged to a different religion – not to a different nation. As Clermont-Tonnerre commented in his celebrated 'Speech on Religious Minorities' in 1789: 'We must refuse everything to the Jews as a nation and accord everything to Jews as individuals.'

If, therefore, the Jews insisted that they belonged to another nation rather than to another religion, their path to full equality in the societies in which they lived would be blocked at worst and impaired at best. They thus accepted the offer on hand, but essentially led 'a dual existence in all spheres of life'.

Jabotinsky immersed himself in learning Hebrew, studying the poetry of Bialik and the essays of Ahad Ha'am. Yet he still felt torn between the prospect of a glittering career as a Russian writer and the accolades of a reading public – and the wilderness of being 'a Zionist leader'.[9] This was an intellectual dissonance which he never fully resolved.

Jabotinsky's frantic rush to educate himself and to formulate a structural framework for his new beliefs led him to read *Autoemancipation* by his fellow Odessan Leon Pinsker, which had been published some twenty years earlier. Pinsker's life story exhibited some parallels which Jabotinsky identified with. Pinsker too had been a Russian liberal who was awakened to the possibilities of a better future by the revolutions of 1848. He had tried to install and to awaken a Jewish national spirit amongst those Jews well on the way to Russification and assimilation. Unlike Jabotinsky he emerged from the cultural milieu of the Haskalah – and was not oblivious to it. Although he was involved with the Society for the Advancement of the Enlightenment of the Jews, the pogrom in Odessa in 1871 and the wave of attacks nationwide ten years later moved Pinsker to a Zionist position. Although Jabotinsky did not write about the Kishinev pogrom[10]

[9] Vladimir Jabotinsky, *Avtobiyografyah: Sipur Yamei*, Ketavim 1, ed. Eri Jabotinsky (Jerusalem, 1947), p. 51.
[10] Stanislawski, *Zionism and the Fin de Siècle*, p. 159.

and later suggested that it did not make an impression upon him[11], a contemporary recalled that it had affected him deeply:

Volodia Jabotinsky completely changed. He began to study his native language, broke with his former environment and soon stopped writing for the general press.[12]

As an advocate of embracing Russian culture, Pinsker like Jabotinsky knew little Hebrew. Pinsker and Jabotinsky had no colleagues to lead them into Zionism, but they instead worked it out for themselves.[13] Pinsker's inspiration for *Autoemancipation* had ironically come from a chance remark by Arthur Cohen, a Liberal MP, president of the Board of Deputies of British Jews and scion of the Montefiore family, on a visit to London.

Jabotinsky's desire for self-education was extended to promoting the education of the next generation. He rejected the rabbinical approach of the past and argued for turning 'a vice into a virtue':

If we want our children's life to be an easy one, if we want to save them from the tragic burden of being different we ourselves carried, it is our duty to educate them in such a manner that the recognition of their ancestry will not be the result of compulsion, but the source of pride and joy. Therefore we have to fascinate them, from their infancy with the exalted glory which we, their elders, discovered at a later age during the painful crisis of adolescence.[14]

REJECTING JUDAIC HISTORY

Another influence on Jabotinsky's early thought was the work of Moses Margolin, who published *Basic Trends in the History of the Jewish People* in St. Petersburg in 1901. He also worked with Jabotinsky as an editor of *Evreiskaya zhizn* when he wrote for the periodical in 1904. Margolin argued that Judaism could 'protect' the Jews when the Land of Israel was

---

[11] Jabotinsky, *Avtobiyografyah*, p. 46.
[12] Letter from Kornei Chukovsky to Rakhel' in Pavlovna Margolina, *Rakhel' Pavlovna Margolina i ee perepiska Korneem Ivanovichem Chukovskim* (Jerusalem, 1978), pp. 19–20, quoted in Alice Nakhimovsky, 'Vladimir Jabotinsky, Russian Writer', *Modern Judaism*, vol. 7, no. 2 (May 1987), pp. 151–73.
[13] Kornei Chukovsky, On Jabotinsky and his Contemporaries: Four Letters to Rachel Margolin, *Ha'uma*, April 1975.
[14] Vladimir Jabotinsky, 'Evreiskoye vospitanie' (Odessa, 1905); 'On Jewish Education', *Our Voice*, 3 November 1971.

lost, but it could not do so when an assimilatory universalism arose in the nineteenth century.

In an article for *Evreiskaya zhizn* in February 1904, Jabotinsky developed the ideas of Margolin. Judaism had been stopped in its creative tracks by the loss of land and sovereignty. Unlike the evolution of Christianity over millennia, its development had been frozen in time. The Jews had survived only through their 'national will' (*narodnaya volya*), but they had not progressed. The idea of 'national will' subsequently assumed a messianic veneer – and the Jews persisted down the centuries. For Jabotinsky, the Land of Israel – not Judaism – was at the core of Jewish history.

Although there were strains of Ahad Ha'am's writings in such ideas, Jabotinsky had little patience for religious tradition. He disparaged the imagery of 'the old maggid in the synagogue', wise but disordered and undisciplined intellectually, jumping from one idea to another – 'and the worst of it is that his audience revels in it'.[15] He was scathing about the time-honoured tradition of the acceptance of suffering. In an article in 1905, he castigated the saintly man who meekly accepted the slaughter of his family as God's will. He was not only a saint, but also a sinner.[16] It was not enough to utter that he had been of no harm to anyone. He also wrote that his newfound faith in Zionism had not been 'culled from the pogroms'. He wrote of being 'happy in his faith – my happiness is such as you have never known and such as you never will know and I want nothing more.'[17] Yet this outpouring of emotion was more than a reaction to the deteriorating situation of the Jews in Tsarist Russia. The pogroms of 1905 and 1906, he pointed out, could not tell him anything that he had not known before.[18] His conversion to Zionism, he pointed out, was an intellectual transformation and not simply a reaction to Tsarist anti-Semitism and the recurring killing of Jews. He maintained his antipathy towards God and Judaism and questioned those who exhibited reverence for the rebbes:

A good many cannot free themselves from the influence of the mystics who gave our ideal a supernatural form.[19]

---

[15] Vladimir Jabotinsky, 'Militarism', *Haynt*, 25 January 1929.
[16] Vladimir Jabotinsky, 'Dva Predatelya', *Khronika evreiskoye zhizni*, vol. 1 no. 43–44 (11 November 1905); 'Two Sinners', *Jewish Herald*, 6 July 1956.
[17] Vladimir Jabotinsky, 'Your New Year', *Odesskie Novosti*, 3 January 1908.
[18] Jabotinsky, 'I Have Faith'.
[19] Jabotinsky, 'Nashi Kritiki'; 'The Critics of Zionism'.

Although he often resorted to religious imagery and well-known Talmudic phraseology to make a political point to his followers, throughout his life he remained contemptuous of God and ghetto:

The ghetto despised physical manhood, the principle of male power as understood and worshipped by all free peoples in history. Physical courage and physical force were of no use, prowess of the body rather an object of ridicule. The only true heroism of the ghetto acknowledged was that of self-suppression and dogged obedience to the Will above.[20]

Jabotinsky distinguished between Jewish history and Judaic history. He lauded the fighter Bar-Kokhba and the Maccabees and ignored the later scholars, the Rambam (Maimonides) and the Ramban (Nahmanides). Yet he also looked to biblical heroes such as Gideon to enlist in his spreading of the Zionist word. In his early poem 'Hesped' (Eulogy) about Herzl, Jabotinsky was happy to mention Rabbah bar bar Hana, a third-century Talmudic sage, to colour his depiction of the late Zionist founder.[21]

Jabotinsky famously wrote that 'in the beginning God created the individual' – essentially a call to action, to take responsibility. But Jabotinsky ultimately believed that it was the individual who created. In 1910, writing through the literary persona of a poet, he commented:

For every day I would feel my might, my sovereignty. I would feel that I have in my power what no one else has – for I create from naught, like God himself – and my creation is more perfect than his.[22]

Jabotinsky's 'poet' argued that he himself had created the 'pure idea' which God's creatures were distant from:

I judge God, nature, kings and heroes – and against my verdict there is no appeal, for it is armoured with rhymes. Centuries will pass and still my poetry will live.[23]

THE COMPANY OF CRITICS

Although Jabotinsky had rejected some elements of positivism in his pre-Zionist days, he now transferred his positivist belief in the Russian intelligentsia to solve Russia's problems to its Jewish counterpart in order to find an answer to the Jewish conundrum. If his explanation of the

---

[20] Vladimir Jabotinsky, Introduction to *Chaim Nachman Bialik: Poems from the Hebrew*, ed. L. V. Snowman (London, 1924) pp. ix–xv.
[21] Jabotinsky, 'Hesped'.
[22] Vladimir Jabotinsky, 'Three Arts' (1910), Jabotinsky Institute Archives, Tel Aviv.
[23] Ibid.

course of Jewish history was correct, then the way to overcome ossification and eventual disintegration was to reconnect with Zion, to return and to reinhabit the Land.

Jabotinsky also had to prove both to himself and to his reading public why other solutions to the Jewish problem were wrong. Several articles swiftly appeared which attacked assimilation; his major foray into this arena was an article entitled 'The Critics of Zionism', which was published at the beginning of 1904. He took issue with the views of the Constitutional Democrat Aleksandr Izgoev and returned to spar once more – this time as a Zionist – with Iosif Bikerman.

Bikerman wanted an accommodation between Russian culture and Jewish tradition. In 1910 he wrote:

The elemental growth of the mighty Russian state and the elemental power of the Jewish people scattered around the world, Peter the First and the Maccabees, the figures of Herzen and the prophet Isaiah exist side by side in pairs in my mind, rising above other contents existing in this world, standing closer to me because they are mine – and there is nothing perverse in this, it is only a little complex, but complexity is universally characteristic of the mind of modern man.[24]

Jabotinsky in his new adherence to Zionism was convinced that such a synthesis was impossible. His reaction to the spate of pogroms throughout Russia – especially after the limited concessions made in the Tsar's manifesto in October 1906 – was fatalistic. He even argued that self-defence groups were a waste of energy and would not fundamentally solve the Jewish question in Russia:

The craters of the exile have opened. The storm has burst. The stranger will have his way with us. All Jewry will be contorted with pain. You will unfold multi-coloured banners of resistance, you will tire out your minds trying to find an escape and there will be moments when you will believe that you have found it. Yet I do not believe in it and it disgusts me to find consolation in such fairy tales. I tell you, coldly and deliberately, there is no salvation. You are in a strange land and right to the end the stranger will have his way with you.[25]

In 1909 a furious literary row blew up concerning Jewishness, anti-Semitism and the place of the Jew in Russian society, ignited by the comments of the playwright Evgeny Chirikov. Jabotinsky was unsparing in his criticism of Russian liberals and their progressive selectivity of chosen causes. He argued that Jews had to 'be vigilant and to organise', to rely

[24] Zsuzsa Hetényi, *In a Maelstrom: The History of Russian-Jewish Prose, 1860–1940* (Budapest, 2008), p. 20.
[25] Jabotinsky, 'I Have Faith'.

upon themselves and not depend on others.[26] The liberal marginalisation
of anti-Semitism he termed 'a-Semitism'.[27] In response to articles by Pyotr
Struve and Pavel Miliukov, he wrote: 'Their affectionate declamation is
drenched in hypocrisy, insincerity, timidity, obsequiousness and for this reason utterly mediocre'.[28] In response to Maxim Vinaver, he called one of the
pre-eminent leaders of Russian Jewry 'the Jewish servant of the Russian
mansion'.[29]

By 1909, Jabotinsky, the Russian writer, was taking his literary idols to
task for the anti-Semitic inferences in their works. He castigated Pushkin,
Turgenev, Dostoyevsky, Gogol and even Chekhov for their often subtle ste-
reotyping of 'the Jew'.[30] This was a far cry from the Russian correspondent
who wrote for the Odessa press from fin-de-siècle Italy.

In 1931 he revisited this theme after a long silence – and perhaps was
even more acerbic. He wrote about the indifference of Russian writers
to the suffering of Jews and other ethnic groups. He attacked Pushkin,
for whom he believed that 'the idea of a Jew was generally repellent', and
Turgenev's negative portrayal in a short story, 'Zhid'. Moreover, the Jew,
he believed, was virtually invisible for too many writers. Thus Nekrassov
mentioned Jews in only one solitary poem, Gogol in a description of a
pogrom in 'Taras Bulba' and Tolstoy in a reference to a Jewish political
offender in 'Resurrection'.[31]

His hostility to assimilation was lifelong and like his antipathy
to Russian writers became more pointed during the inter-war years.
Invoking both Czech nationalism and Indian nationalism, he regarded
assimilation as merely the first step towards a national awakening. It was as if the Jews had been living for 'many days in a cellar'
before emerging into the sunlight.[32] The appearance of 'the Jewish
Communist' preaching assimilation and a relegation of Jewishness particularly grated. Indeed, when two of Herzl's children – both assimilated and estranged from their Jewishness – committed suicide in 1930,

[26] Vladimir Jabotinsky, 'Draft Without a Title', *Rassviet*, 7 June 1909.
[27] Vladimir Jabotinsky, 'A-Semitism ', *Slovo*, 9 March 1909.
[28] Vladimir Jabotinsky, 'The Bear Leaves Its Den', *Rassviet* 15 March 1909.
[29] Aleksandr Solzhenitsyn, 'Two Hundred Years Together', *Common Knowledge*, vol. 9,
     no. 2 (Spring 2003), pp. 204–27.
[30] Vladimir Jabotinsky, 'letifa ha-Rusit', *Al sifrut ve-omanut*, Ketavim 6, ed. Eri Jabotinsky
     (Jerusalem, 1958), pp. 88–96.
[31] Vladimir Jabotinsky, 'Jewish Types in Russian Fiction', *Jewish Chronicle Supplement*,
     5 June 1931.
[32] Vladimir Jabotinsky, 'A Lecture on Jewish History', *Haynt*, 13 May 1932.

Jabotinsky asked, 'What's the difference if one commits suicide with a pistol or with thoughts?'[33]

In 1903 Jabotinsky took issue with Karl Kautsky, who was the pre-eminent Marxist thinker at that time in Europe – a far cry from Lenin's condemnatory 'the renegade Kautsky' of the early Soviet period. The Polish social democrats Rosa Luxemburg and Adolf Warski asked Kautsky to address the problem of anti-Semitism in the aftermath of the Kishinev pogrom. These assimilated Jews wished to challenge the Bund's authority amongst Jewish workers. Kautsky's article 'The Kishinev Massacre and the Jewish Question' duly appeared in several Polish and German Marxist periodicals as well as in Lenin's *Iskra*[34] – almost simultaneously with Jabotinsky's conversion to Zionism.

Kautsky believed that the assimilation of Jews and non-Jews in Eastern Europe was the solution to anti-Semitism. The masses were kept in ignorance, isolated from the rest of the world where the assimilation of the Jews was proceeding apace. The Jews did not have a homeland and were therefore no longer a nation. Class solidarity between Jew and non-Jew was the defining factor – not ethnicity or nationhood. Kautsky had a long record of opposing anti-Semitism and trying to frame a theory for the Jewish question. He strongly supported Jean Jaurès in defending Dreyfus while other socialists demurred. Significantly he did not quote Marx's 'On the Jewish Question' in any of his writings for fear of being tainted by its apparent anti-Jewish projection.[35] However, his closeness to Engels and the solution of assimilation continued and he developed the views of his mentors. Jewish identity was formed through historical factors and would eventually disappear. He argued that Jews were essentially city dwellers and that anti-Semitism was really the accentuated difference between the urban Jew and the rural non-Jew. For Kautsky, Zionism was a distraction and a marginal phenomenon. It would never solve the problem of the Jewish working class. Kautsky's Jewish heroes were Spinoza, Ricardo and Marx – those who either were excommunicated or converted to Christianity.[36]

In his newfound nationalist zeal, Jabotinsky responded to Kautsky's idea of the blending together of all nationalities. If the problems of

[33] Vladimir Jabotinsky, 'His Children and Ours: On Herzl's Children', *Haynt* 26 September 1930; *Hadar*, nos. 1–3, February 1940.

[34] *Iskra*, no. 42, June 1903.

[35] Jack Jacobs, *On Socialism and the Jewish Question after Marx* (New York, 1992), pp. 9–10.

[36] Karl Kautsky, 'On the Problems of the Jewish Proletariat in England', *Justice*, 23 April 1904.

hunger and want were solved – as they both desired – was it not likely that peoples would remain in their homelands and not emigrate? He commented:

Not to a coalescence of nationalities does the natural process lead, but to a security of complete independence. Wars will cease, custom houses will be abolished, but individual dissimilarity, innate in a people will never disappear; eternally maintained by differences of soil and climate, it will not in the least prevent the friendly progress and mutual respect of nations.[37]

Jabotinsky also did not address Kautsky's thesis as to how different peoples emerged or 'how much of different racial ingredients entered into them'. While the past mattered, it was superseded by the present. Jabotinsky argued that the crucial point was how the Jews considered themselves at this point in time – not how they had evolved.

Kautsky's theoretical template about the Jews was taken up by Lenin in an issue of *Iskra* in October 1903, probably at the same time that Jabotinsky was penning his response to Kautsky:

Absolutely untenable scientifically, the idea that the Jews form a separate nation is reactionary politically. Irrefutable practical proof of that is furnished by generally known facts of recent history and of present-day political realities. All over Europe, the decline of medievalism and development of political liberty went hand in hand with the political emancipation of the Jews, their abandonment of Yiddish for the language of the people among whom they lived, and in general their undeniable progressive assimilation with the surrounding population. Are we again to revert to the exceptionalist theories and proclaim that Russia will be the one exception? – although the Jewish emancipation movement is far broader and deeper rooted here, thanks to the awakening of a heroic class consciousness among the Jewish proletariat. Can we possibly attribute to chance the fact that it is the reactionary forces all over Europe, and especially in Russia, who oppose the assimilation of the Jews and try to perpetuate their isolation?[38]

Lenin similarly wanted the Jews to amalgamate with other nations, yet unlike Kautsky's, such views appeared superficial and seemingly not based on any rigorous research. In part, it was an addendum to his confrontation with the Bund and part of his broader plan to dominate the Russian Social Democratic Labour Party (RSDLP). He seemed unaware of the influx of Marxist Zionists into Palestine at the turn of the century. Like Kautsky he preferred to quote assimilated and acculturated Jews such as the French Comptean positivist Alfred Naquet rather than genuine

[37] Jabotinsky, 'Nashi Kritiki'; 'The Critics of Zionism'.
[38] V. I. Lenin, 'The Position of the Bund in the Party', *Iskra*, no. 51, 22 October 1903, in Hyman Lumer, ed., *Lenin on the Jewish Question* (New York, 1974).

representatives of the Jewish workers. Indeed, probably the only Jews with whom he had been acquainted were those who had relegated their Jewishness long ago. He projected the idea that such Russified Jews, often with little Jewish awareness, were the true leaders of the Jewish proletariat despite the developing national conscientiousness of the Jewish masses in Russia.[39]

Like Marxism-Leninism, Zionism wanted to transform the Jews. Both were a revolt against the inertia of the ghetto and the passivity of its inhabitants. Jabotinsky wanted the Jew to become a different type of Jew. Lenin wanted the Jew to become a different type of non-Jew.

The RSDLP, the Bund and the Zionist Organisation had all been founded within months of each other in 1897–1898. Each purported to solve the Jewish problem in Russia and beyond. The Balfour Declaration, which promised a home for the Jews in part of Palestine, and the October Revolution, which promised universal redemption appeared within days of other in 1917. These events promised profoundly different pathways for Jews to follow during the twentieth century.

Both Jabotinsky and Lenin had coincidentally set up their ideological stalls at the end of 1903. Both were Russian intellectuals emerging from the ideological confusion of fin-de-siècle Tsarism. Jabotinsky promised particularism, Lenin offered universalism. Both were seductive to any Jew with a modicum of knowledge of the history and traditions of the Jewish people. Each accused the other of utopianism. As Jabotinsky commented in 1908:

Long ago I had a strong sense of the beauty in the sovereignty of a free person, who has no label on his forehead, who owes nothing to anybody on earth, whose attitude to members of his own people is the same as to members of another people, the sovereignty of a man who moves according to his own will and not of others. I still see its beauty. But for myself I have given it up.[40]

Yet this was not entirely true. Jabotinsky was unable to totally discard his pre-Zionist liberal views. As late as 1926, he condemned 'the ghetto' for its narrowness and suspicion – its inhabitants often blissfully unaware of the wonderful world outside.[41] His last quasi-autobiographical novel,

---

[39] Colin Shindler, *Israel and the European Left: Between Solidarity and Delegitimisation* (New York, 2012), pp. 16–30.

[40] Vladimir Jabotinsky, 'Your New Year', *Odesskie Novosti*, 3 January 1908, in Shmuel Katz, *Lone Wolf: A Biography of Vladimir Ze'ev Jabotinsky*, vol. 1 (New York, 1996), p. 75.

[41] Vladimir Jabotinsky, 'The Roots of the Crisis', Speech to the Second World Conference of the Revisionist Movement, Paris 1926, in *Neumim, 1905–1928*, Ketavim 4, ed. Eri Jabotinsky (Jerusalem 1957–1958), p. 322.

The Five, sketched out the different paths open to a purposeless Jew in fin-de-siècle Odessa. In a preface entitled 'Instead of a Preface,' Jabotinsky relates:

> I'm a child of my age,
> I understand the good and the bad in it,
> I know its splendour and its decay:
> I'm its child
> And I love all its blemishes, all its poison.[42]

In contrast, Jabotinsky's public demand not to stray beyond Zionism or to entertain any hyphenated hybrid such as Marxist-Zionism ironically mirrored the dilemma of numerous Marxist Jews who tried throughout their lives to transcend their Jewishness. As early as 1872, Pavel Axelrod exclaimed:

What significance, it seemed to me, could the interests of a handful of Jews have in comparison with the 'idea of the working class' and the all-embracing, universal interests of socialism. After all, strictly speaking, the Jewish question does not exist. There is only the question of the liberation of the working masses of all nations, including the Jewish. Together with the approaching triumph of socialism the so-called Jewish question will be resolved as well.[43]

For both Jabotinsky and Axelrod, the suppression of other views, often publicly rejected, was also a private unresolved issue.

THE POGROMS

Jabotinsky spent the years 1904–1908 travelling to centres of Jewish population and promoting the cause of Zionism. He often engaged in debates with proponents of other solutions to the Jewish problem such as adherents of the Bund, Russian liberals and Jewish assimilationists. However, all this was overshadowed by a wave of pogroms in Russia. The Kishinev pogrom during Easter 1903 was the template, followed by another in Gomel later in the year. In 1904 some forty-three pogroms occurred, a majority of which were sparked by disappointment with the Russian performance in the Russo-Japanese War.[44] It was further

---

[42] Vladimir Jabotinsky, *The Five*, trans. from the Russian by Michael R. Katz (New York, 2005).

[43] V. S. Voitinskii et al., eds., *Iz arkhiva P.B. Aksel'roda, 1881–1896* (Berlin, 1924), p. 217, quoted in Erich E. Haberer, *Jews and Revolution in Nineteenth Century Russia* (Cambridge, 2004), p. 68.

[44] Shlomo Lambroza, 'The Pogroms of 1903–1906', in John D. Klier and Shlomo Labroza, eds., *Pogroms: Anti-Jewish Violence in Modern Russian History* (Cambridge, 1992), p. 213.

argued that this was retribution for the part played by the American Jewish banker Jacob Schiff in underwriting loans to the Japanese government, without which Japan's economy would have surely collapsed. The war in turn catalysed workers' strikes in St. Petersburg and the killing of 150 participants in Father Gapon's demonstration. The onset of the Revolution of 1905 created a loose coalition of opponents of Tsarist autocracy, including the Jews. This culminated in forcing the Tsar to accept an extension of civil liberties and to consider the prospect of a constitutional monarchy. Following the publication of his acceptance of these demands in the October Manifesto at the end of 1905, there was an eruption of pogroms, organised by newly established right-wing bodies, including the Union of the Russian People and the 'Black Hundreds'. The pogroms of 1905 and 1906 took the lives of 3,100 Jews, a quarter of whom were women, and some 1,500 children were orphaned. Eighty percent of these pogroms occurred within sixty days of the publication of the October Manifesto. Most of the violence took place in the Pale of Settlement, where the cost of the destruction of Jewish property was estimated at 57.84 million roubles.[45] The Jewish self-defence groups much vaunted by the Bund and others proved unable to stop this tidal wave of assaults on Jews and their homes.

For Jabotinsky, all this confirmed his view that Jews had no place in Russia and that Zionism was the sole solution. This period of pogroms thus forced Jabotinsky to clarify his own views on Russian political affairs and to take issue with others who saw the Jewish future differently.

By early 1905 he was already castigating liberals and socialists for having no interest in 'the national soul'[46] and attacked Jews who were involved in reforming Russia as part of 'a mad adventure'.[47] He remained fatalistic about the possibility of changing Russia and considered it a waste of Jewish energies. He wondered how the Russian masses would react to a visible Jewish participation in the revolutionary forces and how the Jews would be 'thanked' if the Revolution was successful. Jabotinsky instead fell back on his pre-Zionist views that the masses would not

[45] Ibid, p. 231.
[46] Vladimir Jabotinsky, 'Zionism and Palestine', *Evreiskaya zhizn*, February 1905.
[47] Joseph Nedava, 'Jabotinsky and the Bund', *Soviet Jewish Affairs*, vol. 3 no. 1 (1973), pp. 37–47; Vladimir Jabotinsky, 'Jewish Rebelliousness', *Evreiskaya mysl*, no. 1, 5 October 1906.

'march in the forefront of ideas' to repair human society. He bluntly argued that they had neither the intellect nor the time:

The proletarian is the last one to join socialism. This casts no aspersion on him; on the contrary, it is a perfectly natural thing for an oppressed and obscurantist class.[48]

At a meeting in St. Petersburg in the winter of 1905, he told his audience that the proletariat had forgotten about the Jews during the pogroms.[49] He urged Jews instead to become Zionist pioneers rather than Jewish immigrants to Palestine and advocated the formation of a new BILU.[50]

Yet paradoxically he wanted to promote his ideas of Jewish autonomy in the Diaspora as a means of capitalising on the upheaval engendered by the Revolution of 1905. He wanted to represent a Zionist constituency in any elections for the Duma. He called for a Jewish constituent assembly which would be the central instrument for the implementation of Jewish autonomy. He argued that his views differed considerably from the more limited approach of the Bund. The latter would not prevent 'pogroms, ostracism, economic repression and anti-Jewish legislation'.[51]

Throughout 1906, he had attacked the Bund in numerous articles, presumably as the opening shots in an election campaign. It also provided the opportunity to clarify his own position with regard to his former self.

Jabotinsky's pamphlet, *The Bund and Zionism*, was published, probably coincidentally, with the publication of the Tsar's October Manifesto. Jabotinsky viewed the Bund as a transitional stage between Marxism and Zionism. He praised the Bund for raising national awareness amongst the Jewish workers, but it had performed its historic task and thereby outlived its usefulness. This was a period when Lenin and his followers were criticising the Bund for adopting a more nationalist approach. As early as 1899, there had been internal debates over the national reflection of the Bund. Under the impact of the pogroms, the national question in Bundist circles was gaining more and more significance. Lenin was also utilising the issue to take over the RSDLP and to eliminate its self-proclaimed

---

[48] Nedava, 'Jabotinsky and the Bund', pp. 40–41; Vladimir Jabotinsky, *The Bund and Zionism* (Odessa, 1906).

[49] Joseph Schechtman, *Rebel and Statesman: The Jabotinsky Story – The Early Years, 1880–1923* (New York, 1956), p. 94.

[50] One of the first pioneering groups that emigrated to Palestine in 1882. Its name was taken from Isaiah 2:5: 'Beit Ya'akov Lekhu ve-Nelkah' – 'O House of Jacob, let us rise up and go.'

[51] Joseph Goldstein, 'Jabotinsky and Jewish Autonomy in the Diaspora', *Studies in Zionism*, vol. 7, no. 2 (1986), pp. 219–32.

right to represent all Jewish workers. Whereas Lenin wanted a centralised party, the Bund offered federalism. Lenin's colleague in opposing the Bund was Julius Martov, the grandson of the Zionist editor of *Hamelitz*, Aleksandr Tsederbaum. Like Lenin, he advocated the assimilation of the Jews and gradually became a harsh critic of the Bund over its creeping awareness of the national question. Martov regarded himself as a Russian intellectual, yet he made a speech on May Day in 1895 which strongly promoted the idea of a separate Jewish workers' organisation. The Jews, he believed, were doubly oppressed because of their nationality and their class. It was important, therefore, to create a separate Jewish body which would lead the Jewish proletariat. Significantly Martov commented:

When the Russian proletariat is forced to sacrifice certain of its demands in order to gain something, it will first give up the demands which concern only the Jew ... such as that for equal rights.[52]

While this statement no doubt became an embarrassment for Martov, since he never again repeated his belief that the Russian workers could potentially betray their Jewish comrades, Jabotinsky alighted upon it with great enthusiasm. Jabotinsky compared the Bund's founding statement on May Day in 1895 to Pinsker's *Autoemancipation* in 1882. He dubbed the Bund's formulation unoriginal and 'a pale imitation' of Pinsker's tract. Jabotinsky was not averse to attacking the Bund by quoting its adversaries in the RSDLP. Extracts from several anti-Bundist speeches at the second congress of the RSDLP in 1903, including that of Lenin, were cited. Plekhanov, whom Lenin believed possessed 'a phenomenal intolerance' towards the Bund, 'a serpent tribe', chaired the session at the conference.[53] Trotsky and twelve 'Jewish comrades' – all assimilated Jews – claimed to represent the Jewish proletariat, much to the astonishment and anger of the Bund's delegates. Jabotinsky was therefore happy to later interview Plekhanov to solicit his well-known criticism that 'Bundists are simply Zionists who suffer from sea-sickness'.

Even when Lenin had resigned from *Iskra* and the editorial board was in the hands of a Menshevik majority, Jabotinsky quoted liberally from an article by Trotsky which demonstrated his opposition to both the Bund and Zionism.[54] Trotsky, however, drew attention to the fact

---

[52] Jonathan Frankel, *Prophecy and Politics: Socialism, Nationalism, and the Russian Jews, 1862–1917* (Cambridge, 1982), p. 193.

[53] Joseph Nedava, *Trotsky and the Jews* (Philadelphia, 1971), p. 51.

[54] Leon Trotsky, 'The Decay of Zionism and Its Possible Successors', *Iskra*, no. 56, 1 January 1904.

that the socialist Zionist organisations were attracting more adherents, and the great fear of the Bund was that they would lose members to the Zionists.[55]

The Revolution of 1905 and its expectations amongst many Jews did not convince Jabotinsky that Jewish salvation was best served through Jewish participation in the revolutionary movement. Invoking Ferdinand Lassalle, he concluded that reforming Russia – while admirable in its intention – would not ultimately solve the Jewish problem.[56] Many Jews, both in support of Zionism and those opposed to it, disagreed with him.

Jabotinsky's position with respect to advocates of other solutions to the Jewish problem clearly hardened as his own convictions solidified. His language became harsher. In a riposte to an assimilated Jewish writer, he commented:

> You went over to the rich neighbour – we will turn our backs on his beauty and kindness … our hardened, condensed, cold-mad determination to stick it out at the post that the others have deserted … and we shall do the job for you as well.[57]

In part Jabotinsky's views on national revolutionary movements as progressive emanated from the European experience of the early nineteenth century, and this is how he also framed Zionism. Yet such views on national movements by the end of the nineteenth century were now viewed as the ideological domain of the Right. Written probably before the first Balkan War in 1912, Jabotinsky suggested that if Garibaldi had lived fifty years later, he would have been ridiculed and labelled as a reactionary. On the eve of World War I, Jabotinsky attacked 'radical Europe' for looking unsympathetically on the cause of national minorities which did not wish to assimilate into their host countries. Italians in the southern Tyrol and Trento wished to be connected to the Kingdom of Italy. The Turks ruled Bulgarians in northern Macedonia and Greeks in Crete, while the Croats were divided into five or six states. There were 2 million Romanians in Hungarian Transylvania. He wrote:

> [Their aspirations] are deemed unnecessary and regarded as harmful fancies. They divert humanity from its real problems, they obscure class consciousness … they are therefore called reactionaries and chauvinists. Only a reactionary can dream of creating new states, when there are already altogether too many old ones. Only a chauvinist can preach that peoples must necessarily be separated

[55] Vladimir Jabotinsky, 'The Bund and Zionism', 1906, in *Ketavim tsiyoniyim rishonim* , Ketavim 8, ed. E. Jabotinsky (Jerusalem, 1949), pp. 247–49.

[56] Jabotinsky, 'Jewish Rebelliousness'.

[57] Vladimir Jabotinsky, 'On the Jews and Russian Literature', *Rassviet* 29 March 1908.

from each other by state boundaries. Only reactionaries and chauvinists are capable of stirring up nationalist passions ... diverting the masses from their urgent tasks and interests.[58]

Jabotinsky pointed out that at the beginning of the twentieth century, Garibaldi would have been placed in the same camp for his nationalist views as the Russian reactionaries and anti-Semites Vladimir Purishkevich and Nikolai Markov. Garibaldi did not argue that there were only two nations in the world – 'the rich and the poor'.

Zionism had been a latecomer to the camp of national revolutionary movements. It had arisen at the same time that many European nations dreamed of empires. Yet Jabotinsky's personal approach to socialism was that it should be limited to 'the product of human labour',[59] but all other problems could be solved within the framework of a capitalist economy. In his polemic against the Bund, he cited the establishment of Poale Zion in Russia in March 1906 and did not disparage socialist Zionism. Significantly he did not establish a political movement until 1925, but always acted in an individual capacity. In part this stemmed from his deepening disillusionment with the Bolshevik control of Russia and the liquidation of freedom of expression. The idealism of the October Revolution influenced many of the early Zionists and especially the labour Zionist movement. While Ben-Gurion was wary of Communist influence, he admired Lenin for carrying out the Revolution with few resources and eulogised him on his death in January 1924. Jabotinsky moved to a more critical view of the Soviet experiment in the 1920s when it became apparent that the Bolsheviks had set out to destroy the intellectual world of his youth.

[58] Vladimir Jabotinsky 'Mrakobes', *Feuilletons* (St. Petersburg, 1913); 'Reactionary' (1912), Jabotinsky Institute Archives, Tel Aviv.
[59] Schechtman, *Rebel and Statesman* p. 99; Vladimir Jabotinsky, 'Sketches without a Title', *Evreiskaya mysl*, no. 2, 12 October 1906.

3

An Army of Jews

THE FUTILITY OF WAR?

First of all in the forefront of the events due to come to Europe is the great war. That war of which the world is so frightened and which at the same time, it expects with such a morbid, painful curiosity. A war in the centre of Europe between two (or more) first rate civilized powers, armed to the teeth with all the grandiose madness of present day technical equipment – with the participation of ground, sea, undersea and air forces. [This will entail the loss] of an incredible number of casualties and such financial losses, direct, indirect and reflected – one gets the impression that there will not be enough figures in the mathematical lexicon to count [them] all.[1]

So predicted Jabotinsky on 1 January 1912. And yet the outbreak of the Great War that changed the lives of untold millions in the twentieth century and the destiny of the Jewish people was more than two and a half years away. He believed that Britain would not accept any challenge to its naval supremacy. 'Young Germany', he wrote, 'is stretching her muscles' and the best solution would be 'a change on the throne of the Hohenzollerns'. With a prescience of the events of 1917 and 1918, he commented that 'what Germany is brewing is a revolution, a revolution on a global scale, designed to move the political axis of the world'.[2]

Jabotinsky's views on the war four years later, in 1916, were ones of deep ambivalence and profound regret:

The war has suddenly poured into the world's cauldron a bucket of some terribly corrosive acid. Not for a long time has humanity been shown so clearly

---

[1] Vladimir Jabotinsky, 'Horoskop', *Odesskie Novosti*, 1 January 1912; 'Horoscope', Jabotinsky Institute Archives, Tel Aviv.
[2] Ibid.

that 'everything is possible'; that principles, agreements, promises, progress, traditions, liberty, humanity are all rot and rust and rubbish. Everything is permissible: you may drown women and children, burn people alive, smoke them out like vermin, turn out tens of thousands onto the high road and drive them the devil knows where, hang and beat and rape. All these are lessons, they 'stick', they sink into minds and hearts, changing the very tissues of human conscience.[3]

Jabotinsky felt that it was a war without purpose. In 1916 he bemoaned the fact the world had changed in the past fifty years. The 1860s, he wrote, bore witness to war in the name of principle – the unification of Italy, the liberation of blacks from the slavery of the American South. And yet this sense of futility about World War I coexisted with the advantage it offered the Zionist cause when Turkey entered on Germany's side in 1914.

Jabotinsky's initial view of the tragedy of the outbreak of war was a studied neutrality – almost 'a plague on both your houses'. His approach was a hope for 'stalemate and peace as soon as possible'. Working for the Zionist cause in Istanbul for several years had convinced him that 'where the Turk rules neither sun may shine nor grass may grow and that the only hope for the restoration of Palestine lay in the dismemberment of the Ottoman empire'. Turkey's participation in the war was therefore the catalyst to take sides and to establish a Jewish legion.

The idea of a Jewish fighting force was not new. The French Revolution had spawned national legions fighting for the independence of their countries. Many started out under the tricolour of France to safeguard the Revolution. Such international armies defeated the Prussians at Valmy and Jemappes in 1792. Then they participated in national struggles or in foreign armies on the basis of 'the enemy of my enemy is my friend'.[4] More than 100,000 Poles fought in Napoleon's Grande Armée during the invasion of Russia in 1812. The development of Zionism as an outcome of the national revolutionary struggles in Europe during the nineteenth century therefore brought with it the inevitability of a Jewish fighting force. Indeed, Adam Mickiewicz, the Polish national poet, proposed the establishment of a Jewish legion in the 1850s which would liberate Palestine.[5] Jabotinsky, of course, drew inspiration from Garibaldi and the Risorgimento, but the refusal of the Poles to give up their struggle for

---

[3] Vladimir Jabotinsky, 'Solveig', *Russkie Vedomosti*, 2 April 1916; Jabotinsky Institute Archives, Tel Aviv.

[4] Colin Shindler, *The Triumph of Military Zionism: Nationalism and the Origins of the Israeli Right* (London, 2006), pp. 78–79.

[5] Michael Graetz, *The Jews in Nineteenth Century France: From the French Revolution to the Alliance Israélite Universelle* (Stanford, CA, 1996), p. 244.

national sovereignty despite one defeat after another was also a political template. Józef Piłsudski, the founder of modern Poland, went to Tokyo to solicit support during the Russo-Japanese War in 1904–1905. Even before the outbreak of World War I, the Hapsburgs supported Piłsudski in establishing the Polish Legion. Three companies of Polish riflemen immediately invaded Russian Poland following the formal declaration of hostilities in 1914.

The past held important lessons for Jabotinsky, a man very much in thrall to the attractions of the age of romantic nationalism. Jews had been forbidden to bear arms in Germany for 800 years, and seemingly the very idea of 'the fighting Jew' had fallen into disuse – at least in the popular Jewish imagination.[6] In the non-Jewish world, it was a laughable and impossible image of the Jew in the late nineteenth and early twentieth centuries. Even within the embryonic Zionist movement which wished to change the course of Jewish history, this view was often promoted. The scholar was preferred to the soldier. In 1894 Bialik had written a poem, 'At the Threshold of the House of Study', which included the lines

> Rather than be a lion among lions
> I prefer to perish among the sheep

Jabotinsky's decision, therefore, to take sides in the conflict did not exactly endear him to any of his colleagues in the Zionist movement apart from Chaim Weizmann. It seemed to contradict the spirit of the times. Indeed, he was totally isolated, and many considered his choice to throw in Zionism's lot with Britain foolhardy in the extreme. There was always a very good chance that Germany and not Britain would emerge as the victor. And what then?

Max Nordau in Spanish exile was lukewarm to the idea of a Jewish legion. The English Zionists Norman Bentwich, Harry Sacher and Leon Simon ridiculed it. Zionist leaders such as Sokolov and Chelenov even blocked Weizmann from facilitating an introduction for Jabotinsky to Herbert Samuel, a member of the British cabinet.[7] In St. Petersburg, on a last visit to Russia, Zionist leaders refused to meet Jabotinsky, since they hoped for the defeat of Tsarism by the armies of civilised Germany. Moreover, there was a real possibility that Russia would seize the ice-free port of Narvik in Norway – a move which would bring Sweden into the war in support of Germany. In his home town of Odessa, he was denounced from the pulpit by pro-Zionist rabbis for voicing the very idea

---

[6] Derek J. Penslar, *Jews and the Military: A History* (Princeton 2013) pp. 17–34.
[7] Vladimir Jabotinsky, *The Story of the Jewish Legion* (New York, 1945). p. 52.

of a Jewish legion.[8] Even within Russia, there was little enthusiasm for the war. The British lion, it was claimed, was prepared to fight to the last drop of Russian blood.

Jabotinsky was not oblivious to the broader consequences of participating in a seemingly irrational conflict. In 1916 he saw an early film, D. W. Griffith's *The Birth of a Nation*, which gave a southern perspective on the American Civil War. On the one hand, he clearly saw through the tugging of emotions in a preordained direction:

And, of course, when all this duly culminated in the inevitable de rigueur assault on a white maiden by an ape-like African, I simply shrugged my shoulders. Equally when the Ku Klux Klan riders appeared on the screen avenging the white man's humiliation, I did my best to remember that, according to what I had always been taught to believe, they had been nothing but glorified hooligans.[9]

On the other, he admitted that an *advocatus diaboli* had conquered him that evening and he began to perceive the complexity of the American Civil War. He asked himself, was there one truth or were there two?

The main question is: need one, may one, should one, consider things objectively? And if so, when? During a conflict? Or only after – many a year after – the conflict?

This perhaps epitomised the lifelong tension between Jabotinsky the Russian intellectual and Jabotinsky the Zionist populist. He further asked:

One shudders to think of it: judging things objectively, what about this Great War? What about the clash between Irish Home Rule and Ulster? Jews and Anti-Semites? Zionism and assimilation?

Jabotinsky quoted from the poem 'The Poet Captain' by the Irish Republican Thomas MacDonagh about a king who had led his followers in battle on many occasions.[10] For Jabotinsky, he fell victim to 'that superhuman gift of hindsight' in which he discovered that there was not one single truth:

And he loved the past that he could pity and praise.
And he fought no more, living in solitude.

The king's followers left him and eventually appointed another in his place.

---

[8] Ibid., pp. 29–56.
[9] Vladimir Jabotinsky, 'Pravda', *Russkie Vedomosti*, 26 May 1916; 'Truth', Jabotinsky Institute Archives, Tel Aviv.
[10] MacDonagh was one of the leaders of the Easter Uprising during Easter 1916 and was subsequently executed by the British. Although Jabotinsky supported Home Rule in Ireland and was probably wary of antagonising the British while trying to solicit their support for a Jewish legion, it is clear that the rebellion of the Sinn Feiners made an impression on him.

THE JEWISH LEGION

Despite all his reservations about the war, the entry of Turkey into the war on Germany's side in November 1914 transformed Jabotinsky from a 'disinterested' journalist to an active advocate of a Jewish armed force to fight for the British. In his quest he was partnered by Joseph Trumpeldor, who had been a professional soldier in the Tsarist army. He had lost an arm during the siege of Port Arthur during the Russo-Japanese War. As a socialist, he had worked on the agricultural collective in Palestine, Degania, practised vegetarianism and was well read in Russian literature. At the Mafruza barracks in Alexandria, Egypt, in 1915, Jabotinsky finally located some 400 refugees from Palestine to formally embark on the establishment of a Jewish legion . However, the British insisted that foreign soldiers could not be admitted to the British army; instead Jabotinsky and Trumpeldor were permitted to form the Zion Mule Corps in April 1915, which saw action in the Gallipoli campaign.

Yet something had changed dramatically. The name of the Zion Mule Corps was now widely known through repeated mention in the international press. For the Jews, the lowly muleteer became the exalted symbol of the courageous Jewish fighter.

In 1915 Jabotinsky had been instrumental in using all his rhetorical powers to persuade the expelled Palestinian Jews to enlist. Yet he was aghast when all the British offered was a mule corps and not a fighting army. While Trumpeldor embraced the proposal, an aggrieved Jabotinsky left for Italy. Jabotinsky later admitted that he had been wrong. He understood that the mere existence of this small transportation unit had elevated the cause of Zionism and broken through the barrier of international indifference. He later wrote:

Until then it had been almost impossible to talk about Zionism even to friendly statesmen: at such a cruel time as that, who could really expect them to worry about agricultural settlements or the renaissance of Hebrew? All that was, for the moment, simply outside their field of vision.[11]

The Zion Mule Corps was disbanded on 26 May 1916 – it had existed for a little more than a year. Yet 120 of its members made their way to London, where they enlisted as the 5th Company of the 20th Battalion of the Royal Fusiliers. Any mention of the Zion Mule Corps now opened

[11] Jabotinsky, *The Jewish Legion*, p. 43.

doors and invited discussion with the British political and military establishment.[12]

The death of Lord Kitchener in 1916 removed another obstacle to a Jewish legion. Jabotinsky and Trumpeldor successfully petitioned Lloyd-George, and the remnant of the Zion Mule Corps became the nucleus of several regiments together with a handful of Russian Jewish émigrés from the East End of London and some Lithuanian Christians.

This was to be the model for something much greater. The February Revolution in Russia had brought about a much more liberal attitude towards Zionism. Trumpeldor therefore intended to ask Boris Savinkov, the new Russian minister of war, for permission to form a Jewish army of 100,000. With the subsequent overthrow of the Kerensky government and the rise to power of the Bolsheviks, the plan was stillborn.

The Jewish Legion eventually developed into a force of 5,000 – 35 percent from the United States, 30 percent from the United Kingdom and 28 percent from Palestine itself. It moved to Palestine via Taranto and saw action at the tail end of World War I on the Nablus front and in the offensive in the malaria-ridden Jordan Valley in 1918.

Jabotinsky's reflections as he travelled through Palestine were very much those of his time, very Eurocentric. Gaza was 'a grey, dusty and dry Arab village', while Rehovot was 'another world, a piece of Europe'.[13] On the one hand, he expressed wonder at gazing upon a harem in the village of Abouein; on the other, he proclaimed the Jews to be both 'the children and the active creators of European culture'.[14] He distinguished between 'Easternness', which he equated with backwardness, and 'the East', seen in purely geographical terms. Indeed, he argued that at one point in history, Baghdad could be regarded as more 'Western' than Rome.[15] He was as harsh on Jews as he was on Arabs in this respect. He railed against attitudes which segregated some bodies of knowledge into no-go areas. He believed that religion should not intrude into every nook and cranny of life, and he regarded women as unfortunately fettered to the superior status of men and their demands. He therefore viewed the British upper-class romantic view of the Arab world as caught in a time warp, a museum attitude. He noted that Lawrence of Arabia was happy

[12] *Jewish Chronicle*, 31 October 2014.
[13] Jabotinsky, *The Jewish Legion*, p. 110.
[14] Ibid., p. 118.
[15] Vladimir Jabotinsky, 'The East', *Rassviet*, 26 September 1926.

to support the Zionists if they went to Palestine as Orientals but not as Europeans.[16]

British policy towards Jewish and Arab nationalism was to support both their aspirations during the war and then to decide where British national interests best lay after the war. While Jabotinsky's 'unpronounceable' name was jovially transformed into 'jug-of-whiskey' by some British colleagues, others ironically labelled him a 'Bolshevik' determined to upset the natural order of things. Even so, he was awarded the MBE (Member of the British Empire) by King George V in recognition of his military service.

General Allenby and the military leadership regarded only the white troops as totally reliable; hence no one in the large Indian force in Palestine was ever given an officer's rank. As the end of hostilities receded, Allenby in Palestine and Curzon in London began to retreat from the pledges made to the Zionists in 1917. This coincided with the ambiguous promises made to both Jews and Arabs during the war. The rowing back from the Balfour Declaration propelled an urgency in disbanding the Jewish Legion and neutralising any possibility of a Jewish military force in Palestine. With the rising passion of Arab nationalists producing numerous armed attacks on Jews, there were growing mutterings from the Zionists that the British were proving incapable of protecting them. During Passover in 1920, a spate of rapes, knife attacks and pillage passed without intervention by either Indian troops or Arab policemen. Six were killed and 200 injured – 'a second Kishinev in Jerusalem'.[17] This induced Jabotinsky to establish a haganah – a self-defence force against further Arab assaults. While 600 enrolled, there were virtually no weapons to be acquired. Yet the three rifles and two revolvers which were located provided the evidence necessary for a British military court in Palestine to try Jabotinsky – and to hand down a sentence of fifteen years, followed by deportation. He was to be moved to Egypt and then probably to the Sudan for the duration of his sentence. However, the uproar from the Jews of Palestine, the British Parliament and the international media brought an abrupt reduction of the sentence to one year. The *Manchester Guardian* called him 'the Jewish Garibaldi'.[18] When Sir Herbert Samuel arrived as the first British high commissioner in Palestine, one of his first acts was to proclaim an amnesty which granted

---

[16] Jabotinsky, *The Jewish Legion*, p. 171.
[17] Ibid., p. 148.
[18] *Manchester Guardian*, 3 May 1920.

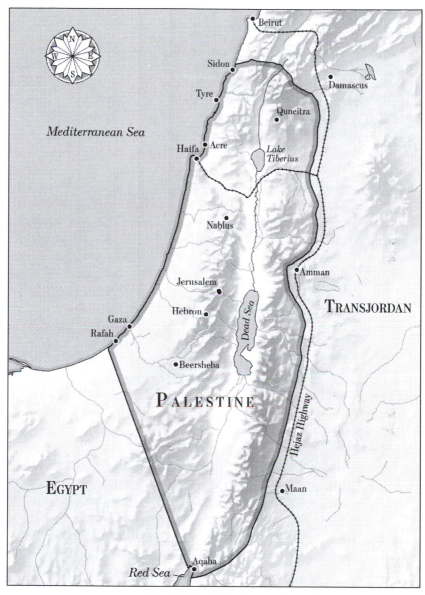

MAP 1. The Original Zionist map (1919).

freedom not only to Jabotinsky but also to those Arabs who had been sentenced for rape.

Jabotinsky was seen by Jews in Palestine and the world over as 'the founder of the Jewish Legion', 'the prisoner of Acre', the man who refused to bow to 'the realities' of the situation.

THE END OF THE ANCIEN RÉGIME

World War I was the destroyer of worlds. The great European empires of
the Romanovs, Hohenzollerns and Hapsburgs shuddered and burst open.
In the East, the Ottomans took their bow and saw the Middle East overrun by the victorious armies of Britain and France, much to the consternation of nascent Arab nationalist movements. The Zionist movement
saw its legitimacy in Palestine endorsed by the colonial powers which it
was both dependent upon and opposed to. History's joke was to encourage both Jewish and Arab nationalism to arise at the same point in time
over the same territory.

In Russia the convulsions were even more dramatic. The question was
immediately asked, 'If the old world has been destroyed, then a new world
will be created, but what sort of new world do we want?' Many sub-
servient nations in the old empire demanded freedom to run their own
affairs. An independent Poland emerged after almost 150 years of Tsarist
subjugation. The Ukrainians attempted the same, but ultimately without success. The collapse of the Romanovs brought forth a new political
landscape. It consisted of nationalist movements, local warlords and deep
ideological hatreds. All this played into the hands of the Far Left in Russia,
which built on this once-in-centuries opportunity to irrevocably change
the nature of humankind. It was guided by the expediency and genius of
Lenin and the military and intellectual brilliance of Trotsky. All this latent
messianism deeply appealed to Jews – an appeal crafted by both historical
experience and Jewish teaching. The passage of Jews into the Communist
Party started as a trickle and became a flood. The mass killing of Jews
during the civil war by anti-Communist forces induced a sympathy for
the utopianism of the revolutionaries. Once Bolshevism was seen as permanent and not a passing political fashion, Jews joined the ranks of the
Revolution in great numbers. Lenin appreciated the possibility of filling
the gaps left by an emigrating bureaucracy with committed and educated
Jews. All the Jews had to do, according to Marxist-Leninist theory, was to
transcend their Jewishness – to relegate Jewish national interests initially
to the demands of internationalism and then later to Soviet national interests. Lenin's understanding of Jews was informed solely by assimilated
and acculturated Jews – and by non-Jewish Jews who had moved beyond
the confines of community. The actual situation of the Jewish masses
per se – their beliefs and interests – was considered less important.

The Balfour Declaration, which promised a Jewish home in Palestine,
and the October Revolution, which promised universal redemption,

occurred within days of each other. This symbolised a great dilemma for most Jews, since both aspirations could be related to Jewishness and Judaism. Many former Zionists who embraced Lenin's view of the future now regarded their former ideological adherence with disdain and abhorrence. There was a psychological and emotional determination to oppose Zionism, as well as a political one. For example, Semyon Diamanstein, head of the Yevsektsia, the Jewish sections of the Communist Party, was a former Lubavicher hassid. The desire to Bolshevise the Jewish street began with the closure of Jewish organisations and developed into the mass arrests of Zionists and their deportation to the embryonic Gulag in the 1920s.

The October Revolution and its legacy deeply affected Jewish life in Russia and often wreaked havoc within families. The messianism of the Jewish Bolsheviks not only turned brother against brother, but ignited a campaign to purge the new socialist homeland of all Zionists. The vehemence of the newly converted bewildered the non-Jewish Bolshevik leadership. In a memorandum to his deputies in March 1924, the head of the Cheka, Feliks Dzerzhinskii, admitted that he was perplexed:

I reviewed the Zionist materials. I must admit, I do not understand at all why they are being persecuted on the basis of their Zionist affiliation. The majority of their attacks on us are based on our persecution of them. Persecuted, they are a thousand times more dangerous for us than they would be not persecuted, developing their Zionist activity among the Jewish petty and large scale speculative bourgeoisie and intelligentsia. Their party work therefore is not all dangerous for us.[19]

The Revisionist intelligentsia which emerged in Palestine during the late 1920s was in part a reaction to the blind zeal, influence and deeds of the Jewish Bolsheviks – and in particular their ideological passion to persecute their former colleagues in the Zionist movement.

Abba Ahimeir (né Geisinovich) came from a family of intellectuals, yet he was the only Zionist amongst them.[20] Following the October Revolution, all his siblings joined the revolutionary cause. His younger brother, Meir, a Communist, died fighting in the Red Army during the Polish campaign in 1920.

During the Polish-Russian War, Bobruisk, the home town of the Geisinoviches, was occupied several times by both the Bolsheviks and

---

[19] Feliks Dzerzhinskii, Letter to V. R. Menzhinskii and G. G. Iagoda, 15 March 1924, in Ziva Galili and Boris Morozov, *Exiled to Palestine: The Emigration of Zionist Convicts from the Soviet Union, 1924–1934* (New York, 2013), p. 91.

[20] Ahimeir's brother, Avraham Gaissinovitch, wrote *Le Revolte de Pougatchev* (Paris, 1938).

the Poles. The street on which they lived was originally called 'Polisa Street' after the police; it was renamed 'Stolypin Street' following the assassination of the Russian premier by a Jewish revolutionary; it then became 'Kerensky Street' after the leader of the February Revolution and finally 'Liebknecht Street' after the German Spartacist murdered by the Freicorps together with Rosa Luxemburg.[21]

His early experience of the Bolsheviks in Bobruisk convinced Ahimeir that this bold aspiration to change human nature would never be achieved.[22] Unlike the rest of his family, he viewed the October Revolution as little more than a Russian nationalist revolt which would lead to tyranny. Despite their differences, Geisinovich deeply mourned his Communist brother, Meir, and Hebraised his name to 'Ahimeir' (my brother, Meir) to memorialise him.

The Hebrew poet Uri Zvi Greenberg was traumatised by the savagery that he had witnessed at the Battle of Cer during World War I.[23] During the pogrom in Lemburg (Lviv, Ukraine) in November 1918, Greenberg and his family were subjected to a mock execution by Poles.

In the Ukraine, a probable 150,000 Jews died in the massacres of 1918–1920.[24] In 1919 there were massacres in Proskurov (January) perpetrated by the Cossacks of the elite Zaporej Brigade. There were further mass killings in Zhitomir (March), Vasilkov (April), Elizabetgrad (May), Teophipol (June), Tulchin (July) and Fastov (September).[25]

Although several poets, such as Yitzhak Lamdan and Avraham Shlonsky, became Zionist pioneers in Palestine, Greenberg was initially reluctant to leave Europe with members of the third aliyah. He became interested in Polish modernism and edited a poetry magazine, *Albatros*, in Warsaw. In some of his poetry he expressed his difficulty in saying 'farewell to Europe'[26] and, beyond this, leaving the home of his childhood – for example:

> Forced to leave all valuables, we dressed for exile
> Slung satchel on shoulder

---

[21] From Ahimeir's 'Prison Diaries, 1934', in Aba Ahimeir, *Atlantidah, o, 'Olam she-shaka': sipurim ve-zikhronot* (Tel Aviv, 1996), pp. 250–53.

[22] Abba Ahimeir, *Herut*, 16 November 1951.

[23] Glenda Abramson, 'The Wound of Memory: Uri Zvi Greenberg's "From the Book of the Wars of the Gentiles"', *Shofar*, vol. 29, no. 1 (2010) pp. 1–21.

[24] Howard M. Sachar, *Dreamland: Europe and Jews in the Aftermath of the Great War* (New York, 2002), p. 18.

[25] Marius Schattner, *Histoire de La Droite israelienne: De Jabotinsky à Shamir* (Paris, 1991), p. 70.

[26] In the second issue of *Albatross*, Greenberg published an essay, 'Farewell to Europe', in which he expressed his ambivalence about leaving.

We sang like new recruits in an army barefoot
On Mediterranean sands
Say it: malaria kills in Zion
Say it: Arabs ambush and murder on the road
Say it: jackals creep into the tent, under the blanket,
Devour the flesh of sleeping men.
Say it again and again: still we came!
We were forced to go.[27]

THE DECLINE OF THE WEST

Both Ahimeir and Greenberg were clearly influenced by Oswald
Spengler's *Decline of the West*. In the Palestine of the 1920s, the translation of Spengler's book into Hebrew stimulated intense discussion about
it in the pages of *Hapoel Hatzair*. After all, Spengler had promoted the
moral East in contrast to the declining West – and many Zionists felt
vindicated in the path they had chosen. Spengler thought that Germany
would emerge victorious in World War I, but that it might subsequently
decline like Rome.

The first volume of Spengler's magnus opus was published in the summer of 1918 before Germany's defeat and the second in 1922 following
a period of intense strife and polarisation in German politics. Spengler
examined 'the twilight of the West' and derived much from Vico and
Nietzsche. The Jews were an oddity, a relic, a fossil. On the other hand,
Mussolini, 'a *condottiere*', was more to his liking. Spengler had a profound scorn for democracy and representative institutions.

Ahimeir's doctoral thesis was devoted to analysing the reactions of the
Russian intelligentsia to Spengler's work. Russia, Spengler believed, had
yet to flower. The nineteenth century, he argued, was an age of preparation and preparedness for unprecedented conflict and war. Large numbers
of men were being mobilised to fill the ranks of ever-expanding armies.
All this culminated in the horror of World War I. Spengler viewed the
previous 100 years as a 'transition from Napoleonism to Caesarism'. In
1918 he viewed Lenin as 'a Caesar figure'.

Yet he was pessimistic about the future. It led him to suspect the intelligentsia, the seekers after utopia, humanists and pacifists. As someone

---

[27] Uri Zvi Greenberg, 'Yerushalayim shel matah' (Earthly Jerusalem), *Hapoel Hatzair*,
18 April 1924; 1 July 1924 in David Aberbach, 'Fanatic Heart: The Poetry of Uri Zvi
Greenberg', *CCAR Journal: A Reform Jewish Quarterly* (Spring 2003), pp. 16–32.

who opposed the scientific laws of history, he rejected the linear progress that socialism envisaged:

Socialism owes its popularity only to the fact that it is completely misunderstood even by its exponents who present it as a sum of rights instead of as one of duties, an abolition instead of an intensification of the Kantian imperative, a slackening instead of a tautening of directional energy.

Ethical socialism is not a system of compassion, humanity, peace and kindly care, but one of will-to-power. Any other reading of it is illusory.

The Stoic adapts himself, the Socialist commands. He would have the whole world take the shape he desires, thus transferring the idea of [Kant's] *The Critique of Pure Reason* into the ethical field.[28]

The future, Spengler rationalised, was one of conflict between democracy and Caesarism:

The coming of Caesarism breaks the dictature [dictatorship] of money and its political weapon democracy. After a long triumph of world-city economy and its interests over political creative force, the political side of life manifests itself after all as the stronger of the two. The sword is victorious over money, the master-will subdues again the plunderer-will.[29]

Moreover, Spengler was clearly not terribly keen on Jews and wrote about their role in 'the moralisation of history'. He tried to explain the emergence of 'the Chosen People':

Vespasian's War, directed against Judea, was a liberation of Jewry. In the first place, it ended both the claim of the people of this petty district to be the genuine nation, and the pretensions of their bald spirituality to equivalence with the soul-life of the whole.[30]

For Spengler, the Jew had evolved into 'the master of the forms of city-economics and city-science'.[31] Tarragon, Toledo and Granada in medieval Spain were in his eyes predominantly Jewish cities. The Jews had become 'civilised and cosmopolitan'. He noted, however, that Jewish civilisation had developed at a different rate to that of other peoples – and this was the reason for 'mutual hate and contempt'. The Jews had lost any attachment to the land.

Instead Spengler wrote about the evolution of a megalopolis – a chain of metropolitan areas – and argued that the Jews built 'metropolitan – proletarian – ghettos'. The Judengasse (Jewish Quarter) was 'a thousand

[28] Oswald Spengler, *The Decline of the West* (Oxford, 1991), p. 186.
[29] Ibid.
[30] Ibid., p. 284.
[31] Ibid., p. 349.

years ahead of the gothic town'. The Jews of the ghetto were 'a coolie-mass characterised by civilised, cold, superior intelligence and an undeviating eye to business'. In this respect, the Jews were no different from the Parsees, the Armenians, the Greeks and the Chinese.

The Jews were unable to feel 'the passion with which Faustians livingly experience the short crowded epochs in which their history and destiny take decisive turns'. Spengler cited as examples the Crusades, the Reformation, and the French Revolution. 'All this for the Jew lies thirty generations back.'[32]

Although Ahimeir rejected Spengler's philosophy of history as far as the Jews were concerned, neither did he believe that the age of theory was drawing to an end. Yet he was undoubtedly attracted to 'Caesarism' and the age of national dictatorship which was unfolding. The man of steel was emerging from the shadows:

The sum of honour and duty, discipline, resolution, is a thing not learned from books, but awakened in the stream of being a living exemplar.

Highest of all, however, is not action, but the ability to command. It is this that takes the individual up out of himself and makes him the centre of a world of action – not Napoleon but Caesar.[33]

Spengler argued that thinkers were essential to the process of guiding, explaining and moulding history. And it was in this role that Ahimeir understood himself:

A thinker is a person whose part it is to symbolize time according to his vision and understanding. He has no choice, he thinks as he has to think. Truth in the long run is to him the picture of the world which was born at his birth. It is that which he does not invent but rather discovers within himself. It is himself over again: his being expressed in words; the meaning of his personality formed into a doctrine which so far as concerns his life is unalterable, because truth and his life are identical. This symbolism is the one essential, the vessel and the expression of human history.[34]

HOMO HOMINI LUPUS

Spengler's ideas also attracted Ahimeir to Jabotinsky. In a remarkable article in 1910, 'Homo Homini Lupus' (Man is as a wolf to other men), Jabotinsky attacked the racism of American whites towards their fellow

[32] Ibid., p. 351.
[33] Ibid., p. 385.
[34] Oswald Spengler, Preface to the revised edition, Blankenburg am Harz, December 1922 (Oxford, 1991), p. xxix.

black citizens.[35] Written as a response to an article in the Russian press about the riots that broke out after Jack Johnson had famously defeated 'the great white hope', James J. Jeffries, in a heavyweight title bout, Jabotinsky commented on the aftermath:

They [the whites] sought to quash black pride and fell upon blacks in a ratio of fifty-to-one. They broke open heads, trampled upon people and even acted cruelly to women and children. 'In other eastern states', the correspondent writes, 'blacks were torn to pieces and hundreds were injured and crushed. In southern states, where the difference between blacks and whites is more strongly pronounced, the number of blacks that were injured probably has reached several thousand.'

Jabotinsky bemoaned the fact that this should occur, in of all places, the United States of America.

Democracy, in and of itself, is good, all of us desire it and make efforts to achieve it. But there is no requirement to see a pie-in-the-sky dream and then make promises based on things that will never come about. Prejudicial racist views are rooted first and foremost in the masses. By investing power to the masses, the situation of those oppressed peoples does not improve … in this situation, with a background of the most idyllic democratic possibility of complete freedom and broad self-rule rights, it is right here that racial hatred exists in all its sinister forms that arouse horror.

Jabotinsky commented that the continuing racism in the United States – the rapes and the lynchings – were far worse than the Kishinev pogrom of 1903. Whereas the wealth of the Rothschilds and the existence of the Viennese 'quasi-Juden' were utilised to justify anti-Semitism in Europe, the impoverishment of American blacks was 'arbitrary, without reason and without cause'.

Jabotinsky was almost fatalistic about the ability of human beings to attack their own – hence the title 'Homo Homini Lupus' and his sympathy with Thomas Hobbes's philosophy that human beings were inherently selfish creatures. Jabotinsky stressed that the pattern of the oppressed masses was not to learn from their situation, but to search for another victim and to convert him into the oppressed's oppressed. In particular he mentioned the attacks of Poles in Galicia on Jews:

In the last decade, many private schools were established to spread the Hebrew language and it is impossible to count the ways by which the Poles attempted to close down these schools including visits to check the sanitary conditions. In 75% of these visits, the inspection team was astounded by the unhygienic situation of the wonderful, but wretched children, leading to the closures … in Lemberg a few months

---

[35] *Odesskie Novosti*, 18 July 1910.

ago, a young lawyer who spoke in public in Yiddish was subjected to disciplinary punishment by the local lawyers' guild. Not for the content of his words, but for the language in which they were spoken.

Jabotinsky pointed out that in Finland – also under the heavy hand of Tsarist autocracy – Jews were permitted to live in only three cities, Helsinki, Vyborg and Turku. Ritual slaughter was banned, Jewish marriages regulated and Jews driven from their homes by Tsarist officials.

Jabotinsky's conclusions were harsh, negative and fatalistic, which reflected reality as he envisaged it in 1910:

A fool is he who believes his neighbour, even a mainly decent and pleasant one. He who trusts integrity and justice is a fool in that integrity exists only for the powerful and the stubborn ... I preach – and will continue to do so – on behalf of separatism, lack of trust, to always be prepared and on the alert, with a stick hidden up my sleeve. For these are the things that allow us to exist among the wolves that fight.

All this struck at the experiences of Abba Ahimeir and Uri Zvi Greenberg during World War I. Distinguishing between theory and practice, universalism and particularism, aspirations and reality was a central factor that moved several Zionists from the left to the right in the 1920s.

Ahimeir joined the non-Marxist Tserei Tsion in 1916 and became a member of its committee in Bobruisk. He attended an important Zionist meeting in Petrograd in May 1917, following the February Revolution.[36]

After completing his doctorate on Spengler at the University of Vienna, Ahimeir left for Palestine. Here the quiet Ahimeir was employed as a librarian for the cultural committee of the General Workers Organization in Zikhron Ya'akov. He taught in Nahalal and lived for a year on Kibbutz Geva. As a natural continuation of his membership of Tserei Tsion, Ahimeir joined Hapoel Hatzair. He soon established a reputation for himself as a thinker and published articles in *Ha'aretz*, *Davar*, *Kuntres*, and the party journal, *Hapoel Hatzair*. His close friend from Bobruisk, Yosef Katznelson, later a stalwart of Maximalist Revisionism, arrived in Palestine in January 1925.[37]

Uri Zvi Greenberg followed a similar path. In Palestine he was a member of the non-Marxist Hapoel Hatzair, fashioned by the Tolstoyan philosophy of A. D. Gordon. His messianic poem about the Land of Israel,

[36] Aba Ahimeir and Yehudah Margolin, *ha-Shenayim: kovets ma'amarim aktu'aliyim* (Tel Aviv, 1981), p. 20.
[37] See Aba Ahimeir, *The Black Prince*, in Yossi Ahimeir, *The Black Prince: Yosef Katznelson and the National Movement in the 1930s* (Tel Aviv, 1983), pp. 21–28.

'Hizdaharut 1926' ('Radiance 1926'), reflected the pioneering passion of Hapoel Hatzair for the Land.

The party opposed Marxist-Zionist Borochovism and Marxism per se from the outset. It also opposed Jabotinsky in the early 1920s, particularly in the socio-economic spheres, but supported Weizmann instead.

Hapoel Hatzair had a troubled history in Russia due to the October Revolution. It split in 1920 into two factions, Tserei Tsion Socialistim and Tserei Tsion Trudoviki. The latter, 'Labour' Tserei Tsion, whose political orientation was more social democratic, renamed itself Hamiflagah Ha'Tsionit Ha'Amlanut and was less well disposed to the Soviet experiment. It was led by Moshe Lurie, Baruch Weinstein and Aryeh Altman, all of whom played key roles in Revisionist Zionism.

On 30 April 1922, the third conference of 'Labour' Tserei Tsion commenced in Kiev. On the fifth day of the proceedings, the security police, the GPU, marched in and stopped the deliberations. Fifty-one participants were arrested and thirty-seven were tried in the club of the prison guards on 26 August 1922. In the dock, they were accused of counter-revolutionary activities and having contacts with Petliura, Poincaré, Lloyd-George and the pope by the revolutionary court.[38] The charge sheet read:

They developed national chauvinistic feelings in the Jews and dulled the consciousness of the working masses so that their interests can only find maximum satisfaction through the creation of a national bourgeois state in Palestine.[39]

The local Yevsektsia, the Jewish Communists, enthusiastically publicised the trial in the Yiddish press and spoke about 'Jewish counter-revolutionaries'. The Tserei Tsion activists believed that their incarceration was linked with the Jabotinsky-Slavinsky Accord of 1921 and their plight orchestrated by the Jewish Communists in order to deal a blow to their ideological enemy, the Zionists.

Maksym Slavinsky, a Ukrainian nationalist, was an old colleague of Jabotinsky from the time of the 1905 revolution. Jabotinsky had met Slavinsky in August–September 1921 and agreed that a Jewish gendarmerie would be attached to Petliura's nationalist forces if a new invasion of the Ukraine was attempted in 1922. Jabotinsky's motivation was to

---

[38] Arieh Rafaeli (Tsentsiper), *B'Ma'avak L'Geula: Sefer Hatsionut HaRusit Mi Mahapehat 1917 ud Yomeinu* (Tel Aviv, 1956), pp. 131–35.

[39] Benjamin West, *Struggles of a Generation: The Jews Under Soviet Rule* (Tel Aviv, 1959), p. 169.

protect Jews from wanton assaults by the Ukrainians and to prevent a repetition of the massacres that had occurred in the Ukraine between 1918 and 1920. Although Jabotinsky later argued that he would also have established a Jewish gendarmerie attached to the Red Army, the fall-out, ranging from Communist Jews to Marxist Zionists, was one of deep outrage that a Jew should cavort with a pogromist.

Jabotinsky's advocacy of a Jewish legion during World War I had been interpreted by many on the left as an indirect alliance with Tsarism. Moreover, many socialist Zionists had heard Jabotinsky paraphrase Mazzini the year before at the Zionist congress at Karlsbad: 'Noi faremo l'Italia anche uniti col Diavolo' – 'For the sake of Palestine, I would willingly ally myself with the devil.'[40] The Yevsektsia, however, wanted to use the accord to indicate to their non-Jewish colleagues that Zionism was indeed counter-revolutionary. The Bolsheviks independently were very worried about Ukrainian nationalism and wanted to put an end to Petliura's influence.

Many Russian Zionists at the time feared that the GPU would respond with mass arrests of Zionists.[41] Yet Jabotinsky was adamant that he would not be scared off by the threat of Soviet reprisals.[42] He justified his approach by arguing that he was told that his effort to establish a Jewish legion would similarly cause pogroms in Palestine – but this did not happen.

Even so, articles in the Communist press attacked him and there was even a call to ban the Jewish youth group Maccabi, since the accord mentioned its members as possible recruits for the Jewish gendarmerie.[43] Despite a tidal wave of opprobrium from many quarters, Jabotinsky never accepted such criticisms.[44] Indeed, he had had a history of association with Ukrainian nationalists. He disagreed with the commonly held view that all were reactionaries and anti-Semites.

Shortly after the assassination in May 1926 of Symon Petliura, the Ukrainian nationalist leader whom most Jews held responsible for the

[40] Joseph B. Schechtman, 'The Jabotinsky-Slavinsky Agreement: A Chapter in Ukrainian-Jewish Relations', *Jewish Social Studies*, vol. 17, no. 4 (October 1955), pp. 289–306.

[41] Joseph B. Schechtman and Yehuda Benari, *History of the Revisionist Movement* (Tel Aviv, 1970). vol. 1, p. 405.

[42] Vladimir Jabotinsky, Letter to Yonah Machover, 18 December 1921, *Igrot, 1918–1922* (Tel Aviv, 1997).

[43] Itzhak Rabinowitch, *Haolam*, 5 August 1943.

[44] Nahum Levin, 'Jabotinsky and the Petliura Agreement', *Jewish Standard*, 9 August 1940.

mass murder of Jews, Jabotinsky reiterated his defence of the Slavinsky Accord and exonerated Petliura from being a pogromist. He said:

He was well acquainted with that type of Ukrainian intellectual nationalist hold-ing socialist views. I grew up with them and conducted a joint struggle with them against anti-Semites and Russifiers, both Jewish and Ukrainian. Neither I nor other thinking Zionists from Southern Russia can be convinced that people of that type can be considered anti-Semites.[45]

Despite Jabotinsky's strongly held views, the Kiev defendants expected the issue to be raised during the trial. Yet the Slavinsky Accord never was. Subsequent arrests and trials were not connected to the affair either.[46] Even so, twelve defendants were given two years' hard labour, while another fifteen were given one year. This was the first show trial of Zionists in the USSR.

This precipitated a further wave of trials in the Ukraine and was fol-lowed by the mass arrests of more than 3,000 Zionists on 2 September 1924.[47] Soviet policy was imprisonment, on the one hand, and expulsion, on the other.[48]

The Soviets had initiated a policy of 'substitution' – substituting inter-nal exile for life abroad. It had begun in January 1922 with a group of Mensheviks. In September of that year, 100 cultural figures were expelled to Germany. By the beginning of 1924, this approach was extended to the Zionists. Zionists left Odessa on vessels of the Black Sea shipping fleet such as the *Novorossiik*, which arrived in Jaffa in July 1924.[49] In December 1924 the steamer *SS Chicherin* brought 500 immigrants to Haifa, including 100 members of Tserei Tsion – some of whom had been imprisoned in Russia for Zionism.

[45] Vladimir Jabotinsky, 'Di "Krim" Kolonizatsye', *Der Morgen Zhurnal*, 4 June 1926. On Jabotinsky's attitude to Ukrainian nationalism, see Israel Kleiner, *From Nationalism to Universalism: Vladimir Ze'ev Jabotinsky and the Ukrainian Question* (Toronto, 2000).
[46] Schechtman and Benari, *History of the Revisionist Movement*, vol. 1, p. 414.
[47] Benjamin West, *B'derech l'geula* (Tel Aviv, 1971), p. 268.
[48] Ya'akov Goren, *ha-'lmut ha-kove'a: ben tenu'at ha'avodah la–tenu'ah ha-revizonyistit be-Erets Yisrael, 1925–1931* (Tel Aviv, 1986), pp. 16–17.
[49] Ziva Galili and Boris Morozov, *Exiled to Palestine: The Emigration of Zionist Convicts from the Soviet Union, 1924–1934* (New York, 2013), p. 22.

4

The Making of the Revisionists

THE LEGACY OF THE OCTOBER REVOLUTION

THE LEGACY OF THE OCTOBER REVOLUTION

The initial euphoria of the Russian Zionists on reaching the Land of Israel was replaced by their astonishment at the pro-Soviet approach of Hapoel Hatzair in Palestine. Their own experience in GPU prisons had been profoundly different from the experience of those who had emigrated during the early days of the October Revolution. They had remained long enough in Soviet Russia to make a distinction between the dream and the reality. Little information about the fate of the Zionists had seeped out, and the leadership of the Yishuv seemed to have more pressing problems.[1] Those who were able to leave had also borne witness to the zeal of the Yevsektsia to uproot Zionism from Soviet soil. They subsequently formed an opposition group within Hapoel Hatzair in Palestine and within the Histadrut called Kvutzot Ha-Amlanim (Trudoviki).

This dissident labour group began to find common ground with the supporters of Jabotinsky. One of those leaders of Tserei Tsion who was tried and sentenced in Kiev, Moshe Lurie, called for the merging of the Amlanim with the pro-Revisionist group of Yaakov Weinshal,[2] who had attended the founding meeting of the Revisionist movement in Paris. While there was no formal merger, there was certainly a meeting of minds.

The Amlanim strongly opposed the visit of Levi Shkolnik (Eshkol), a member of Hapoel Hatzair, to the Moscow conference of the Communist

---

[1] In September–October 1927, Arthur Ruppin visited the USSR ostensibly as an individual and recorded his views in his diary. Alex Bein, ed., *Arthur Ruppin: Memoirs, Diaries, Letters* (London, 1971), pp. 232–34.

[2] *Rassviet*, 26 April 1925.

Cooperative Movement in 1925 while Zionists were still sitting in Soviet prisons. Yet Tserei Tsion representatives met Shkolnik when he visited Moscow.

In July 1925 Hapoel Hatzair demanded the dissolution of the Amlanim, who responded by publishing a letter in *Davar*, the newly founded daily of the Histadrut. It accused Hapoel of deserting its labour roots to become a socialist party. It was signed by Arieh Altman, Baruch Weinstein and others who had been victimised in Russia. Moreover, the Amlanim accused Hapoel Hatzair in Palestine of suppressing freedom of expression within the party. They established the Histadrut ha-tsiyonim ha-Amlanim in early 1926, which mirrored many Revisionist principles but argued for Palestine to be built on labour pioneering principles. It rejected the Marxist approach regarding the relationship between labour and capital. It further opposed the enlargement of the Jewish Agency. Zionism, in its opinion, should be a classless national movement. The solution to industrial strife should not be sought though strikes but through national arbitration. It argued that the Histadrut should be a non-political organisation which dealt solely with trade union matters.[3] It also argued that Zionist labour parties should not affiliate to the Socialist International.

The Amlanim were attacked by the labour establishment. Moshe Beilinson wrote an article entitled 'Amlanim-Revisionistim' and thereby automatically merged the Amlanim with the newly founded Revisionist movement.[4] It was in a sense prophetic. Jabotinsky arrived in Palestine in October 1926 and met the Amlanim. Jabotinsky rejected their suggestion of a federal structure and argued instead that they should join a centralised organisation. In mid-January 1927 they decided to dissolve their own party and join the Revisionists as individuals.

Another group, Menorah, comprising the first two groups of Latvian members of Betar who had emigrated in late 1925 and in 1926, was also imbued with labour pioneering ideals. Riga had been the birthplace of Betar when Jabotinsky had visited in November 1923. Yet the 'Latvians' were distant from Betar in Palestine. Menorah wanted to remain within the Histadrut, whereas the Amlanim wanted a separate organisation. Menorah worked in the orange groves in Petah Tiqva and also draining the marshes in Binyamina:

[3] Joseph Schechtman and Yehuda Benari, *History of the Revisionist Movement*, vol. 1 (Tel Aviv, 1970), p. 198.
[4] Moshe Beilinson, *Davar*, 6 March 1926.

The agricultural centre assigned to us a small plot of land on which to erect our own tents. Each member of the group worked only one day a week. To conquer the market for Jewish labour, the Betarim agreed to receive a lower salary than that earned by the Arabs. We were able to survive only thanks to strict military regime which we introduced in the camp. In order to economise on breakfast and supper, we arose at 11 am and went to bed at 6 pm. Only members engaged in the day's work received an additional food ration. It was decided not to accept assistance from the national institutions.[5]

Ahimeir and the intellectuals, the Amlanim and Menorah were all influenced by the October Revolution. Their point of reference was the third aliyah rather than the fourth. This was shared by a group from Nes Ziona which was led by former Zionist prisoners in the USSR. This was the ideological difference with the originators of Revisionism.

The labour movement initiated a bitter campaign against the Revisionists, accusing them of wishing to introduce fascism into the Histadrut. Jabotinsky, however, was popular with a cross section of the Jewish population in Palestine. When he visited in October 1926, a reputed 6,000 people attended a rally at the Maccabee sports ground to hear him speak.[6]

Moreover, in 1925 there had been a dispute between the Histadrut and the settlement of Nahalat Yehudah over allocating part of the settlement's land to another pioneering group. The Histadrut enacted economic sanctions against the settlement, closing down the health services of Kupat Holim and the kindergarten.[7] The Amlanim supported Nahalat Yehudah against the Histadrut.

A Revisionist faction was represented at the third Histadrut conference in July 1927. But the Amlanim wanted to establish a separate labour group initially within the Histadrut – Gush Avodah HaRevisionisti. In February 1928 Gush Avoda Revisionisti was founded at a conference at Nahalat Yehudah. Abba Ahimeir, Uri Zvi Greenberg and Yehoshua Hirsh Yeivin appeared at the gathering and formally joined the Revisionists.[8] They pressed the Amlanim to establish an independent trade union, whereas the Revisionists wanted the Gush to position itself within the Histadrut. The compromise was to remain within the Histadrut while an independent labour exchange would be set up by the Revisionists.

[5] Y. Ophir, *Sefer HaOved haLeumi* (Tel Aviv, 1959), p. 43, in Schectman and Benari, *History of the Revisionist Movement*, vol. 1, p. 203.

[6] *Jewish Telegraphic Agency*, 21 October 1926.

[7] Schechtman and Benari, *History of the Revisionist Movement*, vol. 1, p. 196.

[8] Ya'acov N. Goldstein, 'Labour and Likud: Roots of Their Ideological-Political Struggle for Hegemony over Zionism', *Israel Affairs*, vol. 8, nos. 1–2 (2002), pp. 79–90.

FIGURE 4. Abba Ahimeir, Uri Zvi Greenberg and Yehoshua Hirsh Yeivin. (June 1927).
Courtesy of the Jabotinsky Institute, Tel Aviv.

This organisation of Revisionist workers made several demands on the Histadrut:

1. The Histadrut should consist of trades union only.
2. There should be a separation of the social and economic institutions from the Histadrut.

3. There should be neutral labour exchanges.
4. A body for compulsory national arbitration should be established which would thereby prevent the necessity of strikes.[9]

The appearance of these three left-wing intellectuals at the conference and the adherence of the Amlanim changed the direction and complexion of the Revisionist movement.[10]

The defection of Ahimeir and his colleagues from the labour camp and the establishment of rival structures, based on different principles, shocked the labour Zionists. It exacerbated the differences between labour and Revisionist Zionism and accelerated an ongoing political polarisation between Left and Right. It laid the basis for bitter disputes and occasional mutual violence.

Davar carried the slogan 'the paper of the workers of Eretz Israel' while *Doar Hayom* carried 'under the editorship of Vladimir Jabotinsky'.[11]

And yet there had always been ideological differences between Jabotinsky and the labour movement. In 1911, on the fiftieth anniversary of the death of the Ukrainian national poet Taras Shevshenko, he argued that the middle class could respond only to nationalism rather than to liberalism or socialism.[12]

Revisionism promoted the vision of a movement above politics and beyond ideology. It dismissed class and ignored religion. Its call for a return to a Herzlian ethos was also an attempt to hold back the lapping waves of factionalism. Its raison d'être was a reaction to Weizmann and the stagnation of the Zionist Organisation. Yet this desire to mould a coherent set of ideas took place in the midst of a profound economic crisis in Palestine as well as during the arrival of the Polish Jewish middle class in the mid-1920s.

In 1925 Jabotinsky wrote 'Basta',[13] in which he lamented the absence of the private sector – and the possibility that this would lead to fascism.[14] In May 1927 he not unexpectedly wrote, 'We, the Bourgeoisie',

---

[9] Ya'acov N. Goldstein, *From Fighters to Soldiers: How the Israeli Defense Forces Began* (Sussex, 1998), p. 180.

[10] Ya'akov Goren, *ha-'Imut ha-kove'a: ben tenu'at ha'-avodah la–tenu'ah ha-revizyonistit be-Erets Yisra'el, 1925–1931* (Tel Aviv, 1986), p. 106.

[11] Ibid., p. 129.

[12] Vladimir Jabotinsky, 'On the Lessons of the Anniversary of Shevshenko', *Odesskie Novosti*, 27 February 1911.

[13] *Rassviet*, 28 June 1925.

[14] Schechtman and Benari, *History of the Revisionist Movement*, vol. 1, pp. 221–22.

which attacked 'the cult of the proletariat'.[15] The reference point for the post-war bourgeoisie of the 1920s, he argued, was the national liberal revolutions of the nineteenth century rather than the October Revolution. Thus he could comment positively on the liberal legacy of Luigi Luzzatti, a former prime minister of Italy, on his death in 1927 and his commitment to nineteenth-century ideology.[16]

Jabotinsky commented that although he had never belonged to a socialist party, he did once believe in socialism. Jabotinsky referred to a booklet, written in 1910, in which he argued that 'the socialisation of the means of production is an inevitable and desirable result of the social process,' but 'I would not say that now. I do not consider the establishment of a socialist order either desirable or inevitable – humanity is not moving towards socialism; it is going in the reverse direction.'

Jabotinsky made a distinction between an ideal and a conviction. Zionism was an ideal even if you had left-wing convictions:

Garibaldi was one of the early dreamers of a League of Nations which would abolish all war, yet he himself directed war during his entire lifetime. I am prepared to believe that the Russian Communists are, in principle, opponents of militarism, nevertheless, they possess one of the largest armies. An ideal is a creation which does not tolerate any competition. You may have as many convictions as you wish, but you can and must serve only one, and all the others, no matter how nice and precious they may be in your eyes, must be abandoned.[17]

He argued that Communism instructed the people of the East that the land belongs to you 'and not to strangers … your enemy must be attacked at the weakest point. Jews are weaker than the English, French or the Italians.'

Jabotinsky had moved from a non-socialist position after 1917 to an anti-socialist position ten years later. In part this was due to a growing revulsion at the Bolshevisation of Russia – concerning not simply the campaign against Zionism by the Jewish Communists, but the loss of the culture and the literature of the old Russia. The dragooning of the anti-Tsarist intelligentsia to serve Lenin and Stalin, the destruction of a free press and the disappearance of the Odessa of his youth – all this embittered Jabotinsky. Despite his trumpeting of the centrality of the Land of Israel, he remained an émigré Russian intellectual:

The essence of Communism is anti-Zionist whether all the Stalins like it or not. Communism must strive to give the Arabs the possibility of making Palestine a

---

[15] *Rassviet*, 17 April 1927.
[16] Ibid.
[17] Vladimir Jabotinsky, 'On Relations with England', *Rassviet*, 22 May 1932.

part of a great Arab state. It cannot be otherwise. And Communism strives to annihilate the only source of our construction capital – the Jewish bourgeoisie – because their foundation is our root and its principle is the class struggle against the bourgeoisie. Not only is it impossible to serve two such movements – one cannot remain theoretically true to one while serving the other.[18]

This growing hostility towards Soviet Russia coincided with the fourth aliyah, the emigration of the Polish Jewish middle class. This took place during the mid-1920s due to the severity of the economic situation in Poland.

During his visit to Poland in 1927 in the aftermath of the Pilsudski coup, Jabotinsky was surprised by the ecstatic welcome that he received. Many Polish Jews saw Pilsudski's takeover as a chance for political stability under a strong leader after the failure of the preceding decade in Poland. Jabotinsky was seen in a similar light. While he did not care for the hero worship that he received,[19] he also began to perceive the possibilities of a mass movement, framed by Polish nationalism.[20] This necessitated developing a public anti-Soviet and anti-socialist stand.[21] Thus his article 'We, the Bourgeoisie' was designed to appeal to Polish Jews. This was followed by his attack on socialist economic theory[22] and his belief that the Jews were a nation of traders and businesspeople.[23] The socialism of his comrade in the Jewish Legion was played down and his military prowess promoted instead.[24]

However, there was also an economic crisis in Palestine, and the influx of Polish immigrants gave rise to a discussion within the Revisionist movement. Jabotinsky supported the ideas of Selig Eugen Soskin regarding intensive agriculture in order to develop the rural sector in Palestine. This evolved into accepting private ownership of land and its development by private capital.

There was correspondence between the Histadrut and the Revisionists about neutral employment exchanges and the non-partisanship of *Davar*, but the ideological gulf began to widen rather than narrow.

[18] Vladimir Jabotinsky, 'Ida Kremer's City', *Jewish Tribune*, 14 May 1926.
[19] Vladimir Jabotinsky, Letter to Anya, 27 February 1927.
[20] Daniel K. Heller, "The Rise of the Zionist Right: Polish Jews and the Betar Youth Movement, 1922–1935" (PhD diss., Stanford University, 2012), pp. 70–83.
[21] Vladimir Jabotinsky, Letter to Yefim Belilowsky, 2 May 1929, *Igrot, 1928–1929* (Jerusalem, 2002).
[22] Vladimir Jabotinsky, 'The Jubilee Idea', *Haynt*, 20 May 1927.
[23] Vladimir Jabotinsky, 'The Shopkeeper', *Haynt*, 5 June 1927.
[24] Heller, "Rise of the Zionist Right', pp. 108–10.

At the Revisionist conference in Vienna in 1928, the idea of national arbitration was discussed. Jabotinsky argued that the basis of colonisation activity was based on private capital. Therefore, if capital was to flow into Palestine and to employ Jewish labour exclusively, then conditions had to be created which did not prevent normal profit making:

The principle of national arbitration provides for the creation of a judicial body, entrusted with the task of fixing in every single instance the limit up to which the wages of the workers and employees can be increased without disturbing the opportunity of making normal profits.[25]

The alternative method of testing the limits of dispute was to go on strike. This, Jabotinsky argued, was not in the national interest of the construction of the Yishuv. The Revisionists viewed the Jewish worker as first and foremost a pioneer who had come to Palestine 'not to fight for his class interests but in order to help produce a Jewish majority.' Building up a Jewish economy which would bring more Jews to Palestine was deemed far more important than the interests of either capitalists or workers. In Palestine both capitalists and workers were 'soldiers, each one playing his particular role in the general plan of upbuilding.'[26]

The Histadrut held the diametrically opposite view. It put class interests before national interests. This, the Revisionists argued, did not mean that the opponents of the Histadrut espoused the cause of the middle class to the detriment of the working class. Indeed, Jabotinsky criticised the Jewish bourgeoisie, which was willing to tolerate such a situation. Moreover, the Histadrut official and the Jewish employer were equally irresponsible if they employed Arab labour. Not only would it deepen the class struggle in Palestine, it would aid the forces of Arab nationalism:

If the employer employs Arab labour, he is just as harmful as the Jewish agitator who organises Arab workers and thus artificially assists them to develop as a dangerous force in the country.[27]

In August 1932, the Revisionists decided to finally form their own rival Histadrut. This would be unaffiliated to any party and be known as a Histadrut Leumit – a national Histadrut. Jabotinsky pointed out that there was a plethora of workers' organisations – social democratic, Communist, Catholic and several others in Germany. There was an entrenched bitterness between labour youth and their opponents – often

[25] Vladimir Jabotinsky, 'National Arbitration', *Moment*, 6 January 1933.
[26] Vladimir Jabotinsky, 'The Rule of the Fist in the Yishuv', *Jewish Weekly*, 4 November 1932.
[27] Ibid.

from Betar. The strike at Frumin's biscuit factory in Jerusalem in 1932 – and the attempt to break it by Jabotinsky's followers – was a case in point.

Jabotinsky used his pen to attack his opponents in the labour movement in articles with provocative titles such as 'Crisis of the Proletariat',[28] 'The Rule of the Fist in the Yishuv',[29] 'Yes, Break It'[30] and 'In the Grip of the Red Swastika'.[31]

Jabotinsky was also clear about the meaning of 'social redemption'. He argued that fifty years hence, in 1984, the advance of technology would have made 'work' superfluous. A few million button-pushers would have to work perhaps three hours a day to operate machines. The central concern of the state was not to tolerate starvation. Moreover, experiments to engineer human nature and to change the economic system could not alter fundamental inequalities – 'one person may possess genius, another may lack it'. He added:

It is no concern of the state that Mr X dwells in a palatial mansion and Mr Y is grumbling why, he, too cannot occupy an equally luxurious place.[32]

Such views did not impress those in an age of ideology who believed that change would come through social evolution instigated by social revolution.

Jabotinsky stood for a Jewish army, urban settlement (since mass immigration could be absorbed only by cities), recognition of the dependency on the Mandatory power, a state on both sides of the Jordan, middle-class support and private enterprise, individualism, monism and opposition to the class war.

He was a stout defender of the Jew as a trader and a shopkeeper. He regarded the Jews as 'a commercial people', quoting the work of Werner Sombart.[33] He frowned upon the almost ideological attitude in the 1920s that the Jewish intelligentsia should desert the world of business and become 'a people of lawyers, a very doubtful promotion and a very dubious eminence'.[34] He further argued that it would damage the economic position of the Jews.

---

[28] *Poslebnie Novosti*, 19 April 1932.
[29] *Jewish Weekly*, 4 November 1932.
[30] *Haynt*, 4 November 1932.
[31] *Rassviet*, 23 October 1932.
[32] Vladimir Jabotinsky, 'Social Redemption', *Our Voice*, January 1935.
[33] Werner Sombart, *Die Juden und das Wirtschaftsleben* (Berlin, 1911).
[34] Jabotinsky, 'The Shopkeeper'.

Jabotinsky stated that the Revisionist movement was profoundly different from the other parties in that it publicly proclaimed that its membership was drawn from different trends in Zionism. It was a *Zweckerverband* – a movement with only one purpose, to reinvigorate Zionism.

Jabotinsky argued that the Revisionist movement wanted the Jews to leave behind two millennia of a Diaspora existence, a fundamental change in the Jewish condition:

A Jewish majority [in Palestine] does not mean that we intend to "rule" over our neighbours; but we want Zion to become a country where the Jew can no longer be overruled. The main characteristic of the Galut [exile] is precisely the fact that everywhere in the Diaspora the Jew can be, and always is, overruled – because the Jews are everywhere in a minority. Zionism would be meaningless if, after all our efforts, we were to face ultimately the same condition in Palestine.[35]

The Revisionist movement had been formally established in 1925 by acculturated Russian Jews in the heart of the Latin Quarter in Paris at the Café du Panthéon. It promised a return to Herzlian dynamism, following the stagnation of Weizmann's diplomacy. Its foundation instantly provoked attacks from the labour camp. In *Kuntres* both Moshe Beilinson[36] (May–June) and Eliahu Golomb (June–July) wrote articles which condemned the inception of Revisionism. Militarism became associated with 'Jabotinskyism'.[37] Weizmann too feared the political resurrection of his one-time colleague and flatmate, Vladimir Jabotinsky. In a letter to his wife, he remarked that the Revisionists were busying themselves with 'parades, protests and playing at soldiers'.[38] The Paris-based Russian-language journal, *Rassviet*, however, brought together many émigrés, and this proved to be the coordinating mechanism around Revisionism.

It was in Palestine itself where the founding of a union of Revisionist Zionists generated great interest. The hopes, engendered by the Balfour Declaration, had been dampened by the reality of the situation in Palestine. Weizmann's belief in England seemed to be misplaced. This disillusionment with plodding diplomacy was matched by the dire economic situation in the 1920s.

---

[35] Vladimir Jabotinsky, 'The Aims of Zionism', *The Zionist*, 14 May 1926.
[36] Moshe Beilinson, 'The Paris Congress of the Revisionists', *Kuntres*, 12 June 1925; 'The New World of Mr. Jabotinsky', *Davar*, 2 September 1925.
[37] Selig Brodetsky, 'Jabotinskyism', *Jewish Chronicle*, 30 October 1925.
[38] Chaim Weizmann, Letter to Vera Weizmann, 28 October 1926, in *The Letters and Papers of Chaim Weizmann*, Series A Letters, vol. 13, March 1926–May 1929 (Jerusalem, 1977).

Ya'akov Weinshal had attended the founding conference in Paris in 1925. He had been a member of the activist faction at the all-Zionist conference in Petrograd in 1917. From 1922, he wrote a regular 'Letter from Palestine' for *Rassviet*. Weinshal developed a discussion group of intellectuals in Tel Aviv in 1923 which interested Zionist youth and those in the liberal professions. He was the link between the Revisionists and disaffected groups within the labour movement such as the Amlanim and Menorah. Weinshal organised the first Revisionist conference in Palestine in Tel Aviv in July 1925.

THE SEEDS OF MAXIMALISM

Following their appearance at the Nahalat Yehudah conference in early 1928, Ahimeir, Yeivin and Greenberg were extremely active within the Revisionist movement in Palestine and in particular were influential amongst the Poles of the fourth aliyah. They also joined the board of *Doar Hayom*.

The Revisionist Executive was to a large extent situated in the Diaspora, whereas Ahimeir and his supporters were rooted in Palestine. Moreover, the founders of Revisionism came from mainly assimilated families. So were Ahimeir, Greenberg and Yeivin – these intellectuals of the Left – true Revisionists?

The intellectual trio undoubtedly introduced a militant anti-Marxist approach which Jabotinsky did not wholly share.[39] Yet Ahimeir was allowed to publish his 'Anti-Ma' (anti-Marxist) column. This was because of a belief in monism that both Ahimeir and Jabotinsky held. Both argued that a simultaneous adherence to socialism would deviate from the struggle by Zionism.

Ahimeir had met Jabotinsky for the first time in Vienna, where he was studying in 1921. Following his emigration to Palestine in 1924, his articles in the labour press gradually became more acerbic and critical of fundamental principles.[40] The shadow of the October Revolution was always there. He wrote about Peter Kropotkin,[41] Mikhail Gershenzon[42] and Felix Dzerzhinsky[43] when they died. On one occasion, he crossed

[39] Schechtman and Benari, *History of the Revisionist Movement*, vol. 1, p. 188.
[40] Mordechai Naor, 'Aba Ahimeir b'itonut hapoalit', in Yossi Ahimeir, ed., *Aba Ahimeir v'hatsionut hamupehanit* (Tel Aviv, 2012), pp. 34–46.
[41] Abba Ahimeir, 'On the Death of Prince Kropotkin', *Kuntres*, 1 April 1921.
[42] Abba Ahimeir, 'On the Death of Mikhail Gershenzon', *Hapoel Hatzair*, 6 April 1925.
[43] Abba Ahimeir, 'On the Death of Felix Dzerzhinskii', *Davar*, 16 August 1926.

swords with Moshe Sharett, who had responded to him.[44] In addition, Ahimeir participated in the debate as to whether Hapoel Hatzair should merge with Ahdut Ha'avodah. He vehemently opposed any connection with the 'Marxist' Ahdut Ha'avodah.

Like Jabotinsky, Ahimeir was an intellectual, political theoretician and literary critic. Benjamin Akzin, a loyal aide to Jabotinsky, later wrote:

Beside the analytical, rational considerations which brought people to espouse the Revisionist cause, it had also attracted many who were drawn to it by temperament, either because of their inclination to assume extremist positions or because they were nonconformists by nature. Jabotinsky's own personality, uniting a first rate logical mind with the soul of a poet dissatisfied with daily humdrum, reflected these two aspects. Many of my Revisionist co-workers shared both characteristics.[45]

This perhaps summed up Ahimeir's enthusiasm for Jabotinsky and for the Revisionists. Like Jabotinsky, Ahimeir wrote about a plethora of literary figures who were responsible for the revival and evolution of Hebrew culture during the twentieth century, such as Elishevah,[46] Sh. Ansky,[47] Max Brod,[48] Yehudah Gur,[49] Haim Hazaz,[50] Shaul Tchernikovsky,[51] Moshe Smilansky,[52] Yosef Klausner[53] and Avraham Reizin.[54]

The inter-war years were, however, polarising and ideologically charged. By 1926 Ahimeir was writing about the turn to dictatorship in Europe with some sympathy:

The recognition that the parliamentary system is detrimental to the realisation of modern ideas and aspirations encourages the creation of a new ideology of democracy.[55]

This was clear, he indicated, in the regimes of Mussolini, Pilsudski and Atatürk .

Like Ben-Gurion, he and Uri Zvi Greenberg admired Lenin for carrying out the Revolution with so few resources. Lenin had convinced the

---

44 Abba Ahimeir, *Davar*, 11 June 1926.
45 Benjamin Akzin, Mi-Rigah li-Yerushalayim (Jerusalem 1989) p. 157.
46 Abba Ahimeir, *Herut*, 8 April 1949.
47 Abba Ahimeir, *Hamashkif*, 19 November 1940.
48 Abba Ahimeir, *Herut*, 11 June 1954.
49 Abba Ahimeir, *Herut*, 27 January 1950.
50 Abba Ahimeir, *Hamashkif*, 11 December 1942.
51 Abba Ahimeir, *Hamashkif*, 27 November 1942.
52 Abba Ahimeir, *Hamashkif*, 17 March 1944.
53 Abba Ahimeir, *Herut*, 26 August 1949.
54 Abba Ahimeir, *Hamashkif*, 17 April 1943.
55 Abba Ahimeir, *Hapoel Hatzair*, 27 August 1926.

sympathetic wing of the Russian intelligentsia 'not only that it was necessary to draw a distinction between morality and politics, but that morality
must also be subordinated to politics'.[56] No one, Ahimeir observed, was
willing to sacrifice him- or herself for Kerensky's regime, but the powerful
attraction of the total transformation of society prepared people to do so
for Lenin.[57] Greenberg had even eulogised Lenin in a poem on his death
in 1924 and was later critical of the freedom of speech in democracies.[58]

The Zionist movement's general belief in self-sacrifice began to occupy
a central, perhaps obsessive place in Ahimeir's beliefs. He looked to the
past century's attempts to overthrow Tsarism. He admired the Decembrists
who had staged an early revolt against authoritarian Tsarism in 1825. He
had read the memoirs of the Narodnik Vera Figner, who had spent two
decades in prison, and he was moved by such idealism. He was impressed
by those imprisoned in the fortress of Schlossburg who took up mathe-
matics and astronomy.

Ahimeir was interested in the Russian social revolutionaries. He dedicated one of his publications to Dora Kaplan, a social revolutionary who
attempted to assassinate Lenin in 1918.

In 1927 just before his departure to the Revisionists, Ahimeir wrote
several critical articles, such as 'The October Terror'[59] and 'The Creator
of the Brest-Litovsk Accord'.[60] These commemorated the tenth anniversary of the October Revolution and Trotsky's fall from grace. He even
announced his disillusionment with socialism by signing his articles 'Aba
Apostata' after the scholarly and reforming Roman emperor, Julian the
Apostate (361–363), who authorised the building of the Third Temple
during his short reign.[61] But perhaps more crucially Julian had abandoned Christianity as the state religion of the empire. Julian's loss of faith
and his attempt to turn the tide was highly symbolic for Ahimeir.

The triumph of Bolshevism and its ascendency both attracted and
repelled Ahimeir. Lenin was to be admired, but clearly 'national dictatorship' rather than Communism was the way of the future. In this manner Ahimeir intellectually tiptoed along a path to Italian Fascism and
embraced the perception that Mussolini was the inheritor of the mantles
of Garibaldi, Mazzini and Cavour. He viewed Italian Fascism – before its

[56] Yonathan Shapiro, *The Road to Power: Herut Party in Israel* (New York, 1991), p. 44.
[57] Abba Ahimeir, *Hapoel Hatzair*, 17 March 1927.
[58] Abba Ahimeir, *Kuntres*, 26 August 1926.
[59] *Ha'aretz*, 8 November 1927.
[60] *Ha'aretz*, 23 November 1927.
[61] *Ha'aretz*, 19 June 1927.

formal adoption of anti-Semitism in 1938 – as fighting Bolshevism. This was something that he bitterly regretted later in life.

The Italian Fascist movement since its earliest days had boasted of Jewish members, often assimilated Jews who considered themselves to be Italian patriots. Mussolini himself blew hot and cold towards Jews and the Yishuv in Palestine. At one point he regarded the October Revolution as Jewish vengeance against Christianity. In the Fascist *Il Populo d'Italia*[62] there were several articles in 1919 and 1920 which equated all Jews with Communism – and were possibly authored by Mussolini. Jewish bankers in the United States were deemed to be in league with the Bolsheviks, and Italian Jews were sometimes accused of double loyalty. Yet Italian interests in the Mediterranean were sometimes seen by the Zionists as a means of placing pressure on the British. Weizmann too met Mussolini on several occasions to discuss this.

During a stay in Rome in July 1922, Jabotinsky wrote a long letter[63] to the Fascist leader in response to a recent article that Mussolini had written in which he raised the possibility of establishing a centre for the pan-Arab movement in Italy.[64]

The Italian Revisionists, led by Leone Carpi, tried to urge Mussolini to be more sympathetic to the Zionist experiment.[65] Addressing him as 'Duce del Fascismo e Capo del Governo', Carpi argued that it was in Italy's national interest in the Mediterranean to support Zionism. Jabotinsky was in favour of developing Betar in Italy.[66]

Unlike that of Weizmann and Jabotinsky, Ahimeir's motivation seemed purely ideological. He was attracted to the idea of developing a 'revolutionary Zionism' which would revive the Zionist experiment, currently residing in the ideological doldrums. He believed that Italian Fascism would provide ideological scaffolding.

Ahimeir became interested in the work of the German political sociologist Robert Michels, one of the advocates of revolutionary syndicalism twenty years before. Following World War I, Michels had moved towards

---

[62] *Il Populo d'Italia*, June 1919; 19 October 1920. See Mario Toscano, 'Italian Jewish Identity from the Risorgimento to Fascism, 1848–1938', in Joshua D. Zimmerman, ed., *Jews in Italy under Fascist and Nazi Rule, 1922–1945* (Cambridge, 2009), pp. 60–63.

[63] Vladimir Jabotinsky, Letter to Benito Mussolini, 16 July 1922, *Igrot, 1918–1922* (Tel Aviv, 1997).

[64] Benito Mussolini, 'La gratitudine del syriani per l'Italia', *Il Populo d'Italia*, 14 July 1922.

[65] Leone Carpi, Letter to Benito Mussolini, 5 November 1931, Jabotinsky Institute Archives, Tel Aviv.

[66] Vladimir Jabotinsky, Letter to Leone Carpi, 7 October 1931, *Igrot, 1930–1931* (Jerusalem, 2004).

espousing Italian Fascism and then joining the party. In 1925 Michels's classic work on political sociology regarding political parties, *Zur Soziologie des Parteiwesens in der modernen Demokratie: Untersuchungen über die oligarchischen Tendenzen des Gruppenlebens*, was published once more. It provided food for thought for Ahimeir:

> History, Michels argued, reveals that the mass of mankind is passive. Only under crisis conditions is the apathetic mass moved to political action. Under such conditions a small minority of men assume leadership and put together ideological formulations calculated to stir the interests and the sentiments of their potential followers. Such leaders, drawn almost exclusively from the bourgeois and petit bourgeois intelligentsia, give shape to the aspirations of the mobilizable masses. The leaders become the embodiment of the revolutionary party's goals and the role models who infuses through mimetic suggestions, an organisational and collective ethic.[67]

Michels spoke of 'the iron law of elites' which governed the organisation of men. He further argued that patriotism arose not out of political history, but out of intellectual history. While Ahimeir moved towards a theoretical framework for his concept of 'revolutionary Zionism', it also placed him in direct opposition to Jabotinsky, who accepted both traditional liberalism and parliamentarianism as well as the myth-making and the galvanising epitomised by revolutionary syndicalism.

In September 1926 Ahimeir promoted the figure of Nahshon ben Aminadav – the first follower of Moses to jump into the unparted Red Sea – as an example for revolutionary youth.[68] Indeed, being a 'Nahshon' in the 1920s was synonymous with being a doer, a leader, an initiator.

Although Ahimeir was fiercely anti-Communist, he revered the Russian revolutionary tradition and its spirit of self-sacrifice. His revolutionary Zionism looked to the fighters of the Second Temple period, on the one hand. It looked to 'Lenin, Trotsky and the Narodnaya Volya', on the other.[69]

In November 1927 – on the anniversary of the October Revolution – Ahimeir wrote an article for *Ha'aretz* entitled 'If I Am Not for Myself, Who Will Be for Me?'[70] Well known as a saying of the Talmudic sage

---

[67] James Gregor, *Young Mussolini and the Intellectual Origins of Fascism* (Berkeley, CA 1979), pp. 64–65.

[68] Abba Ahimeir, *Hapoel Hatzair*, 22 September 1926.

[69] Yosef Zahavi, 'Revolutionary Zionism: From Berit Ha-Biryonim to Etzel', in Yossi Ahimeir, ed., *The Black Prince: Yosef Katznelson and the National Movement in the 1930s* (Tel Aviv, 1983), p. 292.

[70] *Ha'aretz*, 15 November 1927.

Hillel, it had been transformed, he argued, into the slogan of the Irish Republican Sinn Fein – and this was also an indication of what should be the Zionist pathway as well. In this article and others which followed, he argued the case for Fascism. He wrote a series of eight articles entitled 'From the Notebook of a Fascist' for *Doar Hayom*.

Although an admirer of Lenin's ability to carry out the Revolution, Ahimeir was less enamoured of what had followed. Ahimeir argued that the 'Red Dictatorships' had failed in Germany and China. The Soviet Union under Stalin was adopting the doctrine of 'socialism in one country'. On the other hand, national dictatorships had arisen in Italy, Hungary, Spain, Poland, Lithuania, Turkey, Persia, Egypt and Yugoslavia:

The national Italian model of dictatorship has flourished instead. Even Yugoslavia, the ancient enemy of Italy, discovered no better way than the Italian system. In the Yugoslav dictatorship we see proof. Parliamentarianism was powerless to solve the country's mass of internal problems. Intrigue destroyed the professional politicians. The king had no choice but to abandon the politicians and to appeal to the military man. 'Come, be our ruler and let this ruin be under thy hand.'[71]

And at the same time, the national dictatorship is striking roots, without claiming any victims. It is absurd to speak of Italian fascism as a murderous regime.[72]

Ahimeir believed that Revisionism was 'a revolution within our people whose political sense has been dimmed'. Moreover, he was more enthusiastic about the national revolutionary movements of central Europe than the cosmopolitan ones of Eastern Europe. Zionists in Palestine, he believed, should learn from Western non-Jews rather than from Jewish socialists in Western Europe.[73]

In an article entitled 'National Dictatorship in the Wider World',[74] Ahimeir argued that parliamentarianism worked only in strong stable countries such as the United Kingdom and France. But in less stable countries, it had been eroded and often superseded by national dictatorship. He noted that there was danger to parliamentarianism in weak regimes such as Weimar Germany.

When Jabotinsky arrived in Palestine in October 1928, Ahimeir in his series 'From the Notebook of a Fascist' entitled an article 'On the Arrival of Our Duce'.[75] Ahimeir argued that Jabotinsky's followers would

[71] Isaiah 3:6.
[72] Abba Ahimeir, 'Rome and Jerusalem', *Ha'am*, 8 May 1931.
[73] Abba Ahimeir, 'Autoemanzipatia', 19 August 1932, in *Revolutionary Zionism* (Tel Aviv, 1965), p. 284.
[74] *Doar Hayom*, 29 January 1929.
[75] *Doar Hayom*, 10 October 1928.

appeal to him in blind faith with a popular quotation from the book of Exodus: na'aseh ve-nishmah, 'We will do [everything that God has commanded] and [then] we will listen.'[76] Ahimeir wrote his first letter to Jabotinsky and addressed him as 'the leader'. In his second letter, on 25 October 1928, he stated that he longed for 'someone superior to stand above me and show me the way ... so why do you consult with us so much? Command us more. We have to obey your orders.'

In his next article he wrote:

Our messiah will not arrive as a pauper on a donkey. He will come like all messiahs, riding a tank and bringing his commandments to his people.[77]

Yet Jabotinsky found the idea of a 'Duce' repulsive. Although he had originally tried to disabuse Mussolini of his crude stereotypes of Jews,[78] by 1926 Jabotinsky was scathing about him:

There is today a country where 'programmes' have been replaced by the word of one man. Whatever he says is the programme. Popular vote is scorned. That country is Italy; the system is called fascism; to give their prophet a title, they had to coin a new term – 'Duce' – which is a translation of that most absurd of all English words – 'leader'. Buffaloes follow a leader. Civilised men have no 'leaders'.[79]

Jabotinsky wrote that he had met 'a fascist acquaintance' in 1925 and chided him with the question: 'And what will you do when your "genius" dies? After all, you yourselves know that you can't get geniuses by the dozen.'[80]

At the same time he recognised that there was a need for the generation of the 1930s to mythologise a figure.[81] A few years later, Jabotinsky argued that there was a romantic longing for adventurism in virtually every nation. This led to the desire to locate 'a leader' and place him on a pedestal. For Jews, Jabotinsky reasoned, this was tantamount to accepting 'the dictates of assimilation'.[82] Yet while the Duce cult was disparaged by Jabotinsky, he also realised that he could utilise its attributes to further his aim of building a mass movement in Poland.

---

[76] Exodus 24:7.
[77] Abba Ahimeir, 'From the Notebook of a Fascist: If He Proves to be a Villain, then Act in the Same Manner to him', *Doar Hayom*, 14 October 1928.
[78] Vladimir Jabotinsky, Letter to Benito Mussolini, 16 July 1922, *Igrot, 1918–1922*.
[79] Vladimir Jabotinsky, 'Zionist Fascism', *The Zionist*, 25 June 1926.
[80] Vladimir Jabotinsky, 'The Unknown Race', *Causeries* (Paris, 1930).
[81] Vladimir Jabotinsky, Letter to Miriam Langer, 27 August 1930, *Igrot, 1930–1931*.
[82] Vladimir Jabotinsky, 'Leader', *Moment*, 3 July 1934.

Ahimeir did not believe in 'England', but in 'national revolution'. He argued that Jews should not rely on 'the kindness of nations'.[83] The defeat of Greece by Turkey and the victory of the House of Saud over the Hashemites suggested to Ahimeir that Britain would not support its friends.

In contrast, Jabotinsky expressed his admiration for the British parliamentary system. Yet his idea of parliament was one which transcended ideology and petty politics. In 1928 he suggested the establishment of 'a professional parliament' to supplement the assembly of elected representatives. This second house, a senate, would deal with practical matters such as the economy and would involve all thoughtful people. The elected parliament, consisting of political parties, would deal with ideological questions. These clear ideological differences between Jabotinsky and Ahimeir would be fought out in the struggle to attract youth to the Revisionist standard.

Even though the initial Arab violence had subsided during the 1920s, the symbol of the Jewish Legion, the Haganah and Jewish self-defence per se remained a potent nationalist symbol. For the Revisionists and its embryonic Maximalist wing, the idea of a Jewish fighting force grew in importance and certainly was an attraction for the newly established Betar in Palestine. Jabotinsky attempted to keep alive the idea of military prowess and self-sacrifice by writing *Samson*, which was published in Hebrew in 1927. Jabotinsky changed the biblical story of Samson, airbrushing God out of the narrative and turning Samson into a universal nazarite hero who implicitly condemns assimilation. Pulling down the Temple is 'no longer a defense of God's honour, it is now a man's sacrifice for his people'.[84]

In November 1926 Menahem Arber, who had served in the Jewish Legion, put forward the outline of a training programme for the sports section of Betar to the third conference of the Revisionists in Palestine. He soon became the head of the section in April 1927 and developed it with the help of Yirmiyahu Halperin, Jabotinsky's aide-de-camp during the Jerusalem disturbances in 1920, and Moshe Rosenberg, a former officer in the Russian White Army. They organised the Bet Sefer le-madrikhim Betar – the school for the Betar guides – and provided military training for twenty-four cadets. From the outset it exhibited an independent

[83] Abba Ahimeir, 'In Place of an Investigation', *Doar Hayom*, 4 October 1929.
[84] Rachel Harris, 'Samson's Suicide: Death and the Hebrew Literary Canon', *Israel Studies*, vol. 17, no. 3 (Autumn 2012), pp. 67–91.

approach and possessed a considerable degree of autonomy. All this created resentment and a tension with the formal leadership of Betar and the Revisionist movement in Palestine. Despite threats from Jabotinsky to expel Halperin and his colleagues, the Bet Sefer continued its independent existence.[85]

The educational input into the training programme came from the intellectuals who had recently joined the Revisionist movement. Abba Ahimeir and his like-minded friend from Bobruisk, Yosef Katznelson, were drafted to lecture to the cadets.[86] As a history lecturer, Ahimeir was by far the most influential and instilled the ideas of revolutionary Zionism.[87] Some of the cadets had lived through the period of the October Revolution and the massacres of Jews in the Ukraine. Just before the serious disturbances of August 1929 when Jews were killed in Safed, Jerusalem and Hebron, the *madrikhim* graduated and the Bet Sefer was disbanded. The personal contacts, however, could not so easily be dissolved and the school continued to exist informally.

Ahimeir considered those Jews killed in Hebron and Safed in 1929 to be similar to those killed in the massacres of Worms, Nemirov and Proskorov. They were, he wrote, 'martyrs to the building of the Jewish homeland'. All this resonated strongly with those who had suffered at the hands of both the Bolsheviks and the Ukrainian nationalists.[88] Ahimeir further asked whether Jewish youth were prepared to do something about this and whether they were up to the task.[89]

[85] Itzik Remba, 'the First Lighters of the Blazing Torch', *Herut*, 25 September 1955.
[86] Zahavi, 'Revolutionary Zionism', p. 293.
[87] Moshe Segal, 'Hashavua l'yad Ha'kotel', in Yossi Ahimeir and Shmuel Shatzky, eds., *Hineinu Sikirikim* (Tel Aviv, 1978) pp. 139–40.
[88] Abba Ahimeir, 'The Desert and the Garden of Eden', *Doar Hayom*, 4 September 1929.
[89] Abba Ahimeir, *Doar Hayom*, 25 September 1929.

5

The Maximalists

On 15 August 1929, the Bet Sefer le-madrikhim organised a march to the Western Wall.[1] Its purpose was to protest the continuous Arab interruption of Jewish religious services at this location – the outer wall of the Temple compound – and to re-energise Jewish claims to it. It acted, however, without consulting the Revisionist Executive or Betar in Palestine. At least 90 percent of the protesters were unaffiliated individuals. The Bet Sefer distributed leaflets, advertising the march on behalf of 'Zionist Revolutionary Youth'. The procession of 300 was led by a young man carrying a black-edged flag and accompanied by a British representative, Major Kingsley-Hitt. The silent march ended as it began, in an orderly fashion.

The following day, however, a Muslim demonstration took place which was anything but orderly. It ended with the dispersal of Jewish worshippers and the burning of prayer books with little interference from the understaffed police.

Ha'aretz considered the Jewish demonstration to have been a catalyst of the Muslim demonstration – and did not mince its words.[2] The secularists and the socialists did not look upon the Wall in the same fashion as the nationalists and the religious. The Zionist Executive meeting at the Zurich congress appealed for calm. The die, however, had been cast. The mufti of Jerusalem, the leader of Palestinian Arab nationalism, attempted

[1] Joseph Schechtman and Yehuda Benari, *History of the Revisionist Movement*, vol. 1 (Tel Aviv, 1970), p. 256.
[2] *Ha'aretz*, 18 August 1929.

to capitalise on this wave of discontent. The mufti's rumour mill about Zionist annexation of the Temple Mount and a multitude of Muslim deaths sparked off a spiral of violence in the Jerusalem area which led to the subsequent killing of 59 Jews in Hebron on 24 August and another 20 in Safed on 29 August. In all 133 Jews were killed in the 1929 disturbances and more than 120 Arabs perished – mainly at the hands of the British.

The Commission of Enquiry under Sir Walter Shaw laid the blame for the violence at the door of the Jews and defined the Jewish demonstration 'as having been more than any other single incident an immediate cause of the outbreak'. In his testimony in camera to the Shaw Commission, Major Alan Saunders, head of the Palestine police, said that after the two demonstrations, he believed that the Arabs were interested only in driving out the Jews:

The whole Arab population wanted to make it clear to the world that they were not going to tolerate the Jews, the old or new ones. If a man was a Jew, it was good enough for him to be killed and stamped out.[3]

Although the dissident Bet Sefer cadets had been the real instigators of the Jewish march, much against the advice of the British police and Jewish Agency officials, Jabotinsky bemoaned the fact that it had not been organised by Betar. He dismissed the charge that such a demonstration had antagonised the Arabs. He was fatalistic: 'the very fact that the Jews in Palestine breathe the same air annoys the Arabs'.[4]

The Shaw Commission, the Hope-Simpson report and the Passfield White Paper in 1930 all attempted to extract British policy from the promises of the Balfour Declaration and to interpret it anew. The Jews of Palestine who had been the actual victims of Arab violence felt aggrieved. Jabotinsky and the Revisionists also felt betrayed by the British and vowed to do something about it. However, it was the teachings of Ahimeir that had fashioned a new force in Palestine – the Bet Sefer cadets, a group of militants who espoused the ideals of revolutionary Zionism. This laid the basis for military action against both the British and the Palestinian Arabs at the end of the 1930s. It was the seed that grew into the Irgun Zvai Leumi (National Military Organisation) and Lehi (Fighters for the Freedom of Israel).[5]

---

[3] Testimony of Major Alan Saunders, Commission of Enquiry on the Disturbances of August 1929; evidence taken in camera; PRO CO 967/91, National Archives, Kew, United Kingdom.

[4] Vladimir Jabotinsky, 'What Happened', *Rassviet*, 23 February 1930.

[5] Yehoshua Ofir, *Rishonei Etzel, 1931–1940* (Tel Aviv, 2002), pp. 28–30.

The network created by Ahimeir's Bet Sefer cadets was formalised with the creation of a new organisation, Berit Ha-Biryonim. The original *biryonim* were the Zealots of the Second Temple period. For some, they were simply radical ruffians. For others, they were the *sicarii*, assassins of the perceived enemies of the Jews – both Jewish and non-Jewish. Significantly those Jews with 'moderate' views were especially deemed worthy of assault.

Uri Zvi Greenberg regarded Zionism as an Eastern revolutionary movement. He had referred positively to the biryonim of antiquity in an article as early as July 1923.[6] Greenberg criticised Bialik on several occasions for not totally devoting his later work to the national struggle.[7] Greenberg bemoaned the absence of 'blood stained biryonim poets'.[8] He had also written a poem about the sicarii in 1929.[9]

Berit Ha-Biryonim reflected Ahimeir's desire for an organisation based on the ideals of revolutionary Zionism. Ostensibly an organisation which originated from Ahimeir's interest in revolutionary and national syndicalism, it was actually Lenin rather than Mussolini who was held up as the exemplar. During one of his lectures to the Berit Ha-Biryonim, Ahimeir commented:

Our teacher is not Herzl or Jabotinsky, but Lenin. We reject the doctrines and philosophies of Lenin and his followers, but they were correct in their practical path. This is the path of violence, blood and personal sacrifice.[10]

Yet Ahimeir rejected Lenin's creation, the USSR and international Communism. In a *Letter to Young Zionists*, he pleaded with the youth to turn away from revolutionary socialism.[11] One factor in the genesis of Berit Ha-Biryonim was the return of several left-wing Zionists to the Soviet Union due to the dire economic situation in Palestine and a disillusionment with its political stagnation in the mid-1920s. The returning group, which eventually settled in the Crimea, was led by Menahem Elkind and it touched a raw nerve as far as Ahimeir was concerned:

I am certain that if the Berit Ha-Biryonim had existed during the split in the Labour battalion, Elkind's people would not have returned to Russia and become

---

[6] Uri Zvi Greenberg, *Haolam*, 27 July 1923.
[7] Uri Zvi Greenberg, *Davar*, 18 November 1927.
[8] Monty Noam Penkower, 'The Silences of Bialik: Zionism's Bard Confronts Eretz Israel', *Modern Judaism*, vol. 26, no. 3 (2006), p. 244.
[9] Uri Zvi Greenberg, 'Sikirikin', *Ezor magen u-ne'um ben ha-dam* (Jerusalem, 1929).
[10] Kalman Katznelson, 'Ha-Dugma: Lenin', in Yossi Achimeir and Shmuel Shatski, eds., *Berit Ha-Biryonim: The First Anti-British Organisation* (Tel Aviv, 1978), p. 130.
[11] *Doar Hayom*, 21 October 1930.

lost to the Zionist cause, but would have found their rightful place within the structures of the Zionist Revolutionary Movement.[12]

Another factor was the decision of the leader of the 'Activists' within the Revisionists in Palestine, Wolfgang von Weisl, to temporarily go abroad. Many from his group then looked to Ahimeir for leadership.[13]

Like Jabotinsky, Ahimeir and Berit Ha-Biryonim believed in 'a Hebrew state on both sides of the Jordan'.[14] Despite all the incendiary language, there was no violence when it came to demonstrations. There was a protest against the visit of Drummond Shiels in October 1930.[15] Shiels was undersecretary of state for the colonies in the Labour government and perceived as responsible for the Passfield White Paper. In addition, in the eyes of Ahimeir and his followers, the symbolism of this White Paper demonstrated the vacuity of social democracy and the failure of the Second International.[16] Ahimeir and two others were arrested at the demonstration.[17]

A year later, Berit Ha-Biryonim staged a protest against the 1931 Census, which they believed was paving the way for the establishment of a representative legislative assembly with an Arab majority.[18]

In February 1932 Norman Bentwich, the former attorney general in Palestine was due to be formally installed as the newly established professor of peace studies at the Hebrew University in Jerusalem. Bentwich had long sympathised with Zionism. In 1916, he wrote:

In Heine's poem on the 'Princess Sabbath', the peddler is changed into a prince when he throws off his pack on the Sabbath eve. And the Jewish people, when in its own land, it throws off the burden of centuries of persecution, will again reveal the excellence which made it of old, a light to the nations.[19]

The Foreign Office regarded Bentwich, a British Jew, as too great a liability in the aftermath of the disturbances of 1929. At a meeting in July 1930, the foreign secretary, Lord Passfield, and the high commissioner,

[12] Yehoshua Heschel Yeivin, 'Mehulal Berit Ha-Biryonim', in Joseph Nedava, ed., *Abba Achimeir: The Man Who Turned the Tide* (Tel Aviv, 1987), p. 34.
[13] Ephraim Even, *The Schism in the Zionist Movement: Why Jabotinsky Established the New Zionist Organisation* (Jerusalem, 1992), p. 103.
[14] Abba Ahimeir, *Hazit Ha'am*, 8 September 1933.
[15] Abba Ahimeir, *Hazit Ha'am*, 10 October; 12 October 1930.
[16] Abba Ahimeir, *Hazit Ha'am*, 5 September 1933.
[17] *Hazit Ha'am*, 16 October 1930; *Jewish Chronicle*, 17 October 1930.
[18] *Hamedina*, 25 September 1931; *Ha'uma*, 2 October 1931.
[19] Norman Bentwich, 'The Future of Palestine', in H. Sacher, ed., *Zionism and the Jewish Future* (London, 1916), p. 207.

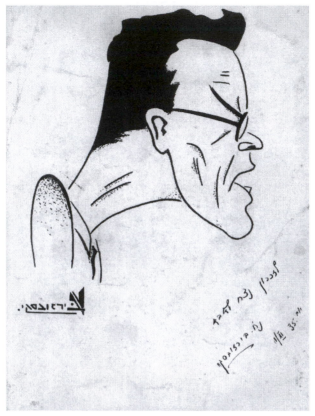

FIGURE 5. Caricature of Abba Ahimeir (November 1935). Illustration by Noah Birzovsky.
Courtesy of the Jabotinsky Institute, Tel Aviv.

Sir John Chancellor, thought it best that Bentwich not return to Palestine after his summer holidays.

Ironically, although a loyal servant of the British crown, Bentwich projected dovish views and hopes of a Jewish-Arab reconciliation. Worse still was his friendship with Judah Magnes, chancellor of the university, advocate of a binational solution in Palestine and leading light in Berit Shalom. The American Magnes had been strongly opposed to U.S. involvement in World War I and was deeply involved in the campaign to oppose it. All this did not recommend him to either Jabotinsky[20] or Ahimeir, both of

---

[20] Vladimir Jabotinsky, 'Bi-National Palestine', 1930, Jabotinsky Institute Archives, Tel Aviv.

whom wrote numerous critical articles about Magnes and Berit Shalom. Ahimeir labelled Bentwich an assimilator and missionary who practised universalism.[21] His inauguration was therefore a red rag to a bull – and Berit Ha-Biryonim barracked Bentwich and attempted to disrupt the ceremony at the Hebrew University. One placard read: 'We don't need a school of peace in the name of Weizmann – what we need is a military academy in the name of Trumpeldor.'[22] Bentwich was told, 'Go from here, you traitor, you despoiler of Israel.'[23]

The university security personnel were unable to contain the situation and the police were called in.[24] In addition to the arrest of Ahimeir, fifteen students were suspended following the disruption. Four belonged to the El Al group and were suspended for two years. Another eleven, members of the Hulda Union, were banned for one term.[25]

WHAT WAS BETAR?

Ahimeir believed that the task of Betar was to be a 'national guard' – a revolutionary vanguard. Nietzsche's *der Wille zur Macht* (will to power), he argued, should be developed in the youth – to take and not receive. Moreover, a central task of Betar was to liberate Zionist youth from left-wing influence. Its outlook should be one of extreme monism, unpolluted by Marxism. Influencing Betar became the raison d'être for Ahimeir's literary outpourings and his political activism. It formed the ideological battleground of the struggle between himself and Jabotinsky.

Ahimeir profoundly believed that the idea of Betar could be found in modern Hebrew poetry – Y. L. Gordon, Tchernikovsky, Shneur, Yaakov Cohen, Bialik and Berdichevsky, even the hero in Max Brod's *Reubeni, Prince of the Jews*.[26] He believed in heroic acts that would awaken the Jews of Palestine from their political slumber:

[A] single deed by a brave young man, a deed that for the usual reasons the writer of these columns does not find it possible to write about – such a deed would raise far greater interest in Eretz Israel.[27]

[21] Abba Ahimeir, *Hazit Ha'am*, 19 February 1932.
[22] Abba Sikra, 'A Diaspora or a Political Mentality?' *Hazit Ha'am*, 16 February 1933.
[23] *Hazit Ha'am*, 12 February 1932.
[24] Norman Bentwich, *My Seventy-Seven Years: An Account of My Life and Times, 1883–1960* (London, 1962), p. 99.
[25] *Jewish Chronicle*, 19 February 1932.
[26] Aba Ahimeir, *Revolutionary Zionism* (Tel Aviv, 1965), pp. 21–24.
[27] Abba Ahimeir, 'Problems of the World Revisionist Conference', *Hazit Ha'am*, 15 July 1932.

Jabotinsky tried to counteract Ahimeir's growing influence by writing several articles about the Jewish Legion.[28] If Ahimeir had viewed 1932 as commemorating 1,800 years since the start of the Bar-Kokhba revolt against the Romans, 1932 also marked the fifteenth anniversary of the founding of the Legion in 1917. This symbolised the different narratives – was Betar an embryonic national liberation movement or the source of manpower for a Jewish army?

Jabotinsky placed his faith in military training – almost as an educational activity – but not in taking it further, not in actual military action against the British or the Arabs. Thus Jabotinsky emphasised military knowledge rather than military action:

If I am told that to shoot is militarism, particularly in the present world which hates militarism and strives for peace – I would not disagree, although I am not certain that the world has truly such peaceful aspirations. I would even concede that it is very sad for us Jews at a time like this to be forced to learn to shoot. But we are forced to it and it is futile to argue against the compulsion of a historical reality which teaches a very simple lesson.[29]

Jabotinsky was conspicuously silent on the struggle of the Irish Republicans against the British. In part, he believed that the revolutionary path of the IRA would damage his diplomatic initiatives with the British and validate the philosophy of the biryonim. In contrast, Ahimeir lauded it at every opportunity. Instead, Jabotinsky reclaimed the proposal of Mickiewicz, the Polish national hero, during the mid-nineteenth century to establish a Jewish legion.[30]

Jabotinsky also made a point of writing in *Hazit Ha'am*, the new journal of Ahimeir, Greenberg and Yeivin, which had started publication in January 1932 in order to reach those who espoused a Maximalist Revisionism.

Significantly Jabotinsky argued that if Jewish youth had responded in 1917 to the announcement in a British government paper, calling for the establishment of a Jewish legion, then Jewish communal leaders would have been unable to play a role. Who was responsible for the procrastination during the war years?

---

[28] Vladimir Jabotinsky, 'The Regiment', *Hazit Ha'am*, 30 August 1932; 6 September 1932; 'The Jewish Legion and Mickiewicz', *Rassviet*, 11 September 1932.
[29] Vladimir Jabotinsky, 'Afn Pripitshek', *Haynt*, 16 October 1931; *Jewish Herald*, 12 September 1947.
[30] Jabotinsky, 'The Jewish Legion and Mickiewicz'.

Not the general leaders, the assimilationists or the Zionists; not the newspaper correspondents, not the preachers, not the rabbis and not the fathers and mothers. True, all these above-mentioned elements manifested themselves then to be short-sighted, petty, politically uneducated. But a living youth possesses a healthy instinct and in a period of great decision does not need any advice from older people in order to run towards the direction which history demands.[31]

Jabotinsky argued that World War I had offered an unprecedented opportunity to recruit an army of 100,000. Yet the Jewish Legion comprised a force of only 5,000. If an army had been created, it would have strengthened the hand of the Zionist negotiators. Jews would then have constituted a majority of the military forces in Palestine at that time. Youth had a different outlook on war and therefore could perform daring deeds, whereas the older generation was much more cautious and conservative.

Jabotinsky did not glorify war, but regarded it as a reality of the times in which he lived. While Jews did not desire war, he argued, should it occur, then 'our youth must be prepared to sacrifice their lives in such a manner and in such a form as to bring us nearer to our national aims'. The presence of a Jewish army on the victorious side would act as a bargaining counter to further Zionist goals. This was the logic which guided Jabotinsky during World War I. It was also the rationale of his call for a Jewish fighting force in 1940. This also reflected the views of some of the Maximalists in the early 1930s who had argued that a war between Great Britain and Soviet Russia was imminent.[32]

In addition, there had been a noticeable lack of progress in the disarmament talks between Britain, France and Germany – even before the rise of Hitler. In an article appropriately entitled 'The Meaning of Preparedness', Jabotinsky argued that 'military training remains the first and most essential raison d'être of the Betar' ... pacifism is worthy of all our moral support; but it does not give us the guarantee of never having, in the future, any physical conflicts, above all in the Levant'.

Each generation must be ready to take immediate action at the moment of the grand opportunity. 'Opportunity!' Dante has called it *Fortuna*. He tells us she passes by rapidly and inscrutably. Her hair is long and by her hair we must seize her. One moment too late and we can no longer grasp her.[33]

[31] Vladimir Jabotinsky, 'The Regiment', *Hazit Ha'am*, 28 August 1932.

[32] Wolfgang von Weisl, 'The Eve of the New World War: Towards the New Roles of Revisionist Policy', *Hazit Ha'am*, 29 March 1932.

[33] *Betar Monthly*, April 1932.

Jabotinsky attacked Ahimeir's notion of an underground organisation. He distinguished between the monism of the period and its goal. It was not 'a pocket monism, a monism of means and methods'. This meant that different paths to the same goal had to be trod and there could not be sole reliance on militant action. The idea of 'only an underground, the rest is unnecessary' he regarded as 'bourgeois impressionism, hysterical and short-sighted'. Furthermore, Jabotinsky promoted the point that Betar was a legal organisation, not an illegal one.

In contrast, Ahimeir wanted a strong leader like Mussolini, and he believed that Jabotinsky could be that person. Following Jabotinsky's rebuff, Ahimeir came to see Jabotinsky as a Kerensky rather than a Lenin because he would not exercise his full authority. Ahimeir wanted to transform monism into a revolutionary Zionism. Moreover, the Maximalists were irritated that the leadership of Betar in Palestine remained loyal to Jabotinsky's vision of the organisation. They railed at the 'lack of motivation and petrification of the "establishment"', and even worse, that 'the young men from the establishment ... follow Jabotinsky blindly'.[34] Even so, Jabotinsky could not be attacked directly. The ire of the Maximalists was directed instead at Meir Grossman, Richard Lichtheim and the other members of the Revisionist Executive.

Ahimeir's advantage over Jabotinsky was that he was closer in age to the youth of Betar. Jabotinsky was then in his early fifties. He clearly recognised this when he commented, 'Every generation is a separate country with a different climate; what we know about ours may not be worth knowing in yours'.[35]

While Jabotinsky – like many Russian émigrés – was hostile to Bolshevism, his point of departure from understanding Communism as the dawn of humanity was that any association detracted from the central goal of establishing a Jewish state. He had disparaged 'the soft-hearted bourgeoisie' who supported the labour movement because it was still under 'the influence of buried Russian memories'.[36] While Ahimeir shared this approach in part, he was deeply opposed ideologically to the Bolsheviks. Indeed, he had called for the expulsion from Palestine of Jewish Communists in 1928.[37]

---

[34] *Hazit Ha'am*, 20 September 1932.
[35] Vladimir Jabotinsky, 'If I Were Young in 1932', *Jewish World*, February 1955.
[36] Vladimir Jabotinsky, 'Revolution or Ruin?' *The Zionist*, 17 November 1931.
[37] Abba Ahimeir, 'From the Notebook of a Fascist: Concerning the Visa for Jabotinsky', *Doar Hayom*, 21 September 1928.

Jabotinsky's problem was that he spoke in two voices: a rationalist political one to his Revisionist colleagues, many of whom were Russian émigrés, and a more incendiary, militant, extra-parliamentary one to the youngsters of Betar in Palestine and Poland. Jabotinsky spoke to different audiences in different ways in the hope of moving them towards the same goal. This approach instead created confusion, which Ahimeir and the Maximalists capitalised on. Such a dissonance in Jabotinsky's public commentary became more accentuated as the situation in both Europe and Palestine worsened and as the stand of Betar became more radical.

In seeking to prevent Ahimeir from influencing Betar, Jabotinsky was willing to adopt a more authoritarian guise and to point out the flaws in the democracies in an age of national dictatorships.[38] Yet Jabotinsky still believed in evolutionary Zionism, parliamentary politics and England. He dismissed as unrealistic the Maximalist demand for a Diaspora boycott of British goods to coincide with the Passfield White Paper.[39] In one sense he remained the Russian liberal of his sojourn in fin-de-siècle Italy. In early 1932 he told the members of Betar:

If we want to lead the world to social justice, this is the best service we can render the cause: to give the specialist a laboratory of his own – a state to the Jewish nation. If I work on this task I work for the salvation of humanity. And if the work demands heavy sacrifices, let it be so.[40]

ON ADVENTURISM

During 1932, Jabotinsky's task was to outmanoeuvre the Maximalists and to control the militancy of the young, but not to eliminate it. He therefore had bowed his head to Ahimeir and referred to him as 'our teacher and master'.

He justified this remark by invoking 'the necessity of adventurism' in the Jewish national movement. He had described adventurers as those 'who refuse to accept a ready-made ladder of life on which to climb, but must create a new ladder themselves'.[41] Moreover, he remarked that when he appointed Ahimeir to the board of *Doar Hayom* in 1928, he should have made it clear that he regarded his ideology as nothing but

---

[38] Vladimir Jabotinsky, 'Zeyde Liberalizm', *Haynt*, 14 October 1932.
[39] Von Weisl, 'Eve of the New World War'.
[40] Vladimir Jabotinsky, 'Memento', *Betar Monthly*, March 1932.
[41] Vladimir Jabotinsky, *The Story of the Jewish Legion* (New York, 1945), p. 157.

'moods'. Jabotinsky initially interpreted the actions of the Maximalists as a tactic towards a common political goal, but not as a rival ideology.

Following the disruption of Bentwich's professorial inauguration at the Hebrew University, Jabotinsky implicitly criticised Berit Ha-Biryonim. He argued that it was far easier to attack Bentwich and Magnes than an external opponent, the British authorities. 'Our war is not against the Jewish slave but against his masters.'[42] Ahimeir, on the other hand, referred to Bentwich as 'an assimilationist and a missionary',[43] while Yeivin labelled Magnes and his Hebrew University colleagues as the equivalent of the Yevsektsia – the Jewish section of the Communist party of the Soviet Union.[44]

Jabotinsky wrote several articles[45] in 1932 in which he explained his endorsement of a selective adventurism and his opposition to a blanket adventurism which was the answer to everything. He rejected 'the ideology of the sansculottes' and argued that while adventurism was necessary sometimes to create a stir and to catalyse activism, it was not the be-all and end-all of working towards the goal of a Jewish state.

Ahimeir responded with a letter to the youth of Betar from his cell in the central prison in Jerusalem.[46] The best of the youth were attracted to Communism or Bundism because it promised a life of revolutionary heroism, war, prison and the gallows – not a monastic passivity. Only a minority followed A. D. Gordon, while the majority looked to the Cheka of Dzerzhinsky and the Red Army of Trotsky. The Zionist youth had not been called upon to make sacrifices.

Ahimeir believed that it was actually the sansculottes who created history. Lenin, Mussolini and Hitler succeeded in coming to power only because of the sansculottes. For Ahimeir, Mussolini had revived the glory of Bonapartism[47] and argued that 'the leader of Italian Fascism, Napoleon and Caesar were democrats in their own way'. In contrast, Jabotinsky was also brutally clear where he stood on the role for Betar:

Adventurism? There are moments when it might bring benefits. An underground? Yes, that too. But Betar is not and cannot be part either of adventurism or of an underground; yet not anti-adventurism and not anti-underground. Betar, as

---

[42] Vladimir Jabotinsky, 'Shir Betar', *Hazit Ha'am*, 22 March 1932.
[43] Abba Ahimeir, *Hazit Ha'am*, 19 February 1932.
[44] Yehoshua Hirsh Yeivin, *Hazit Ha'am*, 23 February 1932.
[45] Vladimir Jabotinsky, 'On Adventurism', *Haynt*, 26 February 1932; 'More on Adventurism', *Haynt*, 29 and 31 July 1932; *Hazit Ha'am*, 5 August 1932.
[46] Abba Ahimeir, 'A Letter to the Youth of Betar', 17 March 1932.
[47] Yonathan Shapiro, *The Road to Power: The Herut Party in Israel* (New York, 1991), p. 45.

I conceived it, is a school with three 'levels' where youth will learn to control their fists, their batons and all other means of defence; to be able to stand to attention and to march well; to work; to foster beauty of form and ceremony; to scorn all forms of negligence – call it whatever you wish, hooliganism or ghetto mentality; to respect women and the elderly; and prayer – no matter what religion, democracy and many other things which may seem obsolete, but which are everlasting. This is the type of school that Betar has to be. Yes, a school like that, for if not, better that Betar not exist at all.[48]

Ahimeir's central focus in 1932 was the forthcoming Fifth World Revisionist Conference in Vienna. He wanted the Maximalists from Palestine to make a strong showing at the conference, to influence the delegates and to move Jabotinsky from his liberal-conservative position.

Several points of reference were brought to fortify the Maximalist position. The anniversary of the start of the Bar-Kokhba struggle against their Roman masters in the year 132 initiated articles about the legacy of the Jewish rebels in contemporary times.

Yehoshua Hirsh Yeivin's article 'The Torah of Bar-Kokhba'[49] commenced with some lines from a poem by Uri Zvi Greenberg which said that the tradition of the fighting Jew had never died even after the fall of the last Jewish stronghold of Betar. Yeivin argued that the history of the Jewish people had been censored by the rabbis in that the Zealots, the freedom fighters, the biryonim were not seen as heroes but as criminals. Some rabbis saw Bar-Kokhba (the son of a star) as the messiah, come to liberate the Jews. A majority did not.

Yeivin commented that if it had not been for Josephus and the early Christians, no one would have known the name of Bar Giora, a leader of the revolutionary forces during the first war against the Romans, 66–70. He also argued that the rabbis had censored the story of the heroism of 'the false messiahs' throughout history, David Alroy, David Hareuveni and Shabtai Zevi. Yeivin turned Jewish tradition on its head in rejecting the perceived passivity of the Jews over two millennia under the guidance of the rabbis:

The Torah of all those who stand in the name of 'the conditions of objective reality' and who instruct us to bow our heads in the corner … this is a false Torah.

Yeivin strongly believed that World War I had mercilessly uprooted old-fashioned liberalism. 'In the trenches, among the graves of ten million corpses, was also buried the optimistic faith in the "Reign of Justice".' He argued that this truth had still not percolated into the thinking of the

[48] Jabotinsky, 'More on Adventurism'.
[49] *Hazit Ha'am*, 4 June 1932.

Zionist leadership. 'They allowed themselves the luxury of retaining their liberal faith twenty years after the words "liberalism" and "progress" had become butts of ridicule.'[50]

Ahimeir took a different view, utilising the example of Lenin rather than Bar-Kokhba. In 1931 he viewed the position of the Zionist movement as replicating the political doldrums that set in after the failure of the 1905 revolution in Russia. Ahimeir logically concluded that Zionists should prepare for 'their own 1917'.[51]

He argued that in 1932 the challenge facing Zionism was similar to that facing socialism during World War I. Most socialists, he remarked, had ultimately betrayed international socialism for being complicit in a war against fellow workers. In 1932 most Zionists betrayed Zionism for not actively opposing the British occupier of Palestine. Therefore, what was needed was not a grandiose Revisionist conference on the model of the first gathering of Zionists in Basel in 1897, but rather a gathering that took as its paradigm the conspiratorial meetings in the Swiss villages of Zimmerwald and Kunterhal where Lenin addressed the faithful few who had attended in preparation for the October Revolution.[52]

Ahimeir still believed in the legacy of national syndicalism, a merging of class and nation within a revolutionary context, and wished to change the face of the Revisionist movement.[53] Ahimeir and Yeivin produced their own manifesto and presented it to the delegates of the Revisionist conference in Vienna. A central objective of the Maximalists was to save Revisionism from the scourge of liberalism. 'To this war of renewal, raise your arm!' – it was a call to activism, but it was also a Fascist salute. Their central demands to the conference participants were as follows:

1. To raise the prestige of the leader to that of dictator
2. To propose that Maximalist Zionist institutions be a tool for national liberation
3. To transfer the political department to one of the centres of the Jewish masses
4. To organise Diaspora youth to fight anti-Semitism[54]

---

[50] Yehoshua Hirsch Yeivin, 'Betar and the Revolution in Zionism', *Betar Monthly*, February 1932.

[51] Abba Ahimeir, *Ha'am*, 14 July 1931.

[52] Abba Ahimeir, 'Problems of the World Revisionist Conference', *Hazit Ha'am*, 15 July 1932.

[53] Abba Ahimeir, *Ha'am*, 5 August 1931.

[54] 'The Declaration of the Maximalists to the Delegates of the Vienna Conference', *Hazit Ha'am*, 9 August 1932.

The Maximalist delegates, Ahimeir, Katznelson, Greenberg and Yeivin, and their Activist allies, led by von Weisl, wanted a purge of Meir Grossman's London group and a dramatic redirection of Revisionist policy. Their presence at the Vienna conference posed for the first time an opposition to Jabotinsky's middle of the road policies. This ideological opposition, carried on by others, stalked Jabotinsky for the rest of his life.

Jabotinsky was well aware of the challenge to his approach despite the attempts of the Maximalists to woo him. Instead of writing another article in *Hazit Ha'am*, Jabotinsky responded privately to Yeivin in a letter and refuted the Maximalist claims that Revisionism had become outdated. He argued instead that the approach of the Maximalists was based on 'forbidden romanticism'. He bluntly stated that this attempt to place sansculottism at the heart of Revisionist ideology was tantamount to a takeover of the movement and would drive him out. If Yeivin succeeded, he would abandon the party. It was a party of nineteenth-century democracy, the conquest of positions. He was prepared to justify revolution only when it was necessary and possible:

It would be difficult to find men in the ranks of Zionism whom I respect and admire as I do, yourself and A. A. [Abba Ahimeir], for your generous spirit of self-sacrifice and your talents. I regard you, and your noble companions who suffer for the sanctity of their hearts, as my teachers and masters in the commandment of self-sacrifice. But your sanctity is mistaken, in my eyes; it destroys the building which I have laboured so long to erect, and in its place creates a shrine which I do not desire. I will not go with you. Nor do you have the moral right to go with me and to be considered as members of the party in which I participate, from the moment when you came to believe that all its basic principles 'had perished' ... your attempts to make your views prevail in Tsohar [Revisionist movement] and Betar in place of the former views are nothing but attempts to drive me out. If these views had triumphed, I would have left the party. Tsohar is a movement founded on nineteenth-century democracy, on the rebuilding of the land, on the conquest of positions, on governmental and patrician education. Its revolutionary nature, which justifies *kremola* [rebellion] when it is necessary and appropriate, is also imbued with this ideology, and will remain so. If it is not – then I will not remain in it.[55]

Yet Jabotinsky clearly believed in a plurality of views within the Revisionist movement and effectively saw the advantage of having

[55] Vladimir Jabotinsky, Letter to Yehoshua Hirsch Yeivin, 9 August 1932, *Igrot, 1932–1933* (Jerusalem, 2006).

a militant group outside the Revisionist movement which carried out independent actions. He continued:

These words of mine are not intended in relation to any particular action: even if I do not always agree with the way in which an action is carried out or the choice of a particular moment for action, I think that a member of the movement is free to decide by himself to take action which the movement does not want to or cannot carry out itself, on the condition that he does not carry out these actions under the movement's flag and on the condition that such action is not against the moral law. This is my personal opinion … and I will defend this view in the governing bodies of our movement. I shall not say, nor agree that others should say, that there is no room within our ranks for those of our members who do more than the official measure and outside the official camp – as long as they act in the name of the same outlook. However, I will not move an inch as regards the principles of this outlook'.

While the Maximalists certainly respected Jabotinsky and hoped to win him over, they did not agree with him. Two days before the opening of the conference Yeivin wrote: 'The majority always wins at conferences, but not always in life – on the contrary, often the minority wins, the minority which is crushed and persecuted.'[56]

Jabotinsky opened the Fifth World Revisionist Conference at the Renz Circus House in Vienna with a two-hour speech. It was directed against the Mandate, which had 'no ethical basis' and constituted a danger not only to Jews, but also to 'the whole of civilisation'. Zionism, he argued was actually stronger than Great Britain because 'we stand for a just and humanitarian cause.'

In contrast, Ahimeir spoke about the evolution and emergence of a neo-Revisionism within the Revisionist movement. He compared its adherents to the Jesuits who had saved Catholicism. He argued that the twentieth century had been forged by dictatorship and youth. Democracy had had its day. It had been defeated everywhere and was now totally bankrupt. In the past, Zionism, he pointed out, had been characterised by the ghetto and by pious declarations – 'the route to the kingdom of Israel is not paved by a bridge of paper, but by a bridge of steel'.[57] He called for a revolutionary Zionism and a dictatorial leadership which would inspire the masses of Jewish youth with the idea of sacrificing everything to secure a Jewish state.[58] He added that 'we have prepared deep roots in Betar'.

[56] Yehoshua Hirsch Yeivin, 'Opposition or Liberation Movement', *Hazit Ha'am*, 26 August 1932.
[57] Abba Ahimeir, 'Address to the Fifth World Revisionist Conference', *Hazit Ha'am*, 13 September 1932.
[58] *Jewish Chronicle*, 9 September 1932.

Other Maximalists called for the resignation of Grossman and other members of the Revisionist Executive.[59]

Ahimeir described the arrival of the Maximalist delegation from Palestine as tantamount to 'a snowflake on the head'. He commented that several delegates were unaware that there was a Revisionist Histadrut and many did not know Hebrew. The Maximalists lobbied the conference delegates to persuade them of the veracity of their views and to marginalise Grossman and his allies. Robert Stricker, the head of the Revisionists in Vienna, was characterised by Ahimeir as a moderate 'who governs in a yamulka [skullcap]'.[60] Both Stricker and Grossman had questioned the autonomy of the Palestinian Revisionists to go their own way for several years. Moreover, they drew attention to the attack on Yiddish speakers in Tel Aviv by members of Betar.[61] Jabotinsky disagreed and spoke about guarding 'the treasure, the Hebrew language'. He argued that the Revisionist movement was nothing less than a federation and granting it a degree of autonomy was a practical necessity. It was also impossible to define the limits of autonomy.

Other Maximalists implicitly criticised Jabotinsky for basing his future programme on resurrecting the Jewish Legion. Jabotinsky was accused of becoming 'inconsistent and of sacrificing the Revisionist idea for the sake of preserving unity in the Revisionist movement'.[62]

Eliahu Ben-Horin strongly criticised the Revisionists in the Diaspora and argued that the independence of the Revisionists in Palestine should not in any way be impaired. He developed Jabotinsky's 'back to basics' approach by inferring that the same should take place within Revisionism. 'To the slogan "Back to Herzl!" we should add the words "Back to Jabotinsky!"'

The delegate from Italy, Leone Carpi, spoke of 'the elective affinities between Fascism and Revisionism'.[63] When Carpi raised his hand in the Fascist salute at the conference, Ahimeir and the Maximalists responded in kind.[64]

---

[59] Wolfgang von Weisl, *Hazit Ha'am*, 13 September 1932; Uri Zvi Greenberg, *Hazit Ha'am*, 20 September 1932.

[60] Greenberg, *Hazit Ha'am*, 20 September 1932.

[61] *Doar Hayom*, 8 October 1928.

[62] *Jewish Chronicle*, 2 September 1932.

[63] Vincenzo Pinto, 'Between Imago and Res: The Revisionist Zionist Movement's Relationship with Fascist Italy, 1922–1938', *Israel Affairs*, vol. 10 no. 3 (2004), pp. 90–109.

[64] *Hazit Ha'am*, 20 September 1932.

All this antagonised the other delegates – and there were reports in the press that there were 'stormy meetings'. Indeed, neighbours called the police to intervene at three o'clock in the morning.[65] Grossman accused Ahimeir of mouthing empty slogans and desiring a 'Fuhrer'.

Jabotinsky responded strongly in his own speech. He disputed the idea that redemption would be brought about only by blood and fire. He asked, 'What about water?' He argued that there were several channels to follow. He rejected the attempts of the Maximalists, led by Ahimeir, and of the Activists, led by von Wiesl, to base the party on a 'leadership' cult. Jabotinsky repeated his approach:

> In our world today, especially among the younger generation, the dream of a dictatorship has become an epidemic. I am taking this opportunity to declare once again that I am absolutely against this dream. I believe in the ideological heritage of the nineteenth century, the century of Garibaldi and of Lincoln, of Gladstone and Hugo. The ideological fashion of today is that man is naturally dishonest and foolish, and therefore should not be given the right to rule himself; freedom leads to destruction, equality to falsehood, so society needs leaders, orders, and truncheons ... I do not want this type of faith. It is better not to be alive at all than to live under such a regime. I would rather disappear and die than to agree to a worldview that sees my son and the son of my neighbour as being of different value, or my son and the cobbler's son as unequal. I stand with all my strength by the democratic nature of our movement.[66]

He once more explained his understanding of leaders and leadership. Jabotinsky added that cattle have a leader, but people have a chairman. Leadership allows people to defer responsibility. He commented, 'Look at Charlemagne. After Big Karl came Short Pepin'.

THE ATTRACTION OF FASCISM

The Maximalists were heavily defeated in the votes at the conference despite making their presence felt. Yet Jabotinsky wanted to keep the Maximalists within the Revisionist movement in almost a catalytic role to stoke the fires of activism in Palestine. He also believed that he could guide the Maximalists despite their freedom of action in Palestine. Indeed, there were issues where he took their side against his colleagues on the Revisionist Executive, such as the question of remaining within the World Zionist Organisation. In summing up, Jabotinsky expressed his belief

[65] *Jewish Chronicle*, 2 September 1932.
[66] Ben-Yerucham, Chaim, ed., *Sefer Betar: Korot u-mekorot*, vol. 2, 'From the People' (Tel Aviv, 1969), p. 425.

that he could wean the Maximalists from their ideological rigidity and their conviction that there was only one path towards securing the state:

If there are among us men for whom this side of fascism [i.e., dictatorship] has truly become a deeply-felt and solid worldview, then there is no place for them among us, and we have no place among them. But such men, even in the maximalist and activist factions, number no more than two or three, and even these two or three – pardon my frankness – I do not believe. It is mere phraseology, not a worldview, for them. Even Mr Ahimeir gives me the impression of a man who will show flexibility for the sake of educational goals ... to this end he has borrowed some currently fashionable (and quite unnecessary) phrases, in which this daring idea clothes itself in several foreign cities.[67]

Yet privately Jabotinsky intensely disliked Ahimeir's flirtation with Italian Fascism even though at that point in time it was not anti-Semitic and Mussolini was not sympathetic to the rise of Nazism in Germany. He continued to defend liberalism and found it difficult to understand the view that democracy had become an irrelevant failure:

It hurts us, it consumes us like fire. My generation grew up in the firm conviction that a regime based on general and equal suffrage for which government is responsible is the best and most complete answer to all political troubles. The only thing that we were not quite sure about perhaps was that democracy could cure anti-Semitism.[68]

Jabotinsky recalled that the 'fasces' – a hatchet with a bunch of rods – was a symbol of coercive discipline to enforce obedience amongst dissenters of all kinds:

Italian fascism is an attempt to reaffirm the principle that the state has the right and the duty to coerce – and the actual power too.

Right or wrong, all this can have no application to Jewish social phenomena. There is no Jewish government, and no Jew can be administratively 'coerced' to obey orders issued by any Jewish leader or committee of leaders. Jewish political organisations are voluntary associations and can be nothing else.[69]

Fascism, he argued, forced people to accept decisions whether they agreed with them or not. It was 'wholly and organically inapplicable to any aspect of Jewish life'.

Yet *Hazit Ha'am* remained captivated by the national dictatorships in Europe. In May 1931, the periodical published an article by John Strachey, a British MP who had followed Oswald Mosley out of the Labour Party

[67] Vladimir Jabotinsky, 'An Evaluation of the Conference', *Hazit Ha'am*, 7 October 1932.
[68] Vladimir Jabotinsky, 'Democracy', *Moment*, 19 October 1934.
[69] Vladimir Jabotinsky, 'Jews and Fascism', *Jewish Echo*, 10 May 1935.

due to the mounting problems of unemployment in the UK.[70] Mosley's New Party also believed that youth were politically more important than their elders – and were regarded by Strachey and others as providing the last opportunity to locate a middle way, based on evolutionary change, in spite of the attraction of Communism and Fascism. Social democracy, as demonstrated by the failure of successive Labour governments, had failed. Strachey lasted five months in the New Party and resigned because of the drift towards Fascism – and in particular its desire to establish a youth movement on paramilitary lines. The New Party was effectively wiped out during the 1931 election and morphed into the British Union of Fascists the following year. This desire to break with the old politics, empower the youth and worship before the altar of discipline impressed the Maximalists.

The Austrian Hitler became a German citizen in February 1932 in order to stand for parliament. The German Federal elections took place on 31 July 1932, and the Nazis emerged as the largest party with 230 seats – more than the seats gained by Social Democrats (133) and the Communists (89) put together. The Nazis thereafter proceeded to overturn the Weimar Constitution and to establish a dictatorship.

Even before the Nazis' electoral breakthrough, Yeivin had described Nazism as a national liberation movement – like the social revolutionaries' brigades of 1905, like the Bolsheviks, like Garibaldi's thousand, like the Czech Sokol and the Polish Legions.[71] Ahimeir pointed out that there was racism in the United States and South Africa as well as in Nazi Germany. He argued once more that 'political heroes create history' and not the other way around. Germany, Italy and Israel, he recalled, all gazed back into their heroic past and saw revolutionary heroes. Israel in particular reclaimed the example of the Maccabees and the Zealots.[72] Both Yeivin and Ahimeir therefore wrote appreciatively about Hitler as the builder of modern Germany.

Following Hitler's appointment as chancellor in January 1933, the Maximalists believed that lessons could be learned from the Nazis' rise to power. *Hazit Ha'am* said that the Jewish press had reacted in a very superficial manner to Hitler and Nazism:

[70] John Strachey, *Hazit Ha'am*, 12 May 1931. I am indebted to Dan Tamir for drawing my attention to this article.
[71] Yehoshua Hirsh Yeivin, 'We are Fighting the People's War', *Hazit Ha'am*, 29 July 1932.
[72] Abba Ahimeir, 'Romantic Realism or Realistic Romanticism?', *Hazit Ha'am*, 30 September 1932.

The difference between Hitler and Thaelmann [the leader of the German Communists] is that one is a subjective and the other an objective anti-Semite.[73]

The Maximalists reminded the reading public in Palestine that Hitler's rise to power would awaken assimilated German Jewry to their origins and that this in turn would probably result in an increased emigration from Germany. Moreover, Nazism was fiercely anti-Communist.

Even before Hitler's appointment as chancellor, Jabotinsky had 'viewed Hitlerism with contempt'.[74] In an unpublished article in September 1932, Jabotinsky bemoaned the passing of the pre-1914 era and the order of the aristocracy. He speculated that von Papen might restore the Hohenzollerns but that to hand over the government to the Nazi 'street enthusiasts' would be nonsensical. Yet he noted that there were 11 million 'Hitlerised' voters because there was no other party which the German electorate felt represented 'strong government, order, discipline, patriotism – "no-nonsense" in short'.[75] A few months later, von Papen had fallen, yet he was able to convince the ailing Hindenburg that he would be able to control Hitler. From the very beginning of Hitler's accession to the chancellorship in January 1933, however, Jabotinsky warned against not taking the Nazis seriously – the view that Hitler would not last long as chancellor, that Hindenburg, Hugenberg and von Papen would run rings around him, that anti-Semitism played an unimportant role.

Jabotinsky had read *Mein Kampf* and regarded the author as someone who was 'without talent, naive and peddling pedestrian ideas'. He attributed Hitler's success in part to the shrewdness of Goebbels, Gregor Strasser and Gottfried Feder in promoting him. Writing in February 1933, he decried those who believed that the Nazis would now drop anti-Semitism as 'excessively optimistic'.[76]

An aghast Jabotinsky angrily responded to the Maximalists in an article in *Hazit Ha'am* in which he argued that anti-Semitism was at the core of Nazism and not at its periphery.[77] The Maximalists believed that Hitler was just another persecutor of the Jews, the latest in a long historical line:

Hitler has not yet treated us badly as Stalin has done ... the anti-Semitic shell must be discarded, but not its anti-Marxist kernel.[78]

---

[73] *Hazit Ha'am*, 3 February 1933.
[74] Vladimir Jabotinsky, 'Extract from the Address at the Fifth Revisionist Conference in Vienna', *Jewish Chronicle*, 9 September 1932.
[75] Vladimir Jabotinsky, 'That "Barons' Government"', 7–21 September 1932, Jabotinsky Institute Archives, Tel Aviv.
[76] Vladimir Jabotinsky, 'Germany', *Hazit Ha'am*, 24 February 1933.
[77] Ibid.
[78] Abba Ahimeir, *Hazit Ha'am* 31 March 1933.

On 1 April 1933 the Nazis enacted the boycott of Jewish businesses, whose entrances were defaced with slogans such as 'The Jews Are Our Misfortune!' German citizens were exhorted not to buy from Jews. The Jews were told to go to Palestine. The Maximalists were shocked at this display of state-sponsored exclusion. Gradually the shades began to fall from their blinded eyes. Berit Ha-Biryonim then attacked the German consulates in Jerusalem and Jaffa – and removed the Nazi flag.[79] The German imperial flag was left untouched.[80] Ironically the German consul general in Jerusalem, Heinrich Wolff, had been a sympathiser of the Zionist movement since his appointment in 1932.[81]

Hazit Ha'am abruptly changed its line back to strong support for Jabotinsky, who opposed the very idea of trade between Nazi Germany and Palestine. Ahimeir, however, continued to praise Italian Fascism, which had not embraced Hitler's anti-Semitism.[82] Jabotinsky remarked that Italy would not stain itself by 'supporting German appetites'.[83]

By mid-April 1933, Jabotinsky had discovered the full extent of *Hazit Ha'am*'s stance after the appointment of Hitler to the chancellorship and wrote an extremely angry letter to the editorial board of *Hazit Ha'am*. Such articles about Hitler and the Nazi movement, he wrote, were 'a stab in the back for me personally and in the backs of all of us'. Such commentary undermined him and nullified all his work. He was scathing about those Maximalists who located elements of a 'national liberation' movement in Nazism and demanded the complete disappearance of 'all this dirty hysteria' from the pages of *Hazit Ha'am*:

If even one more line is published in *Hazit Ha'am* that could be interpreted as an attempt by small-minded Jews to find favour before such a crude tyrant who happened by chance to be elected, I will insist on removing the newspaper from the party and will cut off all personal contact with those who are causing my work to flounder for the sake of such cheap mass sarcasm.[84]

He compared the Maximalists of 1933 in Palestine to the Externists of 1903 in Russia. The Externists were Jews such as Berl Katznelson who

---

[79] Ben-Zion Shoshani, 'Kvutsat Haiguf', in Yossi Achimeir and Shmuel Shatski, eds., *Berit Ha-Biryonim: The First Anti-British Organisation* (Tel Aviv, 1978), pp. 150–51.

[80] *Hazit Ha'am*, 19 May 1933.

[81] Francis R. Nicosia, *Zionism and Anti-Semitism in Nazi Germany* (New York, 2008), pp. 80–85.

[82] Abba Ahimeir, *Hazit Ha'am*, 5 May 1933.

[83] Vladimir Jabotinsky, 'The Revisionist Movement and Germany', *Hazit Ha'am*, 12 May 1933.

[84] Vladimir Jabotinsky, Letter to the Editors of *Hazit Ha'am*, 17 May 1933, *Igrot 1932–1933*, Tel Aviv 2006.

had abandoned traditional Jewish learning for the study of revolutionary theory and often travelled long distances to meet their new 'rebbes' – leading Jewish revolutionaries. It was only the Kishinev massacre that had awakened them from their worship of false gods.

Jabotinsky argued in several articles that there was now 'a war between Judah and Germany', and the Revisionists had to play their full part in bringing about the downfall of Nazi Germany. 'The Jewish voice', he argued, 'will truly be the sound of the human conscience without introducing any selfish ambitions.'[85]

Yet many both inside and outside the Revisionist movement asked what would have been the stand of the Maximalists towards Nazism if Hitler had not been an ideological anti-Semite.[86] The damage had been done. The Maximalists had tarred the Revisionists with the 'fascist' brush – and the accusation was put to good use by Jabotinsky's enemies. Ben-Gurion had told a meeting of the Executive Committee of the Histadrut in March 1933 that 'if he only could, Jabotinsky would do to us what Hitler is doing to the socialists in Germany'.[87]

[85] Vladimir Jabotinsky, 'The Revisionist Movement and Germany', *Hazit Ha'am*, 12 May 1933.

[86] *Hazit Ha'am*, 6 May 1933.

[87] David Ben-Gurion, Minutes of the meeting of the Histadrut Executive Committee, 29 March 1933, in Benny Morris, 'Response of the Jewish Daily Press in Palestine to the Accession of Hitler, 1933', *Yad Vashem Studies*, no. 27 (1999), pp. 363–407.

6

The Legacy of Abba Ahimeir

THE MURDER OF HAIM ARLOSOROFF

Following the killing of his former colleague, Haim Arlosoroff, the rising star of the labour movement, in June 1933, Ahimeir and his followers in Berit Ha-Biryonim were immediately viewed by the British as self-evidently the assassins. Within a few days of the killing, Ze'ev Rosenblatt was accused of the actual assassination, and a new arrival from Brest in Poland, Avraham Stavsky, was charged with shining a torch in Arlosoroff's face before the fatal shots were fired. On the same day *Hazit Ha'am* had published a provocative article entitled 'Berit Shalom-Ben-Gurion-Hitler'.[1]

In the eyes of Berit Ha-Biryonim, Arlosoroff had been responsible for the transfer agreement so that Jews leaving Nazi Germany could depart with some of their belongings. In return, German goods would be marketed in Palestine. Jabotinsky and the Revisionists passionately supported the anti-German boycott. Ben-Gurion had taken a pragmatic view that the Zionist movement should not provoke the Nazis by initiating 'an irresponsible battle against Hitler'. After all, even Stalin's Soviet Union maintained diplomatic relations with Hitler's Germany.[2]

Moreover, in the eyes of the leaders of Mapai, Arlosoroff was a bright star in the socialist firmament, potentially a future prime minister of Israel. Ahimeir, on the other hand, was seen as the *éminence grise*, the inspiration for the dark deed. Five weeks later the police seized the Revisionist archives and some of Ahimeir's writings.

[1] *Hazit Ha'am*, 16 June 1933.
[2] David Ben-Gurion, *Davar*, 27 August 1935.

On the evening of the assassination, Ahimeir was lecturing at the Revisionist Club in Jerusalem. Avraham Stavsky had recently arrived in Palestine and was lodging with Ahimeir. Stavsky did not attend Ahimeir's talk because he 'was not a high brow and did not speak Hebrew'.[3] On the night in question, Stavsky was staying at the Turjeman Hotel in Jerusalem. The police believed that he had slipped out unnoticed, travelled to Tel Aviv, committed the act and returned swiftly. Rosenblatt said that he was at a social gathering in Kfar Saba. Eventually Avraham Stavsky and Ze'ev Rosenblatt were charged with the murder of Arlosoroff. Ahimeir was also arrested and went on a hunger strike for a prolonged period. In a letter to Chief Rabbi Kook from Jaffa prison, Ahimeir claimed that he and his co-defendants were 'the Dreyfus and Beilis of our generation' and upbraided Kook for remaining silent.[4] Ahimeir felt that he and his defendants were being made scapegoats because of their political activities. He drew upon the analogy of the intended sacrifice of the biblical Isaac[5] and urged the members of Betar to recall the deaths of Sara Aaronson[6] and Yosef Trumpeldor.[7]

After months of investigation, the evidence proved flimsy. In the end all the members of Berit Ha-Biryonim were either released or acquitted.[8] The suspicion between Left and Right, however, deepened. Some members of Mapai labelled Jabotinsky 'a Jewish Mussolini' and his followers 'fashistlekh' (little fascists), seeking to overturn the hope of a socialist tomorrow.[9] Berl Katznelson told a private meeting that even if Stavsky was innocent, a group of 'terrorists' had attached themselves to the Revisionist body. In turn the Right saw Mapai as devious, untrustworthy, ideologically subversive and willing to use any dirty trick to entrap leading nationalists.

This built on a smouldering mountain of mistrust and suspicion. Earlier in the year there had been clashes between members of Betar

[3] *The Arlosoroff Murder Trial: Speeches and Relevant Documents*, Committee for Assisting the Defence (Jerusalem, July 1934), p. 90.

[4] Abba Ahimeir, Letter to Avraham Yitzhak Kook, 12 February 1934, in *Ha-Mishpat* (Tel Aviv, 1968), pp. 228–29; Shnayer Z. Leiman, 'R. Abraham Isaac Ha-Kohen Kook: Letter on Ahavat Yisrael', *Tradition*, vol. 24, no. 1 (Fall 1988), pp. 84–90.

[5] Genesis 22: 7–8, in Ahimeir, *Ha-Mishpat*, p. 190.

[6] Abba Ahimeir, Letter to World Betar, 18 October 1933, in *Ha-Mishpat*, p. 227.

[7] Abba Ahimeir, Avraham Stavsky, and Zvi Rosenblatt, Letter to World Betar, 5 March 1934, in *Ha-Mishpat*, pp. 230–32.

[8] Colin Shindler, 'Zionist History's Murder Mystery', *Jewish Chronicle*, 13 June 2013.

[9] Daniel K. Heller, 'The Rise of the Zionist Right: Polish Jews and the Betar Youth Movement, 1922–1935' (PhD diss., Stanford University, 2012), p. 85.

FIGURE 6. Avraham Stavsky being taken into custody (June 1933).
Photo: Zvi Oron; courtesy of the Jabotinsky Institute, Tel Aviv.

and local socialists at Tel Hai over Trumpeldor's grave. The locals stated
that Trumpeldor was a committed socialist, whereas the members of Betar
viewed him as their inspiration and symbolic founder. On another occasion,
a local gathering of Revisionists was met by demonstrators who handed out
leaflets, castigating 'the Jewish Hitlerites'.[10]

Jabotinsky waited a few days and then came out in open support of
Ahimeir, Stavsky, Rosenblatt and other members of Berit Ha-Biryonim
under suspicion in an article in the Yiddish Warsaw publication *Moment*,
suitably entitled 'Kalt und Fest' (Cool and Steadfast).[11] Jabotinsky compared the accusations to the blood-libel case of Mendel Beilis some twenty
years before. He also invoked the Dreyfus affair and the Sacco-Vanzetti
trial as examples of blatant miscarriages of justice. A few days later he compared the climate of fear to a Stalinist inversion of truth.[12] While describing
Arlosoroff as 'an honest, quiet, hardworking Jewish patriot', he described
the case against Berit Ha-Biryonim as 'sheker en lo raglaim' – 'a lie which
has no legs to stand on'. Jabotinsky suspected that the killers had been
Arabs and that the murder had been part of a chain of events, starting with
the killings during August 1929 and ending more recently with the arson in
the Balfour forest and a murder in Nahalal.[13]

[10] *Hazit Ha'am*, 28 March 1933.
[11] *Moment*, 22 June 1933.
[12] Vladimir Jabotinsky, 'Moscow-Style Methods', *Moment*, 25 July 1933.
[13] Vladimir Jabotinsky, 'Murder in Nahalal', *Rassviet*, 8 January 1933.

Despite their inability to make the charges stick, the British authorities had carried out extensive searches and located sufficient seditious material to arrest Ahimeir once more. Although the indictment related to the killing of Arlosoroff was formally dropped on 16 May 1934, Ahimeir was charged on several counts of sedition on 12 July 1934.

Clearly there was a desire to suppress any overt opposition to British authority in Palestine. Jabotinsky himself had been prohibited from returning to Palestine in 1930, following a speech in Tel Aviv. In it, he had castigated the Zionist leadership and commented that the Revisionists would not allow 'that national asset, the fury of the masses, to be wasted ceaselessly'.[14] Moreover, there were reports in the European press that he had stated that there would never be peace between Jews and Arabs in Palestine – a claim which he subsequently strongly denied.[15]

Uri Zvi Greenberg had written to Yeivin in February 1932 that Berit Ha-Biryonim held the key to 'the fate and order of rescue'. Berit Ha-Biryonim was in a position to disturb the peace and quiet that Britain ardently desired in Palestine –

not as the Communists who are agents and slaves to Russia, but as the ancient biryonim in the name of the Zionist belief in their Jerusalem.[16]

This letter became evidence in the new case against Ahimeir, Yeivin and other members of Berit Ha-Biryonim.

The British had uncovered *Megilat ha-sikarikin*, the 'Scroll of the Sicarii', which Ahimeir had written in 1926 while still a member of Hapoel Hatzair. It was dedicated to Charlotte Corday and Dora Kaplan. The former had famously assassinated Marat in his bath in 1793, while the latter had wounded Lenin in 1918. Both were swiftly executed. It commenced:

The person with a sicarii spirit turns to the assistance of the sword, the revolver, the bomb because the present day Sicarii believe in the hero who makes history no less than the supporter of the present rule ... the philosophy of the history of the sicarii is based on the accentuation of heroes and heroic acts.[17]

---

[14] Vladimir Jabotinsky, Speech in Tel Aviv, 23 December 1930, PRO 733/186, National Archives, Kew.

[15] Vladimir Jabotinsky, Letter to *Reichspost*, Vienna, 2 February 1930, Jabotinsky Institute Archives, Tel Aviv.

[16] Uri Zvi Greenberg, Letter to Yehoshua Yeivin, 19 February 1932, Exhibit Z.R. 25, Jabotinsky Institute Archives, Tel Aviv.

[17] Abba Ahimeir, *Megilat ha-sikarikin*, Exhibit Z.R. 26, Jabotinsky Institute Archives, Tel Aviv.

In contrast, he pointed out that Marxism disliked heroes and devalued any heroic act by an individual.

Ahimeir argued that the legacy of the sicarii was that history changes its course because of 'the work of negative heroes – not the divine, but the satanic'. No organisation stood behind the sicarii of the past, and it was conviction that drove them 'to kill and be prepared to be killed'. Charlotte Corday removed Marat and instigated the end of the French revolutionary process. Ahimeir asked how Corday's solitary 'contribution' compared with that of Mirabeau, Danton, Marat, Robespierre and Napoleon. 'Zero', he wrote, yet she removed Marat from the political equation and the onward march of history. He also lauded self-sacrifice:

What is death? The discontinuation of life in this world, against the unerased name in history. This is the modern conception of everlasting life.

Ahimeir argued that history seemed to permit killing if it was deemed to be for the public good but criminal if conducted for personal reasons. He gave as examples the assassinations of Julius Caesar, Henri of Navarre, William of Orange, Alexander II and Wallenstein. Raskolnikov in *Crime and Punishment* thus killed someone for personal reasons and was punished. Napoleon, however, caused hundreds of thousands of deaths, ostensibly in the cause of revolutionary France. Moreover, he suffered no pangs of conscience. Ahimeir tried to sort out this intellectual conundrum. Why was there a difference between the individual and the group?

Yet Ahimeir also wrote that there was 'no public movement today which based itself on the sicarii'. The last movement which did so, he remarked, was that of the Russian Social Revolutionaries of 1905. In the past, he pointed out, there was much more public sympathy for the assassination of a tyrant in the national cause. The Bible was replete with examples.

In an article in *Hazit Ha'am*, Ahimeir expressed understanding of the assassination of the French president Paul Doumer in May 1932 by a Russian émigré, Paul Gorguloff – a character in the mould of the heroes of Dostoyevsky.[18] One of Gorguloff's motives was that France had not supported the Whites against Bolshevism. He was guillotined and his plea of insanity was rejected.

In their search to imprison Ahimeir and eliminate Berit Ha-Biryonim, the British discovered such themes in Ahimeir's published and unpublished

[18] Abba Ahimeir, 'The Assassination of Paul Doumer', *Hazit Ha'am*, 2 August 1932.

writings. Ahimeir maintained that these ideas were all within the realm of theory and intellectual discourse. In the context of the murder of a leading opponent, Haim Arlosoroff, the British police were not so sure.

One tract which the police discovered, entitled 'The ABC of Revolutionary Zionism', started with a quotation by Ernest Renan: 'Moderation has never saved the homeland'. Another comment was:

Whoever is not with us, is against us. The truth is 100% with us. Whoever agrees to our truth by only 99% is not only not with us, but our opponent.[19]

Ahimeir also committed to paper the intimidation Revisionists felt in the aftermath of the killing of Arlosoroff. Like Jabotinsky, he mentioned the Beilis affair. He wrote about a pogrom-like atmosphere, an expected carnage, a civil war between Jews.[20]

He was sentenced to twenty-one months in Jerusalem Central Prison and released in August 1935.[21]

THE WATERSHED OF THE KATOWICE CONFERENCE

There were other divisions within the Revisionist movement which went beyond the differences between the Executive and the Maximalists. Two of these proved to be the death knell of the movement and its fragmentation. One issue was whether the Revisionists should remain within the Zionist Organisation. Another was the granting of autonomy of action to the Revisionists of Palestine, who were dominated by Ahimeir and the Maximalists. All this came to a head at a conference in Katowice in March 1933, attended by forty delegates from all over Europe, including Palestine.

The Revisionists in Palestine called upon the conference delegates

to be the ones who fight its war of honour and existence to the point of self-sacrifice, to be a large revolutionary force that will bellow the cry of the nation and its demand that the wicked world will fully fulfil the redemption not through words but in actions and active political warfare.[22]

They had already appealed to the world body not to lose sight of the goal and not to get bogged down in the bureaucracy of the establishment

[19] Abba Ahimeir, 'The ABC of Revolutionary Zionism', Exhibit Y.T. 10, Jabotinsky Institute Archives, Tel Aviv.

[20] Abba Ahimeir, Notebook, Exhibit B.S. 84, Jabotinsky Institute Archives, Tel Aviv.

[21] Yossi Ahimeir and Shmuel Shatzki, *Hinenu Sikirikim* (Tel Aviv, 1978), pp. 226–35.

[22] *Hazit Ha'am*, 10 March 1933.

Zionist organisations. They argued that Jabotinsky should take personal control of the running of the Revisionist movement.[23]

From the very inception of Revisionist Zionism, Jabotinsky had great reservations about its participation in the Zionist Organisation, but he had been in a minority within his movement – and specifically within the Revisionist intelligentsia.[24] The manifesto of the Revisionist movement at its founding in 1925 insisted that it was part and parcel of the Zionist Organisation.

Meir Grossman and the Revisionist Executive argued that the movement was defined by its back-to-basics Herzlian character and that it should be free of political factions. By re-creating the idea that all were General Zionists, this organisation within an organisation would grow until it eventually supplanted Weizmann's approach.

Jabotinsky profoundly disagreed. In a letter to his sister in 1927 he argued that even success at a Zionist congress would be meaningless, since the organisation was tantamount to 'a cart that is hopelessly stuck in the mud'.[25]

The third side of this triangle was Ahimeir and the Maximalists. Ahimeir and his supporters also wanted to leave the Zionist Organisation. At a conference of Palestine Revisionists in November 1930, motions were passed that the Revisionists should leave unless it accepted the idea of a Jewish commonwealth as the basis of Zionist activity.[26] The Maximalists wished to utilise Jabotinsky's opposition to bring him into their camp – a prospect which he resisted for many years.

Even so, at the Seventeenth Zionist Congress in 1931, there was so much dissatisfaction with Weizmann that he narrowly lost a no-confidence motion. Much to the consternation of his colleagues, Jabotinsky said that he would join the Zionist Executive only if it passed a Revisionist motion that stated that the goal of Zionism was a state with a Jewish majority. It did not. The delegates differentiated between Weizmann's general policies and his diplomatic approach on this central question. Despite the fact that the Revisionists had tripled their vote, Jabotinsky tore up his delegate's card and stormed off. This widened the split in the Revisionist

[23] *Hazit Ha'am*, 17 March 1933.
[24] Vladimir Jabotinsky, Letter to Joseph Schechtman, 4 June 1925; Letter to Solomon Jacobi, 11 September 1925, *Igrot, 1922–1925* (Jerusalem, 1998); 'Conversation with the Devil', *Rassviet*, 17 and 24 October 1926.
[25] Vladimir Jabotinsky, Letter to Tamar Jabotinsky-Kopp, 27 July 1927, *Igrot, 1926–1927* (Jerusalem, 2000).
[26] *Jewish Chronicle*, 28 November 1930.

movement, since many now wished to leave the Zionist Organisation. Sokolov was elected as Weizmann's caretaker successor.

Jabotinsky's long-term colleagues, the intellectual elite within Revisionism, Grossman, Lichtheim and the others, still wished to conquer the Zionist Organisation from within. Grossman saw the disappearance of Weizmann as a great opportunity to take over. In contrast, Jabotinsky felt that it heralded the eventual exodus of the Revisionists and reiterated his opposition to participating in the Zionist Organisation.[27]

Figures such as Max Bodenheimer who had worked with Herzl believed that Jabotinsky had 'fallen under the spell of Wolfgang von Weisl and Abba Ahimeir'.[28] The chasm between Jabotinsky and his colleagues on the Executive visibly widened. Grossman believed that Jabotinsky's promotion – and politicisation – of Betar and his embrace of the youth was no more than a lever to be used against his opponents. Jabotinsky struggled to keep his movement together, but clearly the prospect of a split was moving towards its denouement.[29]

Jabotinsky's numerous moves towards the Maximalists and then back again to the Executive were conditioned by his fear of being entrapped by Ahimeir and his supporters. Articles such as 'Independence or Decay'[30] were explained away afterwards. Yet there were other areas of alignment between Ahimeir and Jabotinsky, such as the autonomy of the Palestinian Revisionists and the emphasis on class antagonism.[31]

The Katowice conference indicated that these differences – particularly on remaining in the Zionist Organisation – could not be resolved. In the Lodz Declaration, Jabotinsky formally suspended the central institutions of the movement and stated that he was taking personal control of the Revisionist movement.

Jabotinsky projected himself as a neutral mediator rather than as someone on one side of a difference of views. He said that many Revisionists had turned to him with a 'kol demamah dakah' – 'a still small voice' – and he had decided to act.[32] Grossman responded that Jabotinsky had neither

[27] Vladimir Jabotinsky, Letter to the Revisionist Executive Committee, 17 August 1931, *Igrot, 1930–1931* (Jerusalem, 2004).
[28] Max Bodenheimer, *Prelude to Israel: The Memoirs of M. I. Bodenheimer*, ed. Henriette Hannah Bodenheimer (London, 1963), p. 314.
[29] Vladimir Jabotinsky, Letter to Meir Grossman, 23 November 1932, *Igrot, 1932–1933* (Jerusalem, 2006).
[30] *Rassviet*, 30 August 1931.
[31] Jan Zouplna, 'Vladimir Jabotinsky and the Split within the Revisionist Union: From the Boulogne Agreement to the Katowice Putsch, 1931–1933', *Journal of Israeli History*, vol. 24, no. 1 (March 2005), pp. 35–63.
[32] Vladimir Jabotinsky, 'Fate of the Revisionists', *Moment*, 26 March 1933.

the legal nor the moral right to do this and his action was tantamount to a putsch.[33] Grossman, Machover, Soskin and Stricker – his colleagues of long standing – further condemned Jabotinsky for arranging a plebiscite to approve the legality of his actions.[34] The Executive viewed this as the zenith of Jabotinsky's authoritarian tendencies, encouraged by his pandering to the anti-democratic sentiments of the Maximalists. The Revisionists split whilst Betar and the Maximalists passionately supported Jabotinsky. Grossman garnered the support of the old guard, the Revisionist Executive and the party loyalists. All this took place at the very time Hitler began to implement his anti-Semitic policies and the economic boycott of Jewish businesses.[35] The Polish press greeted the news with the headline 'The Jews Have a Dictator'.

Even before the Katowice conference, Grossman had started to publish his own journal, *Hamatarah*.[36] He now formally established the 'Democratic Revisionists' and commented acerbically:

It is hard for me to grasp how democratic principles can be reconciled with the dictatorship of a single person who changes his coats in the same way as an oriental dancer changes her veils.[37]

Thus at the next Zionist congress in Prague, the official Revisionists sent forty-five delegates while the Democratic Revisionists were represented by seven.

The Maximalists in Palestine, however, were overjoyed.[38] This, they believed, verified the veracity of all their arguments; Jabotinsky had finally seen the light and now openly declared his support for their stand. *Hazit Ha'am* speculated that Jabotinsky might now head a Betar faction 'that is totally devoted to his discipline'.[39] Jabotinsky was viewed as returning to his roots, the energised and assertive leader.

Jabotinsky had stripped himself of the support of colleagues who did not see things in the black-and-white scenario of the Maximalists and a large proportion of the youth. Meir Grossman primarily endorsed the parliamentary road to a state, while Ahimeir rejected it in favour of direct action. Jabotinsky, however, believed in the possibility of different

---

[33] *Jewish Chronicle*, 31 March 1933.
[34] Declaration of the Executive Committee of the World Union of Zionist Revisionists, 5 April 1933, Jabotinsky Institute Archives, Tel Aviv.
[35] Ibid.
[36] *Hamatarah*, 7 March 1933.
[37] *Haynt*, 26 March 1933.
[38] *Jewish Telegraphic Agency*, 22 July 1933.
[39] *Hazit Ha'am*, 31 March 1933.

paths to the ultimate goal of a state – which could coexist. Jabotinsky also entertained the idea that the civil disobedience of Berit Ha-Biryonim could awaken the youth.

When a Betar demonstration in Tel Aviv in December 1933 against the limits placed on Jewish immigration to Palestine resulted in attacks on the police, arrests and hospitalisation – Jabotinsky sent the organisers a telegram:

> Your righteous outbreak and sacrifice will remain in Jewish history as the date of birth of the decisive world onslaught smashing anti-Zion rule in Zion and bringing the dawn of the Jewish state.[40]

He later qualified this by appealing to his followers not to use physical force against opponents – not on ethical grounds, but on tactical grounds. Despite Jabotinsky's support for such actions, Ahimeir was seen as a hero by many and such activism was a redeeming feature in a period of stagnation.[41]

The Revisionists in Palestine were increasing their support. In the 1931 elections for the Asefat Nivharim, the elected body of Palestinian Jews, they quadrupled their support – in less than a decade.[42] Jabotinsky had always insisted that the Palestinian Revisionists needed their autonomy to pursue their own independent actions. This put him at odds with Revisionist moderates who believed in an evolutionary Zionism. Indeed, a number of Revisionists had signed a letter to *Doar Hayom* in which they stated that they did not recognise the authority of 'the extremist Zionist Revisionist Executive in Palestine'.[43]

Jabotinsky's task, as he saw it, was to divert the energy of the Maximalists into productive channels. He therefore opposed any criticism of Ahimeir and his supporters. In March 1931 he chastised the German Revisionists' criticism of their Palestinian counterparts.[44]

GROOMING THE YOUTH FOR LEADERSHIP

Ahimeir believed that 'whoever has the youth has the state'.[45] Jabotinsky also believed that youth held the key to the future if their actions were

[40] *Jewish Chronicle*, 15 December 1933.
[41] Vladimir Jabotinsky, Letter to Baruch Weinstein, 26 May 1932, *Igrot, 1930–1932* (Jerusalem, 2006).
[42] *Doar Hayom*, 7 January 1931.
[43] *Jewish Chronicle*, 11 September 1931.
[44] Vladimir Jabotinsky, Letter to Richard Lichtheim, 20 March 1931, *Igrot, 1930–1931*.
[45] *Ha'am*, 19 July 1931.

politically constructive, but he also did not dismiss older, often wiser heads who saw alternative paths to the ultimate goal of a state. Even though Jabotinsky and Ahimeir projected different paths to the Jewish state, both viewed Betar as the container for nationalist youth. Indeed, the very first Betar newsletter was appropriately called *Massuot* (Beacons) when it was published in Riga in April 1927.

Jabotinsky invested time and energy in speaking to groups of young people and convincing them to take on a military persona – albeit educational. In speaking to a student group in Vienna in 1927, he was aghast when he was told that they were going to do away with all the paraphernalia of a military imagery. He responded:

You can abolish everything – the cap, the ribbons, the colours, heavy drinking, the songs, everything, but not the sword. You are going to keep the sword. Sword-fighting is not a German invention, it belonged to our forefathers. The Torah and the sword were both handed down to us from heaven.[46]

In a letter to the youth of Wloclawek in Poland, he told them that 'all Hebrew youth, whether a boy or a girl – each one is a soldier of the people'.[47] This was coupled with the sense of 'moral hadar' (dignity and self-respect) with which a member of Betar acted.[48] Jabotinsky perceived Betar as a non-political youth group whose military training would allow it to become the nucleus of a future Jewish legion. At eighteen, a member of Betar could formally declare his or her political allegiance by joining the Revisionists.

The killings of 1929, followed by the negative proposals of the Shaw Commission, the Hope-Simpson report and the Passfield White Paper, all created a sense amongst the youth that only civil disobedience and rebellion would be successful against the British. Jabotinsky's more militant tone in his writings and speeches reflected this. But it was also a question of not being outflanked by Ahimeir.

For this generation now growing before our eyes and on whose shoulders will fall the responsibility for the greatest turning point in our history, the Aleph-Bet is very plain and simple: Young men, learn to shoot!

But if we are told that we should all be educated people and learn to plough the land and to build houses and all be able to speak Hebrew and know our whole

---

[46] I. Z. Kantor, 'Jabotinsky and the Student Corporations', *Hamashkif*, 20 August 1940.
[47] Vladimir Jabotinsky, Letter to the Hebrew youth of Wloclawek, 29 March 1927, *Igrot*, 1926–1927 (Jerusalem, 2000).
[48] Vladimir Jabotinsky, Letter to Betar in Riga, 5 November 1928, *Igrot*, 1928–1929 (Jerusalem, 2002).

literature from the songs of Devorah until Avigdor Hameiri and Shlonsky, and yet not know how to shoot then there is no hope.[49]

Jabotinsky and Betar became very attractive to Jewish youth after 1929. Menahem Begin's father had been chairman of the left-wing Zionist Hashomer Hatzair in Brest-Litovsk, while Yitzhak Shamir's parents had been supporters of the anti-Zionist socialist Bund.[50] All became less enamoured of socialism and answered the call of stand-alone nationalism. Their sons soon became heavily involved in Betar.

Jabotinsky expected the members of Betar to be disciplined members of a collective, ready to obey any command, but at the same time to remember that 'in the beginning God created the individual'.[51] He spoke about Garibaldi and Trumpeldor. Jabotinsky expected an iron discipline and the only elected official was Jabotinsky himself as Rosh Betar.[52]

Ahimeir's heroes, in contrast, were Aaron and Sarah Aaronson of Nili, the World War I espionage group which passed on information to the British. Their goal was to facilitate the invasion of Palestine and drive out the Turks. A majority of the Jews of Palestine at that time held a different view. They were worried that they would be next on the list for retribution after the Armenians. Jamal Pasha, the Turkish governor, was determined from the outset to institute traditional reprisals against perceived rebellious minorities, to expel Jews from Palestine and to end the Jewish and Christian presence in Jerusalem. The Jews were protected only by the German military commanders in Palestine, Erich von Falkenhayn and Friedrich Kress von Kressenstein.[53] Despite this, the exploits of Nili, it was reasoned, would provoke reprisals from the Jamal Pasha and the enraged Turks. The members of Nili stood alone and were shunned by the Zionist leadership and most of the Jewish community.

This made a great impression upon Ahimeir, who clearly identified with the non-socialist Aaron Aaronson. The youth, he argued, must be prepared for self-sacrifice and accept prison or even the gallows.[54] Indeed,

[49] Vladimir Jabotinsky, 'Afn Pripitshek', *Haynt* 16 October 1931; *Jewish Herald*, 12 September 1947.
[50] Interview with Yitzhak Shamir, Tel Aviv, 25 July 2000.
[51] Vladimir Jabotinsky, *Avtobiografiya*, Ketavim 1, ed. Eri Jabotinsky (Jerusalem, 1958), p. 38.
[52] *Jewish Chronicle*, 24 April 1931.
[53] *Ha'aretz*, 1 August 2014.
[54] Abba Ahimeir, Speech to the conference of Revisionists in Palestine, *Hazit Ha'am*, 29 April 1932.

he spoke of replacing 'salon Revisionism' with 'prison Revisionism'.[55] Ahimeir regarded Nili as first and foremost an indigenous movement, unaffected and untainted by the cosmopolitanism which many revolutionary Zionists brought with them to Palestine.[56]

Following the Katowice conference in March 1933 and the split in the Revisionist movement, he advocated a third stage of Zionism.[57] He regarded the events at Katowice as an endorsement of his approach at the Revisionist conference in Vienna in 1932. Ahimeir envisaged two possible paths for a dissident Revisionism in opposition, composed of Jabotinsky, the Maximalists and Betar. It could become yet another version of General Zionism – a General Zionist *gimel* – or it could embark on a third stage of Zionism which embraced Maximalism and upheld the ideas of the national movements of Atatürk, Pilsudski and De Valera. The third generation of Zionists after Katowice should therefore follow a revolutionary path, the path of national liberation.

POLAND

In 1932 Jabotinsky had written to a critic of the Maximalists that 'the enormous moral influence of the Ahimeir spirit in the Diaspora' should not be underestimated.[58] Indeed, following the Vienna conference when Maximalism had first made its mark, Ahimeir was in contact with admirers via various channels in Poland to create new organisations such as Berit Bar-Kokhba and Berit Ha-Cana'aim which would spread the gospel of Maximalism – youth groups following his political philosophy rather than that of Jabotinsky.

The 1931 census indicated that Pilsudski's Poland had a population of 3,113,900 Jews, of whom 2,732,600 spoke Yiddish. One in ten Polish citizens was therefore Jewish – from the assimilated and converted to the Communist and Zionist. It was a microcosm of 'Jewishness' and Jewish life in the Diaspora. It boasted strong ideological movements, from Bundism to Marxism-Zionism. There were, for example, regular demonstrations outside the British Embassy in Warsaw over its policies in Palestine in 1930.[59] Moreover, 75 percent of all Revisionists lived in

---

[55] Joseph Heller, '"Monism of the Goal" or "Monism of the Means": The Conceptual Debate between Ze'ev Jabotinsky and Abba Ahimeir, 1928–1933', *Zion*, no. 52 (1987), pp. 315–369.

[56] Abba Ahimeir, 'Hashluv hashlishi', *Hayarden*, 18 October 1935.

[57] Abba Ahimeir, 'Hahistadrut hatsionit Hashlishit', *Hazit Ha'am*, 28 March 1933.

[58] Vladimir Jabotinsky, Letter to Baruch Weinstein, 26 May 1932, *Igrot, 1932–1933*.

[59] *Jewish Chronicle*, 7 November 1930.

Poland, and the vast majority sided with Jabotinsky following the schism at the Katowice conference. During the inter-war years, Revisionist Zionism published almost 120 journals in a wide variety of Polish cities and towns in Hebrew, Yiddish and Polish.[60]

Although marginalised by a resurgent Polish state, the Revisionists admired Polish nationalism and utilised it as a model, while the Left began to detest it for its reactionary views.

Seventy percent of the population consisted of ethnic Poles. There was an ongoing campaign, therefore, to Polonise the country, much to the detriment of the rights of Ukrainians, Byelorussians, Germans and smaller minorities. There were periodic outbursts of popular anti-Semitism in the new Poland. There were attacks on Jewish students at the Anatomical Institute and at the Warsaw Institute of Dentistry. A sign was put up: 'No Jews permitted to enter.'[61] There were even rumours that Poland intended to purchase Angola so that it could send its Jews there to colonise it.

A dire economic situation, coupled with a 'Poles First' policy, accelerated the impoverishment of thousands of Polish Jews. By the mid-1930s, it was estimated that three-quarters existed partially or totally on the goodwill of philanthropic organisations. Some 300,000 Jewish schoolchildren were thought to be suffering from malnutrition. In Vilna, 80 percent were found to be anaemic.[62] Many Jews wanted a better life for their families – in North America, in Western Europe and in Palestine. The great Revisionist hope was to organise the emigration of the Jewish masses from Poland and other countries of distress in Eastern Europe and to settle them in Palestine. With Pilsudski's death in 1935, the situation of Polish Jewry worsened.

Jabotinsky believed that the salvation of Polish Jewry lay in the promise of a mass movement to Palestine. Jabotinsky argued that the Polish dislike of Jews was 'the anti-Semitism of things', caused essentially by the economic situation. This was profoundly different from 'the anti-Semitism of men', an ideological racism as typified by Nazi Germany.[63] The Poles believed that it was in their national interests to welcome a gradual departure of their Jewish minority. For these reasons, Jabotinsky eulogised Pilsudski in a meeting at Krakow after his death. He compared him to Trumpeldor.[64]

[60] Mina Grauer, ed., *Haitonut shel hatenuah haRevizionistit b'shanim*, 1925–1948 (Tel Aviv, 2000), pp. 211–55.

[61] *Jewish Chronicle*, 21 March 1930.

[62] Howard M. Sachar, *Dreamland: Europeans and Jews in the Aftermath of the Great War* (New York, 2002), p. 60.

[63] Vladimir Jabotinsky, *The Jewish War Front* (London, 1940), pp. 55–66.

[64] Vladimir Jabotinsky, 'Speech to the Betar Conference in Kraków *Hayarden*, 25 August 1935.

Pilsudski in Jabotinsky's eyes was neither kosher nor non-kosher – he was simply indifferent to Jewish interests:

Pilsudski was neither a friend of the Jews nor their enemy: he was politely indifferent – 'politely' at all events in public. One cannot help suspecting (although he never said so) that he would not have thought it regrettable had Poland had only 1% of Jews instead of 10%; and as there were never enough jobs to go round, one may imagine (though he never mentioned it) that he wanted them to go to the Poles and not to the Jews. But pogroms and ghetto laws and such things were to him like a boil on the tip of a beloved's nose: Pilsudski would not have them in his Poland.[65]

Pilsudski, however, was admired for his successful struggle in securing independence for his people. The Polish national spirit was an example for the Revisionists.[66] The Polish brigades of 1914 were undoubtedly a model for the Jewish Legion of 1917. The Legion, heroism and militarism were seen as intrinsically Polish qualities. Both were diasporic peoples – Polonia stretched from Lodz to Chicago. Jabotinsky admired the Polish role in the French revolutionary wars. Moreover, Jews had fought in the Polish revolts of 1794, 1830 and 1863.

Literature and poetry coloured and reflected the struggle. A few years after the defeat of Napoleon, which put an end to dreams of independence, the Polish national poet Adam Mickiewicz wrote 'Ode to Youth', which impressed Jabotinsky and many of his followers:

> Heartless, soulless – these are nations of skeletons
> Youth, give me wings
> Let me soar above a dead world
> To the heavenly land of illusion
> Where enthusiasm works miracles
> Strews the flowers of new things
> And clothes hope in golden pictures[67]

Jabotinsky believed that literature served a national purpose and gave as the exemplar Henryk Sienkiewicz's historical novel *By Fire and Sword*.[68] Indeed, he argued that Hebrew literature, as it existed in 1919, was not ready to illuminate the national role. Uri Zvi Greenberg, on the other hand, was seen as a visionary poet in the Polish tradition in

[65] Jabotinsky, *The Jewish War Front*, p. 72.
[66] Vladimir Jabotinsky, 'Poles and Jews', *Odesskie Novosti*, 12 October 1910.
[67] Alexander Bruce Boswell, *Poland and the Poles* (London, 1919), pp. 217–18.
[68] Vladimir Jabotinsky, 'Books', *Hadashot Ha'aretz*, 8 October 1919.

the same light as Polish visionary poets such as Mickiewicz and Yuliusz Slowacki.[69]

In 1905 Jabotinsky had met the Polish writer and Nobel Prize nominee Eliza Orzeszkowa, who had written *Eli Makower* (1875), which illustrated the relations between the Jews and the Polish aristocracy, and *Meir Ezofowicz* (1878), which described the conflict between Jewish orthodoxy and modern liberalism. Jabotinsky admired her *Patriotyzm i kosmopolityzm* (1880).[70] He told her that he supported an independent Poland but was critical of Polish attitudes towards national minorities. He therefore rejected the views of the Polish nationalist leader, Roman Dmowski, who disliked Jews and opposed the representation of national minorities.

Ahimeir also looked to Poland. In contrast to Jabotinsky, he admired the young Pilsudski, the freedom fighter, the organiser of the Bezdany train robbery in 1908 rather than the later legionnaire and president. Ahimeir also believed that Polish nationalism had been untainted by foreign influences, unlike Zionism, which had absorbed the cosmopolitanism of Russian and German culture. 'Goethe, Dostoyevsky and Tolstoy poisoned us', Ahimeir wrote, but Polish culture was different and its national spirit would have aided the Zionists.[71]

The new Poland appealed to both Jabotinsky and Ahimeir because it had stood as a bulwark against the advance of the Red Army into the West, its anti-Communism mingled with its centuries-long detestation of Russian imperialism. The fourth aliyah of the Polish Jewish middle class during the mid-1920s was therefore coloured by Polish anti-Communism. Significantly, 48 out of the 141 delegates at the contentious Vienna conference in 1932 came from Poland.[72] There was a natural affinity for Revisionism.

Many Polish Jews left the Histadrut in 1933 to establish the National Workers' Federation. They incorporated corporatist ideas. The workers were a revolutionary element in making the national revolution.

A couple of weeks after the opening of the Katowice conference, a group of leading members of Betar appended their signatures to an appeal entitled 'What Do the Maximalists Want?' Its central demand was the militarisation of Jewish youth. It argued that normative Zionism had

[69] Yaakov Shavit, 'Politics and Messianism: The Zionist Revisionist Movement and Polish Political Culture', *Studies in Zionism*, vol.2, no. 6 (1985), pp. 229–46.

[70] Jabotinsky, *Avtobiyografiya*, Ketavim 1, pp. 61–62.

[71] Abba Ahimeir, 'Poland in Palestine', *Hamashkif*, 24 January 1941.

[72] Zouplna, 'Vladimir Jabotinsky and the Split within the Revisionist Union.'

betrayed the idea of the Jewish state as the solution to the Jewish problem. The Revisionist Executive, which had just been removed in Katowice, was no better, since it had compromised and viewed itself as no more than an appendage of the World Zionist Organisation. Revisionism had distanced itself from 'active resistance', and 'the great permanent revolution in Zionism' had come unstuck mid-way.

The Revisionist movement should be reconstructed on the basis of hierarchy, discipline and total obedience to the senior leadership – and relating to Jabotinsky 'first and foremost to the only dominant force, the creator of Revisionism'. The movement should be brought under the absolute rule of the leader, 'the genius of our era of national revival'. He should guide the movement along 'the route of recovery from its childhood illnesses'. The signatories concluded with the request that 'the youth after the war want to be commanded and they will obey'.

The Polish Maximalists made several demands on the Revisionist movement. They wanted an end to cooperation with England, since it was 'a government of occupation'. The Revisionist movement in Palestine should be autonomous and outside the Zionist Organisation. They demanded a strengthening of the role of the National Labour Union, which should be based on national syndicalist foundations. It should fight against the monopoly of the Histadrut and 'the Marxist camp in Eretz Israel'. They demanded the establishment of a stable defensive force in Palestine to ensure security. Youth should be involved in sports and there should an association for demobbed Jewish soldiers. This memorandum of the Polish Maximalists was signed by Betar leaders from Warsaw, Lutsk, Pinsk and Danzig. It was also signed by Menahem Begin from Brest-Litovsk.[73]

---

[73] Memorandum of the Polish Maximalists to the Katowice Council, 7 April 1933, Jabotinsky Institute Archives, Tel Aviv.

7

The Arabs of Palestine

Jabotinsky grew up in a city of minorities and even subconsciously was attuned to their demands and differences. In particular his interest in Ukrainian nationalism led to his contribution to numerous Ukrainian intellectual journals, and this was the background to his accord with Maxym Slavinsky. The Ukrainian nationalists opposed the role of the assimilated Jewish intelligentsia as well as many Russian liberals per se in advocating Russification. This mirrored the resolve of many Jewish intellectuals to marginalise their Jewishness and the desire of Russian liberals to dismiss Zionism as a solution to the Jewish question. Jabotinsky identified with the Ukrainians on this issue and was scathing about the general attitude towards minorities in the Tsarist Empire.[1]

He believed that there should be a rapprochement between Ukrainians and Jews in Galicia. He therefore fought not only for cooperation but also for reciprocity. He sided with the Ukrainians against Polonisation and expected in return Ukrainian support for Jewish rights within the Tsarist Empire.

Jabotinsky understood that the Jews could be authoritative on this issue and had something to contribute in a wider sense on the issue of national minorities in Russia. In a series of articles entitled 'Our Tasks', written for *Khronika evreiska zhizn'*,[2] he put forward ideas for resolving the question of the rights of national minorities living in a multi-national empire.

[1] Vladimir Jabotinsky, 'On Russian Liberalism', *Ukrainskaia zhizn'*, nos. 7–8, 1912.
[2] *Khronika evreiska zhizn'*, 15 and 29 June; 6, 13 and 20 July 1906.

This evolved into the Helsingfors Programme, which was adopted at the third conference of the Russian Zionist Organisation in Helsinki in December 1906. Its participants stated that they had originally expected Palestine to be given to them immediately, and this lack of realism had taken them away from 'the mundane problems of the present life'. The Russian Zionists were therefore forced to recognise the developmental nature of Zionism and to examine the current situation of Jews in Russia.

The Helsingfors Programme did not seek to alter the majority culture of the Russian state, but it did advocate a universal application of its principles which would serve all minorities in multi-national states. It demanded

the overall democratisation of the state apparatus, based on the principle of parliamentarianism with wide-ranging liberties, autonomy for regions with a specific national character and a guarantee of national minority rights.[3]

Jabotinsky had studied the works of theorists such as Richard Charmatz and Georg Jellinek on the nationalities question, but he was also highly influenced by the works of Karl Renner (Rudolf Springer), an Austrian socialist who had developed the idea of personal autonomy in a multi-national state. Renner had first-hand experience of the problem, since Austro-Hungary consisted of fifteen nationalities living in many mixed areas. Moreover, there had been a tremendous influx of national minorities, including a large number of Jews into Vienna after 1848.

The conventional idea was that there should be a territorial base from which a nationality could develop its cultural life. Yet classic liberalism had real problems with the idea of ethnic autonomy if it wasn't expressed in territorial terms. The assimilatory melting pot model was preferred. Marxists such as Lenin and Stalin rejected the idea of non-territorial autonomy. Yet Renner pointed out that Catholics, Protestants and Jews could coexist in Vienna with their own institutions, provided they did not claim territorial exclusivity.

Renner's ideas were provoked by the German-Czech dispute within the Austro-Hungarian Empire. He dismissed the belief that 'voluntary reconciliation between disputants' was possible and labelled it utopian:

The nations shall be constituted not as territorial entities, but as personal associations, not as states but as peoples, not according to age-old constitutional laws, but according to living national laws.[4]

[3] Jan Zouplna, 'Revisionist Zionism: Image, Reality and the Quest for Historical Narrative', *Middle Eastern Studies*, vol. 44, no. 1 (June 2008), pp. 3–27.
[4] Karl Renner (Rudolf Springer), 'Nation and State', in Ephraim Nimni, ed., *National Cultural Autonomy and Its Cultural Critics* (London, 2005), p. 29.

On the other hand, Renner did not dismiss the territorial principle as 'wrong' as a formula for nation-state formation, but it was not a solution to the nationalities problem in Austro-Hungary.

In his *Der Kampf der oesterreichischen Nationen um den Staat*, published in 1902,[5] Renner was able to construct a model which effectively did away with the idea of national minorities and the desire to protect them. All citizens, he argued, should declare their nationality when they reached voting age. Regardless of where they lived, they should possess all the institutions necessary to deal with national cultural affairs in a multi-national state. There should be 'proportional access to office to the organised national councils', and German should be the official language of the state. Yet Renner did not pronounce on the question of the Jews as a nation – only Judaism as a model for national-cultural autonomy.

Jabotinsky was very much taken by such ideas in his understanding of the Jewish problem in Russia. Indeed, Jabotinsky wrote the introduction to the Russian version of Renner's 'Nation and State'. Even more so, he clearly believed that it could also be applied to a future state of the Jews wherein the Jews constituted a majority of the population. Indeed, as Renner pointed out, 'The nationalities struggle is the competition between national groups for the dominant influence within the state.'[6]

Jabotinsky did not view Renner's work as a vehicle to allow the Jews to remain in the Diaspora as a national minority. Even as early as 1906, he predicted that the history of the Jews in the twentieth century would demand that jurisdiction over territory be 'fundamentally germane to the continuity of peoplehood.'[7] He argued that a people without territory cannot truly claim absolute autonomy, but it could demand self-government, regarding its national life as well as representation in the Reichsrat and in the Sejms. It should have its national language recognised in the courts and schools and be represented on elected bodies.

Jabotinsky held to his views about national minorities, based on the Helsingfors Programme, throughout his life.[8] After World War I ended, when the clash of Jewish and Arab nationalism over Palestine grew and became more intense, Jabotinsky returned to the ideas that he had first advocated in 1906. He believed that by 2030 all states would be multi-national and would have to confront the question of the rights of national minorities. However, he disagreed with figures such as Judah Magnes as to the

[5] Ibid.
[6] Ibid., p. 33.
[7] Geoffrey Brahm Levey, 'National Cultural Autonomy and Liberal Nationalism', in Nimni, ed., *National Cultural Autonomy*, p. 154.
[8] Vladimir Jabotinsky, 'The Helsingfors Programme', *Odesskii Novosti*, 12 August 1912.

meaning of 'binationalism' and the role of the majority national group in such states. In an article in January 1926 entitled 'On a Bi-national Land of Israel',[9] he mentioned the Helsingfors Programme in the context of the different nationalities that populated Poland, Belgium and Switzerland. Not only could the Programme apply to the Arabs in a state of the Jews, stretching across both banks of the Jordan, but it would also apply to the Circassians of TransJordan. In addition to Hebrew, Arabic and Circassian would be the official languages of the future state. In a speech in Zion Hall in Jerusalem in February 1929,[10] Jabotinsky argued that the internal autonomy of national minorities should be guaranteed and that their schools and other institutions should be maintained by the state.[11]

In contrast to such a vision, Jabotinsky was often fatalistic about a solution to the problem of states with several national groups. Jabotinsky said that he was not an optimist and did not believe in 'love' between national groups, only in common interests between them.[12]

However, by 1938, in the midst of the Arab Revolt, Jabotinsky wrote that after more than thirty years no one had successfully applied the Springer theory:

Even the Czechs under the leadership of Masaryk, the teacher of all autonomists, could not or would not do it ...

Among the Arabs, even their intellectuals have never heard of this theory, but these same intellectuals would know that a minority suffers everywhere – the Christians in Turkey, the Muslims in India, the Irish under Britain ... so that one must be intoxicated with rhetoric to expect the Arabs to believe that the Jews, of all the peoples in the world, will alone prove able or will, at least honestly intend to, realise an idea that has not succeeded with other nations who are with much greater authority.[13]

Despite his pessimism, Jabotinsky still advocated the implementation of the Helsingfors Programme, even though all precedents had clearly failed. He hoped 'that the first country in which it will be given effect will be our Palestine'. He also believed that the Arabs would not agree to it:

But what will the Arab answer be: 'No! These are empty words. It is not a question of rights. It is purely a question of numbers. Who will be the majority in Palestine?' And our Arab brothers will be right.

[9] *Rassviet*, 3 January 1926.
[10] *Doar Hayom*, 18 February 1929.
[11] Vladimir Jabotinsky, 'Empty Words', *Haynt*, 12 September 1930; *Jewish Standard*, 19 September 1941.
[12] Vladimir Jabotinsky, 'Non Multum, Sed Multa', *Ukrainskii vestnik*, 16 July 1906.
[13] Jabotinsky noted these various points in an unpublished article, dated 10 July 1938. He significantly did not advise publication. Jabotinsky Institute Archives, Tel Aviv.

He said that a state with a big Arab majority would be an Arab state. The Jews as a majority would want a Jewish national state – and 'no bi-national constitution will mitigate against that':

It is not possible to delimit the whole of the state life into national spheres. Only cultural affairs and those of an intellectual character, like the school system, can be taken out of the competence of the State Parliament and transferred to the special nationalities administration.

Areas such as the economy, declaration of war, immigration have to remain in the hands of the state parliament and government – and these in turn will be in the hands of the majority nationality.

THE IRON WALL

Jabotinsky's views on Islam – and by extension on the Palestinian Arabs – were conditioned by his sympathy for the ideas of Marinetti and the Futurists. In 'The Iron Wall' he commented that the Palestinian Arabs were 500 years behind the Jews culturally. 'They have neither our endurance nor our determination'.[14] This was based on the prevailing Eurocentric mood and a general disdain for religion. He was disparaging of married religious Jewish women who wore the sheytl, a wig to ward off attention from predatory men other than a husband, and the refusal to shake the hands of men. He condemned *kashrut*, the religious dietary laws governing the eating of solely kosher food. For Jabotinsky, this was obscurantist. Zionism was Western, secular and activist. However, he viewed the preservation of Jewish observance as a national value. He believed that Jews were the originators and purveyors of European culture – a European people which was now returning to the Orient.[15] He spoke about the Jews being covered by 'the dust of the West'.[16]

In his early writing, Jabotinsky utilised the character of Cervantes's Don Quixote to argue that there was a human need to worship an abstraction, to create a personal living God 'and to commit acts of heroism in His name.'[17] He condemned 'organised religion'[18] and believed that certain practices of Judaism were part of Eastern civilisation which he regarded as incompatible with the liberal traditions of Europe.

---

[14] Vladimir Jabotinsky, 'The Iron Wall', *Rassviet*, 4 November 1923.
[15] Vladimir Jabotinsky, 'The Arabesque Fashion', *Rassviet*, 23 January 1927.
[16] Vladimir Jabotinsky, 'The East', *Rassviet*, 26 September 1926.
[17] Vladimir Jabotinsky, 'The Ten Books', 1904, in *Al Sifrut Ve-Omanut*, Ketavim 6, ed. Eri Jabotinsky (Jerusalem, 1958), pp. 13–45.
[18] Jabotinsky, 'The East'.

Jabotinsky criticised the customs of both Jews and Arabs. In the 1920s, he referred to 'the 700,000 Arabs of Palestine' as 'primitive and polygamous'.[19] He extended such views to Islam, which he characterised as both 'a great and positive moral force' and 'religious zealotry blended with nationalist zealotry'.[20] The Ottomans had proclaimed a jihad against the Allies in November 1914, yet Indian Muslims actually helped the British during World War I. When the Ottoman Empire began to fall apart, no Muslim countries came to its aid.[21] Neither did Christendom have a good record. Christian kingdoms never helped each other when the Ottomans came from the East, such as during the sieges of Vienna in 1529 and 1683. Jabotinsky thereby argued that while pan-Islamism was a force to be reckoned with, words spoke louder than actions.

Jabotinsky believed that the Turks lost World War I because they did not value technological advance. Yet this was not the same as an inherent racism. In an article published in 1911,[22] Jabotinsky depicted an intense discussion between a Russian and a Jew which referred to the editor Alexandr Stolypin's controversial article 'An Inferior Race'. The Jew commences with the statement:

There is no such thing as an inferior or superior race. Each race has its own characteristics, its particular aptitudes, and I am convinced that if it were possible to find an absolute standard and precisely evaluate the inborn qualities of each race, in general, it would turn out that they are more or less equal.

In the 1930s Jabotinsky wrote about 'the spiritual mechanism' that defined a people which had nothing to do with its so-called purity:

The quality of the 'spiritual mechanism' depends on the 'race', the strength of the intellect, a stronger or weaker leaning to search for new ways, the preparedness to be resigned to the prevailing situation or the daring which urges to invent; the stubbornness or on the contrary the character that gets tired with the first failure. The supreme means of production is in itself a product of race. This is why each race has an explicit uniqueness, and aspires to become a nation.[23]

[19] Vladimir Jabotinsky, 'The Aims of Zionism', *The Zionist*, 14 May 1926.
[20] Vladimir Jabotinsky, 'Islam', *Rassviet*, 19 April 1924.
[21] Vladimir Jabotinsky, 'Awesome Islam', *Morgen zhurnal*, 26 June 1927.
[22] Vladimir Jabotinsky, 'An Exchange of Compliments', *Feuilletons* (St. Petersburg, 1913), trans. Alice Nakhimovsky, in Maxim D. Shrayer, ed., *An Anthology of Jewish-Russian Literature, 1801–1953: Two Centuries of Dual Identity in Prose and Poetry* (New York, 2007), pp. 150–58.
[23] Vladimir Jabotinsky, 'A Lecture on Jewish History', *Haynt*, 13 May 1932; in *Uma V'Hevra*, Ketavim 9, ed. E. Jabotinsky (Jerusalem, 1949–1950), pp. 159–70.

In his early articles, Jabotinsky focussed mainly on the return of the Jews to their historic homeland.[24] The Jews, he argued, were forged from 'the fragments of other peoples'.[25] They became a people only when they settled in the Land of Israel. Everything emanated from being tied to the soil.

Although far from being religious, Jabotinsky, like many early Zionists, tried to reclaim the national spirit of the Jews from biblical heroes such as Gideon and from ancient Jewish history.

Following his resignation from the Zionist Executive in 1923, he began to pursue his own independent line – an approach free from dreams of joint Arab-Jewish cooperation. In an article entitled 'Majority', he was unequivocal in advocating the belief that the Zionist experiment would succeed only if there was a Jewish majority in Palestine.[26] This was the precursor of two articles which advocated the erection of an 'Iron Wall' behind which the Jews would build a Palestine in which a majority of Jews would dwell.[27]

In 'The Iron Wall', he argued that there were two nations in Palestine, and their rights should be observed in accordance with the Helsingfors proposals. What was applicable to Diaspora Jews in Russia was also applicable to Palestinian Arabs in a Jewish state. Jabotinsky proposed the taking of an oath that no one should be expelled. In the Russian original of 'The Iron Wall', Jabotinsky wrote about 'Palestine' and not about 'Eretz Israel', which recognised 'the unique character of Palestinian national existence'.[28]

On the question of peace between Zionist Jews and Palestinian Arabs, Jabotinsky said that the future depended on the approach of the Arabs and not on the attitude of the Jews. His hope was that once a Jewish majority had been attained in Palestine, everything would fall into place; the Arabs would accept this fait accompli and negotiate a rational peace agreement.

Given the realities of 1923, Jabotinsky concluded that it was unlikely that there would therefore be a voluntary agreement in the near future.

[24] Vladimir Jabotinsky, 'Zionism and Palestine', *Evreiskaya zhizn'*, February 1904; *Evreiskaya zhizn'*, January 1905; *On Territorialism: Zionism and Palestine* (Odessa, 1905).

[25] Vladimir Jabotinsky, 'Tsiyonut ve-Erets Yisra'el', *Ketavim Tsionim Rishonim*, Ketavim 8, ed. E. Jabotinsky (Jerusalem, 1949), p. 123.

[26] *Rassviet*, 21 October 1923.

[27] Jabotinsky, 'The Iron Wall'; 'The Ethics of the Iron Wall', *Rassviet*, 11 November 1923.

[28] Jan Zouplna, 'Revisionist Zionism: Image, Reality and the Quest for Historical Narrative', *Middle Eastern Studies*, vol. 44, no. 1 (June 2008), pp. 3–27.

This was a time when Lenin's Bolshevik regime was seen as a permanent fixture and when there was a growing awareness that the victory of the Allies in World War I had not fundamentally changed the conditions of ordinary people, yearning for a better life. The philosophy of many socialist Zionists in 1923 was that it was self-evident that Jews and Arabs would come to a rational compromise and build a bright new future.

Jabotinsky was blunt in attacking such well-intentioned notions. He ridiculed those Jews 'who were born blind', because there would be no voluntary consent from the Arabs. Moreover, he maintained that it did not depend on the conduct of the Jews. It did not matter whether Jews acted decently or like 'brigands' as in the time of Yehoshua Bin Nun during the invasion of Canaan. He gave the example of the native Indians of North America who fought the Pilgrim Fathers. It did not matter that they wanted to share the country with the indigenous population or that there was enough land for all, given the small population of the Indian tribes.

In 'The Iron Wall', Jabotinsky castigated 'our peacemakers' for their attitude towards Arabs in that they were either corrupt or could be bribed economically:

To imagine as our Arabophiles do that they [the Palestinian Arabs] will voluntarily consent to the realisation of Zionism in return for the moral and material conveniences which the Jewish colonist brings with him, is a childish notion which has at bottom a kind of contempt for the Arab people. It means that they despise the Arab race which they regard as a corrupt mob that can be bought and sold, and are willing to give their homeland a good railway system ...

We may tell them whatever we like about the innocence of our aims, watering them down and sweetening them with honeyed words to make them palatable, but they know what we want, as well as we know what they do not want. They feel at least the same instinctive jealous love of Palestine as the old Aztecs felt for ancient Mexico and the Sioux for their rolling prairies.

He attacked the notion of 'a misunderstanding' between Jews and Arabs which Sokolov had suggested in a speech in Palestine in 1920. The Arabs simply did not want minority status. 'Colonisation can have only one aim and the Palestine Arabs cannot accept this aim.' The Jews in return could not offer any adequate compensation to the Palestinian Arabs. Colonisation could proceed only behind an 'Iron Wall' of protection which the native population was unable to breach. The 'militarists' amongst the Zionists, he pointed out, believed that it should consist of Jewish bayonets. The 'vegetarians' felt that it should instead be composed of Irish (British) troops. A third group advocated Arab bayonets.

Jabotinsky drew the analogy of the Italian irredentists who wanted Trento and Trieste but who remained part of the Hapsburg Empire despite the unification of Italy. They never gave up the struggle and finally achieved their goal in 1918. Therefore, it did not ultimately matter if Baghdad, Mecca and Damascus eventually agreed to give up Palestine and renounce its Arab character; the Palestinian Arabs would still fight on for what they considered to be their homeland. Jabotinsky concluded that when the Arabs finally accepted the notion that they could not rid Palestine of the Jews – only then would there be meaningful negotiations with concessions.

He further argued in 'The Iron Wall' that the Zionists needed the support of a great power. For this reason, to join the Arab nationalist movement in order to oust Britain and France 'would be suicide and treason on our part'. Moreover, 'justice that is enforced does not cease to be justice.'

In another article the following week, entitled 'The Ethics of the Iron Wall', Jabotinsky gave the example of a dispute in the Babylonian Talmud:[29]

If two obstinate people found a piece of cloth at exactly the same time and neither would give way, the Talmudic solution was to divide the cloth. However, if the exercise is repeated, this time with one obstinate person and one reasonable person, the latter says magnanimously, 'Let us divide the cloth since we found it at the same time.' The obstinate person refuses. The Talmud rules that it is now only half the cloth that is in dispute and rules that this should be divided in half. The obstinate person ends up with three-quarters of the cloth while the reasonable person ends up with only a quarter.

The Jews, Jabotinsky believed, had to be realistic. At the end of the day he believed that they could offer little to the Arabs. Even if the Jews looked for another country such as Uganda, the same situation would occur. While there were no uninhabited islands in the world, there was also no law which stipulated that 'the landless must remain landless for eternity'. This reflected Jabotinsky's belief that World War I had effected a sea change and that the Versailles decisions were symptomatic of a redivided globe wherein small nations could seek justice: 'The soil does not belong to those who possess land in excess, but to those who do not possess any.'

Jabotinsky took the long view of history. He asked whether someone who had seized a piece of land should remain there for all time while the evicted person must remain homeless for all time. Should there not be a

[29] Baba Metziah 1:2.

revision of the distribution of the earth among the nations he asked, such that 'those nations who have too much should have to give up some to those nations who have not enough or have none so that all will have some place to exercise their right to self-determination?'. While there were 38 million Arabs in the Arab world, there were 15 million landless Jews in the world in 1923. The area of Eretz Israel was 1/170th of the Arab Middle East.

Jabotinsky believed that the presence of an 'Iron Wall' was imperative for the creation of the infrastructure of a state in which the Jews would constitute a majority of the inhabitants. The alternative was for the Jews to remain a minority during a period of growing Arab nationalism. If this came to pass, they would once more become 'slaves to Pharaoh'.[30]

Jabotinsky always looked to the Helsingfors Programme as the template for dealing with Palestinian Arab minority rights and questions of personal autonomy, the Palestinian national unit within a wider Arab people, but he also believed that the Jews needed to come to a modus vivendi with the Arabs.[31]

WEIZMANN AND THE BRITISH

Jabotinsky understood the role of the British in Palestine differently from the British themselves. He believed in a 'colonisation regime' in that the British should actively help the Zionists in Palestine and not simply coexist with them. Jabotinsky did not view Palestine in 1923 as merely another British colony on the traditional model.

On the one hand, Jabotinsky emphasised the symbiotic relationship between the British and the Jews and certainly recognised 'white settlements' in Palestine as akin to other British colonies. On the other, he recognised the national rights of the Palestinian Arabs. Moreover, Jabotinsky argued that the British upper class was inane if its members believed that they could hold onto any colony forever. 'They are yeshivah bahurim (seminary students) in occidental guise, just as provincial in their outlook as our own boys and as ignorant'. Yet despite his sarcasm, he still believed in England. A state with an Arab majority would simply be the beginning of further Arabisation.[32] If there was a plebiscite, he surmised,

[30] Israel Zangwill, *Times*, 17 May 1921.
[31] Vladimir Jabotinsky, Letter to Frederick Kisch, 4 July 1925, *Igrot, 1922–1925* (Jerusalem, 1998).
[32] Vladimir Jabotinsky, 'Binational Palestine', Jabotinsky Institute Archives, Tel Aviv.

then the Arabs would vote to join a union of other Arab countries, but the Jews would vote to join the British Empire.[33]

Jabotinsky believed that the Yishuv would evolve and grow. By 1950 he imagined that there might well be a sufficient degree of statehood, possibly within the British Empire or within another 'civilised commonwealth of nations' or possibly even within the League of Nations.[34] Jabotinsky's supporter in the House of Commons, Josiah Wedgwood, put forward the idea of a seventh dominion of the British Empire:

Palestine is the Clapham Junction of the British Empire. It will become the Jewish Dominion of the Empire in the same sense as South Africa is a Dutch dominion and Canada French. It seems clear that Palestine must remain attached to the British Empire since it needs protection from other peoples to a greater extent than do other parts of the Empire.[35]

Other leading Zionists were more circumspect about even mentioning the term 'Jewish state'. The First Zionist Congress had indeed expressed support for an 'oeffentlich-rechtlich gesicherte heimstaette', a diplomatic euphemism, though the Balfour Declaration took its cue from this.

Weizmann was very wary about making a difficult situation worse with regard to the British and the Palestinian Arabs:

It is impossible to expect Zionist successes before we have more favourable conditions in which the principles presented by President Wilson will again have come to life. Mr Jabotinsky would have been right if we had to colonise Rhodesia not Palestine which is a sensitive world nerve and has an Arab population within an Arab world. Our mission is to open up the Near East to Jewish initiative by way of Palestine and a policy of justice is therefore essential.[36]

The differences between Weizmann and Jabotinsky began to widen with the establishment of the Revisionist movement in 1925 and certainly when it allied with the Maximalists after 1933. Unlike Weizmann, Jabotinsky would never compromise his belief that the Jews needed both banks of the Jordan to accommodate all the Jews of Eastern Europe. It would house a population of millions as it had done in Roman times. His poem 'The Left Bank of the Jordan', written for the Yardena student group in Kaunas in November 1929,[37] speaks about both sides of the

[33] Vladimir Jabotinsky, 'On the Jewish Agency and the Seventh Dominion', *Jewish Chronicle*, 2 August 1929.

[34] Vladimir Jabotinsky, 'Zionism: Its Aims and Methods. Palestine and the Jews, the True Basis of Colonisation', *Jewish Chronicle*, 19 June 1925.

[35] *Jewish Chronicle*, 7 January 1927.

[36] *Jewish Chronicle*, 28 August 1925.

[37] *Doar Hayom*, 11 April 1930.

Jordan, stretching from the desert to the sea, with the river Jordan as its spine. In paraphrasing the traditional injunction to remember Jerusalem, it includes the line 'Let my right hand wither if I forget the East Bank of the Jordan'. In essence all Revisionists including the Maximalists and their opponents concurred with this sentiment.

Yet Weizmann too had argued for the inclusion of the East Bank before it had been hived off by the British to accommodate the Hashemites. In a letter to Churchill in 1920, Weizmann wrote about 'the fields of Gilead, Moab and Edom with the rivers Arnon and Jabbok, to say nothing of the Yarmuk' being historically, geographically and economically linked to Palestine.[38] British interests, however, came first. Weizmann quickly concluded that he could not afford to alienate the British and subsequently focused on western Palestine. At the end of 1922, Jabotinsky called for the nullification of the plan to exclude TransJordan from the Jewish national home.[39] He strongly opposed setting up Abdullah as the emir of a newly created country.

While there was relative quiet in the Middle East, the differences between Jabotinsky and Weizmann were muted. The events of 1929 and the deepening hostility between Arab and Jew proved to be a catalyst which moved Jabotinsky openly towards a more critical position, but at the same time attracted a lot of disaffected youth to his standard.

Following the killings in Hebron, Safed and Jerusalem in 1929, Jabotinsky gave a speech at Beit Ha'am, Tel Aviv, at the end of December.[40] He addressed several general arguments and once more was brutally straightforward in his approach. He argued that the model of intercommunal relations which worked best was one in which there was a minimum of daily contacts between Arab and Jew. He gave the example of the Jewish city of Tel Aviv next door to Arab Jaffa.

He then addressed the proposal to cantonise Palestine, which Weizmann and the Jewish Agency had raised. If the Arabs accepted the principle of cantons, he continued, would Jews be allowed to settle in the non-Jewish cantons? Jabotinsky argued that there was little hope that this would be accepted by the Palestinian Arabs and it would certainly not bring peace:

---

[38] Chaim Weizmann, Letter to Winston Churchill, 1 March 1921, *The Letters and Papers of Chaim Weizmann*, Series A Letters, vol. 10, *10 July 1920–December 1921* (Jerusalem, 1977).

[39] Vladimir Jabotinsky, Memoranda, 4 November, 12 December, 29 December 1922, Central Zionist Archives, CZA S25–2073, Jerusalem.

[40] *Doar Hayom*, 24 December 1929.

The rebuilding of Palestine is a question of a race between two horses and it is very important that our horse should gain on the other. It is still more important because the second horse had a clear start before the beginning of the race.

He also addressed the notion that 'a little peace and quiet' would solve the problem:

If you don't solve a problem that confronts you and close your eyes to it, then you must not think that your opponent will also close his eyes and will not think about it.

Jabotinsky was unsparing in his criticism of the British. He reminded his audience that Balfour had been delegated by the British government in 1917 to convey its sympathy with Zionist demands to Lord Rothschild, but what were Zionist demands at that time if not a state? The preamble to the Mandate spoke of recognising the grounds for reconstituting the Jews' national home in Palestine. The desire was not to establish a new ghetto. Instead the British had been given a unique opportunity to address 'the thousands of years of exile and suffering'.

All this was too much for Sir John Chancellor, the high commissioner and Sir John Shuckburgh, head of the Middle East Department in the Foreign Office. The speech provided an opportunity to eliminate Jabotinsky from the political equation within Palestine itself. The speech was subsequently labelled 'seditious' rather than harshly critical of British policy. It was used to bar Jabotinsky from returning to Palestine from a trip abroad. Despite periodic appeals, including one to King George V, Jabotinsky never set foot in Palestine again.[41]

Weizmann, however, similarly rejected Jabotinsky's fatalism and argued that an agreement with the Arabs was still possible on the basis of parity. While he argued that parity did not mean a binational state, he was categorical about Jabotinsky's repeated belief in the goal of a Jewish majority, which he feared would lead to the erroneous idea that the Zionists desired a wholesale expulsion of the Palestinian Arabs.

I have no sympathy or understanding for the demand for a Jewish majority. A majority does not necessarily guarantee security. We may have a majority and still be insecure. A majority is not needed for the development of Jewish civilisation and culture. The world will construe this demand only in one sense that we want to acquire a majority in order to drive out the Arabs.[42]

---

[41] *Jewish Chronicle*, 16 March 1934.
[42] *Jewish Chronicle*, 10 July 1931.

At the Seventeenth Zionist Congress in 1931, Weizmann said that
he had never neglected an opportunity to meet Muslims and Arabs and
explore all avenues:

With a strong national home in Palestine, built up peacefully and harmoniously,
we may expect, in cooperation with the Arabs, also to open up for Jewish endeavour the vast areas which for their development need intelligence, initiative, organisation and finance. We shall, with mutual benefit to the two races, contribute
towards the establishment of a belt of flourishing countries stretching from the
Mediterranean to the Indian Ocean, where the two races, which stood together at
the cradle of civilisation, may cooperate in peace and harmony. Surely this is an
ideal worthy of an ancient race! It is not merely Zionism in the narrower sense;
it is a large and human conception and one which must enlist the sympathies of
thinking people.[43]

He even suggested the establishment of a department for Arab relations
within the Palestine Executive. In contrast to Jabotinsky's approach, he
commented:

Anything savouring of domination by physical force, whatever form that force
may assume, anything even remotely resembling the colonising methods which
were freely practised during the last two centuries, would in our case be intolerable and would belie our history.

This belief in an eventual rapprochement with the Arabs sounded both
utopian and unrealistic to Jabotinsky's ears. As he tried to build up Betar,
Jabotinsky's differences widened with his old friend Chaim Weizmann and
with the labour movement of David Ben-Gurion. Internally the schism
within the Revisionist movement was growing almost daily. By 1934,
Jabotinsky was isolated, with only the Maximalists and impressionable
youth for allies. Yet they too were rejecting the gradualist dream of building
a Jewish majority in Palestine. His relationship with the British had worsened as well. On the one hand, he still believed in British fair play and viewed
negotiations as the only way forward. On the other, the Warsaw *Haynt*
published Jabotinsky's article 'Disobedience', in which he urged the Jews
of Palestine to pursue a policy of disobedience regarding any government
measures which might hinder the establishment of a Jewish national home.

THE PROSPECT OF PARTITION

The formal split in the Zionist Organisation with the establishment of
the New Zionist Organisation made little sense at a time when Arab

---

[43] Ibid.

nationalism was in full flight and the storm clouds over Europe were becoming very dark indeed. Yet in his last years Jabotinsky continued to plough this path, and the gaps both within and without became magnified.

In his testimony to the Palestine Royal Commission (Peel Commission) in February 1937[44] Jabotinsky enunciated his understanding of the conflict between Zionist Jews and Palestinian Arabs over the same territory. He argued the case for 'a Jewish state' – meaning that a majority of the inhabitants had to be Jewish. Palestine in 1937 contained 1,600,000 inhabitants – of whom 1 million were Arabs.

An increase in the Jewish population would come from a mass Jewish immigration from the countries of distress in Eastern Europe where the Jews were facing 'an elemental calamity, a kind of social earthquake'. There was 'an inherent xenophobia' – an 'anti-Semitism of things' – which was occurring and would reoccur. Both sides of the argument, Jabotinsky inferred, had a case to argue and the Commission had to strike a balance. For the Jews, however, the decisive factor was need.

If both sides of the Jordan were colonised, then based on the population density of Wales, the area could hold 8 million people. At the population density of England, it would increase to 18 million. With an influx of Jews, the Arabs of Palestine would become a minority. It would certainly be a disappointment, Jabotinsky pointed out, but it would not be a hardship.

The industrialisation of Palestine and the development of its economy in the 1930s had induced Arab immigration into the country from surrounding regions. Jabotinsky said that a million places in the economy would be reserved 'for their progeny' and this would make 'the Arabs happy'. Such amelioration did not impress one member of the Commission, Sir Laurie Hammond:

You can make the Arabs happy? If that is the case, why is it that the surrounding Arab states, Syria, Iraq, Trans-Jordania, do not welcome the Jews and ask them to come and give them the great happiness?

Hammond also asked Jabotinsky whether the Arabs as well as the Jews had needs.

Jabotinsky castigated the Zionist Left for its idealism in that, at the end of the day, Arabs would see the benefit of the Jewish presence in Palestine.

---

[44] Testimony of Vladimir Jabotinsky, 11 February 1937, *Palestine Royal Commission: Minutes of Evidence Heard at Public Sessions*, Colonial no. 134 (London, 1937).

'Some Jews think that they can bamboozle the Arabs. They can't. You can only carry Zionism through straightforward methods.'

He told the Commission members that the Jews were unable to make any meaningful compromise. What could be the concession made by an Oliver Twist? 'It is the workhouse people who have to concede a plate of soup,' he told them.

When the Commission said that more than two-thirds of Palestine belonged to the Arabs, Jabotinsky responded by stating that the Mandate was given to Britain independently of the Arab attitude. The Balfour Declaration was given solely to the Jews. If Britain was simply unable rather than unwilling to carry out the tenets of the Declaration, then it should hand the Mandate back and allow another country as 'a colonisation regime' to administer Palestine.

Jabotinsky was disdainful of Britain's ability to protect the Jews from Arab attack and asked for the legalisation of Jewish self-defence units. The Arab Revolt would have been stopped in its tracks in April and May 1936, he told the Commission, if 5,000 Jewish youth had been mobilised.

The Peel Commission's report proposed the partition of Palestine. Jabotinsky, it appears, was undecided initially and was prepared to consider the question of partition.[45] On this issue, he concurred with Weizmann and Ben-Gurion. Jabotinsky was attracted by the Commission's implicit recognition of the meaning of the Balfour Declaration – a state with a Jewish majority. It would certainly provide a shelter from the Nazi onslaught. Yet Jabotinsky rejected the establishment of a Palestinian Arab state. Partition, yes, but territorial autonomy, no.[46]

His colleagues in the New Zionist Organisation were less convinced. This was the public line that was followed, yet clearly Jabotinsky had reservations about it. Menahem Begin, Abba Ahimeir and the Maximalists had no such qualms. Demonstrations against partition were organised in Poland and Palestine.[47] The borders of the proposed much-reduced state would be impossible to defend, it was argued, but perhaps more central to the objection was the prospect of ideological and territorial

---

[45] Itzhak Galnoor, *The Partition of Palestine: Decision Crossroads in the Zionist Movement* (New York, 1995), pp. 109–10.
[46] Joseph Heller, 'Weizmann, Jabotinsky and the Arab Question: The Peel Affair', *Jerusalem Quarterly*, no. 26 (1983), pp. 109–26.
[47] *Hayarden*, 6 August 1937.

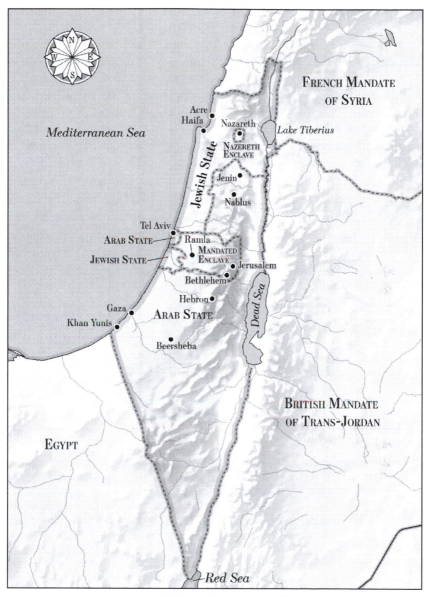

MAP 2. Peel Commission proposal (1937).

compromise. If 10,000 Jews were allowed to immigrate each year, even by 1970 the Jews would still be a minority of 41 percent.

Denouncing the report as 'irresponsible',[48] Jabotinsky now publicly took on the role of the vociferous opponent of partition, enlisting the

[48] Vladimir Jabotinsky, 'On the Partition', *Hayarden*, 13 August 1937.

help of Eamon De Valera, who saw the proposal in terms of the partition of Ireland.[49] The issue of reversing the first partition, which gave rise to TransJordan, was placed in abeyance and replaced as to how to avert a second partition. Some 20 percent of Palestine would be transformed into a Jewish state with a further 10 percent, including Jerusalem and the Christian holy places, to be administered by Britain. The Jewish state would comprise the Galilee, the Jezreel Valley and part of the coastal plain. In addition, Britain would have responsibility for four cities in the Jewish area, Haifa, Tiberias, Safed and Acre, which had substantial Arab populations. Sir Herbert Samuel himself described the geographical depiction of the two states as 'entwined in an inimical embrace like two fighting serpents'.[50] In a speech at Parliament on 13 July 1937, Jabotinsky asked if the Jews would now suffer the fate of the Armenians and the Assyrians. 'No Jew would renounce Jerusalem, Hebron and the land of Gilead, east of the Jordan.'

Jabotinsky found himself joining forces with labour Zionists such as Berl Katznelson and Golda Meir, General Zionists such as Menahem Ussishkin and Marxist Zionists such as Yitzhak Tabenkin in Palestine in opposing any hint of partition – as did the leaders of American Zionism, Stephen Wise, Abba Hillel Silver, Robert Szold, Julian Mack and Louis Brandeis.

Since any 'Jewish' state would essentially be a binational state, the Peel Commission recommended that 225,000 Arabs be transferred to the Palestinian state. Jabotinsky strongly opposed this. In general he opposed both compulsory and non-compulsory transfer of the Arabs, essentially on ethical grounds,[51] but also because he feared that it would set 'an instructive precedent indeed for Jew-baiters all over the world':[52]

They may call me an extremist, but at least I never dreamed of asking the Arabs who live in a Jewish country to emigrate. It would be a most dangerous precedent, extremely harmful to the Jewish interests in the Diaspora.

He also was concerned about provoking the Islamic world:

Inevitably, therefore, the question must arise of 'transferring' those Arabs elsewhere so as to make at least some room for Jewish newcomers. But it must be

[49] Shulamit Eliash, 'De Valera and the Palestine Partition Plan', *Cathedra* (September 2000), pp. 117–48.

[50] Howard M. Sacher, *History of Israel: From the Rise of Zionism to Our Time* (Oxford, 1977), p. 205.

[51] Vladimir Jabotinsky, 'A Talk with Zangwill', *Jewish Herald*, 4 August 1939.

[52] Joseph B. Schechtman, *Rebel and Statesman: The Jabotinsky Story – The Early Years, 1880–1923* (New York, 1956), p. 324.

hateful for any Jew to think that the rebirth of a Jewish State should ever be linked with such an odious suggestion as the removal of non-Jewish citizens.[53]

The Peel Commission report spoke about 'the instructive precedent' – 'that compulsory "exchange of population" between Greece and Turkey to which Greece was forced to agree after the 1923 disaster'.

The statement of the New Zionist Organisation (NZO) on the Peel Commission report suggested that Arabs would want to live and work in the industrialised and probably more prosperous state – it would be highly unlikely that they would leave voluntarily without coercion. In his articles in the late 1930s Jabotinsky occasionally mentioned the Turkish-Greek exchange of populations in the 1920s, yet he was clearly impressed by the proposed voluntary transfer of the southern Tyrol Germans from Italy to Germany, following an agreement between Hitler and Mussolini in June 1939. More than 70 percent opted for the transfer.[54] This reflected the approach of a broad spectrum of both proponents and opponents of the Peel report. They drew a distinction between the forcible expulsion of the Greeks by the Turks in the 1920s and a voluntary agreed departure with compensation if this is what the Arabs desired. The NZO statement on partition commented:

We regret that the Report should mention, in a very suggestive paragraph, 'the instructive precedent' of that 'compulsory exchange of population' between Greece and Turkey to which Greece was forced to agree after the 1923 disaster.[55]

By the late 1930s, thoughts about cooperation between Arabs and Jews which had been so prevalent were now considered unrealistic. The swift rise of Arab nationalism instead of Arab socialism had convinced many labour Zionist leaders – even if they voiced the same sentiments in the public arena.

Jabotinsky asked how this new 'Pale of Settlement' would be defended:

Most of it is lowland whereas the Arab reserve is all hills. Guns can be placed on the Arab hills within 15 miles of Tel Aviv and 20 miles from Haifa; in a few hours these towns can be destroyed, the harbours made useless and most of the places overrun whatever the valour of their defendants.

[53] Vladimir Jabotinsky, 'Points from V. Jabotinsky's Address', Dublin, 12 January 1938, Jabotinsky Institute Archives, Tel Aviv.

[54] Schechtman, *Rebel and Statesman*, p. 325.

[55] Memorandum on the Partition of Palestine, submitted to the Permanent Mandates Commission on behalf of the New Zionist Organisation, London, July 1937, Jabotinsky Institute Archives, Tel Aviv.

In contrast to the labour Zionists, Jabotinsky reiterated his view that the clash between the Jew and the Arab was inevitable and that this was the fate of all colonisations. He berated the British for a certain hypocrisy:

The history of the world is a history of colonisations ... (there has never been one example where the population on the spot 'agreed' to their country being colonised). You Anglo-Saxons colonised half the world, but you never colonised with the consent of the people in the countries which you colonised ... so how can we Jews colonise Palestine or Uganda or any other country without a contest of wills with the population on the spot? That is how all colonisations have been done – and should that be a crime, then it follows that America is a crime, this country is a crime, all Europe is a crime and our Bible history is the story of a crime.

Therefore the question is: is the Jewish colonisation necessary or not? Is it just or not? If it is necessary and just, then any local inhabitant who wants to obstruct something necessary and just must be prevented from using violence.[56]

At a meeting in Manchester in January 1938, he pointed out that 97 percent of the population of Alsace-Lorraine opted to stay under Prussian rule after its conquest.[57]

Jabotinsky drew a comparison with his Italian heroes, Garibaldi, Mazzini and Cavour, who disparaged the views of their partitionists. He ridiculed the very notion that a small state would permit expansion later on:

This will be a Jewish Piedmont, they dream, after that will come in turn Tuscany, Lombardy and so on ... today no nation allows successful penetration into their states, especially not to Jews. Arab irredentism will covet the capture of the Pale. The Jews would not emulate the citizens of Piedmont but would suffer the fate of the Armenians [at the hands of the Turks] and the Assyrians [at the hands of the Iraqis].

Jabotinsky argued that a state situated in the lowlands would allow the Arabs to occupy the highlands and position their guns on the hills. In contrast, he promoted his 'evacuatzia' plan. If the Jews were allowed to settle in TransJordan, they would transform the country within ten years 'with a solid majority of some 2 million Jews and 1.3 million Arabs'.[58]

---

[56] *Jewish Standard*, 12 September 1944.
[57] *Jewish Herald*, 7 January 1938.
[58] Vladimir Jabotinsky, 'Al tokhnit Ha-evakuatsyah', *Neumim, 1927–1940*, Ketavim 5, ed. Eri Jabotinsky (Tel Aviv, 1957–1958), pp. 197–212.

The broad opposition to partition was based on a plethora of reasons.[59] Some indicated that Eretz Israel – the Land of Israel – was a single unit, historically and geographically, and that the River Jordan did not divide its parts but joined them. Given the proposed dimensions, such a state would not be economically viable. Water sources would be lost and it would effectively ghettoise the Jews such that a large army would be required to defend its borders. Moreover, its small size would not attract further Jewish immigration. On the other hand, if this proved incorrect and 100,000 immigrants a year did actually come, then the population would be three times as dense as that of England – the densest in Europe.

The Zionist Left, on the other hand, rejected the report's contention that Jews and Arabs could not live together. They believed that it was only Jabotinsky's nationalists and their Arab counterparts who were essentially responsible for the impasse. Moreover, any form of partition would be bitterly resisted by the Arabs. It would have to be imposed upon them. Why then initiate conflict?

There were even those who understood that a state in 1937 was crucial to save those in the lands of distress in Eastern Europe but who opposed partition. Any immigration to such a narrow area would have to be based on a 'deluxe Zionism'. It would be selective and discriminate between those who possessed influence, wealth and standing and the masses, who did not.

British interests in the run-up to war turned to ensuring the supply of oil needed by its fighting machines to face Nazism. It was imperative, therefore, to halt Hitler's cultivation of Arab nationalism. Moreover, Jabotinsky perceived that Britain felt that the Palestine problem had become more trouble than it was worth. There was a sense of frustration and fatigue.

As the situation worsened in Europe, Jabotinsky's last years were taken up with opposing Britain's increasingly pro-Arab line, as evidenced by the White Paper of 1939. Jabotinsky raised the spectre of intercommunal conflict if Britain imposed an Arab government in Palestine, declaring that it would resemble the civil war in Spain:[60]

---

[59] Maurice J. Karpf, 'Partition of Palestine and Its Consequences', Address to the Regional Conference of the Council of Jewish Federations and Welfare Funds, Minneapolis, 24 October 1937 (American Jewish Committee, New York, 1938).

[60] Vladimir Jabotinsky, Speech at a meeting in North London, *Jewish Herald*, 6 January 1939.

For an Arab government to take control of the Jewish Yishuv, it will have to conquer, with arms and with blood, every street of every settlement and every backyard in the streets of towns.[61]

For Jabotinsky, the imperative was a Jewish majority with fair play and genuine representation for the Arab minority of 20–25 percent of the population. In his last book, Jabotinsky argued that Palestine could have an Arab deputy prime minister.

[61] Vladimir Jabotinsky, 'Vanity of Vanities', *Hayarden*, 2 February 1939; *Jewish Herald*, 17 February 1939.

8

The Road to Active Resistance

During the early 1930s, Jabotinsky began to devote time to determining how he could harness the energy of youth to power the cause of Zionism. The killings in 1929, the implacability of rising Arab nationalism and the rapid backtracking of the British from the commitment given in the Balfour Declaration attracted many young Jews to the Revisionist standard. Yet Jabotinsky understood that in the wider world, where the twin ideals of Fascism and Communism had mobilised European youth, 'a bald head is a rarity'.

Like the rest of his generation Jabotinsky believed that 1918 saw the dawn of a new peace, that World War I was truly the war which would end all wars. H. G. Wells's *Joan and Peter: The Story of an Education*, published in 1918, greatly impressed Jabotinsky. Wells wrote:

Mankind must learn the duties of human brotherhood and respect for the human adventure or waste and perish ... if in peacetime we cannot learn and choose between alternatives then through war we must.[1]

In contrast, the generation of the 1930s was one he found difficult to fathom. Andrè Gide's *The Counterfeiters* (1925) was a work he considered 'bad and unpleasant' – and symptomatic of the succeeding generation:

[1] H. G. Wells, *Joan and Peter: The Story of an Education* (London, 1918), p. 447.

All that marked youthful thinking at the beginning of the century – the torturing pangs of Nietzsche, Futurism, Russian Marxism, emotional strain, asceticism – all this has disappeared.[2]

Young people in 1930, he wrote, preferred to 'stand to attention and take clear, short, indisputable orders'. And whoever gave them orders was awarded the title of 'leader'. Jabotinsky commented that this word would not have been found 'in our vocabulary thirty years ago'. The young generation was simply not interested in parliament, freedom of the press and free speech. 'All the recent fashionable dictators have relied on young people.'[3] Fascism and Communism, he pointed out, were the choices of youth:

An entire people sometimes shouts for 'bread and circuses' and it later turns out that the chief trait of the time was a thirst for a new religion. It is far from seldom that people, especially in their youth, do not exactly understand what it is that they thirst for, while it is this 'thirst', the tastes and appetites of a generation which define its 'soul'.[4]

His youthful interest in Italy never left him. He had read Ernest Hemingway's *A Farewell to Arms* about the disastrous Italian campaign in World War I. Hemingway's masterpiece left him quite depressed at what had transpired. The work of Italian authors such as Guido da Verona, a Jew who signed the manifesto of Fascist intellectuals, distressed him. Italy had changed under Mussolini. 'All young Italians are itching for a fight,' he wrote. All this was a far cry from his experience of his own days in Rome.[5]

Yet following the Katowice conference, Jabotinsky lost all his old comrades on the Revisionist Executive who wished to remain within the Zionist Organisation. Grossman, Machover and the others formed the Jewish State party in August 1933. Jabotinsky now found himself boxed in and allied to both the impressionable youth of Betar and the Maximalists. Despite his desire to forge a youth movement uninfluenced by either Fascism or Communism, Betar was perceived as no more than an ideological clone. Following the Vienna conference in September 1932, one highly critical editorial in a Jewish weekly commented:

Inclined towards the dramatic and spectacular, [Jabotinsky] encouraged Jewish youth to [adopt] the current methods of flash and splash such as uniforms,

[2] Vladimir Jabotinsky, 'The Unknown Race', Jabotinsky Institute Archives, Tel Aviv; *Causeries* (Paris, 1930), pp. 101–18.
[3] Ibid.
[4] Ibid.
[5] Ibid.

military salutes and other forms of outward display – unwholesome manifestations borrowed from undesirable outside sources wholly contrary to Jewish ideas and ideals. Having been taught to react, the daily routine of Zionist work as too slow and too dull, the Revisionists are now clamouring for the adventurous and exciting methods which they learned to expect, but which their leaders cannot provide; their teaching to the youth has not been that kind of impatience that moves one to do his duty to the ideal he believes in by steady work, but rather the impatience which produces stupid recklessness and irresponsible acts on the part of those who have some courage if no wisdom, or, if bereft of both, who find expression in foolish words ... The anarchy they have introduced is beginning to recoil on their own heads as they must have learned from the wild talk of some of their adherents at the Vienna Conference to whom they had to appeal for discipline and loyalty which they themselves have taught them to despise.[6]

The First World Conference of Betar had taken place in Danzig in April 1931. Delegates from eighteen countries were present, representing 22,000 people, more than 14,000 of whom came from Poland. Jabotinsky faced in different directions at the same time. On the one hand, he argued in the 'Song of Betar' that the new Jew would be 'proud and generous and cruel'.[7] On the other, he proclaimed:

Hatred of war is our heritage; our prophets were the first to protest against mass murder; we accept their teachings and no one is thinking of training a generation that will love war'.[8]

Jabotinsky wanted tough, trained, disciplined young Jews who abhorred war and would defend their people at a moment's notice. He wanted Betar to be 'a Jewish army in the making'. His model was not the youth groups of Mussolini's Italy or indeed any other authoritarian country, but the Sokol youth movement of Masaryk's Czechoslovakia. He was impressed by Masaryk's memoirs, which depicted thousands of youth in the Ringplatz, Prague:

Some thousands of young men and girls stood in the great Ringplatz, equidistant from each other, like chessmen, all dressed uniformly, and immobile as if they had been carved of granite. Then the leader blew a whistle and all those thousands of men and women extended first the left hand and the right foot. That was all. But they did it all as one man, 'like a machine'.[9]

The Danzig conference instructed Betar's work brigades to include security service. Such imagery appealed to Jabotinsky – and to his sympathy

[6] *Jewish Chronicle*, 16 September 1932.
[7] Vladimir Jabotinsky, 'Song of Betar', *Hazit Ha'am*, 14 and 22 March 1932.
[8] Vladimir Jabotinsky, 'Militarism', *Haynt*, 25 January 1929.
[9] Ibid.

with Futurism, whose evolution he had followed both in pre-war Russia and pre-war Italy.

Le Figaro in Paris in 1909 had published the Futurist manifesto by the Italian poet Filippo Tommaso Marinetti. It celebrated change, difference and innovation. It also glorified 'aggressive action'. It lauded technology and its seductive power. It advocated a destruction of the past and an embrace of an unconventional future. The manifesto's rhetoric was acerbic and uncompromising. The movement also drew its inspiration from Georges Sorel's *Reflections on Violence*. In 1915, Marinetti commented:

With us has begun the reign of the man whose roots are cut, the multiplied man who merges himself with iron, is fed by electricity and no longer understands anything except the sensual delight of danger and quotidian heroism.[10]

In Russia, Futurism found advocates in Velimir Khlebnikov and Vladimir Mayakovsky. They called their manifesto 'A Slap in the Face of Public Taste'. As early as 1912 Jabotinsky was utilising Futurist ideas in a discussion about the philosophies of Rousseau, Montesquieu and Machiavelli.[11] The ideological leader, he argued, was the primary cog in the machine, without which it could not move. Jabotinsky's former colleague from Odessa, Kornei Chukovsky, reviewed and supported the Futurists in his articles.

Vladimir Mayakovsky commented that 'in every young man, [there is] Marinetti's gunpowder'. Futurism revelled in youth and exhorted its followers to maintain a state of perpetual youth. T. S. Eliot and James Joyce were influenced by Futurism.[12] Jabotinsky regarded it as a forerunner of Mussolini's Fascism, but not fascism itself.

Such ideas were already in circulation when symbolism began to fall out of favour in fin-de-siècle Russia. Even in his early Zionist phase, Jabotinsky wrote that 'with a hundred thousand hammers we shall strike ... the very earth shall tremble'.[13] While Marinetti was arguing for a new Italian, disciplined and strong – a person who with his or her comrades would be synchronised like a machine, Jabotinsky took elements of Futurism in forging Betar.[14]

[10] Jonathan Galassi, 'Speed in Life and Death', *New York Review of Books*, 19 June 2014.
[11] Vladimir Jabotinsky, 'Podzhigatel', *Odesskie Novosti*, 15 June 1912.
[12] Galassi, 'Speed in Life and Death'.
[13] Vladimir Jabotinsky, 'Hesped', *Evreiskaya zhizn*, no. 6, June 1904.
[14] Arye Naor, 'Jabotinsky's New Jew: Concept and Models', *Journal of Israeli History*, vol. 30, no.2 (September 2011), pp. 141–59.

Jabotinsky wanted to change the imagery and the habits of the Jew:

The average Jew has no particular grace in walking, in wearing his clothes, in his way of eating or his social intercourse; it shows badly when he has to deal with some hierarchy, when he has to talk to a high dignitary, even when it happens to be of his own people; he feels that he must show him some special mark of respect, and he does not know how to do it without losing his dignity, so that the result is that it looks very much like insolence or cringing.[15]

The ideas of Marinetti, he argued, were more pervasive than the bluster of Mussolini's Fascism.[16] Jabotinsky applied this idea of everyone working together as a machine to Betar in the 1930s. The example of the Czech Sokol was often quoted as the exemplar of voluntary discipline.

Unity in the struggle for a state was all-important. Jabotinsky's view of Betar was that it should 'act in unison born of a single desire'. Moreover, unlike coercive Fascism, the individual members of a nation should come to this conclusion voluntarily. If a national group, Jabotinsky argued, did not know how to become a machine by its own volition, then it was simply no better than an unruly mob. The members had to be whatever the struggle for the establishment of a Jewish state required of them.

The idea of a new Jew influenced Zionists across the political spectrum. Jabotinsky was influenced in this respect not only by Futurism, but also by nineteenth-century romantic nationalism, the writings of Nietzsche and early Zionist writers such as Micha Berdichevsky rather than Ahad Ha'am, who wrote about the Jewish talent for morality as opposed to seeking a political solution to the Jewish problem.

The life and works of Max Nordau were rebranded for the Betar generation. Yet Jabotinsky had vehemently disagreed with him on a number of issues over the years, such as his ambivalence in 1915 to the establishment of the Jewish Legion[17] and advocacy of unrestricted immigration into Palestine in 1919.[18] In later years he depicted Nordau differently:

They still learned from his writings that profound insolence in the face of any veil, any mask, the essential abomination that lies behind any altar, the now all-but-forgotten refusal to forgive, rejection of compromise, rage and hatred of

---

[15] Vladimir Jabotinsky, 'Militarism', *Haynt*, 25 January 1929.
[16] Vladimir Jabotinsky, *Avtobiyografyah: Sipur Yamai*, Ketavim 1, ed. E. Jabotinsky (Jerusalem, 1958), p. 29.
[17] Michael Stanislawski, *Zionism and the Fin de Siècle: Cosmopolitanism and Nationalism from Nordau to Jabotinsky* (Berkeley, 2001), pp. 239–48.
[18] Vladimir Jabotinsky, 'Aliyah', *Hadashot Ha'aretz*, 14 November 1919.

ugliness and untruth – in short, they learned from him the secret of revolution ... Nordau was the ruler of the rebellious spirits.[19]

On the one hand, Jabotinsky promoted that each and every downtrodden Jew was a king and the heir to King David. On the other, each had to voluntarily act as a reliable component of a human machine. At a Betar conference in Warsaw in May 1939, he commented on the individuality of the Jew:

A king is nobody's subject. That the Jew organically hates being a subject and hates taking orders is a well-known complaint even in our present days; in our olden days, our Bible called us stiff-necked.[20]

Yet quoting from the first book of Samuel, he told his audience that the leaders of the Jewish people desperately desired a king to rule over them, and Samuel rebuked them in the strongest terms in that they would eventually be oppressed by a monarch.[21] It was, Jabotinsky pointed out, the earliest record of a clash between 'the love of freedom and the need for constituted authority':

[Our ancestors] had to bow before the necessities of common defence against invaders and of order amongst themselves, which meant a state with a monarch, but they hated it and believed that God Himself hated it, and they would have liked it much better to obey God only – which would have meant, at least in theory, obeying one's own conscience.[22]

ON MILITARY ACTION

Jabotinsky's vision of Betar meant controlled activism rather than military actions. It meant preparing for a Jewish army rooted in nineteenth-century independence movements rather than a Jewish underground. In order to maintain his direction for Betar, polarisation and radicalisation had to be prevented. Yet numerous factors mitigated against eventual success. Jabotinsky's theoretical approach was sophisticated and complex, not a black-and-white scenario which all could understand. The lack of progress with the British and the increasing belligerence of Arab nationalism attracted Zionist youth towards a radical position – towards Ahimeir's

---

[19] Jabotinsky, *Avtobiyografyah*, Ketavim 1, p. 112. English translation in Stanislawski, *Zionism and the Fin de Siècle*, p. 241.
[20] *Hamedina*, 12 May 1939.
[21] 1 Samuel 8:1–22.
[22] Vladimir Jabotinsky, 'The Betar View on State and Social Problems', *Hadar*, November 1940.

revolutionary Zionism rather than to Jabotinsky's evolutionary approach through negotiations. Moreover, the fallout from the Katowice conference meant that all Jabotinsky's long-time experienced colleagues who by and large professed similar views were now outside his political orbit. The youth of Betar and the Maximalists were now the dominant voices within Revisionism and were pressing Jabotinsky to adopt the policies and persona that he was fundamentally opposed to.

While he was opposed to Ahimeir's acceptance of dictatorship and the negation of democracy, he appreciated Ahimeir's ability to imbue youth with the passion of revolt. Jabotinsky therefore warmed to the demonstrations of Berit Ha-Biryonim,[23] and in a speech to the Second World Conference of Betar in Kraków at the beginning of 1935, he told them how much he appreciated Ahimeir.[24] He also supported the student disruption of Bentwich's inaugural lecture:

Could you have looked on in silence when a Jewish institution was being turned into a nest of vipers for sanballats, a centre for the destruction of the national movement, an agency for Passfield's helpers?[25]

The article was vitriolic and directed at Bentwich. It supported the action and praised Ahimeir, 'our teacher and master'.

Did Jabotinsky become more antagonistic towards the British after the disturbances of 1929, the negative reports of 1930, the frustration and lack of advance at the Zionist congress? Was it MacDonald's letter in February 1931? Moreover, did he really believe that freedom of speech in the case of Bentwich's inaugural lecture was unimportant? This was the first time that Jabotinsky had endorsed dubious actions. It seemed that Jabotinsky and Ahimeir were in agreement in criticising such internal enemies.

In his well-known article 'Afn Pripitshek', first published in Warsaw in October 1931, in which he advised his followers 'to learn to shoot', Jabotinsky was almost fatalistic about the need to be trained for armed warfare:

A few years ago, I would not have said this, for it was then clear that hardly anyone would have acknowledged it. Now, however, it is clear. The bitter truth has been learnt by all without exception – religious Jews, left Jews, Jewish Communists, pacifists, assimilationists – it is even clear to them that the rebirth

[23] Vladimir Jabotinsky, 'The Worthless Congress', *Hazit Ha'am*, 15 September 1933.
[24] *Hayarden*, 15 and 16 January 1935.
[25] Vladimir Jabotinsky, 'On Adventurism', *Haynt*, 26 February 1932.

FIGURE 7. Betar members in Vilna (1929).
Courtesy of the Jabotinsky Institute, Tel Aviv.

as it was dreamed about for thousands of years cannot be achieved if we do not
know how to shoot.[26]

Betar was concentrated in Poland, and it was here that Polish nationalism ironically served as a model even though members of Betar were
barred from entering its portals. Both Menahem Begin and Yitzhak
Shamir knew and were inspired by Mickiewicz's patriotic poems, such as
'Konrad Wallenrod' and 'Pan Tadeusz'.[27]

Jabotinsky had held highly critical views of Polish nationalism
in the debate with Dmowski and his followers.[28] With the rise of the
new Poland, Józef Pilsudski had been the great teacher and guide of his
people – something Jabotinsky could identify with:

Ritual demonstrates man's superiority over beast. What is the difference between
a civilized man and a wild man? Ceremony. Everything in the world is ritual.
A court trial – ceremony. How else is a case conducted in court? The judge opens
the session and gives the floor to the prosecutor; then to the counsel for defence ...
It may be that the most important of all the new ideas which Betar has given to

[26] *Haynt*, 16 October 1931; *Jewish Herald*, 12 September 1947.
[27] Menachem Begin, *White Nights: The Story of a Prisoner in Russia* (London, 1957), pp.
174–175; Yitzhak Shamir, *Summing Up* (London, 1994), p. 6.
[28] Joseph B. Schechtman, *The Jabotinsky Story: Rebel and Statesman – the Early Years,
1880–1923* (New York, 1956), pp. 148–49.

the Jewish ghetto is the idea of ceremony. The special uniform seemed strange to the Jewish public fifteen years ago. And so did all our other habits – standing upright, walking straight, and so on.[29]

On Pilsudski's death in 1935, Jabotinsky compared him to Trumpeldor in a public eulogy in Kraków.[30] Jabotinsky was alone in doing so, for many parties in the Zionist movement in Poland had visibly recoiled from eulogising Pilsudski. A majority view was that Polish nationalism had taken a wrong turn into a sectarian dead-end street. Jabotinsky's depiction of Polish dislike of Jews as 'the anti-Semitism of things' was balanced by a quiet admiration for Polish nationalism. The members of Polish Betar, whether consciously or not, were influenced Pilsudski's nationalism.[31]

Jabotinsky argued that the Jews had given birth to messianism and told the members of Betar:

In the earliest history of the Jews we find Israel, the man who fought with God and conquered, because not everything in God's world was created as it should be. We have to improve that world; and for 3,000 years we have been wandering and aspiring for perfection. We are specialists in this matter …

If you want to serve entire humanity – serve your nation and build for it a laboratory of its own.[32]

Betar's close identification with Poland – and especially a misplaced confidence in its military ability – fuelled a secular messianism about the Jewish future.

The unusual synthesis of a monist Zionist nationalist with a universalist Russian intellectual meant that Jabotinsky's fashioning of Betar was always hedged with a qualifying commentary. Thus Jabotinsky warned at the beginning of 1929 that 'the cult of ritual may encourage at first a tendency to futile and needless arrogance of pomp and mummery. That may sometimes prove extremely distasteful.'[33]

Despite the attempted recruitment of religious Jews to his movement, he continued to enunciate his belief that it was the national spirit that had preserved the Jews down the centuries and not Judaism and the rabbis. He maintained that reading works by the early Zionists, Smolenskin,

[29] Vladimir Jabotinsky, 'Address to the First World Conference of Betar', Danzig, April 1931, *Hadar* November 1940.
[30] Vladimir Jabotinsky, 'Address to a Revisionist Conference in Warsaw', *Medina Iwrit*, 22 May 1936.
[31] Israel Eldad, *Ma'aser Rishon* (Tel Aviv, 1976), pp. 340–41.
[32] Vladimir Jabotinsky, *Hadar*, November 1940.
[33] Jabotinsky, 'Militarism'.

Gordon, Pinsker, Ahad Ha'am, Herzl and Nordau, was important in order 'to instil European culture in the place of obscurantist orthodoxy'.[34] In strongly defending freedom of the press in the 1930s, he argued that the biblical equivalent was the Prophets' defence of liberty. The Prophets should not be seen as 'clergymen delivering regulation sermons', he pointed out, but as free men who opposed and criticised and commented on the issues of the day:

Lots of [their commentaries] sound so violent that no censor now would [allow them] if those men were our contemporaries in any country where censorship exists; in their own lifetime they were also persecuted, as often as not, by the powers of the state, of riches, and of the mob. Yet their words were carefully recorded and preserved: our Old Testament is a mighty monument to the sanctity of free revolutionary speech.[35]

For all his advocacy of monism, Jabotinsky lived in and was acutely aware of the outside world. This stood in distinct contrast to the world-view of his parochial Polish acolytes. Jabotinsky did not see the state as an end in itself, but as a means of redeeming the Jewish people. This in turn would assist in furthering human progress.

Jabotinsky spoke about the three stages of Zionism, the last of which would be the creation of a culture which would contribute to the world. At the founding of the New Zionist Organisation in September 1935, Jabotinsky invoked the Prophet Isaiah and told his audience, 'Out of Zion shall go forth the Law'.[36]

From the inception of the Revisionist movement, Jabotinsky had stressed the importance of working with non-Jews and indeed criticised the Zionist movement for its narrow attitude towards the non-Jewish world:

Theirs is a typical ghetto mentality which regards all non-Jews as goyim, as enemies. With such a mentality nothing can be achieved. It is time that the Jewish people began to have confidence in the goyim. The goyim have not produced only Hamans; they have also produced great idealists who have given their blood for the cause of humanity. I say morenu ve-rabenu ha-goy – our teacher and mentor, the gentile.[37]

[34] Vladimir Jabotinsky, 'A Social Countenance', *Doar Hayom*, 28 January 1929.
[35] Ibid.
[36] Vladimir Jabotinsky, Speech on the Founding of the New Zionist Organisation in Vienna, 7 September 1935, *Neumim, 1927–1940*, Ketavim 5, ed. E. Jabotinsky (Tel Aviv, 1957–1958), p. 180.
[37] Vladimir Jabotinsky, 'Speech to the Second World Conference of the Revisionist Movement', *Rassviet*, 9 January 1927; *Jewish Daily News Bulletin*, 27 December 1926.

The cosmopolitan Jabotinsky coexisted with the fatalistic Jabotinsky. In 'Homo Homini Lupus' in 1911, he indicated his disillusionment with classical liberalism. In a sense Jabotinsky was also a man of his times, as Dubnov had written in 1905:

Take into account this direct sense of the people, this psyche of the sufferers, these emotions and moods, which, more than abstract ideas, are the driving force of history! And this popular consciousness, which grasps recent events more correctly, tells us 'Do not trust Amalek, be it the government, or as the people, because the old Russia can appear as the new!³⁸

Jabotinsky was seen by his opponents as the mesmerising orator whose inspiring words would divert his young charges into unthinking channels. In the 1930s Jabotinsky used his rhetoric and charisma to tremendous effect. Yet privately – at least at the beginning of the Revisionist movement – Jabotinsky railed against the hero worship that was being directed towards him. He complained that he was being turned into a myth, a modern-day *wunder-rebbe*.³⁹ This promotion of the cult of personality angered him.⁴⁰ Yet he permitted it to develop unbounded in the 1930s, possibly because he believed that this was the way of this generation of youth. If he wished to build a movement, if he wished to keep young Jews away from worshipping Mussolini and Stalin, then perhaps this was the price that had to be paid. It also implicitly distinguished him from the approach taken by Grossman, who was more grounded in his attention to party matters.

The New Zionist Organisation, founded in 1935, was supposed to be an answer to the inertia of the 'old' Zionist organisation of Weizmann and Sokolov. It proved to be a hollow and radicalised version of the Revisionists. It was bereft of finance, ill-organised in the absence of Grossman and his former colleagues, and Jabotinsky found it increasingly difficult to control the youth, both in Betar and in the Irgun.

---

³⁸ Simon Dubnov, *Voskhod*, 1 December 1905, in Sophie Dubnov-Erlich, *The Life and Work of S. M. Dubnov: Diaspora Nationalism and Jewish History* (Bloomington, IN, 1991), p. 19.

³⁹ Vladimir Jabotinsky, Letter to Joanna Jabotinsky, 27 February 1927, *Igrot, 1926–1927* (Jerusalem, 2000).

⁴⁰ Vladimir Jabotinsky, Letter to Miriam Lang, 27 August 1930, *Igrot, 1930–1931* (Jerusalem, 2004); *Ha-Umma*, vol. 3–4, no. 61–62 (September 1980), pp. 332–337, in Yaakov Shavit, 'Fire and Water: Ze'ev Jabotinsky and the Revisionist Movement', *Studies in Zionism*, no. 2 (Autumn 1981), p. 224.

MENAHEM BEGIN AND THE MAXIMALISTS

The clear-cut activism of Ahimeir and Berit Ha-Biryonim set the pattern for Betar in Poland. By 1932 Berit Ha-Biryonim had become increasingly popular in Poland. Ahimeir visited Poland to speak to many enthusiastic followers, and there was further radicalisation when Uri Zvi Greenberg moved to Warsaw to edit *Di Velt*, the Revisionists' Yiddish publication.

One young Betar leader, Menahem Begin from Brest-Litovsk, wholeheartedly identified with the cause of Maximalist Zionism in Palestine and adhered to only those of Jabotinsky's policies which followed this direction.

The Council of Regional Commands of Betar had met in Warsaw shortly after the Katowice conference. In 1933, there were thirteen regional commands. The most active was the eastern Galicia region around Lvov with 128 cells. Begin's section command for the Polsia region contained 59 cells. At the conference Begin praised the training at Betar 'institutions' – the agricultural school in Vilna, the carpentry workshop in Szczecin and the foundry in Suwalki. Begin at that time was involved in questions of organisation for Betar.[41] Its members were informed that there were more than 30,000 'brothers and sisters' in Poland.[42]

As a signatory to the Polish Maximalists' collective letter following the Katowice conference, Begin believed that normative Zionism under Weizmann and Ben-Gurion had blurred the vision of a Jewish state as the central solution to the Jewish problem. The Revisionist Executive, which had just been removed at the conference in Katowice, had similarly compromised the purpose of Zionism by opting to remain within the Zionist Organisation. Begin believed that 'the great permanent revolution in Zionism' had become mired in the mud since Revisionism had distanced itself from 'active resistance'. Polish Betar had kept its distance since its earliest days when it rejected becoming part of the Revisionist movement at its first gathering in January 1929. Indeed, there was an understanding that Betar would be autonomous and not engage in political activity as an independent faction.[43]

---

[41] Mo'etset ha-mifkadot ha-gelilot shel Berit Trumpeldor be-Polina, Warsaw, 8 June 1933, Begin Heritage Center Archives, Jerusalem.

[42] On 11 February 1932, there were 33,422 members. Begin Heritage Center Archives, Jerusalem.

[43] Vladimir Jabotinsky, Letter to the Revisionist Executive, 17 August 1931, *Igrot, 1930–1931*).

Begin was involved with Betar from its very beginnings. Originally a member of Hashomer Hatzair, his father enforced his departure when the movement moved to the left in Palestine in the mid-1920s.[44] Hashomer had originally been an apolitical movement. However, a poem in its journal, *El-Al*, expressed Polish Jewish youth's desire to break away from the past and from parental authority. This unnerved religious circles in Poland, particularly in the aftermath of the October Revolution. It was then a short step from advocacy of a counterculture to the embrace of Marxism as a third way between labour Zionism and Communism.[45]

In parallel with the Amlanim of Hapoel Hatzair, a national breakaway group was established which gradually moved towards Revisionism.[46] A former Hashomer member, Ruben Feldschu (Ben Shem), was engaged in appealing to the Polish Jewish intelligentsia to join Jabotinsky's movement in the late 1920s. He wrote *Czerwone dusze* (Red souls), which dealt with the changes in Hashomer Hatzair.[47]

In July 1929 Menahem Begin came to Warsaw to participate in ceremonies to commemorate the twenty-fifth anniversary of Herzl's death. Accompanied by martial music, the members of Betar marched through the streets of Warsaw to Pilsudski Square, where they laid a wreath on the Tomb of the Unknown Soldier.[48]

In *Betar and Its Message: A Letter to Jewish Parents*, written in 1933, Begin railed against 'the red poison' and claimed that 'Betar's actions are non-revolutionary'.[49] Yet Begin and his Maximalist co-signatories, following the Katowice conference, argued that the Revisionist movement should be reconstructed – this time on the basis of hierarchy, discipline and total obedience to the senior leadership – and this meant 'first and foremost to the only dominant force, the creator of Revisionism [Jabotinsky]'.

---

[44] Aviva Halamish, 'The Historic Leadership of Hakibbutz Ha'artzi: The Power of Charisma, Organisation and Ideology', *Journal of Israeli History*, vol. 30, no. 1 (March 2012), pp. 45–66.

[45] Ofer N. Nur, 'The Relevance of Countercultures and Visions of the Future: Examining the Historical Example of Hashomer Hatzair', in Joerg Forbrig, ed., *Revisiting Youth Political Participation: Challenges for Research and Democratic Practice in Europe* (Council of Europe, March 2007), pp. 37–42.

[46] Daniel K. Heller, 'The Rise of the Zionist Right: Polish Jews and the Betar Youth Movement, 1922–1935' (Ph.D. diss., Stanford University, 2012), pp. 60–62.

[47] Laurence Weinbaum, 'Shaking the Dust Off: The Story of the Warsaw Ghetto's Forgotten Chronicler, Ruben Feldschu (Ben Shem)', *Jewish Political Studies Review*, vol. 22, nos. 3 and 4 (Fall 2010), pp. 1–32.

[48] Amos Perlmutter, *The Life and Times of Menachem Begin* (New York, 1987), pp. 57–58.

[49] Ibid., p. 64.

There was no place for amateurs and hangers-on. Revisionism, he argued, must be the advance guard of the Jewish people.

All this adhered far more to the 'revolutionary Zionism' of Abba Ahimeir than to the approach of Vladimir Jabotinsky in his declining years. In only the second edition of Betar's weekly, *Hamedina*, founded in February 1933, Ahimeir was described as the 'head of the Sicarii', 'the Great Zealot, the darling of Jewish youth'. He was quoted approvingly on his views on the direction that the members of Betar should follow – 'to cleanse the soul of idolatry, to form battalions for the war against anti-Semitism ... to learn from Garibaldi, Pilsudski, Gandhi, and especially, from de Valera ... a revolutionary Zionism must be created'.[50]

Begin contributed a few early articles – mainly in Yiddish – to *Hamedina* and to *Unzer Welt* in which he developed his Maximalist views and in particular railed against socialist Zionists.[51] Indeed, he informed Jabotinsky that his socialist critics assailed him with the epithet 'Vladimir Hitler'. He also inferred that Ahimeir offered an alternative pathway.[52]

Jabotinsky's task allotted by the Polish Maximalists was therefore to guide the movement along 'the route of recovery from its childhood illnesses'. 'The youth after the war want to be commanded and they will obey.' There was thus a short step from Ahimeir's revolutionary Zionism to Begin's embryonic military Zionism. Indeed, by the end of 1934 Begin was already writing articles which extolled the virtues of militarism and patriotism.[53]

Betar in Catholic Poland was much more traditionalist than Jabotinsky and his former colleagues on the Revisionist Executive – all assimilated and acculturated Russian Jews who had embraced Zionism. Despite this, a reaction to the anti-religious zeitgeist of the early socialist Zionists was often translated into a more benevolent attitude towards religious Jews and religious Zionism.[54] Polish Betar voted overwhelmingly to side with Jabotinsky during the post-Katowice rift with the Revisionist Executive.

Jabotinsky came and spoke to them – after his declaration at Lodz and his dispute with the other Revisionists. He told them:

This is the third attempt to forge the Zionist movement. Pinsker made the first attempt, Herzl the second, and we are currently engaged in the third. The Tsohar movement will develop and grow. It will first become a majority within Zionism,

50 *Hamedina*, 19 February 1933.
51 Menahem Begin, *Hamedina*, 1 December 1933; *Unzer Welt*, 21 July 1935; 21 May 1937.
52 Menahem Begin, *Hamedina*, 16 February 1933.
53 Menahem Begin, *Hamedina*, 25 October 1934.
54 Eliezer Don-Yehiya and Charles Liebman, 'Zionist Ultra-nationalism and Its Attitude toward Religion', *Journal of Church and State*, vol. 23, no . 2 (1981), pp. 250–73.

and then will become Zionism itself. Betar will be the moral and spiritual law-giver for all Jewish youth.[55]

While Begin distanced himself from Ahimeir's sympathy for Italian Fascism and pro-Franco views,[56] he also wanted an end to any cooperation with England. The administration in Palestine was no more than a government of occupation. The Polish Maximalists demanded a strengthening of the role of the National Labour Union based on national syndicalist foundations. It would fight against the monopoly of the Histadrut and 'the Marxist camp in Eretz Israel'.

They further called for the establishment of a stable defensive force in Palestine to ensure security. The existence of strong support for the Maximalists in both Poland and Palestine meant an increasing cooperation. Indeed, Ahimeir believed that the number of emissaries of the Revisionists and Betar visiting Poland far exceeded the number of functionaries going in the opposite direction.[57]

At the Revisionist World Conference in Poland in February 1934, Begin spoke in favour of the 'Betarisation' of the movement. Jabotinsky fundamentally placed his hope in England and in negotiations. His supporters did not adhere to this belief and desired instead the gun and the bomb.

Jabotinsky was elated by the vibrancy of the youth movement that he had nurtured. At the same time he was depressed by its inability to see beyond the polarised views of black and white, right and wrong. This may well have been a factor in his attempt to douse the flames of conflict between his supporters and those of Ben-Gurion – especially when Nazism was gathering strength and influence. On another level, Jabotinsky attempted to rival the Maximalists in terms of public relations rather than policy.[58]

Yet his attempts to find common ground with Ben-Gurion were unexpectedly successful. In a letter to Edna Jacobi – in whose London home Jabotinsky met Ben-Gurion to conduct quiet negotiations – he commented, 'Our mutual friendliness and cordiality is a surprise to both of us'.[59] Yet such bonhomie was not conveyed to either leader's followers, and their accord was rejected in shock and disgust.

[55] Chaim Ben-Yerucham, ed., *Sefer Betar: Korot u-mekorot*, vol. 2, '*From the People*' (Tel Aviv, 1969), pp. 441–45.
[56] Abba Ahimeir, 'Alcazar and Restraint', *Hayarden*, 6 November 1936.
[57] Abba Ahimeir, *Moto shel Yosef Katsnelson* (Tel Aviv, 1974), p. 91.
[58] Vladimir Jabotinsky, 'Maximalism', *Moment*, 1 February 1935.
[59] Vladimir Jabotinsky, Letter to Edna Jacobi, 4 November 1934, in Rodney Benjamin and David Cebon, *The Forgotten Zionist: The Life of Solomon (Sioma) Yankelevitch Jacobi* (Jerusalem, 2012), p. 175.

Menahem Begin adamantly refused to consider any rapprochement with labour Zionism. Instead he propagated the approach of Ahimeir rather than that of Jabotinsky. In the days before the founding conference of the New Zionist Organisation, Begin wrote to Ahimeir and congratulated him on his release from prison. Seemingly speaking in the name of Polish Betar, Begin asked him to attend the conference.[60] Ahimeir did not respond to this invitation.[61] At the same time Begin penned an adulatory article in Yiddish about Ahimeir.[62] The time for Ahimeir's ideas was fast approaching, and not least his belief that the third stage of Zionism, military Zionism, was the only way forward.[63] The presence of Abba Ahimeir, Uri Zvi Greenberg and Avraham Stern in Poland provided an intellectual nucleus for the radicalisation of Polish Betar. It also provided an ideological template for Menahem Begin.[64]

With the outbreak of the Arab Revolt in 1936 and the deteriorating situation in Poland, Begin began to speak out against Jabotinsky's reliance on diplomacy and to place the emphasis on the armed struggle. He spoke of it as 'a mission of heroic desperation'.[65]

Betar in Poland was heavily involved in the Revisionist campaign in 1937 to oppose the Peel Commission's plan to partition Palestine into Jewish and Arab states. Begin was arrested and imprisoned for several weeks following a demonstration outside the British consulate in Warsaw.[66]

Just before the first conference of the NZO in Prague at the beginning of 1938, Menahem Begin, Avraham Stern and others published the manifesto of the 'Activist-Revisionist Front'. While they acknowledged the debt they owed to Jabotinsky in calling themselves 'the spiritual sons of the iron typewriter of Jabotinsky', the manifesto was also an undisguised attack on his policies:

When it was founded and during the first years of its existence, Revisionism was understood by the Jewish masses, especially by the youth, as a revolutionary fighting movement, aiming at national liberation by means of uncompromising military action, both against the external enemy and against the internal traitors

[60] According to the testimony of Yohanan Bader, Begin refused to attend the NZO conference in Vienna. Testimony of Bader, 9 December 1992, Israel State Archives, quoted in Avi Shilon, *Menachem Begin: A Life* (London, 2012), p. 16.

[61] Perlmutter, *The Life and Times of Menachem Begin*, p. 71.

[62] Menahem Begin, *Unzer Welt*, 9 August 1935.

[63] Abba Ahimeir, 'Hashluv hashlishi', *Hayarden*, 18 October 1935.

[64] Menahem Begin, 'Der Shames', *Hamedina*, 15 July 1935.

[65] Perlmutter, *The Life and Times of Menachem Begin*, p. 81.

[66] Menahem Begin, *Metzudah* July 1937.

and unbelievers. However, in recent years Revisionism has restricted itself to the method of secret diplomacy, which we have mocked so much, in the direction of a completely pro-British orientation. The postulate of mass pressure on the external political factors has been completely forgotten. Within the Jewish people, the party executive has pursued an unceasing policy of seeking peace, thus ignoring the historic chances for a victorious crusade against liquidatory Zionism.[67]

It berated any attempt to come to terms with Ben-Gurion and his party. Instead it signalled an approval of the Irgun, 'our fighting units in the Land of Israel, who adopted the way of active opposition in their war against the mandatory government', and stated that they had been abandoned by the NZO. What was needed, Begin and his supporters argued, was a remodelling of Revisionism on revolutionary lines:

The Revisionist movement must be completely rebuilt, from the foundations upwards. It will cease to be a mass movement and become a closed pioneering group of faithful members, ready for self-sacrifice. Therefore the focus will be transferred from the branch to the individual member. Entrance into the movement will be made more difficult, and everyone who enlists will have to pass through several levels of status until he becomes a member of the Union of Zionist Revisionists with full rights.

In a separate address to members of both Betar and the Irgun who were present at the Prague conference, Jabotinsky attempted to explain his understanding of the adjective 'revolutionary'. It did not impress his audience, which understood another interpretation. Begin significantly supported Yonatan Ratosh's desire to immediately proclaim a Hebrew republic.[68] Moreover, a spell in prison helped to cement his radical credentials.

THE ALTERCATION

The Third World Conference of Betar took place in Warsaw in September 1938. It attracted 130 delegates from sixteen countries. The gathering occurred in the aftermath of the hanging of Shlomo Ben-Yosef by the British in Palestine, the Munich crisis and the lauding of appeasement and the wave of Irgun attacks in Palestine.

Begin utilised the occasion to articulate a clear alternative to Jabotinsky's policies. In his speech, he stated that 'we have had enough of renunciation; we want to fight – to die or to win'. Betar, he surmised, now stood

---

[67] Manifesto of the Activist-Revisionist Front, *Le-Ma'an Ha-Moledet*, 14 January 1938.
[68] Colin Shindler, *The Triumph of Military Zionism: Nationalism and the Origins of the Israeli Right* (London 2006), pp. 197–98.

at the threshold of a new era, the era of military Zionism. In a nod to Jabotinsky's espousal of the Risorgimento, he pointed out that Italy would not have gained its independence if it had depended solely on the diplomacy of Cavour – the military campaign of Garibaldi was equally if not more important. Begin demanded an amendment to the Betar oath which Jabotinsky had formulated in 1934. Clause four had originally read: 'I will train in order to fight in the defence of my people, and I will only use my strength for defence.' Begin proposed instead: 'I will train to fight in the defence of my people and to conquer the homeland.' This move from defence to conquest could only mean the use of military force in an armed struggle against the British and the Palestinian Arabs. Betar, he announced, had reached the age of military maturity and attributed its development to Jabotinsky. 'We must follow in the footsteps of the one who taught us.'[69]

Jabotinsky, for all his fading authority, was not about to become an appendage to Begin's new direction. He interrupted Begin several times and made a distinction between Garibaldi's Italy and present-day Palestine. He asked Begin how he would guarantee the unhindered passage of the soldiers of Betar into Palestine without the help of an outside power. The Arabs, he pointed out, had the advantage of territorial contiguity and could move as they wished. While recognising the value of Garibaldi's example, he commented:

We began Zionism in disgrace – and the disgrace lies in the fact that we are not in the Land of Israel. And even if we become heroes, against whom shall we rise up? The question of getting into the Land of Israel comes before outbursts of heroism. We have come to the Land of Israel by the power of non-Jewish humanity's conscience, and thanks to this, some of us have the audacity to say such things today …

No strategist in the world would say that in this situation we could do something like Garibaldi and De Valera. It is nonsense. Our situation is very different from that of the Italians or the Irish, and if you think that there is no other way than for Mr Begin to offer you weapons – you are committing suicide. If there is no longer conscience in the world – there is the Vistula and there is communism.

Jabotinsky underlined the importance of appealing to the conscience of the world, to the good in humanity. While recognising what he called 'the gold and the thorns in reality', he commented:

Obviously, heroism is important in order to educate and to prove a point. Its aim is to educate the non-Jews, with an education based on the hope or the illusion of

[69] Stenographic Notes of the Third World Conference of Betar, Warsaw 1938. The speeches of Begin and Jabotinsky are taken from the original handwritten notes. Jabotinsky Institute Archives, Tel Aviv.

conscience. To say that conscience no longer exists – this is despair. It is not even worth publishing an article about this. We will sweep this idea away. Obviously each of us is allowed to express his opinion, but there is a limit to this. Conscience rules the world. I respect it. It is forbidden to mock it and ridicule it. I understand the pain, but to sink into despair because of it is dangerous. It is a useless and unnecessary squeaking of the door.

Jabotinsky accused Begin of being detached from this reality. Even so, despite a moving elegy for Shlomo Ben-Yosef, Jabotinsky's eloquence fell on stony ground. A year before the outbreak of World War II, militant and frustrated Jewish youth in Poland were no longer willing to accept the logic of Zionism's wunderrebbe. It was clear to Jabotinsky that Begin and the heirs of Maximalism had won the day:

Both this speech [of Begin] and the applause that it received are like the squeaking of a door, with no sense and no benefit. There is no place in Betar for this kind of nonsense. Sometimes such squeaking can even be attractive, but we should beware of it. The things said here by Mr Begin is squeaking of this sort, and all such squeaking should be cruelly rejected. The face of reality is terrible.

Israel Scheib (Eldad) from Lvov reminded Jabotinsky that a squeaking door alerted the householder to the presence of thieves and drew an analogy with those who had 'broken into' the Zionist movement. Scheib also drew a distinction between the romanticism of the noble conduct of Shlomo Ben-Yosef on the way to the gallows and the reality that it was the British who had killed him. Scheib candidly told the audience of Betar members that there was little difference between Jabotinsky's New Zionist Organisation and Weizmann's 'old' Zionist Organisation and that 'we do not believe in diplomacy'.[70] But the unkindest cut of all – at least from Jabotinsky's point of view – was Scheib's comment that there was a profound distinction in outlook between those who had been born in the nineteenth century and those who came of age after World War I.

Jabotinsky saw himself as the realist and Begin, the dreamer. Begin and his supporters, however, believed the total opposite. The doctrine of military Zionism had triumphed, but Jabotinsky's youthful acolytes were not without remorse:

On the morrow, we, the anguished, triumphed over him, the angel [Jabotinsky]. We, whose youth had not flowed to the beat of Pushkin and Lermontov, whose hearts did not bleed as his heart had bled for the cruelties of the Russian Revolution; we, who had no leisure between the First and Second World Wars

---

[70] Protocols of the Third World Conference of Betar (Bucharest, 1940), p. 88, Jabotinsky Institute Archives, Tel Aviv.

FIGURE 8. Jabotinsky in Betar uniform (September 1938).
Courtesy of the Jabotinsky Institute, Tel Aviv.

to enjoy the melodies of Italy and its skies, who did not care whether the fascist regime was good or not, and did not understand, with our dry political analysis, why he refused to meet Mussolini; we, who were not from the generation of those who fought for the freedom of the citizen, for liberalism and parliamentary democracy, who did not grasp the secret of his sympathy for the democratic British regime and the freedom of the individual and respect for the individual in Britain itself. This was the psychological background to the argument and the struggle that went on at the conference on that day.[71]

The Warsaw conference in September 1938 was the beginning of the end for Revisionism and, after Jabotinsky's death two years later, the selective reworking of the historic Jabotinsky by Begin and the Irgun. Following his dramatic speech, Scheib was asked by Natan Yellin-Mor to meet Avraham Stern, who had also attended the conference. It was the

---

[71] Israel Eldad, *Ma'aser Rishon* (Tel Aviv, 1950), pp. 21–22.

first meeting of the future leaders of Lehi, the Fighters for the Freedom of Israel – or, as the British called it, the Stern Gang.

For Stern, Begin's intervention was a threat to the inroads made by the Irgun into Polish Betar. For Begin, his intervention meant a rallying of Polish Betar to his political standard and nominal support for its revered leader, Jabotinsky.

For Jabotinsky himself, 1938 was doubtless an annus horribilis. His dreams of creating a strong umbrella organisation which would rival Weizmann's Zionist Organisation were dissipating rapidly. There was no mass evacuation from Eastern Europe and a confrontation with Nazi Germany was growing ever more likely. Palestine was in disarray and the Irgun was asserting its political and military independence. His ability to restrain militant youth had been severely weakened, but he was still not prepared to abandon his approach, only to await better political times.

The onward march of the Irgun was reflected by a visit of a delegation to the United States to raise funds. At the end of January 1939, Jabotinsky called a meeting in Paris between the NZO, Betar and the Irgun. David Raziel, head of the Irgun in Palestine, attended but remained silent throughout the discussions. The decision was made that Raziel should become head of both Betar and the Irgun in Palestine. Control of Betar had thus moved from the NZO to the Irgun. A department of military education would be established in the Diaspora which would facilitate the channelling of members of Betar to the Irgun. Much to Raziel's chagrin, Jabotinsky became the first director of this department.

Although Begin and Stern were not present, Irgun cells were still being organised in Poland. In the weeks after the Paris gathering, the Irgun was clearly still not confining itself to Palestine, but making political statements in open press conferences in Warsaw.[72] The Paris gathering was seemingly a defeat for the Revisionists of the NZO, who still believed in diplomacy. Aharon Propes, the long-time leader of Betar in Poland, found his position to be untenable and requested a leave of absence. After a delay an unenthusiastic Jabotinsky appointed Begin in his place.[73] Begin began to preach a very different role for Betar – one of national liberation, one which espoused the doctrine of military Zionism.[74] Begin

[72] Vladimir Jabotinsky, Letter to Solomon Jacobi, 16 March 1939, in Benjamin and Cebon, *The Forgotten Zionist*, p. 201.
[73] Bader's testimony, Shilon, *Menachem Begin*, p. 21; *Hamedina*, 3 April 1939.
[74] Menahem Begin, 'Ven Der Soyne Drot', *Hamedina*, 21 April 1939; Tertium Non-Datur', *Hamedina*, 28 April 1939.

like Raziel, however, remained a Jabotinsky loyalist and unlike Stern was prepared to remain within the fold.

The 1939 White Paper of Malcolm MacDonald, the secretary of state for the colonies, was a bitter blow to all Zionists – the immigration rate into Palestine was limited to 15,000 per annum and after a five-year period would require the approval of the Arab majority. The British realised that the Arab world was far more important to them in the event of war than were the Jews. Regardless of the deteriorating situation of European Jewry, British national interests came first. For the Irgun, this proved to be a radicalising influence, and Avraham Stern hoped to establish training camps for Irgun officers all over Eastern Europe. From there, he intended to bring 40,000 Jews to Palestine, hopefully with the blessing of the Poles, the Italians and the Turks.

Arms and ammunition were shipped to the Irgun in Palestine from the Polish port of Gdynia near Danzig on the Baltic Sea. In particular there was the favoured RKM wz.28 Browning light machine gun.

Jabotinsky was not to be outmanoeuvred and proposed a rival plan – albeit with qualifications and caveats – in early August 1939 to Irgun representatives. An armed revolt would be launched in Palestine with Jabotinsky landing with illegal immigrants in Palestine. Government buildings would be occupied, the Zionist flag hoisted and the position defended for twenty-four hours. The Irgun's task was to prevent the arrest of Jabotinsky. In European capitals and in the United States, the existence of a provisional government would be proclaimed.

Jabotinsky convinced most Irgun commanders to support the plan and argued that the Zionist establishment would eventually fall in behind its consequences. Avraham Stern inevitably opposed it, but David Raziel supported it. Whether Jabotinsky would have put such a plan in action in October 1939 is an open question because the outbreak of war intervened and scuppered it. Given Jabotinsky's approach throughout the 1930s, it is unlikely that it would have taken place. It reflects more a shrewd if desperate move by Jabotinsky to reclaim the situation from those of his young opponents. The expectation that this revolt would be quickly suppressed was reminiscent of the Easter Uprising of the Irish Republicans – a revolt which Jabotinsky throughout his life had distanced himself from. Even so, it resonated with Jabotinsky's impassioned exhortations to Jewish youth and conjured up the romantic imagery of other successful struggles. For Begin and many members of the Irgun, this was the blueprint for the *Altalena* ten years later.

With Germany's invasion of Poland on 1 September, Menahem Begin eventually left Warsaw and found refuge in Vilna, which was occupied by the Red Army when it invaded eastern Poland a few weeks later. *Hamedina* was published once more and Begin continued to write articles for it.[75]

Initially Begin seemed to be unaware that Jabotinsky strongly supported the war effort. On the second day of the war Jabotinsky had sent a message of support to Ignacy Mościcki, the president of Poland. Begin was not of the same mind. He believed that Britain's weak position in 1940 should be exploited. In a letter to Shimshon Yunitchman in Palestine, he wrote that 'Zionist support for Great Britain was unrealistic' during the war. 'This war is not our war.'[76] Unlike Stern, he did not regard the enemy of my enemy as 'automatically' my friend.[77]

The death of Jabotinsky in New York in August 1940 was a grievous blow to Begin despite their political differences. This was followed by the split in the Irgun into the opposing camps of Raziel and Stern.

After a year of relative inactivity, Menahem Begin was arrested by the NKVD and sentenced to eight years in the Gulag. Hitler's attack on the USSR in the summer of 1941 and the subsequent formation of General Anders's army saved him from many long years in a Soviet strict-regime labour camp. In April 1942 the army arrived in Palestine and Begin was reunited with his wife. Almost eighteen months later, he was appointed commander of the Irgun.

[75] Menahem Begin, 'Farshvendung', *Hamedina*, 16 April 1940.
[76] Menahem Begin, Letter to Shimshon Yunitchman, 8 January 1940, Jabotinsky Institute Archives, Tel Aviv.
[77] Joseph Heller, *The Stern Gang: Ideology, Politics and Terror, 1940–1949* (London, 1995), p. 92.

9

Retaliation, Violence and Turmoil

THE ENGLISHMAN

In August 1926, Jabotinsky published a remarkable article entitled 'The Englishman: His Virtues, His Flaws' in which he dissected the nature of 'Englishness' and related it to British governance, both in Whitehall and in Jerusalem. He distinguished the English from other Europeans in that they did not remain attached to a political position as 'a point of honour'. They were not afraid of losing face in changing an opinion, were willing to laugh at themselves and elevated 'muddling through' to a permanent method of operating. England was a conservative country but also a progressive one because of a century of radical reforms. Yet bloodless upheaval brought about movements such as that of the Chartists and the General Strike of 1926. Indeed, Jabotinsky wrote that England possessed 'an incomparably liberal colonial administration'.

I write for intelligent people and I expect to be understood. I do not say that all who have demands they want to make England agree to, must resort to violence, smash windows, make themselves a nuisance. We Jews cannot do such things, and if we did, it would not be any use. But at the same time we must not overlook the moral that emerges from the Suffragette agitation. What is important is not the method employed, but the essential fact, which is, that if you deal with England you must not take 'no' for your answer. Try again. Never give the impression that you have accepted the negative answer because the Englishman will interpret it as evidence that your need is not really acute.[1]

He castigated those of his followers who wanted to confront England, 'to threaten, to stamp their foot and beat their fist on the table'. He recalled

---

[1] Vladimir Jabotinsky, 'The Englishman', *Moment*, 6 and 13 August 1926.

the struggle to establish the Jewish Legion: 'We did our work politely. No one was threatened, we never shouted down any cabinet minister. We never hit anybody.' Jabotinsky concluded that 'the Englishman with all his faults is the best partner in the world, for those who understand his ways'. The Englishman was someone who expected his opponent to drive a hard bargain, and this earned his respect. The Zionists, Jabotinsky remarked, would be in contact with the upper-class Englishman, the colonial administrator, for a long time. 'I myself hope it will be for many years, for I do not regret the alliance.'

Jabotinsky pointed out that the days of a mass English emigration to the newly established colonies was long past and the Mandate authorities had lost the expertise of colonisation. The English administrator also had little idea how to deal with Jews:

The average British official has by special training over several generations evolved a particular way of dealing with the native. He has learned it from his father and grandfather – and Eton, Harrow and Winchester provided excellent training for this type of colonial administrator. But as soon as the British administrator is called upon to deal with a civilised and educated foreign community, he is at a loss as to what to do.

The stereotypical Jew was unkempt, unconventional, undisciplined, yet could quote long passages from Carlyle to the unsuspecting administrator. The Jew was stubborn, prone to arguments and could inconveniently mobilise international opinion.

Jabotinsky pointed out that John Galsworthy's play *Loyalties* demonstrated very well how ultimately the allegiance of members of the English upper class was to themselves. They would show loyalty to one of their own rather than to any notion of 'fair play' and justice. It made no difference that Lloyd-George saved the nation during the Great War; he was still an outsider to the upper class. Jabotinsky related this imagery to the attitude of the British military towards Jews between 1918 and 1920:

Generals who wear the King's uniform, judges who have taken the oath, all stand together, to whitewash their own and to rout the insolent 'outsider'.
Yet the insolent 'outsider' won. Not because he is powerful. Jews are not a weak people, but this was not a question of strength. We won that time and we will win in the future again because above and beyond all the faults of the English they have one great virtue – and I claim your indulgence if the name I give it recalls our own internal political differences – the law of revision.

The events of 1929 and the subsequent Shaw Commission, the Hope-Simpson report and the Passfield White Paper moved Jabotinsky's youthful followers, particularly in Palestine, in a completely different direction. The growing influence of the Maximalists and Jabotinsky's own desire to utilise the unquestioning loyalty of the youth against both Grossman and the Revisionist Executive as well as Weizmann and the Zionist Organisation led him towards a more critical public attitude to the British. Despite the rhetoric, Jabotinsky's views essentially remained the same. His belief that the British would deliver one day was not shared by his acolytes.

This was a time of deep reflection within both the labour Zionist establishment and Jabotinsky's Revisionists. It boiled down to two questions: Why had the British not protected the Jews in 1929 and prevented a wholesale slaughter? What was the meaning of the Arab nationalist assault?

Its immediate effect was a radicalisation of nationalist youth and its growing allegiance to the idea of military Zionism and its belief in national liberation through the force of arms. The events of 1929 led to an awareness that Arab nationalism was far more important for British national interests than Zionism – and hence a reinterpretation of the vague wording of the Balfour Declaration. Apart from Judah Magnes's Berit Shalom and the Marxist Zionists' Hashomer Hatzair, the cry for peace between the two national movements became increasingly hollow even if labour luminaries such as Ben-Gurion continued to pay lip service to it. Instead there was a turning away towards building national institutions and looking after vested interests.

A few weeks after the killings in Hebron, Safed and Jerusalem in 1929, Jabotinsky argued that the British police were incapable of defending Jews because the police were so few in number and the Jewish settlements were so spread out. Jabotinsky concluded that the British should establish a special Jewish section of the Palestine police force with a larger number of Jewish police. Jabotinsky recalled that he had argued in *Ha'aretz* in 1919 that Jews should join the police force without any reservations. Yet the decade in between had indicated a different reality. Moreover, Jabotinsky candidly pointed out that while Jews had become increasingly unwilling to join up, the British police in turn projected more than an ambivalent attitude to the prospect of more Jewish recruits:

On the one hand, the Government will complain that the Jews regard themselves as superior, refuse to be ordered about and the like, and on the other hand, the Jewish police will themselves try to find a way of getting out of the service which isolates them from the Jewish environment and compels them to adapt themselves not only to the material, but to the spiritual life of the oriental middle ages.[2]

---

[2] Ibid.

In 1929 he therefore argued that Jewish self-defence should be reorganised and legalised:

An illegal self-defence is bad for self-defence, bad for Zionist policy and bad for the State.

The British taxpayer was unhappy about paying in money and in lives, he argued, to protect the Jews in Palestine. If British battalions were to stay permanently in Palestine, 'there will be no stopping the anti-Zionist agitation in England'. The Zionists would be depicted as 'exploiters living on the backs of the British taxpayers, and as poltroons and parasites who have no right to build a land of our own because we skulk behind other people's backs. It will poison the entire atmosphere.' The government, he predicted, would inevitably bow to this storm.[3]

THE IRGUN ZVAI LEUMI

Sure enough, the dissent within the Haganah fermented, and the defence organisation split in April 1931, with Avraham Tehomi assuming the role of the first commander of 'Haganah Bet' or the 'Irgun Zvai Leumi'. He had been appointed head of the Jerusalem branch of the Haganah in 1929 and desired a more activist approach to Arab attacks. He was also frustrated by the policies of Ramsay MacDonald's Labour government – in which the labour Zionists had placed high hopes in their fellow social democrats. Tehomi gave voice to his reservations about British Labour – 'socialist Jesuits' – and this was not appreciated by others in the Haganah who believed that this was the path away from socialism towards Jabotinsky's Revisionists.[4]

Tehomi, like his successors as Irgun leaders, David Raziel and Avraham Stern, had arrived in Palestine in the 1920s and was well acquainted with the reality of the Bolshevik experiment.

This creation of the Irgun coincided with the First World Conference of Betar in Danzig. Jabotinsky's followers had grown tremendously in number since the events of 1929 in Palestine, but never more so than in many areas of pre-war Poland – with new Betar branches in remote locations such as Ozierany – while the Revisionist party found support in provincial

[3] Vladimir Jabotinsky, 'Defence Problems in Palestine', *Doar Hayom*, 17 October 1929.
[4] Martin Sicker, *Pangs of the Messiah: The Troubled Birth of the Jewish State* (Westport, CT, 2000), p. 108.

towns – Brzozow, Skierniewice and Jezierzany – and rivalled labour Zionism in its influence.[5]

This first Betar conference in April 1931 brought together adherents from Germany, Poland and Eastern Europe in general. There was even a delegate from China.[6] It followed a usual format – an inspiring address from Jabotinsky, a membership drive, the emphasis on spreading the word about Zionism. It reflected Jabotinsky's template for a youth group in his own image. At the same time his Maximalist opponents in Palestine were arguing cogently that following the events of 1929, Betar should be the human material from which a national liberation movement, a Jewish underground, would spring.

By the end of the year, Jabotinsky was trying to steer the youth into equally attractive channels by urging them 'to learn to shoot'. One of his best-known articles, 'Afn Pripitshek',[7] was based on the popular song of the Yiddish poet Mark Warshawsky, exhorting Jewish children to learn the *aleph-bet*, the Hebrew alphabet:

> When you grow older, children,
> You will understand by yourselves,
> How many tears lie in these letters,
> And how much lament.
> When you, children, will bear the Exile,
> And will be exhausted,
> May you derive strength from these letters,
> Look in at them.

Jabotinsky reinterpreted Warshawsky's lyric for the new Jew, the member of Betar who would build the Jewish state. As learning the Hebrew alphabet was a childhood induction into Jewishness, so bearing arms and being prepared to use them was a rite of passage into the new Jewishness. Jabotinsky's attempt to bury the imagery of the weak, helpless Jew of the past was, however, not a call to prepare for a rebellion against the British. Instead he placed military training primarily in the context of building up the self-esteem of his young followers. It was to be the seed from which a new Jewish legion would grow, a disciplined military force which would defend Jewish settlements. Instead of drawing young people away from the approach of Abba Ahimeir and his supporters, this initiative had the opposite effect of stimulating a discussion about the

---

[5] *Revisionist Bulletin*, no. 7, ser. 2, 14 January 1931.
[6] Mordechai Olmert.
[7] *Haynt*, 16 October 1931.

meaning of military Zionism. It inadvertently attracted many members of Betar to the newly formed Irgun. Given the admixture of militant Arab nationalism in Palestine and the deteriorating situation in the Europe of the dictators, this was almost an inevitable outcome. Moreover, it was a struggle that Jabotinsky was bound to lose.

The Irgun came into existence because its members wanted a more active policy after the killings of 1929. David Raziel, later the Irgun commander for the Old City of Jerusalem, had guarded the dead as a young yeshivah student in 1929.[8] Its members also wanted the new organisation to be independent of party control and not allied to the newly formed Mapai of the labour Zionists. The Irgun supervisory board therefore included the General Zionists, Mizrahi, the Revisionists, the Jewish State party and Agudat Yisrael.

Although he reluctantly attended the meeting when the supervisory board was established, Jabotinsky kept his distance and rejected all attempts to involve him. He was opposed to illegal actions and profoundly disliked the idea of an underground. The notion of self-restraint – the doctrine of *havlagah* – and not retaliating had some veracity because Jabotinsky still exhibited a deep confidence that working with Britain would eventually deliver a Jewish state. Above all, he did not want a military confrontation with the British in Palestine, since this would undoubtedly create problems for any future relationship and open up another front. It might also inhibit the influx of capital into the Yishuv. In addition, a clash with Arab nationalists would provide the British with the excuse that a civil war existed in Palestine and therefore place a halt on Jewish immigration into the country.

Even so, despite continuing protests, Britain did not stop Jewish immigration after Hitler's accession to power in Germany, as had been the case in 1921 and in 1929. Immigration increased from 4,000 in 1931 to well over 60,000 in 1935.

On the other hand, Jabotinsky understood that the very idea of self-restraint was self-defeating. How could he preach to young Jews that they were the proud descendants of King David, but then ask them to do nothing against those who repeatedly carried out acts of violence against them? Moreover, Jabotinsky reasoned that suspending havlagah might well unite the divided Arab factions in Palestine.

Yet Jabotinsky's influence amongst youth in Palestine was beginning to wane. He was forced by the British to live outside Palestine, and many

---

[8] Daniel Levine, *David Raziel: The Birth of the Irgun Zvai Leumi* (Jerusalem, 1991), p. 52.

FIGURE 9. David Raziel (date unknown).
Courtesy of the Jabotinsky Institute, Tel Aviv.

young people looked for a more militant approach. The Irgun therefore proved an attraction.

Both David Raziel and Avraham Stern had been involved in right-wing politics as students at the Hebrew University in Jerusalem and had taken part in protests such as the disruption of Bentwich's inaugural lecture at the beginning of 1932. Raziel was a member of Berit El-Al,[9] founded by the academic Yosef Klausner, and close to the official Revisionists, while Stern belonged to Hulda, independent of any party, but with an affinity for Ahimeir's Berit Ha-Biryonim.[10]

As members of the Irgun, they formed a discussion group, Suhba, which published a journal, *Metzudah*. This acted as a coordinating medium between the intellectual Right of Yeivin and Klausner and activist students such as Raziel, Stern and Hillel Kook.[11] They emphasised the value of military training, educated themselves in the discipline by

[9] Ibid., pp. 57–62.
[10] Yakira Ginosar, *Lo bi-shevilenu shar ha-saksofon: 'al shire Ya'ir, Avraham Stern* (Tel Aviv, 1998), p. 45.
[11] Arye Naor, *David Raziel: Ha-mefaked ha-rashi shel ha-Irgun ha-Tseva'i ha-Le'umi be-Erets Yisra'el; hayav u-tekufato* (Tel Aviv, 1990), pp. 61–70.

using the Hebrew University library, importing books from Britain, and eventually began to teach instructors' courses on the subject to all those who were interested. In 1933 Raziel and Stern wrote a military training manual, *Ha'Ekdakh*, under the pseudonym D. Rash – an amalgamation of their surnames.

In the second issue of *Metzudah*, Stern published his poem 'Hayalim Almonim' – 'Unknown Soldiers' – which became the anthem of the Irgun. Stern had originally written in Russian but changed to Hebrew in the 1930s for his odes. Influenced by Mayakovsky and Yesenin, he mirrored their themes of love and revolution. Both had died at a young age by their own hands. Upon entering the political arena as an MA student at the Hebrew University, Stern coloured the Irgun with sketches from his literary imagination. Many poems therefore spoke of self-sacrifice and dying nobly for the good of the cause. Thus 'Hayalim Almonim' contained the line 'Our Dream is to die for our Nation'.

In another line, he wrote about raising the Zionist standard in towns and villages and inscribing upon it 'Defence and Conquest'. The inclusion of 'Conquest', as well as inferring a desire for a clandestine military underground, was clearly at variance with Jabotinsky's advocacy of a legalised Jewish force which would defend settlements and complement negotiations with the British.

In 1936 this situation changed dramatically. It was the year of the Arab Revolt against British occupation and Zionist colonisation. The Palestinian Arabs wanted a state like any other in the region. Arab nationalism in Palestine had come of age, but it embarked on the armed struggle rather than diplomacy. Moreover, it suddenly dawned on observers in 1936 that a future war with Nazi Germany was becoming a distinct possibility, that Hitler was no transient figure of fun. Britain therefore needed to ensure that Palestine was sufficiently stable to preserve the passages to India, south-east Asia and British bases generally in the Middle East. The number of Jewish constables was therefore increased and the Haganah was allowed to defend Jewish settlements.

The Arab Revolt revived Betar in Palestine, empowered the declining Maximalists and invigorated the Irgun. Tehomi had developed the Irgun with help from sympathisers within the Revisionist movement, and both funding and arms flowed in from Poland, Czechoslovakia and Finland. Younger members such as Raziel and Stern were now playing a key role.

During the first half of 1936 Jabotinsky signalled that he was not ready to contemplate retaliation because he did not want a conflict with the British.[12] Later in the year the British began to float solutions to the Palestine problem – and there were strong indications that the Peel Commission would propose partition as had happened in Ireland.

At the same time, there had been a closer relationship between members of Betar and the Irgun in Palestine. An unofficial dialogue between the two groups had commenced as early as 1935. In December 1936 there was a five-point agreement between Jabotinsky and Tehomi in Paris. Jabotinsky would become the supreme commander of the Irgun. It endorsed eventual reunification with the Haganah when there was a united Yishuv. Before reunification, it proposed that a round table conference take place.[13] In the meantime the Irgun would maintain its independence.

Jabotinsky, however, also requested that the Irgun not act against the political interests of the Revisionists – in effect, the Irgun would move from an independent status to affiliation with the New Zionist Organisation. Tehomi feared that if he did not agree to this fundamental shift, Raziel, Stern and Betar would cause a split in the Irgun by taking over its arms dumps.

In early 1937, after an initial silence, Jabotinsky came out in clear opposition to partition and promoted a return to the original mandate for Palestine including both banks of the Jordan. Partition implied complex security dangers and havlagah might now have to be opposed if the situation radically changed. Disdainful of Zionist support for partition by such leading figures as Ben-Gurion and Weizmann, Jabotinsky wanted the flexibility of an independent force. The New Zionist Organisation said that although it spoke 'in the name of 700,000 Jewish voters, most of them in the main countries of distress', the denial of the historic right of the Jews to settle in all the Land, outweighed 'the boon of immediate statehood'.[14] Despite attempts by close colleagues like Colonel Patterson to persuade Jabotinsky to the contrary, he remained unmoved.

Tehomi, on the other hand, had been engaged in negotiations with the Haganah. He seemed convinced that a Jewish state was within reach, and therefore the formation of a Jewish army which should include the Irgun

[12] Vladimir Jabotinsky, 'The Last Week', *Moment*, 28 May 1936.
[13] Agreement between Vladimir Jabotinsky and Avraham Tehomi, 5 December 1936, Paris, Jabotinsky Institute Archives, Tel Aviv.
[14] 'Memorandum on the Partition of Palestine', New Zionist Organisation', July 1937, Jabotinsky Institute Archives, Tel Aviv.

was imminent. An inevitable split in the Irgun took place, with Tehomi returning to the Haganah with at least a quarter of its members.[15]

Despite Jabotinsky's attempts to avert such a crisis,[16] on 10 April 1937 Tehomi left the Irgun. In July Jabotinsky met his successor, Robert Bitker, in Alexandria, together with Moshe Rosenberg and Avraham Stern. Jabotinsky concurred that there was now more than enough justification for retaliation, but he remained deeply concerned about the moral aspects of killing civilian bystanders.[17]

THE MEANING OF TERROR

Jabotinsky finally agreed that he would approve an act of retaliation by the Irgun by sending a telegram stating, 'The deal is concluded', and signed 'Mendelson'. Yet Jabotinsky's clear distaste for this course of action paralysed him politically and intellectually during his last years. In one sense, the liberal Russian intellectual was in clear conflict with the fatalistic nationalist Zionist whose speeches electrified audiences. He cancelled the sending of this telegram, having previously authorised it, on several occasions. His most common explanation was that being outside Palestine made it difficult to appraise the situation and to make a concrete decision.

Jabotinsky was always wary about associating himself directly with Irgun actions, which could be construed as endorsing acts of terror. He was also the head of three different organisations – the New Zionist Organisation, Betar and now the Irgun – which differed in their attitude towards both military Zionism and retaliatory action. But above all, as someone personally committed to the political path and negotiations, he wanted to keep within the letter of the law.

He was also critical of the Irgun for relying solely on armed struggle. Jabotinsky regarded this as akin to Weizmann's sole reliance on diplomacy. He remarked, 'In the beginning God created politics.'[18]

The Irgun also wanted to control aliyah bet, the illegal emigration from Europe, from start to finish. Jabotinsky wanted Betar to initiate it in the Diaspora and the Irgun to conclude it in Palestine.

---

[15] Shmuel Katz, *Days of Fire* (London, 1968), p. 16.
[16] Vladimir Jabotinsky, Letter to Avraham Tehomi, 9 April 1937, *Igrot, 1937–1938* (Tel Aviv, 2013).
[17] Schechtman, Joseph B., *Fighter and Prophet: The Jabotinsky Story – The Last Years, 1923–1940* (New York, 1961), pp. 449–50.
[18] Ibid., p. 457.

The Irgun under Bitker, however, was composed entirely of Revisionists and those further to the right. The adherents of other parties had left with Tehomi and returned to the Haganah. An aging Jabotinsky was now saddled with an organisation which was moving away from his control and which was less susceptible to his rhetoric and charisma during a period of political impotence for Jews in Palestine and in Europe.

The polarisation between Jabotinsky and his supporters in both the Irgun and Betar became more acute in 1937. Bitker was involved in a controversial episode entailing former members of Berit Ha-Biryonim who robbed Bank Hapoalim in Tel Aviv. The unexplained death of Zvi Frankel,[19] an Irgun member whose body was found floating in the Yarkon, forced Bitker's dismissal from his post.[20] Bitker's temporary replacement was Moshe Rosenberg, who then made way for David Raziel and Avraham Stern. The killing of individual Jews such as Rabbi Eliezer Gerstein on his way to pray at the Western Wall in Jerusalem fuelled the demand for retaliation.[21] Raziel faced the same problems as Bitker – how to manage independent actions by members of the Irgun or those close to it. On 9 September 1937, five Jews were killed while working in the fields of Kibbutz Kiriat Anavim. A counter-attack killed thirteen Arabs. While there was a month of havlagah observed by the Irgun High Command, Raziel was pressured to act, and he thereby authorised the bombing of Arab coffee houses in Haifa and Rosh Pinah, attacks in several districts of Jerusalem and centres of militancy, including the nearby village of Lyftah, and the shooting at buses on the Tiberias-Safed route.

The attacks began at first light on 14 November 1937 – 'Black Sunday' – on Arab pedestrians in Aza Street in Jerusalem's Rehavia district.[22] The Irgun symbolically related it to the uprising of Judas Maccabeus against the Hellenism of the Seleucids some 2,000 years before.[23] It was a significant episode in the development of the Zionist Right. Raziel pointed out that the Irgun had moved from a position of 'passive defence' to one of 'active defence':

Even if those who are fighting have no desire to suppress others but merely wish to preserve their own freedom and honour, there is only one path open to them,

[19] Levine, *David Raziel*, pp. 112–13.
[20] Yehoshua Ofir, *Rishonei Etzel, 1931–1940* (Tel Aviv, 2002), pp. 108–110.
[21] David Niv, *Ma'arakhot ha-Irgun ha-Tseva'i ha-Le'umi: mi-haganah le-hatkafah, 1937–1939*, vol. 2 (Tel Aviv, 1965), p. 24.
[22] Naor, *David Raziel*, p. 103.
[23] Statement of the Irgun Zvai Leumi, 14 November 1939, Jabotinsky Institute Archives. Tel Aviv.

to attack. They must charge the enemy and destroy his strength and will. Before the enemy has a chance to attack, the possibility of attacking must be taken away from him. The conclusion is that as regards methods of warfare there is no difference between assailant and defender since the defender must attack in order to avoid servitude. The difference between them lies in the motive for going to war whether it is the desire to subjugate others or the wish to live in liberty and honour.

Defence through attack, in order to deprive the enemy of the opportunity to attack, is called active defence.[24]

Jabotinsky seemingly was ignorant of this initiative, but subsequently attempted to distance the NZO from it while proclaiming 'understanding' of the action.[25] Yet the British did not arrest members of the Irgun following Black Sunday, but mainly Revisionists, including Jabotinsky's son and Abba Ahimeir.

At the Prague conference of the NZO in January 1938, Jabotinsky depicted Black Sunday as 'a spontaneous outbreak of the outraged feelings of the nation's soul and must never be attributed to one party alone'.[26] He welcomed the abandonment of havlagah, but buried any mention deep in his speech. He also pointedly attacked the Peel Commission's recommendations to partition the Land of Israel and argued that there would not be any future opportunities to expand its borders. 'Only an idiot would believe that a [future] military occupation would be a possibility.'[27]

Both Menahem Begin of Polish Betar and Avraham Stern of the Irgun attended the conference, and indeed there were discussions between the two groups. While Begin sympathised with the actions of the Irgun, he also wished to avoid an erosion of Betar's membership and to put a stop to Stern's growing influence. Begin's speech at the conference elevated preparation for an armed uprising against the British over diplomacy. Begin attacked Benjamin Akzin, one of Jabotinsky's aides, for his caution, moderation and sounding too much like Weizmann.[28]

Jabotinsky was only half-aware of developments and continued to walk the diplomatic tightrope between the three organisations which he headed. When Begin asked whether there was a specific ruling regarding

[24] Niv, *Ma'arakhot ha-Irgun ha-Tseva'i ha-Le'umi*, p. 24.
[25] Vladimir Jabotinsky, Speech at Shoreditch Town Hall, East London, 23 November 1937, *Zionews*, 24 November 1937.
[26] *Zionews*, 28 February 1938.
[27] Vladimir Jabotinsky, Opening speech at the NZO conference, Prague, September 1938, *Neumim, 1927–1940*, Ketavim 5, ed. Eri Jabotinsky (Jerusalem, 1958), p. 298.
[28] Binyamin Akzin, *mi-Riga l'Yerushalayim* (Jerusalem, 1989), p. 288.

havlagah, Jabotinsky responded that first of all 'one should ask one's father's permission'.

The situation in Palestine was clearly deteriorating. In July 1937, the Arab Higher Committee formally rejected the Peel Commission's proposals for partition, and Lewis Andrews, district commissioner for Galilee, was killed in Nazareth in September. The following month, the mufti was removed as president of the Supreme Muslim Council and fled to Lebanon. The Arab Higher Committee was declared illegal and it moved to Damascus. All this, however, left a political vacuum and there was no central command. A second wave of attacks then began, mainly in rural areas and on roads linking centres.

In the first half of 1938, there was a broad Arab assault on Jewish settlements, British patrols and Arab opponents. This was led by Abdul Rahim Haj Mohammed, who was independent, and Aref Abdul Razzik, who represented the mufti.

The Foreign Office in London replaced its civilian and military leadership in Palestine. At the beginning of March 1938, Sir Harold MacMichael started his term of office as high commissioner of Palestine, and a few weeks later Major-General Robert Hadden Haining was appointed general officer commanding Palestine and TransJordan. Both men were determined to make a difference in Palestine.

The polarisation of the situation in Palestine increased support for the Irgun. In Poland it had begun to attract large numbers of Jewish youth who were influenced by its philosophy of armed struggle as the means to secure the state. Avraham Stern arrived in Warsaw in 1936, bearing a letter of recommendation from Jabotinsky and began to establish Irgun cells in Polish Betar. They had to swear an oath of allegiance to obey the Irgun solely – there was no mention of Jabotinsky.[29] The Irgun journals, *Di Tat* and *Jerozolima Wyzwolona*, were established in the summer of 1938, while Betar and NZO loyalists were bypassed. In May 1938 Stern signed an agreement with the Polish consul in Jerusalem which would provide for the training of Irgun members in Poland.

Stern's military Zionism was opposed to the views of Jabotinsky – a figure he compared to Hindenburg, yesterday's man. Raziel, however, remained a Jabotinsky loyalist, albeit a critical one. Most Irgun people were unaware of the differences.

---

[29] Schechtman, *Fighter and Prophet*, pp. 455–56.

Stern established courses for Irgun instructors which were overseen by the Polish military. They took place at Andrychów, Warsaw, Zofiówka, Poddębice – and Jabotinsky knew nothing about them.

THE HANGING OF SHLOMO BEN-YOSEF

Members of both the Irgun and different Arab groups began to target public and private transport on roads in Palestine. In one sense both suffered from a lack of disciplined central control, but were driven by a desire to initiate tit-for-tat retaliation. The Safed-Rosh Pinah Road in particular had been a target of attacks. Betar members in Rosh Pinah believed that Arabs from the nearby village of Jaouni had been responsible for the killing of Jews and the rape of women who were travelling on the road. On 21 April 1937 Abraham Shein, Shlomo Ben-Yosef (Tabacznik) and Shalom Zurabin mounted a freelance attempt at avenging the killing of Jewish civilians. Their attempt was hopelessly incompetent – the first bus passed by them and Ben-Yosef's grenade refused to explode near the second one. On being apprehended by police, the young men proclaimed their guilt.[30] Another member of Betar, Yehezkiel Altman, had recently had his death sentence commuted after he had shot dead an Arab boy. But these were changed times, given the determination of the new leadership of the British authorities to suppress violence. Ben-Yosef, a recent immigrant from Poland, was sentenced for his intentions by a military court and hanged at the end of June 1938. The British action was designed to indicate to Ben-Gurion that if the Jewish Agency was unable to control events, the British authorities would do so themselves. The unspoken message was that they should act to suppress the Irgun.

Ben-Yosef's body was turned over to his friends in Betar, public mourning banned and, under heavy military guard, the coffin taken to Rosh Pinah, where a funeral service was held. General strikes were called in Jerusalem, Haifa, Tel Aviv and other cities. In Jerusalem there were clashes, with many Jews carrying black flags of mourning. In Tel Aviv, the banks, the Harbour Authority and the town hall were all closed – with municipal and Jewish organizational buildings displaying black flags.[31] In Kovno, Lithuania, there was a demonstration outside the British consulate in which the windows were smashed.

---

[30] Ofir, *Rishonei Etzel*, pp. 150–57.
[31] *Jewish Telegraphic Agency*, 30 June 1938.

As in the Easter Uprising, the British had badly miscalculated and instead created a wave of sympathy. While Betar now had a martyr, the British action further undermined Jabotinsky's authority and his ability to control the Irgun. In a plea to Malcolm MacDonald, the colonial secretary, to save Ben-Yosef's life, Jabotinsky wrote:

The whole atmosphere is madness. The Jewish people would never get reconciled to a situation which first drives them to the verge of madness and then hangs them. This kind of martyrdom would only serve to release thousands of similar urges, ill-mastered even now which would only set a match to trails long laid.[32]

At a mass meeting in London to mourn Ben-Yosef, Jabotinsky warned:

I declare to the British: Be careful. Jews are beginning to think whether Ben-Yosef's way is the best. Be careful! This has happened before in history. A martyr became a prophet and graves became shrines. Be careful! Ben-Yosef's example may prove too much for suffering Jewish youth. Is Jewish youth dust or is it iron? The hangmen of Ben-Yosef think it is dust. We shall see![33]

Jabotinsky asked whether the sword must rule human destiny and not reason. He quoted from Ferdinand Lassalle's socialist drama, *Franz von Sickingen*, that throughout history it had always been the case:

> It was the sword that David, Samson and Gideon laboured with.
> Thus, long ago, as well as since, the sword
> Achieved the glories told by history;
> And all that's great, as yet to be achieved.
> Owes, in the end, its triumph to the sword![34]

Jabotinsky's anguish at the situation had persuaded him to send a message to David Raziel before Ben Yosef's execution: 'If final, invest heavily, Mendelson.' The Irgun did invest heavily – seventy-six Arabs, forty-four Jews and twelve members of the security forces were killed in three weeks in July 1938. Jabotinsky was aghast at this outcome, and he was particularly outraged by the killings in a marketplace in Haifa where no warning had been given. Jabotinsky's private protests were ridiculed by the youthful Irgun leadership. His diminishing influence both amongst his own followers and with the British was all too apparent.

---

[32] Vladimir Jabotinsky, Letter to Malcolm MacDonald, 3 June 1938, Jabotinsky Institute Archives, Tel Aviv.
[33] *Jewish Herald*, 8 July 1938.
[34] Ferdinand Lassalle, *Franz von Sickingen*, trans. from German by Daniel De Leon (New York, 1904), p. 58.

On 10 July 1938 Jabotinsky met Eliahu Golomb, head of the Haganah, in London to discuss the situation. Jabotinsky evaded addressing the question of his responsibility for Irgun actions. He disingenuously asked whether Golomb thought Jews were responsible and not agents provocateurs. Golomb responded that it was not necessary to stick to such imaginary suppositions. Jabotinsky commented:

Were I now a terrorist in Eretz Israel, I would have felt exactly the same after the [Ben-Yosef] trial to do something against England – in this case it is precisely the Arabs who have not given any reason for actions against them. I do not say that one had to do something, but that there is logic in it.[35]

Golomb responded that the Haganah, the Jewish Agency and Weizmann had all tried to intervene on behalf of Ben-Yosef. Jabotinsky told Golomb in turn that Major-General Haining had told the colonial secretary, Malcolm MacDonald, that the only person who truly believed that the hanging of Ben-Yosef had been a legal mistake was Jabotinsky. Jabotinsky admitted that the Ben-Yosef affair had touched him so deeply that he was seriously considering a change in 'our orientation towards England'.

Golomb informed Jabotinsky that the Haganah could have used force to prevent acts by the Irgun, but that would have meant civil war, so it felt constrained at the moment. Next time, he warned, it might well be different. Despite Jabotinsky's admonition that he was not competent to issue orders from afar to the Irgun, Golomb had come to see him with the expressed purpose of reining in the Irgun.

Golomb stressed the value of a legal Jewish military force. The Haganah's preparations now would lead to a strong military force, he argued, which would be crucial in the event of an outbreak of war in Europe. Yet the Irgun's undisciplined displays of violence would derail such a development. Jabotinsky and Golomb finally agreed that a common body should be established which would adjudicate on any proposed reprisal.

Hundreds of members of the Irgun had been arrested by the British, and Jabotinsky realised that the Haganah promise to crack down was no idle threat. In an article in August 1938 Jabotinsky warned that 'an internal Jewish pogrom will result in an internal Jewish self-defence' and that this would not be limited to Palestine.[36] Despite this bravado, his position was considerably weaker.

[35] Notes on the meeting between Jabotinsky and Eliahu Golomb, 10 July 1938, Jabotinsky Institute Archives, Tel Aviv.
[36] Vladimir Jabotinsky, 'Vereitelt den Buergerkrieg in Palätina!', *Medina Ivrit*, 29 August 1938.

The discussion, however, bore fruit. An agreement to tentatively unite the Haganah and the Irgun was arrived at in Tel Aviv on 20 September 1938. A joint Haganah-Irgun committee would decide on any possible reprisals. Jabotinsky agreed, but to Golomb's amazement, Ben-Gurion rejected the proposal. Ben-Gurion wanted nothing less than both the NZO and the Irgun to be placed under the control of Mapai and the Haganah. He understood the weakness of Jabotinsky's position – even his young followers in Betar had opposed him at their conference in Warsaw – and pressed home his advantage. In a letter to Eliahu Dobkin, who had been involved in the negotiations with the Revisionists, Ben-Gurion did not mince his words:

These biryonim imitate the tactics of the Nazis. They are our sworn enemies. When you speak to them, you should always remember that you talk to an enemy lacking a conscience.[37]

THE END OF THE ROAD

After the Ben-Yosef affair and the White Paper, Jabotinsky was less inhibited publicly about the activities of the Irgun. 'The Irgun is your salvation … it is the strongest form of protest'.[38] He also said:

The blackest of all the characteristics of exile is the tradition of the cheapness of Jewish blood, hadam hamutar, the permitted blood, the spilling of which is not prohibited and for which you do not pay. To this an end has been made in Palestine. Amen.[39]

On another occasion, Jabotinsky attacked official Zionism for the absurdity of 'passive resistance'.[40] There were also more biting comments about British policy in his article. Yet in private Jabotinsky was torn about the Irgun's approach.

In June 1939 he wrote 'A Call to the Jewish Youth' – 'The Only Way to Liberate Our Country Is by the Sword'. Youth would register in Poland and in Palestine. This was not published for fear that it would alienate the Polish government, which wished to preserve its good relations with Britain. Jabotinsky argued that the choice was between retaliation against a hostile population and not retaliating at all. It was impossible to punish just the guilty ones. To justify this view, Jabotinsky quoted

[37] Niv, *Ma'arakhot ha-Irgun ha-Tseva'i ha-Le'umi*, p. 116.
[38] Schechtman, *Fighter and Prophet*, p. 478.
[39] Vladimir Jabotinsky, 'Amen', *Moment*, 9 July 1939.
[40] Vladimir Jabotinsky, 'What Has Been Evacuated', *Jewish Herald*, 28 July 1939.

the example of the British attack on Karlsruhe in reprisal for attacks on London during World War I.

The 1939 White Paper indicated to the Irgun that Jabotinsky's policy of belief in Britain was in reality a complete failure. All sections of the nationalist camp vented their anger against the British move in a demonstration in Tel Aviv.[41] Raziel ordered the resumption of attacks on Arabs – on the village of Bir Adis near Kfar Saba and the bombing of the Rex Cinema in Jerusalem – before he was finally arrested by the British.[42] With Raziel in prison, Stern steered the Irgun towards attacking the British as well as the Arabs. This precipitated a worsening of relations between the two men which was accentuated by the outbreak of war.

Stern and other members of the Irgun High Command were soon arrested and joined Raziel in prison. Raziel viewed the Nazis as the main enemy and from Sarafand prison camp endorsed Jabotinsky's approach in supporting the war effort 'under British colours'. He informed the Irgun of his views[43] and was immediately met by bitter opposition. The Maximalist elements in the broader Revisionist movement – Ahimeir, Yeivin, Greenberg – initially found common cause with Raziel's opponents. They viewed Raziel's stand as a reversal of the Katowice conference in 1933.[44]

Raziel's alignment with Jabotinsky eventually led to the suspension of the Irgun's armed struggle, his release from prison and participation in the war against Hitler alongside 'the British occupier'. For Stern, however, the British enemy was still the British enemy, and he believed that its distraction through war should be exploited. Indeed, he was highly impressed by the early Nazi victories and the ease with which Hitler now bestrode Europe. Even before the outbreak of war, he had instructed one of his followers to make contact with the Italian consulate in Jerusalem.[45]

Despite this, the Irgun intensified its efforts to illegally bring in immigrants from war-torn Europe. It had facilitated the emigration of 7,000 Jews, mainly from Balkan ports, during the first part of 1939.[46] But the purchase price of these often unseaworthy vessels increased as the desperation of the trapped Jews increased. While some managed to avoid the British blockade of the coast of Palestine, others were stopped and

[41] *Ha'aretz* 18 May 1939.
[42] Naor, *David Raziel*, pp. 203–15.
[43] Ibid., pp. 226–29.
[44] Joseph Heller, *The Stern Gang: Ideology, Politics and Terror, 1940–1949* (London, 1995), pp. 64–66.
[45] Naor, *David Raziel*, p. 239.
[46] Katz, *Days of Fire*, p. 43.

their passengers interned. Still others, such as those on board the *Atlantic*, were sent to Mauritius in December 1940.

Jabotinsky understood very quickly that Poland had collapsed as a result of the twin invasions of the Nazis and the Soviets. The only reservoir of Jewish support that could now make a difference in a desperate situation resided in the United States. In an aide-memoire on the outbreak of war,[47] Jabotinsky proposed to lead a delegation to the United States for the following purposes:

1. To form an association under the name of the 'Jewish Army' which would negotiate with both the U.S. and Allied governments for Jewish troops to participate 'on all fronts'. There would be no separate command for the Jewish troops. The conditions would be that Jews would be represented at 'the Peace Conference'.
2. To organise a campaign for U.S. intervention in the war.

Despite his admiration for the British and Churchill's determination to fight on the beaches and the landing grounds, Jabotinsky feared that Britain would capitulate after Dunkirk and seek a peace treaty with Hitler. He feared for Western civilisation, for European Jewry and for his dream of a Jewish army. In June 1940, Jabotinsky started a 'Help the Allies' campaign in the United States. Its immediate objective was to create 'a Jewish army with a Jewish air force as its first constituent component'. The Jewish war effort would solicit funds to purchase airplanes for this purpose. The training of its pilots would take place with the help of British government – and this was the period of the Battle of Britain.

The status of the Jewish Agency would be similar to that of the Polish government in exile. It would be an integral part of the Allied Forces and would command 150,000 men. The initial nucleus would consist of one division of 12,000 infantry plus two air force squadrons.

In view of this profound danger, the squabbling between Raziel and Stern in Palestine paled into insignificance. Raziel had clearly had enough and resigned as head of the Irgun. There was an appeal to the authority of Jabotinsky to make a clear-cut decision. On 28 July 1940 Jabotinsky reappointed Raziel as commander of the Irgun. Jabotinsky collapsed and died of heart failure a few days later at the age of fifty-nine. The Irgun split a few weeks later into the Irgun Zvai Leumi of David Raziel and the Lehi of Avraham Stern.

---

[47] Vladimir Jabotinsky, Aide-memoire, 10 September 1939, Jabotinsky Institute Archives, Tel Aviv.

The Irgun and the Lehi

THE SAGA OF RAZIEL AND STERN

At the beginning of 1938, Jabotinsky told his followers that the Great Powers would not desert Czechoslovakia. A few weeks later Hitler marched unopposed into Austria. In an unpublished article, Jabotinsky noted how easy it was for a small country such as Austria to be swallowed up and to disappear from history in a matter of hours. The Anschluss convinced Jabotinsky that it was important 'to stand fast' and 'to weather the storm'. Remaining neutral was not an option, and he was convinced in 1938 that 'the Jews are going to pay'. The appeasement of Britain and France was anathema to his philosophy:

We are living in a world of universal cowardice. Its worst feature is that the gangsters are also cowards and would never have attempted any of their exploits, had there been the slightest chance of trouble.[1]

Yet in his public pronouncements, Jabotinsky proclaimed that his hopes still resided in 'the conscience of the world'. His opponents were not so sure. As early as 1936, in his poem, 'To the British Empire', Uri Zvi Greenberg had predicted the flight of 'Amalek eagles over Westminster' – a foresight of the Battle of Britain. As war loomed, many of Jabotinsky's youthful followers began to question his public pronouncements. In Palestine they viewed him as an outsider abroad and considered his approach similar to that of Ben-Gurion.[2]

[1] Vladimir Jabotinsky, *Felix Austria*, Unpublished article, 1938, Jabotinsky Institute Archives, Tel Aviv.
[2] Yitzhak Shamir, *Summing Up* (London, 1994), p. 30.

Avraham Stern articulated this dissent and was one of Jabotinsky's harshest critics. He went further and was also critical of Ahimeir and Ratosh, who were closer to him ideologically. The emergence of a separate organisation, the Irgun B'Yisrael (the Irgun in Israel), therefore was viewed as an act of political purification. Stern's central tenet of faith was the use of force – and against the British.

The arrest of David Raziel in the early summer of 1939 meant that Stern was effectively left in control of the Irgun. He thereby determined its military path, and this meant initially an invigorated confrontation with British. He also put forward his programme 'Principles and Conclusion' in the summer of 1939. Yet within three months, Stern too was apprehended by the British authorities. Stern's incarceration coincided with the outbreak of war and led to a widening ideological gap between himself and Raziel.

The war brought complexity, and this was a phenomenon which Stern would not recognise. He believed that both the British and the Germans were enemies. Zionists should not choose between them, but rise above the situation and seek ways to exploit it. This stand was similar to that of both the Stalinists and the Trotskyists in the international Left.

Unlike Stern, Raziel sided with Jabotinsky when Hitler invaded Poland, and he duly signed an agreement with Alan Saunders, the inspector general of police and prisons, in Palestine in October 1939.[3] He signed the document as (Eliezar) 'Ben-Hanania' after one of the leaders of the first revolt against the Romans. Moreover, Raziel inclined towards the idea of a Jewish army rather than an underground. The Zionists had no hinterland, and there would be no armed force marching from the Diaspora in the direction of Palestine – as Jabotinsky had implied in his speech in Warsaw in September 1938. In addition, the Arabs were considered to be enthusiastically pro-German, since Hitler's armies would drive the British from Palestine. Stern, however, pointed out that the existence of Jabotinsky's Jewish Legion during the Great War did not inevitably lead to a Jewish state. Stern believed that Raziel's move was simply a throwback to the ideas of Meir Grossman, and this had clearly infected the Revisionist movement. It diluted the maximalism of Abba Ahimeir and ridiculed the idea that the Irgun should be a revolutionary underground. Yeivin even wanted to revive *Hazit Ha'am*. Yet it was Arieh Altman,

---

[3] Documentation, located in the Haganah archives, by Eldad Haruvi suggests that the agreement was made with another police official, Arthur Jales. See Tuvia Friling, 'A Blatant Oversight? The Right Wing in Israeli Holocaust Historiography', *Israel Studies*, vol. 14, no. 1 (Spring 2009), p. 166.

head of the NZO in Palestine, rather than the lofty Jabotinsky who bore the full brunt of Stern's anger. He compared Altman to Sergei Zubatov, who had made the transition from revolutionary to senior figure in the Okhrana, the Tsar's security apparatus.

On his release from prison, Raziel was reappointed by Jabotinsky commander of the Irgun and attempted to regain control, but very few supported the displacement of Stern. Even before the outbreak of war, many Irgun members tended to be more disposed to a position of neutrality in the war than to one of overtly siding with Britain – 'as long as Great Britain remains the ally of the Mufti'.[4] The official Irgun journal, *Ba-herev*, was therefore critical of Jabotinsky's approach in encouraging Jews to enlist.

It was the relevant issue of military prowess in 1940 which impressed members of the Irgun – whether it was the rapid German military victories over Britain and France in 1940 or the unexpected resistance of the Finns to the advance of the Red Army.[5]

In contrast, Jabotinsky was extremely worried. He constructed a synopsis of a book entitled *Jews after the War*. If the Nazis won the war, Jabotinsky predicted:

European Jewry will face either destruction or expulsion to some kind of big concentration camp; unless the conquerors prefer to let them rot slowly where they are under a reinforced ghetto regime.

Two chapters were to be devoted to the prospect of Nazi victory. He also contemplated whether there could ever be 'a negotiated peace between the Nazi phenomenon and the Jews as an entity'.[6] His response to the deteriorating situation in Europe was to launch a campaign in North America to urge the British High Command to establish a Jewish army, which would initially be based in Canada, but expanding to 150,000 men and two air force squadrons.[7] The inaugural convention for the campaign was due to be held in New York at the beginning of September 1940.[8] Neither his book nor his plans for a Jewish army convention were realised. Jabotinsky died suddenly in August 1940.

---

[4] *Hamashkif*, 28 July 1939.
[5] Joseph Heller, *The Stern Gang: Ideology, Politics and Terror, 1940–1949* (London, 1995), pp. 67–70.
[6] Vladimir Jabotinsky, Synopsis for *Jews after the War* (1940), Jabotinsky Institute Archives, Tel Aviv.
[7] Vladimir Jabotinsky, 'ABC of the Jewish Army', *American Jewish Chronicle*, 20 June 1940.
[8] Vladimir Jabotinsky, *Essentials of the Jewish Army Scheme*, 1940, Jabotinsky Institute Archives, Tel Aviv.

On 10 June 1940 Italy entered the war on Germany's side after Hitler had defeated France. On 18 June Stern was released from prison. On 26 June Stern signed Communiqué 112,[9] regarded as the genesis of the Irgun B'Yisrael, which later evolved into Lehi (the Fighters for the Freedom of Israel). The British labelled the group 'the Stern Gang'. While a majority did not follow Stern out of the organisation, the split induced an apathy which rendered the Irgun inactive.

On 5 July Stern appealed to Jabotinsky to bring Raziel into line and prevent a split 'in the family of Mendelson'. The letter was never delivered to Jabotinsky because of the latter's death a few weeks later. Raziel was criticised for his silence on crucial issues – British actions to prevent Jewish emigration, the trials of Irgun fighters, the introduction of laws regarding the Land of Israel. Jabotinsky was informed that the 'executive committee' had elected Stern in Raziel's place and asked him to ratify this. On the one hand, Jabotinsky was told about 'dissatisfied plotters who take his name in vain'. On the other, Jabotinsky was urged to prevent 'a war of brothers'.[10]

Stern's followers clearly felt that despite the common Nazi enemy, Jewish national interests were not the same as those of the British – and there were some things which could not be glossed over. Britain had declared war against Germany not to save the Jews but to defend and protect its own position and security and that while Britain was fighting the Nazis it was doing its utmost to bar the gates of salvation to millions of Jews trapped in Europe.[11]

Stern argued that the British authorities facilitated the persecution of the Jews in Europe by cutting off the escape routes to Palestine. In November 1940, hundreds of Jewish refugees had drowned when the *Patria* was sunk accidentally by the Haganah. The following month more than 1,500 Jews without documentation were deported to Mauritius. Moreover, mobilisation for the war effort meant that fewer fighters would engage in the struggle against the British.

Stern regarded Raziel's agreement with the British as the worst of betrayals. The relationship between them had changed from one of close comrades to that of sworn enemies. The Arab Revolt had brought them together; Hitler's advance had forced them apart.

---

[9] Communiqué 112, 26 June 1940, Jabotinsky Institute Archives. Tel Aviv.

[10] A 549/13, Stern Archive, Central Zionist Archives, Jerusalem. 'Mendelson' was Jabotinsky's code name and Raziel's was 'Dr. Neumann'.

[11] *The Fighters for the Freedom of Israel*, Undated pamphlet, Jabotinsky Institute Archives, Tel Aviv.

Raziel, however, was bitter about Stern's actions. He called him 'this delicate playboy' and 'a super-demagogue'.[12] There was clearly a difference in temperament between Raziel and Stern. In Stern's eyes, the war against Nazism should not complicate an uncompromising and determined ideological clarity in fighting the British. Raziel, however, had little respect for Stern's romanticism and all-consuming immersion in an ideology of self-sacrifice.

STERN'S APPROACH TO NATIONAL LIBERATION

Stern came from a literary background. His grandfather Rafael Groshkin had contributed to journals such as *Hamelitz* and *Der Idishe Stimme*. In his poetry, Stern, however, promoted the spirit of self-sacrifice, the shedding of blood and the acceptance of death in the cause of national liberation. Indeed, he viewed himself as 'a poet and soldier':

> Yes
> I am both a soldier and a poet
> Today I write with a pen, tomorrow I will write with a sword
> Today I write in ink, tomorrow I will write in blood
> Today on paper, tomorrow on the torso of a man
> Heaven gave us the book and the sword
> Fate has decreed it
> Soldier and poet[13]

Stern's poem started with a quotation from the first book of Samuel and noted King Saul's search for a young man 'who is skilful in playing [the harp] and a heroic man of valour and a man of war'. This young man became the future King David. Stern prefaced the poem with a fragment of a poem from the Greek mercenary and poet Archilochus: 'I am a follower of my Lord Enyalius [the God of war], and I understand the lovely gift of the Muses.' Archilochus's famous comment, 'The fox knows many things, but the hedgehog knows one big thing', was clearly relevant to Stern's understanding of Zionism and his struggle against the British.

Stern signed several of his poems Eleazar Ben-Yair, who according to the historian Josephus exhorted his followers to kill each other on Masada in the year 73 when surrounded by legions of Rome.[14] Stern also

---

[12] Heller, *The Stern Gang*, p. 74.
[13] Avraham Stern, 'Florence', 20 June 1934, *Be-damai la-'ad tihyi: shirim* (Tel Aviv, 1976), p. 40. See also file 98/25–29, Stern Archive, Central Zionist Archives, Jerusalem.
[14] 102/12 Stern Archive, Central Zionist Archives, Jerusalem.

FIGURE 10. Avraham Stern in Suwalki (1934).
Courtesy of the Jabotinsky Institute, Tel Aviv.

admired the ultimate sacrifice of Sara Aaronsohn, a participant in the Nili espionage group who shot herself while in Turkish custody in 1917.

Stern attempted to identify the solitary figure of the freedom fighter who lived unseen and unknown deep in the underground with the religious symbolism of the lonely man of faith. Faith in God became faith in the struggle against the British. It could be neither questioned nor challenged. There was no room for atheists in the Stern group.

Stern's poetry was influenced by the Russian Futurist Vladimir Mayakovsky[15] and the leader of the Easter Uprising in Dublin in 1916, Paidrig Pearse.[16] Quite often, Stern prefaced some of his poems with appropriate quotations from a wide range of literary figures, such as Uri Zvi Greenberg, Homer and Alexander Blok. But it was the Hebrew Bible

---

[15] Yaira Ginossar, *Lo bi-shevilenu shar ha-saksofon: 'al shire Ya'ir* (Tel Aviv, 1998), p. 77.
[16] Ibid., p. 81.

that was not only a source of traditional motifs but also of contemporary relevance.

The daily 'Shema' prayer begins with 'Hear, O Israel: 'The Lord our God, the Lord is One'. In Stern's poem, it became

> Hear, O Avenger: the Voice of the Lord
> Smash your enemy's head with your hand held aloft
> Let his word be engraved upon your heart
> Make holy the weapons of war[17]

Jewish festivals were utilised as poetic themes to promote the idea of resistance. In his poem 'Simhat Torah'[18] (the festival of the Rejoicing of the Law), he writes of resting his head on *Baba Kama* – a tractate from the Babylonian Talmud which refers to damages caused by criminal acts – with a Mauser pistol within reach.

In another poem about Succot[19] (the festival of Tabernacles), he converts the imagery of holding the *lulav* (date palm) and the *etrog* (citron) into weapons of war:

> The field is our synagogue
> The prayer: the realm of Zion restored
> In my left hand, the lulav-rifle
> In my right hand, the etrog-handgranade

Even the oath of betrothal at Jewish weddings was transformed into an oath of allegiance whereby the bride was replaced by the homeland:

> Behold, you are consecrated to me, O Homeland, according to
> the laws of Moses and Israel.[20]

Other poems were defined by the ritual annual cycle which defined Jewish life. Repentance on Yom Kippur[21] and the concluding blessing, Havdalah,[22] at the end of the Jewish Sabbath were also themes. Stern's poems, such as 'To Our Mothers', were often infused with messianic expectation and redemption.[23] As a youth in Suwalki,[24] he had played the part of the false Jewish messiah, Shabtai Zevi, in Jerzy Żuławski's play

---

[17] Stern, 'Hear O Avenger', *Be-damai la-'ad tihyi*, p. 27.
[18] Ibid., p. 69.
[19] Ibid., p. 68.
[20] Ibid., p. 53.
[21] 3-15/1, Stern Archive, Central Zionist Archives, Jerusalem.
[22] 81/1, 2, Stern Archive, Central Zionist Archives, Jerusalem.
[23] Stern, '*Be-damai la-'ad tihyi*, p. 105.
[24] Heller, *The Stern Gang*, p. 318 n. 58.

Koniec Mesjasza (The End of the Messiah).[25] This drama examined the limits of martyrdom in the cause of nationalism.

There were also messianic tendencies in his 'Principles of Renaissance' which all of Stern's followers were commanded to adhere to. Stern looked to the Bible rather than to the British Mandate to define the borders of Israel.[26] The new state would stretch from 'the river of Egypt to the great river, the Euphrates'. As in the days of Joshua, the new state would be established through conquest and not through diplomacy. Stern further invoked his own interpretation of the midrashic commentary that 'the Sword and the Book came down intertwined from Heaven'.[27] The last of the eighteen Principles committed the Stern group to the rebuilding of the Third Temple.

Such messianic tendencies became more pronounced following the break with the Irgun.[28] Stern invoked the writings of Maimonides, the medieval philosopher, and his comments on the appearance of the messianic king who would save the Jews from 'the descendants of Esau' and gather in the dispersed remnant of Israel.[29]

Yet Stern's religiosity was tempered with affection for European cultural romanticism. He could also laud Irish republicanism and Russian Futurism. Stern respected Boris Savinkov, the anti-Bolshevik social revolutionary whose advocacy of political violence mirrored his own views. He also respected the principle of individual elimination – the assassination of British officials – which had been enacted by the Narodnaya Volya in Tsarist Russia and written about by Abba Ahimeir. He pointed to the example of several small nations – Greece, Bulgaria, Serbia, Czechoslovakia – which had liberated themselves by the use of force.

Within a year Jabotinsky was dead from a heart attack in New York while Raziel had been killed in Iraq – ironically helping the British. Stern was thus able to develop his views and his organisation without the restraints and biting criticism of his main opponents. Stern's turn towards an almost mystical approach allowed him to interpret Raziel's death as 'a decree of Providence' for abandoning the armed struggle against the British.[30] His interest in the legends of messianism thus

---

[25] *Ha-Boker*, 13 February 1942.
[26] Genesis 15:18.
[27] Devarim Rabbah 4:2.
[28] Avraham Stern, 'The Messianic Movement in Israel', *Ba-Makhteret*, nos. 4 and 5 (January–February 1941).
[29] Maimonides, 'Hilkhot Melakhim UMilkhamotehem', *Ha-Yad Ha Hazaka*.
[30] Israel Scheib (Eldad), *Ma'aser Rishon* (Tel Aviv, 1950), p. 70.

became accentuated.[31] In Stern's view, both Herzl and Jabotinsky had performed the role of Moses, who had led the people out of bondage. Like Moses, they died before their time, envisaging a future state of the Jews but not entering its portals. Stern believed that he and his followers carried the burden of playing the role of David, tasked with actually establishing the state.[32] Moreover, he may well have seen himself in the role of Meshiah ben Yosef, a catalytic messianic figure destined to fall in battle so that another messianic figure, Meshiah ben David, would finally emerge, wage a successful struggle against the enemies of the Jews and usher in a golden era of world peace.[33] Moreover, his belief that Britain – and not Germany – was the central enemy hardened to such an extent that he declared the Balfour Declaration null and void. His solution to the complexities of the Arab-Jewish struggle over the same land was centred in a population exchange.

STERN'S LAST YEARS

It seemed to Stern in 1940 that Britain was on its last legs and would eventually sue for peace with Nazi Germany. This therefore necessitated a swift agreement with the victors. He perceived the template for any agreement to be the World War I treaty of Brest-Litovsk whereby the Bolsheviks ceded huge tracts of territory to the Germans. His exemplars in making contact with the enemy of my enemy was Nili's collaboration with the British against the Turks, Herzl's meeting with von Plehve in 1903 and even Jabotinsky's discussions with the Ukrainian nationalists in 1921. Why, Stern asked, should Hitler and Mussolini be any different from past enemies of the Jewish people?

The entry of Italy into the war and its advance on Egypt impressed Stern. He believed that Mussolini's regime could become a partner in the plan to oust the British from Palestine. The bombing of Haifa and Tel Aviv in September 1940 further coloured his reasoning. In addition Stern psychologically glossed over Italian anti-Semitism. The Italians, he believed, would train a Jewish army, and 'a corporate regime' would be established in Palestine. The Vatican would control the Old City of Jerusalem, and Mussolini would facilitate the transfer of Jews in occupied Europe to Palestine. Such pipedreams turned to dust when he was confronted with

---

[31] Ibid., p. 75.
[32] Ibid., p. 74.
[33] Heller, *The Stern Gang*, p. 105; (Moses) Maimonides, *Mishneh Torah, Sefer Shoftim, Hilkhot Melakhim Umilkhamotehem*, ch. 11.

the reality of Italy's military debacle in the Western desert and in Greece at the end of 1940.

Other national movements, such as the IRA, the precursors of the Egyptian Free Officers movement and the Indian National Congress, refused to align themselves with the war effort and wished to exploit the difficulties of the British at this time. Some collaborated with the Nazis – for the good of the cause. The Indian nationalist Subhas Chandra Bose, like the mufti of Jerusalem, spent the war years in Germany and in his writings and broadcasts was oblivious to the fate of the Jews.[34] Even in Palestine, there was the Berit Spartacus, a Trotskyist group which campaigned against enlisting in the British forces. The prime concern of all these groups was overthrowing the imperial master and securing independence.

Stern likened the world war to the titanic struggle between Gog and Magog in the book of Ezekiel[35] and argued that British weakness should be exploited. The difference between Palestine and other national liberation movements was that the Nazis were opposed to Jews as a people per se. This did not impinge on the national interests of the Irish, Egyptians and Indians, but it did have meaning for Jews worldwide. Even so Stern did not regard Hitler as an exterminator in 1940, but solely as a persecutor who could be assuaged.

Stern initially attempted to steer a neutral path but then veered towards presenting favourable proposals to the Germans and Italians. He sent Naftali Lubenchik to Beirut, where he met the German representative Otto von Hentig, an adherent of the old school of German diplomacy and not a member of the Nazi Party. In a memorandum of their conversation afterwards, it was claimed that Nazi Germany simply wanted to secure the emigration of the Jews from Europe, which was Stern's aim as well. Even so there might well be cooperation between the new volkisch-nationalen Hebraertum and Nazi Germany. Stern promised participation on the German side, but he required 40,000 European Jews for the conquest of Palestine. Stern referred to a recent speech by Hitler that the Fuhrer would exploit any situation to isolate and defeat Britain.[36]

In May 1941, he believed that Rommel's victory in the Middle East was imminent and that Palestine would fall to the Germans. A few weeks later he predicted that Operation Barbarossa would precipitate the

---

[34] Roman Hayes, *Subhas Chandra Bose in Nazi Germany: Politics, Intelligence and Propaganda, 1941–1943* (London, 2011), pp. 165–67.

[35] Ezekiel 38.

[36] Heller, *The Stern Gang*, pp. 84–91.

collapse of the USSR. *Ha'aretz* accused Stern and his followers of being 'quislings'.[37] This propelled a second – unsuccessful – attempt to contact the Germans at the end of the year.

Despite the noose tightening around him, Stern's willingness to continue the war against the British resulted in the killing of Jewish passers-by in an attempt to rob a bank. Another operation to kill officers of the British Criminal Investigation Department (CID) using landmines resulted in the deaths of two Jewish policemen. The Palmah's commander, Yitzhak Sadeh, met Stern in October 1941 and warned him that if he continued on his path, a clash would be inevitable.

Alienated from an unsympathetic Yishuv which still offered sanctuary to him, even the official Revisionists published a 'wanted' photograph of Stern plus details of the reward offered.[38] Stern was discovered in a south Tel Aviv apartment by British detectives in February 1942 and met his end, confronting his self-defined enemy.

Yet the manner of Stern's killing was questioned. It led to the suspicion in the Yishuv that he may have been murdered by the British CID. It was followed a few weeks later by the sinking of the *Struma*, an unseaworthy vessel chartered by the NZO to bring Jews out of Romania. The British prevaricated about allowing the passengers into Palestine. The Turks towed the ship out of Istanbul after failing to repair its engines and allowed it to drift. A Soviet submarine which was authorised to attack all ships entering the Black Sea, following the Nazi invasion of the USSR, then fired a torpedo at the 'enemy vessel'. The majority of almost 800 passengers were trapped below deck while the handful who escaped died in the cold sea because of the lack of instant action by the Turkish authorities. The captain and crew of the submarine were commended by their superiors for 'their courageous act'.[39]

In one sense the tragedy of the *Struma* encapsulated the helplessness of the Jews and the indifference of the world. It appeared to many that an unholy if inadvertent collusion between the Romanians, British, Turks and Soviets had thwarted an escape from Nazi persecution. The dead Stern was reborn as an icon of resistance who had fought while others buried their heads in the sand. It also stirred the conscience of the Irgun.[40]

[37] *Ha'aretz*, 12 May 1941.
[38] *Hamashkif*, 30 January 1942.
[39] *Jerusalem Post*, 18 August 2000.
[40] *Ba-herev*, March 1942.

THE SHOAH AND THE WAR AGAINST THE BRITISH

The ideological differences between Raziel and Stern were symbolised by an identification with the Hebrew rebels of antiquity. Raziel signed the agreement with the British as (Elazar) Ben-Hananiah, and (Elazar) Ben-Yair was the nom de guerre of Stern. Both historical figures, they represented different factions in the first war against the Romans (66–70 CE). Ben-Yair emerged as the leader of the Sicarii, who espoused the assassination of leading Jews predisposed to a political settlement. Ben-Hananiah opposed the radicalism of the Zealots, and such differences led to an internecine civil war as the Romans closed in on Jerusalem. The Temple was destroyed in the year 70, and three years later Ben-Yair, according to Jewish tradition, met his end at Masada in a mass suicide. In one sense it was this legacy which was taken up by the political heirs of Raziel and Stern.

Menahem Begin was fortunate enough to have escaped both from Nazi-occupied Poland and from Stalin's Gulag. He was fortunate politically to have reached Palestine after Vladimir Jabotinsky, David Raziel and Avraham Stern had all been lowered into their graves. Moreover, he had not participated in the split in 1940 and was initially seen as a neutral political figure.

A few months after his arrival, Begin resumed his political activities. Abba Ahimeir was in contact early on.[41] A CID report of August 1942 noted that Begin spent most mornings at the Betar headquarters in Tel Aviv. Moreover, it was clear that some members of the NZO were unhappy with Begin's presence in Palestine and had advised the CID that he was 'an extremist who merits careful supervision'.[42] The Haganah also kept a watchful eye on Begin.

A few days before his death, Jabotinsky admitted that his movement was falling to pieces and that his authority was waning.[43] Yet for those who remained in the Irgun, the burden of the war against Nazism psychologically rendered them inactive even if they felt unable to participate in the British war effort. The Irgun journal, *Ba-herev*, thus commemorated Black Sunday in November 1942 by recalling the martyrs to the

---

[41] Abba Ahimeir, Letter to Menahem Begin, 27 September [?] 1942, Begin Heritage Center Archives, Jerusalem.

[42] Intelligence Summary no. 15/42, Inspector General, CID Headquarters, Palestine Police, Jerusalem, 3 August 1942, Begin Heritage Center Archives, Jerusalem.

[43] Vladimir Jabotinsky, Letter to Arieh Altman, 28 July 1940, Jabotinsky Institute Archives, Tel Aviv.

cause – Jabotinsky, Raziel, Ben-Yosef and members of the Irgun who had been killed in the struggle against the British.[44]

Stern's legacy – and his ideological perspective – had not died with him. It had been continued intellectually and theoretically by Israel (Scheib) Eldad in his writings. Eldad called Stern 'a Prometheus' and 'the Euclid of National Geometry'. Yonatan Ratosh wrote a poem commemorating Stern. In September 1942 Yitzhak Shamir and Eliahu Giladi, leaders of Lehi, escaped from prison. Slightly more than a year later Natan Yellin-Mor, Stern's main aide in Poland in the pre-war years, also escaped from British incarceration at Latrun.

Lehi was resurrected, but there was an unspoken policy to follow a different path from Stern's while maintaining his legacy and his implicit martyrdom. Although Eldad continued to laud Stern in his own writings, the romanticism and indeed mysticism were replaced by a hard-headed pragmatism. Shamir and Yellin-Mor ruthlessly presided over a tight structure.[45] It was further understood that public opinion had to be courted and that the isolationist 'lonely man of faith' approach of Avraham Stern was impracticable. Eliahu Giladi, however, was more sympathetic to Stern's approach and influenced by the nihilism of the Russian thinkers Pisarev and Nechaev. In addition, Giladi was seen as unpredictable, which resulted in his execution by his comrades in Lehi.[46]

Even so, despite the unfolding tragedy of European Jewry, Lehi still regarded England as 'enemy number one of Hebrew nationalist aspirations' – with scores to settle with Nazi Germany and Soviet Russia.[47] Lehi made a distinction between 'individual liquidation' to achieve a political purpose and killing for personal motives. It took note of the praise showered on the Czech resistance in assassinating Heydrich in June 1942.[48] Political assassination, often of Jews, became Lehi's trademark. Yellin-Mor assumed the nom de guerre of 'Ehud' after the biblical Ehud Ben-Gera, who assassinated Eglon, king of Moab.[49]

British political figures such as Oliver Lyttleton, the resident minister of state for the Middle East, was already targeted during Stern's lifetime.[50] Alan Saunders, who was Raziel's co-signatory to the agreement

---

[44] *Ba-herev*, 14 November 1942.
[45] Ya'akov Banai, *Hayalim Almonim* (Tel Aviv, 1958), p. 335.
[46] Heller, *The Stern Gang*, pp. 113–14.
[47] He-Hazit: Iton Lohamei Herut Israel, no. 2, August 1943.
[48] Ibid.
[49] Judges 3:9–11.
[50] Nachman Ben-Yehuda, *Political Assassinations by Jews: A Rhetorical Device for Justice* (New York, 1993), pp. 167–69.

for the Irgun to cooperate with the British authorities, featured in Lehi's attempts in April 1942. Stern's death, however, triggered a desire for revenge. There was a plan to kill Jeffrey Morton, one of the British detectives who had arrested Stern. With Shamir in charge, there were operations to kill those who were believed to have betrayed Lehi members to the British. Avraham Vilenchik, a Lehi bank robber, was killed in February 1943, while Yitzhak Pritsker, formerly the head of an Irgun intelligence section in Haifa, was eliminated the following September.[51] Jews who were believed to be working for British intelligence, such as Ze'ev Falsh (March 1944) and Haim Gotowitz (May 1944), were also killed by Lehi gunmen.

In addition, there were numerous attempts to kill the British high commissioner, Sir Harold MacMichael, in 1944. Lehi planted a mine as he entered St. George's Cathedral in Jerusalem in February 1944, and he was sprayed by machine gun fire after a farewell party in Jaffa the following August. He emerged unscathed and returned to Britain.

Like MacMichael, the newly appointed British resident minister of state for the Middle East, Lord Moyne, was seen – almost certainly inaccurately – as an anti-Zionist and an anti-Semite by Lehi.[52] Regardless of his actual opinions, he was viewed by Lehi as paradigmatic of British intransigence in Palestine. In 1944 he was gunned down in Cairo by Eliahu Hakim and Eliahu Bet-Tsouri, who had been sent by Shamir. They were found guilty in January 1945 and executed in March.

This campaign of 'individual liquidation' was designed to demoralise and weaken the British in Palestine. Such exploits, which rebelled against the passivity of the diplomatic process, impressed Jewish youth and attracted them to the ranks of Lehi. The demands of defendants in the dock to be regarded as prisoners of war and to defend themselves in court earned respect from the general public.

On the diplomatic front, Weizmann was aghast at the turn of events. Only a few days before the murder of Moyne, the British cabinet had received a report which recommended a state for the Jews. Weizmann's ties with a resentful Churchill had been ruptured. Churchill informed the British cabinet and told the House of Commons that if this was the way of the future he would have to consider his long-held views in support of Zionism.[53]

---

[51] *Ha'aretz*, 5 September 1943.
[52] Bernard Wasserstein, 'New Light on the Moyne Murder', *Midstream*, March 1980.
[53] *Times*, 18 November 1944.

BEGIN'S REVOLT

By mid-1942 the first indications of the systematic mass extermination of the Jews began to reach Palestine. A detailed report of the killings in Poland was presented by the Polish government in exile to Britain and the United States.[54]

Although Begin had been separated from his family and friends for almost three years, he began to resume his political work in the summer of 1942. He told Betar representatives on 8 August 1942 that they should establish a Jewish army rather than enlist individually in the British military forces. He contributed articles to *Ha-Madrikh* under the pseudonym 'Menahem Ben-Ze'ev'. Several were clearly reflections on his experiences under the Soviets and his disdain for the 'one-sided Jewish love' of the left-wing Zionist Hashomer Hatzair and Jewish Communists who continued to worship Stalin.[55]

At the end of September 1942, he spoke at a meeting of the NZO which was attended by sixty people. He argued that Jews should serve in their own army under their own flag, ready for the opening of a second front, and not in the British army during World War II. Ignorant of the magnitude of the Shoah, he argued that 15,000 members of Betar still remained in Poland and should be brought to Palestine straightaway after the war. He also added that there were 800,000 Jewish refugees in Russia, 200,000 of whom were fit to serve in the army. Like Jabotinsky at the end of World War I, he argued that it was important that a standing Jewish army be present in Palestine by the war's end.[56]

All this was a continuation of Begin's projection of 'military Zionism' – that a military revolt was a necessity and the only way forward.[57] In Poland he had appointed a liaison officer to cement contacts between Betar and the Irgun. On the eve of the German invasion of Poland, the Romanian authorities issued a small number of visas to the Jews encamped on their borders. Begin instructed that only Betar youth of

[54] Office for Emergency Management, Executive Office of the President, 21 July 1942, Jabotinsky Institute Archives, Tel Aviv.
[55] Menahem Ben-Ze'ev, 'Russia and Zionism', *Ha-Madrikh*, February 1943; 'Ha-Komintern', June 1943, in *Ha-Irgun Zvai Leumi b'Eretz Israel*, vol. 6, ed. I. Alfassi (Jerusalem, 2002), pp. 71–76.
[56] Haganah intelligence (Shai) report, 2 October 1942, Haganah Archives, Tel Aviv.
[57] Menahem Begin, 'We Must Shoot', *Hamedina*, 12 June 1938.

conscription age should receive them so that they should fight in a Jewish army rather than in a Polish one.[58]

By October 1942 Begin still believed that 100,000 could be enrolled in a Hebrew army. He envisaged a Jewish army which would fight to liberate the Jews in occupied Europe.[59]

In December 1942 the Yishuv observed three days of mourning. Uri Zvi Greenberg questioned God about his indifference and inaction:

> Who am I to add a rung to the ladder of Hebrew prayer
> Of my holy mother, my holy father and their children,
> For whom you had no pity on that day
> The goyim slaughtered them
> When they looked to you where you sat in heaven on high![60]

In all quarters of the Yishuv, there was a sense of frustration that their families had been abandoned to their fate and that the Jews of Palestine had been unable to do anything about it. This inevitably led to a search for scapegoats. Even though Jabotinsky had neither anticipated the outbreak of war nor the Shoah, his evacuation plan and his urgent advocacy of the mass emigration of Polish Jewry in the late 1930s were recalled. The struggles against Weizmann and the sluggish 'old Zionism' were remembered. Mapai was blamed not simply for inaction and lack of foresight, but also for ideological distraction. Its emphasis on class rather than nation was highlighted. A nascent sympathy for the Soviet Union and a silence on the fate of the Jews of the USSR were perceived as another symptom of this malaise. Abba Ahimeir attacked Mapai's universalist concerns, such as assisting the Spanish Republic in its conflict with Franco.[61] All this was transformed into a reductionist indifference to the fate of the Jews in occupied Europe. Such accusations resonated with Begin and many others in the midst of Jewish impotence.

Initially many believed that a proportion of the 3 million–strong Jewish community of Poland would survive and that even rescue was possible.[62] Even as this prospect began to fade, many Jews in Palestine

[58] Ned Temko, *To Win or Die: A Personal Portrait of Menachem Begin* (New York, 1987), p. 54.

[59] M. Ben-Ze'ev, *Ha-Madrikh*, September 1942; October 1942.

[60] Uri Zvi Greenberg, 'To God in Europe', *Rehovot Ha-nahar* (Jerusalem, 1951), p. 237, English trans. Robert Fried in S. Y. Penueli and A. Ukhmani, eds., *Anthology of Modern Hebrew Poetry*, vol. 2 (Jerusalem, 1966).

[61] Abba Ahimeir, 'Ul Da'ugtam le-Madrid', 27 November 1936, in *Revolutionary Zionism* (Tel Aviv, 1965), pp. 123–28.

[62] *Herut*, 1 February 1943.

asked why the British insisted on bolting the gates and refusing entry. The complicity of the British in impeding escape became synonymous in the minds of many a member of the Irgun and Lehi as collaboration with the actions of the Nazi exterminator.

Begin had argued for a specifically Jewish fighting force since the beginning of 1940. By the end of 1942, when the reality of mass extermination had begun to sink in, Begin changed the focus of his political actions. The Yishuv held three days of mourning and there were accusatory articles about the role of the Jewish Agency in the Revisionist press. Begin began to drop any pretence of supporting Jabotinsky's pro-British orientation and considered Britain to be as guilty as Germany. In February 1943, Begin argued that Herzl, Nordau and Jabotinsky – but not the mainstream Zionists – also foresaw the mass murder. In his *Herut* article in February 1943, Begin argued that only the immediate establishment of a state could be a remedy for the plight of the Jews. In his second article in *Ha-madrikh* he argued that the Jews had no one to rely upon apart from themselves. In Begin's eyes, his approach to Jabotinsky at the Betar conference in Warsaw in September 1938 had been justified.[63] The failure of the Bermuda conference in April 1943 implied indifference to the fate of European Jewry by both the British and the Americans. This coincided with the uprising in the Warsaw Ghetto. These events further convinced Begin that appeals to 'the conscience of the world' were meaningless. In May 1943 Begin wrote an article bearing the acerbic title 'The British Regime Prepares for a Massacre of the Jews in the Land of Israel'.[64]

In 1943 the military fortunes of the Allies turned and it was now possible to predict the defeat of Hitler. Yet this prospect was tarnished by the Allied belief that only a total victory over Nazism would save the Jews. Neither the British Royal Air Force nor the Red Air Force attacked the railway lines to Auschwitz. In the interim the Nazis accelerated the extermination of European Jewry. After the turning of the tide at Stalingrad, Begin believed that the British were now relaxing into their old colonial ways. The British maintained their stand on the White Paper of 1939 in refusing to allow Jewish refugees into Palestine.[65] The Bermuda conference in April 1943 on the question of Jewish refugees had ended in failure. A few weeks later the Warsaw Ghetto Uprising began. The juxtaposition

[63] Amir Peleg, 'Menahem Begin and the Holocaust: The Formative Years, 1939–1948' (MA thesis, Ben-Gurion University of the Negev, 2007), pp. 87–91.
[64] Menahem ben-Ze'ev, *Herut*, 17 May 1943.
[65] *New York Times*, 30 April 1943.

of such events radicalised both the Irgun and Lehi. It sharpened their animosity towards the British in Palestine.

Begin proclaimed 'the Revolt' weeks before the termination of the White Paper's five-year period which allowed for a total immigration of 75,000 Jews. After 31 March 1944, the immigration of Jews into Palestine would require Arab approval.

In October 1940 the British cabinet had approved a plan for a Jewish military force, 10,000 strong, of whom 3,000 would be recruited in Palestine. The commanding officers would be approved by Weizmann and the British War Office. Hebrew was to be the language of instruction, and the Star of David would be emblazoned on the Union Jack. By August 1941 the British backtracked on this proposal because of the concern that such a force would be both a threat to their interests in the Middle East and a bargaining counter for the Zionists in post-war Palestine.[66]

It was only in September 1944, nearly five years after Jabotinsky had raised the prospect of a Jewish army, that the Jewish Brigade was finally established. It entered service on the Italian front shortly afterwards and ultimately assisted in aiding Holocaust survivors to reach Palestine.

CRUSHING THE DISSIDENTS

On the political front, Mapai demanded a reckoning. Although originally opposed to a campaign against Lehi at the beginning of 1944, Ben-Gurion embraced it by the year's end. Indeed, he was unequivocal in his assault on the *porshim* – the dissidents – and spoke about a knife being plunged into the back of the Jewish people. In no uncertain terms, he proclaimed that it was either the way of terror or the path of political struggle. In several forums, the prospect of collaboration with the British to root out the members of Lehi was discussed – and the *saison*, the hunting down of the *porshim*, subsequently initiated. It was opposed by both the General Zionists and the religious Mizrahi, as well as by Ahdut Ha'avodah and Left Poale Zion on the Left. Ben-Gurion called upon the Yishuv 'to spew out' the dissidents and called for anyone who aided them to be thrown out of work and struck off the labour exchange register. Young people were not exempt from Ben-Gurion's directive:

If any student be known to take part in murder or marauding, or only distributes the poisonous effusions of the terrorists among his fellows – tear the wretched

---

[66] Stephan E. C. Wendehorst, *British Jewry, Zionism and the Jewish State 1936–1956* (Oxford, 2012), p. 202.

leaflets from his grasp and burn them! Expel them, so that he may feel, and his parents and companions, how we abhor his traitorous felony.[67]

Moshe Sharett, Zionism's primary diplomat, regarded the saison as an inevitability.[68] Both Eliahu Golomb and Moshe Sneh had met Begin in October 1944 and warned him that the Irgun was damaging Zionist interests in the international community, but it was to no avail. Begin offered only a temporary ceasefire. The killing of Lord Moyne had irrevocably changed the situation.

Unlike Ben-Gurion and the Haganah, Begin believed that the enemy in late 1944 was the British and not Arab nationalists. Ben-Gurion condemned Begin's political direction by refusing to meet him. Begin, he believed, constituted the central political threat, while Lehi was no more than a peripheral nuisance. A year before, the Haganah had been instructed not to join Am Lohem, the first attempt at forming a joint military front. Through an agreement between Golomb and Yellin-Mor in December 1944, Lehi remained dormant for the following year while the hunt for dissidents was directed instead at Menahem Begin and the Irgun.[69]

Ironically Begin had initially condemned the killing of Lord Moyne and was profoundly opposed to the assassination of individuals without due process of law beforehand. Operating under the pseudonym of Ben-David, recalling David Raziel, Begin made several attempts to heal the breach in the Irgun and to reintegrate Lehi. He perceived the split in 1940 to be more 'a family affair' than a difference in ideology. He believed that Israel Eldad was the central obstacle to reunification, and after his arrest Begin pursued Lehi with several proposals and plans. Yet there were fundamental differences.

Lehi above all wanted to remain independent and to follow Stern's broad teachings. Begin had regarded Stern as a rival in Poland, and Lehi deeply resented the absence of any mention of Stern in the Irgun announcement of the Revolt. It was as if Stern had never existed and that Lehi's actions against the British had never taken place. Moreover, Lehi regarded itself as post-Jabotinsky and did not view the political process of persuading the British as central. Even in the light of the first revelations of the extent of the exterminations in 1944, Lehi never wavered

---

[67] David Ben-Gurion, *Medinat Yisrael Hamehudeshet* (Tel Aviv, 1969); Martin Sicker, *Pangs of the Messiah: The Troubled Birth of the Jewish State* (Westport, CT, 2000), p. 174.
[68] Heller, *The Stern Gang*, p. 141.
[69] Ibid., p. 138.

in its belief that Britain was still the central enemy of the Zionists. In contrast, Begin was aware that the Jews of Hungary and Romania were still under threat by the Nazi extermination machine. Immigration offices, tax offices and police stations, rather than British military locations, were therefore targets for the Irgun.

For all his rhetoric and accusatory commentary, Begin was not ready to renounce the path of politics. Moreover, he was ready neither to ditch Jabotinsky as a mentor and icon nor to espouse 'individual liquidation'. Begin was highly reticent about igniting civil war between Jews in Palestine – he was mindful of the destructive conflict between Ben-Hananiah and Ben-Yair 2,000 years before.[70] There was also an internationalist dimension to Lehi which Begin dissented from – perhaps to carry the conflict with Britain to London, perhaps to look for anti-imperialist partners similarly trying to free themselves from the colonial yoke.

Although both Begin and the leaders of Lehi had adhered to the ideas of the Maximalists back in 1932, the realities of World War II had intervened. It was the interpretation of those realities which defined the way forward. By 1944 there was thus a profound ideological difference between the Irgun and Lehi.

The character of Menahem Begin was a further obstacle. His sense of formality, reminiscent of Polish cultural norms, also irked. Begin was keen on pomp and ceremony and was not good in personal relationships. Indeed, in contrast to the Irgun, there were no ranks, no hierarchy, no saluting in Lehi – a far cry from Begin's ideal of a hierarchical Jewish army. Begin was thought to be vacuous by the leadership of Lehi, drawn to the lofty phrase and the applause of the crowd. As Shamir later commented:

I disliked his acceptance of flattery and fawning and wished, always in vain, that he were not so hungry for popularity. In fact, it surprised me that Begin had survived as he did, quite undiminished, the months he spent in the underground, in deep cover, deprived of such stimulus.[71]

Yellin-Mor was even more scathing in his appraisal:

Begin imagines himself standing on a high hill, carrying his utterances to those at its foot, whose eyes are uplifted to him. If they gaze at him with enthusiasm and admiration, he gives the one who so gazes a fatherly caress.[72]

---

[70] Menahem Begin, 'There Will Not Be a Civil War', *Herut*, 3 December 1944.
[71] Shamir, *Summing Up*, p. 86.
[72] Sasson Sofer, *Begin: An Anatomy of Leadership* (London, 1988), p. 250.

In turn, Begin ridiculed Eldad's rebranding of Stern as 'a new Jesus'.[73] Both organisations were condemned by the official Revisionists, the New Zionist Organisation. The Irgun maintained its link to the NZO until the outbreak of the Revolt. Begin believed that the NZO, like Lehi, would eventually come round to his way of thinking and unite with the Irgun. He commented in October 1944:

The leadership of Revisionism is not our kind of Revisionism. We still believe in Revisionism as the only movement which in the end will see eye to eye with us and the moment of crisis will support us. After all, it is Jabotinsky's movement.[74]

Despite Begin's hopes, the NZO was implacably opposed to the Irgun in 1944. Lehi had broken away long before. The 'Jabotinsky movement' had well and truly fragmented.

Lehi ultimately defined itself as a separate movement through the assassination of Lord Moyne. The Irgun defined itself through the oppression of the saison and the Haganah's collaboration with the British authorities. The polarisation appealed to Begin's sense of glorious defiance. The saison cemented his growing belief in himself as a leader who continued to oppose a vicious, official leadership and a muddle-headed majority of Jews in the Yishuv.[75]

---

[73] Heller, *The Stern Gang*, p. 103.
[74] Amos Perlmutter, *The Life and Times of Menachem Begin* (New York, 1987), p. 148.
[75] Menahem Begin, 'Herzl and Jabotinsky', *Herut*, 25 July 1944.

The Fight for Independence

MENAHEM BEGIN'S STRUGGLE

Since his very arrival in Palestine, Menahem Begin was clearly a marked man. A Haganah intelligence operative who listened to one of his talks in the autumn of 1942 excoriated him as 'a demagogue'.[1]

Begin admired and emulated the post-1933 Jabotinsky who had dismissed the Revisionist Executive at the Katowice conference. This was the Jabotinsky he knew – not the 'Revisionist' Jabotinsky. The selective Jabotinsky was adopted as 'the father of the Revolt'.

Significantly, in August 1944, when the Irgun was at a low ebb, having suffered numerous reverses, there was still a military parade of the Irgun to commemorate Jabotinsky's death.[2] Begin had also declared the Revolt before the end of the war against Hitler. The Irgun was fighting the war against the British, who were fighting the Germans, who were deporting the Jews en masse from Budapest. In this sense, he was following Stern's path at the beginning of the war, but Begin was also discerning. He forbad an attempt to bomb the Iraqi pipeline and argued that it would harm Britain's war effort.[3]

When the Revolt commenced, there was little public support and the Irgun's demands that the Yishuv declare a general strike and refuse to pay taxes fell on deaf ears. The sheet newspaper, Herut, periodically pasted on walls, was ignored. Perhaps more important, the official Revisionists – ostensibly unfurling the dead Jabotinsky's standard – were adamantly

[1] Haganah intelligence (Shai), Report 2, October 1942, Haganah Archives, Tel Aviv.
[2] Zionism, no. 4 (1976), pp. 400–405.
[3] Avi Shilon, Menachem Begin: A Life (New Haven, CT, 2012), p. 84.

opposed. Both Ben-Gurion and Arieh Altman, the Revisionist leader, feared British military reprisals and a reversal of any political progress. In October 1943 Churchill indicated to Weizmann that partition was a potential solution and that the Zionists might even receive part of Jordan.

Begin, however, saw the Revolt as enhancing the political process in securing an eventual British withdrawal from Palestine. The Revisionists and the labour movement generally were more disposed towards achieving a diplomatic solution through negotiation – although military action was not ruled out. Military force, Ben-Gurion reasoned, should be mobilised against a future Arab threat, not expended on the British, whose control of the Empire was being challenged daily in the post-war world. Begin believed that the Arab world would accept minority status for their brethren in Palestine and even supported the idea of transfer to Iraq when it was momentarily mooted in 1944. While Begin drew on past examples of a dedicated fighting few, as in the cases of the Risorgimento and the IRA, the disregard for the majority irked many. As one labour academic commented:

They are not merely trying to drive the British out of Palestine. They are trying to set down the political demands of the Jewish people, whether or not they can get a majority to back them – to set these demands down at the point of their guns, to define what are the objectives of the Zionist movement by threat of using force against any solution that they don't agree with, even if the majority does.[4]

Members of the Zionist movement had met at the Biltmore Hotel in New York in May 1942 and had proclaimed the prospect of a future Palestine 'integrated in the structure of the new democratic world'. For the Irgun, this was an irrelevance and far removed from the reality. In 1944 the Irgun concentrated on attacks against civilian and military outposts of the British administration. Following a failed attempt to assassinate the British high commissioner, Sir Harold MacMichael, Lehi succeeded in killing Lord Moyne, the British resident minister in Cairo.

Ben-Gurion regarded Begin's mixture of romanticism and fatalism with disdain. Begin argued, 'If we do not fight, we shall be destroyed. To fight was the only way to salvation.'[5]

---

[4] Ben Halpern, Talk to Pioneer Women, 1947, in Mark A. Raider, '"Irresponsible, Undisciplined Opposition": Ben Halpern on the Bergson Group and Jewish Terrorism in Pre-State Palestine', *American Jewish History*, vol. 92 no. 3 (September 2004), pp. 313–60.

[5] Menachem Begin, *The Revolt* (London, 1979), p. 85.

The saison proved broadly unpopular within the Yishuv, and even the liberal *Ha'aretz* was opposed. Begin's 'natural' allies, the General Zionists and the religious Zionists of the Mizrahi, condemned Ben-Gurion's move – and threatened to resign their positions on the Jewish Agency Executive. Even on the labour side there was a general reticence about moving against the Irgun for fear of provoking a civil war. Yet the saison disrupted Irgun activity up to the summer of 1945.

In placing the Irgun fighters beyond the pale, Ben-Gurion's strategy also assisted in defining the Irgun's own sense of self-sacrifice and raison d'être. Ben-Gurion's attack on the Irgun did not convince everyone. Regardless of a dislike of Begin and his policies, handling over Jewish fighters to the British was a step too far.

In 1945 Clement Atlee and the British Labour Party displaced Winston Churchill and the Conservatives as the party of government. This was due to a sense that progressive policies were required in the post-war period that would not allow the status quo ante to raise its jaded head. The welfare state and the National Health Service were introduced. The first steps in decolonisation to convert an empire into a commonwealth were taken. Its advocates lay mainly to the left of the party, where there were many supporters of a socialist Jewish state. However, the man appointed as foreign secretary was Ernest Bevin, a former right-wing trade union leader who viewed the disproportionate number of Jews in the international Communist movement with great displeasure. There were also vested interests in the Arab world which a post-war impoverished Britain hoped to exploit.

Bevin's approach was predicated on disconnecting the disarray of Jewish survivors in Europe from the salvation of immigrating to Palestine. Bevin believed that the problem of the Jewish displaced persons could be solved by returning them to their countries of origin. The enormity of the Shoah and the hostility towards returning individuals in countries such as Poland indicated that this was not a viable solution. There was also a retreat to the quota restrictions of the 1939 White Paper in preventing immigrants from reaching Palestine. Jewish immigration was now restricted to 18,000 annually, and Jews could not exceed more than one-third of the population.

In early 1946 the Anglo-American Committee recommended that 100,000 immigrants be allowed into Palestine and that the Mandate become a UN trusteeship as an interim measure. While the Americans concurred, Bevin refused to implement the report and strongly defended his policy at the Labour Party conference in 1946.[6] The British Labour

---

[6] *New York Tribune*, 13 June 1946.

Party in 1944 had been passionately pro-Zionist in the wake of the revelations of the mass extermination of the Jews, but the responsibility of power, shouldered by politicians unsympathetic to the Jewish plight amidst a myriad of other post-war problems, had engineered a pronounced volte-face. All this had catalysed a reconciliation and an uneasy military alliance between the Haganah, the Irgun and Lehi which operated until August 1946. Begin had been very careful to avoid any merger between the Irgun and the Haganah. The Irgun concentrated on destabilising British rule, such as sabotaging the Haifa oil pipeline and disrupting transportation by blowing up bridges and railway lines, while the Haganah focused on illegally bringing Jewish immigrants to Palestine.

Lehi appropriated arms from arms dumps and destroyed aircraft at Kfar Syrkin in February 1946. The Irgun similarly took war materiel from the air force base at Rosh Ha'ayin in November 1945. The depleted Irgun coffers were replenished by attacks on the gold exchange in Jaffa and a train robbery in January 1946. The Jewish Agency had a veto over operations it considered would harm the Zionist cause; even so, the Irgun also operated independently by attacking CID offices in Palestine.

Begin introduced the idea of reciprocity into the conflict with the British authorities. When two members of the Irgun were sentenced to death, the Irgun captured five British officers as bargaining counters in June 1946. Despite a large number of arrests, including those of members of the Jewish Agency Executive, the Irgun refused to give way. Eventually the death sentences were commuted to life imprisonment, and the British officers were released. In December 1946, an Irgun member was sentenced to eighteen lashes of the whip. The Irgun responded by flogging a British major who had been seized from a Netanya hotel. Two sergeants were subsequently flogged in Rishon L'Zion and in Tel Aviv. In January 1947 the British policy was discontinued.

At the beginning of 1946, there were 80,000 British troops in Palestine – a tremendous financial burden for a weakened post-war Britain. The British military responded to the joint actions of the Haganah, the Irgun and Lehi with mass arrests and searches on 29 June 1946, dubbed the 'Black Sabbath'. Weapons dumps were uncovered and documents located which implicated the complicity of the Jewish Agency in military activities. The documents were duly transferred to the King David Hotel. On 22 July 1946, it was blown up by the Irgun, with 91 dead and 476 injured – including British officials, as well as Jewish and Arab administrators. The Irgun blamed the British for not heeding warnings. The British blamed the Irgun for having instigated the attack in the first place.

The Haganah blamed the Irgun for an incompetent, botched job and for lack of good communication between them.

The original idea had been for the Haganah to attack the arsenals, Lehi to take over the Palestine Information Office and the Irgun to destroy the government headquarters in the King David Hotel. Moshe Sneh, head of the Haganah, had originally agreed to the operation, but twice asked Begin to postpone it. Did the Irgun give sufficient warning to the British to evacuate the hotel? Was the British commander too arrogant to move sufficiently quickly? Did Begin deliberately not respond to Sneh's pleas? Who was Sneh acting on behalf of – Ben-Gurion, the Haganah, himself? Apparently Begin was shocked by the number of deaths, but his line was that the joint resistance movement had approved the attack. The Jewish Agency moved quickly to condemn the attack. The political damage, however, was done.

The King David Hotel attack set the pattern for future events. An inexperienced Begin relied on his military advisors – in this case Gidi Paglin – followed by an explanation to redirect the blame.

A few days later, Operation Broadside was mounted. Twenty thousand British troops marched into Tel Aviv, imposed a curfew and conducted a search of the Jewish Agency headquarters, which resulted in the arrests of nearly 800 people. Jewish Agency leaders were imprisoned in Latrun. Several others, including Yitzhak Shamir, were sent to East African camps. The Haganah ships *Yagur* and the *Henrietta Szold*, bringing illegal immigrants, were turned back and their passengers imprisoned on Cyprus.

The British intensified its coastal blockade to prevent Jews from reaching Palestine. It also requested foreign governments to stop Jews from leaving if they did not possess the correct documentation. In Europe, Italy, France, the United Kingdom and U.S. zones of Germany complied, but significantly the USSR and the Eastern Europeans did not.

At the beginning of September 1946, the leadership of the Jewish Agency was released from Latrun. The Haganah stopped supporting the armed struggle. Lehi and the Irgun, however, continued it. There were now attacks in Europe as well as in Palestine. There were Irgun branches in more than twenty countries.

Ben-Gurion had concluded that the armed struggle against the British had run its course and become counterproductive. Moreover, Weizmann had seen all his diplomatic efforts dissipate due to the situation. He threatened to resign if the attacks on the British continued.

In his address to the Zionist congress in Basel in December 1946, Weizmann commented:

Zionism is a modern expression of the liberal ideal. Divorced from that ideal, it loses all purpose, all hope. When we invoke the Jewish tradition as support for our national claim, we are not free to shake off the restraints of that tradition and embark on courses which Jewish morality cannot condone. Assassination, ambush, kidnapping, the murder of innocent men are alien to the spirit of our movement. We came to Palestine to build, not to destroy; terror distorts the essence of Zionism. It insults our history; it mocks the ideals for which a Jewish society must stand; it sullies our banner; it compromises our appeal to the world's liberal conscience.[7]

Weizmann pointed out that Masada, the last site of resistance to the Romans almost two millennia before, was, for all its heroism, 'a disaster in our history'. The sense of urgency, typified by Begin without and Ben-Gurion within, had sounded the death knell for Weizmann's unerring belief in diplomacy and the good intentions of the British. His views were seen as out of touch.

Weizmann increasingly viewed Begin as a wrecker of his diplomatic schemes. After reading an interview with Begin in the *New York Herald Tribune*, Weizmann wrote in a letter that 'the impression one gets in reading an interview is that you deal with a man who is a megalomaniac suffering from a messiah complex. Whether he is just a fanatic or a charlatan or both is hard to say.'[8]

Despite Weizmann's eclipse, his past efforts yielded dividends when Truman announced his support for a Jewish state on 4 October 1946, dismissing the profound opposition of the Atlee government.

THE EMERGENCE OF HILLEL KOOK

The British refusal to allow Holocaust survivors to immigrate deeply angered the Jewish population of Palestine and in the Diaspora as harrowing tales of Nazi atrocities began to sink into the post-war consciousness. This provoked a growing respect for the Irgun for its bloody-mindedness despite its policies. The Anglo-American Committee of Inquiry report

[7] Chaim Weizmann, 'Address to Twenty-Second Zionist Congress', 9 December 1946, *Presidential Address* (Jewish Agency, London, 1946).
[8] Chaim Weizmann, Letter to Blanche Dugdale, 18 March 1947, in Barnet Litvinoff, Joseph Heller, Nechama A. Chalom, eds., *The Letters and Papers of Chaim Weizmann, May 1945–July 1947*, Series A, Letters vol. 22 (New Jersey 1979).

had been rejected by Atlee and the subsequent Morrison-Grady report proved unacceptable to all. In the midst of a political stalemate in 1946, the Zionist calls for partition became louder and more numerous. For both Bevin, who believed in a unitary state, and for Begin, whose borders encompassed the original British Mandate before the separation of TransJordan, this was anathema.

Menahem Begin discovered that he had a rival as leader of the militant Right. Hillel Kook had worked for the Irgun in Poland in the late 1930s. He was born in Jerusalem, and his encounters with Jabotinsky attracted him to the Zionist cause. He followed Jabotinsky to the United States in 1940, where he began to work for the establishment of a Jewish army which would fight alongside the Allies. Jabotinsky, depressed by the news from Europe, was assuming a quasi-figurehead role. Kook, using the pseudonym 'Peter H. Bergson', formed the Committee for a Jewish Army of Stateless and Palestinian Jews at the end of 1941. His associate, Shmuel Merlin, had worked for the Revisionist Executive in Poland and then became an editor of the Irgun journal, *Di Tat*. Another member of the group was Eri Jabotinsky, son of their late mentor.

When the news of the mass extermination of Polish Jews began to reach the United States in the summer of 1942 and the killings were confirmed by the U.S. government in November, it became clear that this was a lesser issue for the American leadership, which believed that its central focus should be on winning the war.

For Kook and his friends, the establishment of a Jewish army now became a secondary concern. As the revelations of the Shoah became apparent, Kook began to focus on raising awareness about what was happening to the Jews and on the question of rescue. Now 'Germany was more our enemy than ... the British.'[9] While he wanted a Jewish army in place after the war, Kook, unlike Begin, was willing to serve in the British armed forces.

Kook undertook a campaign in the United States that was both dramatic and radical. Only provocative, outrageous and sometimes offensive comment would lodge in the public psyche and bring about change through public pressure. Kook published hard-hitting advertisements in the *New York Times*, having enlisted the writer Ben Hecht to produce the copy. He was also able to solicit the support of well-known stars of stage, screen and the theatre. Several were assimilated Jews who had been busy

⁹ David S. Wyman and Rafael Medoff, *A Race against Death: Peter Bergson, America and the Holocaust* (New York, 2002), p. 61.

trying to create their personal American dream, often in an anti-Semitic environment. The first revelations of the exterminations awakened their buried Jewishness, and Kook was able to utilise their talents in a meaningful fashion. Many had found it difficult to relate to the traditional Jewish organisations, and Kook's organisation provided them with a vehicle in which to act. Unlike the Jewish organisations, Kook did not fear offending the non-Jewish public.

In February 1943, the *New York Times* reported that the Romanian government had offered to move 70,000 Jews from Transnistria to Palestine and would provide the ships, but it expected payment of $130 per refugee.[10] The Romanian government had made a similar offer a month before to the Jewish Agency, which had informed the British Foreign Office. In turn the British Embassy in Washington had been instructed to inform the State Department, which seemingly shelved the proposal. The State Department investigated superficially and concluded that 'it was without foundation'.[11]

A few days after the original *New York Times* item, an advertisement appeared in the paper entitled, 'For Sale to Humanity: 70,000 Jews – Guaranteed Human Beings at $50 Apiece':

Rumania is tired of killing Jews. It has killed one hundred thousand of them in two years. Rumania will now give Jews away practically for nothing.[12]

This was followed by the pageant *We Will Never Die*, written by Ben Hecht, produced by Billy Rose, directed by Moss Hart and narrated by Paul Muni and Edward G. Robinson. This was the voice of the intellectuals, Jews in the arts and those who mixed with the wider world, rather than 'official Jews'.

Yet the Bergson group of young Palestinian Jews had absolutely no mandate to represent U.S. Jews. While the group had previously published advertisements in support of a Jewish army, their pronouncements and mass events now presented the fate of the doomed Jews of Europe in harsh monochrome. Their efforts were designed to prick the conscience of U.S. citizens. Feeling both undermined and criticised, the Jewish organisations, the British Embassy and the State Department bristled and attempted to find a way of deporting Kook and his friends. While such public relations undoubtedly raised the consciousness of

[10] *New York Times*, 13 February 1943.
[11] David S. Wyman, *The Abandonment of the Jews: America and the Holocaust, 1941–1945* (New York, 1984), pp. 82–83.
[12] *New York Times* 16 February 1943.

ordinary Americans about the tragedy that was unfolding in Europe, Jewish luminaries such as Stephen Wise and Nahum Goldmann argued that Kook's emotive and evocative pronouncements cancelled out the unglamorous, painstaking efforts of Jewish diplomacy. Like Begin, Kook refused to accept the discipline of the Zionist Organisation. The Allies' policy of rescue through victory raised the question 'what if there were no more Jews to save?'

As the situation in Europe became more desperate and with no prospect of rescue in sight, Ben Hecht's lines became more biting and uncompromising, his general approach more unapologetic. In September 1943, he published the 'Ballad of the Doomed Jews of Europe':

> Four million Jews waiting for death
> Oh hang and burn but – quiet, Jews!
> Don't be bothersome; save your breath –
> The world is busy with other news
>
> Four million murders are quite a smear
> Even our state department views
> The slaughter with much disfavour here
> But then – it's busy with other news
>
> Oh world be patient – it will take
> Some time before the murder crews
> Are done. By Christmas you can make
> Your peace on earth without the Jews.[13]

In July 1943 Kook organised the 'Emergency Conference to Save the Jewish People of Europe', which was attended by Mayor La Guardia and former president Hoover. By the end of 1943, Hecht's texts inevitably began to criticise the Allies' conduct. The White House was not amused.[14]

Like Begin in Palestine, with the end of the war in sight Kook changed the direction of the campaign from the rescue of European Jewry towards securing a Jewish state in Palestine and the withdrawal of the British.

In May 1944 Kook acquired a former embassy building to be the headquarters of the Hebrew Committee of National Liberation – the government in exile of the Jewish state. At the same time Kook established the American League for a Free Palestine for Jews and non-Jews who supported the goals of the Hebrew Committee, which attracted the support of Eleanor Roosevelt and Groucho Marx. All this was a red flag

---

[13] *New York Times*, 14 September 1943.
[14] Ben Hecht, 'My Uncle Abraham Reports ... ', *New York Times*, 5 November 1943; 'How Well Are You Sleeping?' *New York Times*, 24 November 1943.

FIGURE 11. Launch of the Hebrew Committee of National Liberation (May 1944). Hillel Kook (centre) is speaking.
Courtesy of the Jabotinsky Institute, Tel Aviv.

waved in the face of many American Jewish organisations. It challenged the Jewish Agency and the Zionist Organisation, as well as the authentic representatives of the Yishuv.

Ben Hecht continued to write emotive pageants, such as *A Flag is Born*, which played in many theatres in the United States and emboldened many individual American Jews to support the Zionist cause. Hecht's support for Begin's Revolt was manifested in anti-British advertisements. In a 'Letter to the Terrorists of Palestine', he wrote:

My brave Friends ... every time you blow up a British arsenal, or wreck a British jail, or send a British railroad sky high, or rob a British bank, or let go with your guns and bombs at the British betrayers and invaders of your homeland, the Jews of America make a little holiday in their hearts.[15]

Yet Kook's views on the Jewish future were decidedly different from those of Menahem Begin. Kook sent his ideas to Begin in 1943,

---

[15] Ben Hecht, *A Child of the Century* (New York, 1954), pp. 615–17.

in particular about the establishment of a 'Hebrew government'. While Begin also wrote about a 'Hebrew government' in his proclamation of the Revolt, there were profound differences between the two men.

Begin feared that the Hebrew Committee for National Liberation would become an alternative focus of power and that figures such as Kook could displace him. He therefore expressed his dislike of pageants and advertisements and expressed his preference for a more subterranean organisation. He urged the Hebrew Committee to raise funds for the Irgun and eventually to unite with its European arm rather than use its resources to buy ships to bring immigrants to Palestine.[16]

Moreover, the two men fundamentally disagreed about the meaning of 'Hebrew'. Kook differentiated the Hebrew from the Jew:

The Jews today who live in the European hell together with the Jews in the Land of Israel constitute the Hebrew nation – there isn't another nation to which they owe their allegiance but the Hebrew nation. We must state it clearly: the Jews in the United States do not belong to the Hebrew nation. These Jews are Americans of Hebrew descent.[17]

Begin, however, saw 'Jewish state' and 'Hebrew republic' as one and the same – alternative terms with the same meaning.

THE QUESTION OF PARTITION

The issue of partition was also important to both Begin and Kook. The rationale for establishing a 'Hebrew government' was to prevent any drift towards partition on the part of Ben-Gurion. Yet the situation had dramatically changed. The revelations of the Shoah and the urgency of dealing with the problem of displaced persons in Europe had changed views within Mapai. Golda Meir, who opposed partition in 1937, now supported it. In 1941 Ben-Gurion advised his followers not to propose partition, but only to discuss it if the British raised the idea first. He also drew some borders:

If Zionists are asked what is meant by a Jewish state, they should say a state in the whole of Western Palestine and not make 'extravagant and indefinite claims

[16] Menahem Begin, Letter to Hillel Kook, 24 May 1946, in Eran Kaplan, 'A Rebel with a Cause: Hillel Kook, Begin and Jabotinsky's Ideological Legacy', *Israel Studies*, vol. 10, no. 3 (Fall 2005), pp. 87–103.

[17] Ibid.

based on "historical boundaries"'. This would include the Negev and the waters of the Jordan and the Litani.[18]

In early 1945 Ben-Gurion and Weizmann spoke about the 'immediate establishment' of a Jewish state after the war. Moshe Sharett addressed a group of Jewish soldiers in Cairo and told them that the Jewish Agency would work for partition. He argued that the East Bank, TransJordan, had been lost to Abdullah and that the loss was now an accomplished fact. Zionists, he said, should adopt the attitude of Gambetta following the loss of Alsace-Lorraine. 'We shall never forget and never speak about it.'[19] Many of the Zionist political parties criticised such comments. However, the political reality eventually began to impinge on their sense of what was possible under the post-war conditions. On 5 August 1946 the Jewish Agency rejected the Morrison-Grady plan and formally agreed that partition was the only way forward. Weizmann consequently wrote to the British secretary of state for the colonies on behalf of the Jewish Agency, stating that the Zionists were ready to discuss a scheme for 'the establishment of a viable Jewish state in an adequate area of Palestine'.[20]

The Treaty of London in March 1946 formally endorsed the new Hashemite kingdom of Jordan. The formalisation of the separation of the East Bank entrenched opposition from the Irgun, Lehi and the official Revisionists. An editorial in a Revisionist paper commented:

We may have been robbed of our territories east of the Jordan, but we will never give up our claim to them and that no power on earth will be able to carve up the territory west of the Jordan ... the Revisionist movement has had no part in the farce of the latest commission. It refuses to recognise the inevitability of any other solution but Jewish statehood in integral Palestine as the way of the present catastrophe.[21]

Arieh Altman, chairman of the NZO in Palestine, declared at the end of April 1946 that 'neither he nor his children nor his children's children' would recognise the changed status of TransJordan. The NZO argued that if TransJordan had been opened to Jewish immigration before the war, then hundreds of thousands of Jews would have been saved. The Irgun extended its denunciation to the Anglo-American Committee of

---

[18] David Ben-Gurion, Memorandum, 15 October 1941, in David Ben-Gurion, *Rise of Israel: Zionist Political Programmes, 1940–1947*, vol. 31 (London, 1987).

[19] *Jewish Herald*, 23 March 1945.

[20] Chaim Weizmann, Letter to George H. Hall, 16 August 1946, in Barnet Litvinoff, Joseph Heller, Nechama A. Chalom, eds., *The Letters and Papers of Chaim Weizmann, May 1945–July 1947*, Series A, Letters vol. 22 (New Jersey 1979).

[21] *Jewish Herald*, 12 April 1946.

Inquiry in decrying the commission as 'an English trick'. In addition to the ideological issues, it reiterated Jabotinsky's view that a partitioned state was a security risk and it posed great danger to the Zionist experiment.

Following the publication of the UN Special Committee on Palestine (UNSCOP) recommendations in 1947, Begin referred to the part of the proposed Jewish state along the coast as 'the ghetto whose density approaches 300 people per sq km'. He further argued that the Negev desert was unsuitable for the immediate absorption of any serious number of immigrants, since it would take decades to develop. Invoking the demographic argument, he predicted that the Arab population of the state would be between 40 and 50 percent even after the displaced persons had immigrated. On the question of transfer to the Arab state, he said that 'this option granted to the Arabs will most certainly remain unused. They will not leave their homes – and rightly so. [It will be] a federal state along the lines of the Morrison plan which means a continuation of the British occupation.'[22]

Lehi stated that those Jewish leaders who accepted partition would not be considered representatives of the Jewish people and that any decision made by them would not bind the Jews. The Irgun described Jewish Agency acquiescence in accepting partition as following in the train of past betrayals such as the handing over of its fighters to 'the British Gestapo' during the saison. A broadcast in September 1947 by the Voice of Fighting Zion, entitled 'Jewish Vichyites', predicted that in the near future 'the people will put the leadership of the Jewish Agency on trial' for their past and present misdemeanours.[23]

Throughout 1947, many stalwart opponents of partition, such as Abba Hillel Silver, bowed to the inevitable. Even the national religious, the ultra-orthodox and the Left found ways of explaining their compromise to their followers. It was the different factions of the Zionist Right, the Revisionists, the Irgun and Lehi which continued to strongly maintain their belief in a Jewish state within the historic borders of the Land of Israel. Moreover, they continued to attack the first partition of Palestine in 1920 which gave rise to the Emirate of TransJordan.

The Irgun played on the notion of separating the Americans from the British. In a memo addressed only to the American members of the Anglo-American Committee of Inquiry, the Irgun pointed out that the

---

[22] Memorandum to all the delegations, except the British and their satellites, at the United Nations General Assembly, September 1947, Jabotinsky Institute Archives, Tel Aviv.

[23] Broadcast on the *Voice of Fighting Zion*, 21 September 1947, Jabotinsky Institute Archives, Tel Aviv.

American Revolution of 1776 was a prime example of how to free a nation from British tyranny. It quoted the U.S. Declaration of Independence and Thomas Jefferson and pointedly asked the American delegates whether they still believed in these truths.[24] Despite Bevin's repeated advocacy of a unitary state, the British hand was seen to be behind partition.

The loss of the East Bank and now the proposed division of western Palestine by UNSCOP was anathema to the Irgun. A broadcast by the *Voice of Fighting Zion* in November 1947 complained:

The Arab state set up by the British enslaver east of the Jordan is now to be supplemented by a second Arab state, west of the Jordan. In the Land of Israel there are to be two Arab states while the Jewish state is to be allocated no more than 14% of the home territory – most of it, a desert waste. Jerusalem, the eternal capital of David, is being handed over to alien rule.[25]

Begin recalled that in Roman times Palestina Salutaris, now TransJordan, had been the granary of the east and it accommodated between 5 and 7 million inhabitants. Today, Begin argued, the land had been reduced to a wasteland with approximately 300,000 inhabitants. In support of its views, the Irgun quoted a statement by Molotov, the Soviet foreign minister, that the decision to absorb the eastern territories of Germany into the Polish state had been taken because they were 'the cradle of the Polish state and of Polish culture'.[26] Begin surmised, therefore, that the decisive factor was history.[27] In an Irgun submission to UNSCOP in the summer of 1947, Begin argued:

This consciousness of historic unity is not a unique phenomenon in our days. It is the consciousness and the feeling of every people. What the field of Kosovo is to the Serb, Grunwald to the Pole, the White Mountain to the Czech, Verdun to the French, Valley Forge to the American, and Borodino – or in generations to come, Stalingrad – to the Russian – the Western Wall, Masada, Modi'in, Betar, Yodefat and the Fields of Gilead are to every one of us. These 'imponderables' are one of the most real factors in human history. Their power is supreme and their influence ineradicable.[28]

[24] Memorandum to the American members of the Anglo-American Committee of Inquiry, undated, Jabotinsky Institute Archives, Tel Aviv.

[25] *Voice of Fighting Zion* broadcast, 30 November 1947, Jabotinsky Institute Archives, Tel Aviv.

[26] Irgun memorandum to the United Nations, 21 April 1947, Jabotinsky Institute Archives, Tel Aviv.

[27] Ibid.

[28] Irgun memorandum to the United Nations Special Committee on Palestine, undated, Jabotinsky Institute Archives, Tel Aviv.

The memorandum spoke of the historic connection to the whole of Eretz Israel. Begin mentioned Jerusalem, Masada, Betar, Gush Halav and Yodefat – all symbols significantly of Jewish military rebellion.

Moreover, Begin believed that the Jews constituted a clear majority of the population on both sides of the Jordan. He reached this conclusion by including 'those of our people, numbering millions, who strive to return to it immediately but are unable to realise their right because the British occupation regime ... has placed itself in their path'.[29]

Throughout 1947, Begin rejected any hint of partition, and yet he finally came round to embrace the idea of 'a Provisional Hebrew government'. Begin, however, qualified his support as long as it was a government of the whole of the Land of Israel, 'and not just a Jewish ghetto in the Land of Israel'.[30] But he also feared that support for Ben-Gurion's provisional government would also mean support for partition.[31] The day after the UN vote, the Irgun stated that it would continue to fight for a state on both sides of the Jordan.[32]

Begin believed that the British wished to remain in the Middle East and to rule by proxy through puppet regimes:

Iran, Baku and the land of the Turkomen ... ruled by various native potentates, advised and financed by the British, free to develop splendour and luxury in their courts and to deal with their people in the old way; but held in complete sub-servience in all spheres connected with the requirements of colonial exploitation (cotton, oil, minerals and other raw materials) and of 'imperial security'.[33]

The Land of Israel, according to Begin, was to be transformed into a strategic base for the imperialists. Begin regarded UN Resolution 181 of 29 November 1947, which proposed the partition of Palestine into two states, as a declaration lacking in legality and believed that it would eventually be annulled. He pledged instead to fight to liberate territory from Dan to Beersheva and from the Mediterranean Sea to the desert of Jordan.

[29] Ibid.
[30] Menahem Begin, Broadcast on the *Voice of Fighting Zion*, 1 October 1947, Jabotinsky Institute Archives, Tel Aviv.
[31] Menahem Begin and Chaim Landau, Letter to Shmuel Katz, 3 October 1947, in Yehiam Weitz, *ha'Tsa'ad ha-rishon le-khes ha-shilton: Tenu'at ha-Herut, 1949–1955* (Jerusalem, 2007), p. 15.
[32] *Hamashkif*, 1 December 1947.
[33] Irgun memorandum to the United Nations Special Committee on Palestine, undated, Jabotinsky Institute Archives, Tel Aviv.

MAP 3. United Nations partition plan (1947).

In contrast Hillel Kook, though opposed to partition, was willing to accept the resolution, since 'the national interest dictates the success of the partition plan and that it is our duty to do everything possible to bring about its early fulfilment.' Kook argued that two positive achievements came out of the UN vote, the recognition of Hebrew sovereignty and the withdrawal of British troops. He said that while the partitioned state was not the ultimate goal, it was certainly a milestone towards achieving a larger state. Although Shmuel Merlin and Eri Jabotinsky disagreed, Kook argued against the sanctity and rigidity of ideological beliefs. Unlike Begin, he was unwilling to fragment the newly found unity of the Zionists for the sake of partition. Moreover, he invoked Jabotinsky to back his pragmatism:

It is my conviction that if in 1939 the British and the League of Nations had offered the independence of western Palestine, provided TransJordan went to Abdullah and the Agency had accepted it, Jabotinsky would have, if not agreed, certainly would not have fought it. He would have done precisely what we have – make formal reservations and then play a major role in the consolidation and liberation of western Palestine.[34]

---

[34] Hillel Kook, Letter to supporters, 3 December 1947, Washington, DC, Jabotinsky Institute Archives, Tel Aviv.

12

From Military Underground to Political Party

Begin remained in hiding and in disguise during the Revolt, writing articles and issuing declarations. He promoted the martyrs of the movement, those whom the British had sent to the gallows.[1] He remembered David Raziel and 'Bloody Sunday'.[2] He commemorated the deaths of Herzl and Jabotinsky and celebrated their political journeys. He railed against Ben-Gurion and the gradual drift towards partition.[3]

Begin considered himself to be primarily a political figure who had been thrust into the role of a commander of a military uprising. His political acumen was therefore called for when explaining away blunders such as the large number of civilian deaths in the bombing of the King David Hotel.

Begin possessed 'an intuitive sense about the interplay between violence, politics and propaganda'.[4] His approach was predicated on a narrow interpretation of what was in the national interest. It meant mourning, for example, solely for the Jewish victims of the attack on the

---

[1] Menahem Begin, 'Shlomo Ben-Yosef', *Herut*, 18 June 1947, *Ba-Makhteret*, vol. 3 (Jerusalem, 1961) p. 125; 'Haviv, Nakar and Weiss', *Herut*, 28 July 1947, *Ba-Makhteret*, vol. 3, p. 228.

[2] Menahem Begin, 'On Safeguarding 14 November', 12 November 1947, in *Ha-Irgun Zvai Leumi b'Eretz Israel*, vol. 4, ed. I. Alfassi (Jerusalem, 2002), pp. 43–44.

[3] Menahem Begin, Broadcast on the *Voice of Fighting Zion* 28 May 1947, in *Ha-Irgun Zvai Leumi b'Eretz Israel*, vol. 4, pp. 194–96.

[4] Bruce Hoffman, 'The Rationality of Terrorism and Other Forms of Political Violence: Lessons from the Jewish Campaign in Palestine, 1939–1947', *Small Wars and Insurgencies*, vol. 22, no. 2 (May 2011), pp. 258–72.

King David Hotel. It meant that any attack on the Jewish Sabbath – a non-working day for the Jews – would cause fewer Jewish casualties.[5] For the secular Zionist Left, Begin became a demonic figure who denied the internationalism of socialist belief. Only the Jews mattered, and the Zionist Left feared that Begin would be content with only a new ghetto, isolated from the other nations of the world. In one sense this was unsurprising, since Betar never followed the model which had fashioned the other Zionist youth groups. Jabotinsky had taught that there should be no mixing with other ideologies during the national struggle to secure the state. This ideological monism was depicted as analogous to the biblical prohibition on mixing different kinds of material such as wool and linen.[6] The idea of a determined people that dwells alone was cultivated: 'Within the Temple where the altar of Zion stands, there is no room for other altars.'[7] The cosmopolitan Jabotinsky did not denigrate the nobility of other excluded philosophies, but argued that these could wait until the state came into existence and became a laboratory for testing ideologies. Until then there could be one – and only one – ideal, that of establishing a state of the Jews.

By early 1947 there was a general hostility in the Yishuv towards the Irgun. Many of its members had been arrested and its funds were dangerously low. Begin's movements were restricted by British surveillance, with the result that his ability to communicate was impaired. Even so, Bevin's transfer of the Mandate to the United Nations provoked a spate of further Irgun attacks.

On 16 April 1947, the British hanged Dov Gruner, Mordechai Alkohi, Eliezer Kashani and Yehiel Drezner from the Irgun. A few days later, Moshe Barazani and Meir Feinstein from Lehi blew themselves up in prison with a smuggled hand grenade placed between them. Gruner, who had been captured in an attack on the Ramat Gan police station, had served five years in the British army.

Two weeks later, the Irgun staged an audacious breakout from the seemingly impregnable prison at Acre. Irgun and Lehi prisoners escaped, but five attackers were captured – Avshalom Haviv, Meir Nakar and Yaakov Weiss were duly executed at the end of July 1947.

The hangings produced martyrs for the Irgun and a broad condemnation in the Yishuv. As with the executions of the Easter Uprising

---

5 Avi Shilon, *Menachem Begin: A Life* (New Haven, CT, 2012), p. 136.
6 Leviticus 19:19; Deuteronomy 22:11.
7 Vladimir Jabotinsky, 'Sha'atnez Lo Ya'ale Alekha', *Haynt*, 18 January 1929.

participants, the British believed that they could decapitate the Revolt. Instead it pandered to the emotions, evoked by the Jewish tragedy down the centuries.

Two British sergeants, Mervyn Paice and Clifford Martin, were captured as bargaining counters in Netanya, but Begin initially baulked at ordering their killings in response to the hangings. Finally, it became a question of maintaining the Irgun's policy of reciprocity to the bitter end, as well as Begin's own credibility. As Jabotinsky discovered in the 1930s, digesting the Irgun attacks in civilian areas was replete with moral judgements. Begin, ten years later, deferred to the stronger convictions of his military people. The sergeants were hanged and the areas around their bodies booby-trapped.

The Irgun depicted the killing of the two sergeants as a sad necessity. Begin was left handling the political backlash and wrote 'A Response to a (Bereaved) British Father', in which he blamed the British for the hangings. They were thirsty for blood and oil. They were responsible for the situation in Palestine and implicitly for the past abandonment of the Jews. Begin advised Mervyn Paice's father to instead address Atlee and tell him, 'You are the murderers! You are the ones who killed my son!'[8] The British placed a price on Begin's head of 10,000 Palestine pounds. In Tel Aviv several Jews were killed during random attacks by British soldiers. In the UK there were several days of attacks on Jewish premises and synagogues. Begin was vilified by his political opponents as someone who bemoaned killings yet authorised them.

All this took place as the British Mandate for Palestine moved towards its gradual denouement. The plight of the *Exodus 1947*, laden with more than 4,000 immigrants, had further dented British prestige. Intercepted by British warships, its passengers were transferred to other ships and taken back to Europe. In France, the passengers refused to leave and declared a hunger strike. Eventually the *Exodus 1947* and the other ships sailed to – of all places – Germany; its passengers were removed and interned in camps at Amstau and Poppendorf. All this took place in full view of the world's press and certainly served Zionist political purposes. The image of a Britain during its heroic period standing alone against Nazism in 1940 had been substituted by one of British soldiers victimising Hitler's victims.

Stalin had perceived the handing of the Mandate to the UN as an opportunity to oust the British from the Middle East and perhaps secure

---

[8] Menahem Begin, Broadcast on the *Voice of Fighting Zion* 30 July 1947, in *Ba-Makhteret*, vol. 3, p. 232.

a deep water port in Haifa. At the UN, Andrei Gromyko was instructed to support partition and the principle of a two-state solution if the conflict proved to be insoluble. Externally the Soviet Union advocated the establishment of a state of the Jews. Internally the NKVD continued to arrest Jews who wished to leave for Palestine and to sentence them to long years in the Gulag. However, without Stalin's support, the Zionists would not have acquired the necessary two-thirds majority in the UN vote.

The rapid pace of events, culminating in the UNSCOP proposals for partition on 31 August 1947, drew attention away from the sergeants affair. Indeed, the Irgun now began to attract urban youth to its ranks. Moreover, there were no more British hangings. On 27 September, the colonial secretary, Arthur Creech-Jones, announced Britain's intention to leave Palestine. All Irgun plans to attack British targets in Palestine were suspended.

Although there had certainly been ongoing conflict throughout 1947, UN Resolution 181 of 29 November, which proposed a two-state solution, was the blue touchpaper which ignited a full intercommunal war between Palestinian Arabs and Zionist Jews. It marked the point in history when the Irgun ceased to be an underground force undermining the British and became a more visible conventional military unit fighting the Arabs. At the beginning of March 1948 the Irgun agreed to operate under Haganah direction. A few weeks later, there was a further agreement on military cooperation with Lehi as well as with the Haganah.

One of the Irgun's first tasks was to take a village on the outskirts of Jerusalem, Deir Yassin, in a joint operation with Lehi. The Irgun attacked from Givat Shaul and straightaway ran into trouble. Weapons did not work. A loudspeaker truck was stuck in a ditch. There was poor communication. Senior commanders were hit and command passed to less experienced ranks. Poorly trained new recruits were unable to cope with this situation, and the lack of military discipline led to a large – and almost certainly inflated – number of Arab civilian deaths. Once again the military responsibility was deferred to others, but Begin, probably quite ignorant of the situation on the ground, was left with the political fallout. He called criticism of the Jews 'a blood libel'. The killings at Deir Yassin, however, served a plethora of purposes:

The Haganah used the rumours to stain the reputation of the dissidents. The Irgun used them to frighten the Arabs and the Arabs used them to disgrace the Jews.[9]

---

[9] Shilon, *Menachem Begin*, p. 108.

The Arab media utilised the killings to full effect to stimulate a mindset amongst Palestinian Arabs that the Jews would murder them in their beds. The best solution for themselves and their families was exodus. It also stimulated a sense of revenge amongst Arab irregulars who fought with the forces of the Arab states. The killing of doctors on the road to Jerusalem and the slaughter of the inhabitants of Kfar Etzion who had already surrendered were accompanied by cries of 'Deir Yassin'.

In late April 1948 the Irgun planned an attack against Jaffa, adjacent to Tel Aviv and an enclave within territory designated for the Jewish state. Begin's concern was that the Egyptians would land forces in Jaffa and attack Tel Aviv, the heart of the Zionist endeavour.

Ben-Gurion was hesitant because of the distinct possibility of a British counter-attack. It was also an uncertain time politically, since a reticent U.S. State Department was moving towards a trusteeship and away from supporting a state with a Jewish majority. Moreover both Ben-Gurion and Begin understood that the political outcome of any attack on Jaffa could affect their future electoral fortunes. A successful assault would certainly win the affection of the voters of Tel Aviv who had already been the target of snipers from Jaffa.

The Irgun wanted to capture the Manshiya Quarter, which abutted Tel Aviv, but the Arab resistance proved to be unexpectedly strong. The Irgun forces, wearing improvised 'rak kakh' armbands, relentlessly mortared the centre of Jaffa. Civilians were killed and fled to the port to escape by boat or moved southwards towards Gaza. The British were concerned by the situation in Jaffa, coming so soon after the Arab flight from Haifa. They were worried that the withdrawing British forces in Palestine would become a target for Palestinian Arab irregulars and more generally Britain would be blamed for the debacle by the Arab world. The British therefore threatened to bomb Tel Aviv unless the Irgun withdrew. A show of force rendered the Irgun mortars silent, and the Irgun was subsequently replaced by the Haganah.[10]

While the Irgun had conquered much of Jaffa, it also catalysed a mass exodus of its Arab inhabitants, who feared another Deir Yassin at the hands of the Irgun. Some 94 percent of the Arab population of Jaffa left.

---

[10] Benny Morris, *1948: The First Arab-Israeli War* (London, 2008), pp. 147–52.

THE BIRTH OF HERUT

Ben-Gurion was aware at an early stage that Begin posed a threat to his vision of a socialist state. The Revisionist tradition of separation and rejection of the discipline of the Zionist Organisation, as exemplified by both Betar and the NZO, reflected a purview of the future that was far different from that of other Zionist parties. The stress on individualism in contrast to the socialist notion of collectivism was paramount. The folklore that it was mainly the Irgun fighting family that had forced the British out of Palestine through courage and sacrifice became the launching pad for a new party. Converting the Irgun into Tenu'at ha-Herut – the Freedom movement – was no easy task. The Irgun had remained united because of the common task of fighting the British occupier. Once the British had left, what was the political glue holding it together?

Like Ben-Gurion, Begin understood that the declaration of independence should not be delayed. Significantly he urged Ben-Gurion to declare independence within the partition borders.[11] Such pragmatism was prompted by the distinct possibility of an Arab invasion and the State Department's move towards the idea of a trusteeship. While some in Mapai were quietly suggesting the postponement of a declaration, Begin effectively supported Ben-Gurion by threatening that a government would instead emerge from the Irgun underground if there was no movement.[12] Even apart from the historic consequence and political significance of publicly proclaiming a state of the Jews, Begin recognised the need for strong leadership at a time of military uncertainty.

On the Saturday night following the declaration of the state, Begin made his 'victory' broadcast, in which he emphasised the role of the Irgun in forcing a British withdrawal:

The Irgun Zvai Leumi which rose up against the regime of British subjugation, smote it, brought about its disintegration, forced its armies of occupation to evacuate the country and thus made possible the sovereignty and independence of the people of Israel in their homeland.[13]

Begin had prepared for this moment and his emotional rhetoric evoked his interpretation of history:

We shall go on our way into battle, soldiers of the Lord of Hosts, inspired by the spirit of our ancient heroes, from the conquerors of Canaan to the rebels of

---

[11] Shilon, *Menachem Begin*, p. 104.
[12] Menahem Begin, *Ba-Makhteret*, vol. 4 (Tel Aviv 1961) pp. 245–47; 325–27.
[13] Menahem Begin, 'The State of Israel has Arisen', *Herut*, 15 May 1948.

Judah. We shall be accompanied by the spirit of those who revived our nation, Ze'ev Benjamin Herzl, Max Nordau, Joseph Trumpeldor and the father of resurrected Hebrew heroism, Ze'ev Jabotinsky. We shall be accompanied by the spirit of David Raziel, greatest of the Hebrew commanders of our day, and by Dov Gruner, one of the greatest of Hebrew soldiers. We shall be accompanied into battle by the spirit of the gallows, the conquerors of death. And we shall be accompanied by the spirit of millions of our martyrs, our ancestors tortured and burned for their faith, our murdered fathers and butchered mothers, our murdered brothers and strangled children. And in this battle we shall break the enemy and bring salvation to our people.[14]

The partition of the Land of Israel was declared to be 'illegal', as the Hebrew homeland was 'a historic and geographical entity'. The coming conflict with the Arab states was more than a question of survival; its raison d'être was to reverse both the first and second partitions of Palestine:

The prime task of Hebrew foreign policy will be to bring about the unification of all parts of our partitioned homeland under sovereign Hebrew rule.

The broadcast was carefully crafted to demonstrate the separatism of the Irgun and its predecessors. The underlying message was that the Zionist Right was neither part of the consensus nor part of a Mapai-led establishment. It exuded a different philosophy and a different way forward. It was a government-in-waiting. The essential point of Begin's speech – a point that Ben-Gurion had long understood – was that the Irgun would now become a political party, Herut.

In one sense, the progressive nature of Herut's social policies – the right to work, the organisation of trades unions, the opposition to monopolies and trusts, a positive attitude to women, the family, the poor, the need to learn Arabic – was secondary. The private ownership of land would be limited; otherwise the state would nationalise it. There would be a progressive taxation of the well-to-do without a hint of support for private enterprise. A central purpose of the broadcast was to announce the dismantling of the Irgun and its transformation into Herut. While clearly there was an echo of the populism of the inter-war radical Right in Europe, Begin had opted for the parliamentary road. The Irgun's Gidi Paglin and Lehi's Israel Eldad would not have been averse to an undemocratic seizure of power based on military prowess. Begin was aware that any rival government would challenge Ben-Gurion's provisional government. It would probably end in civil war and the emergence of a new underground. National unity in 1948 was deemed more important than

[14] David Niv, *A Short History of the Irgun Zvai Leumi* (Jerusalem, 1980), pp. 108–09.

an internecine armed struggle. Working through the political system, Begin surmised, would eventually overturn partition.

Begin's well-laid plans to launch a new political movement from the ashes of the Irgun Zvai Leumi were upset by the *Altalena* affair. He had already addressed large audiences in Ramat Gan and Be'er Ya'akov. He had spent several days in an attempt to cultivate and lure the official Revisionists into joining Herut. The Revisionists were divided, with a majority totally opposed to Begin.

On 11 June 1948, the day after the first ceasefire, the *Altalena*, which had been purchased by Kook's Hebrew Committee, sailed from the Port-de-Bouc near Marseilles with almost a thousand volunteers on board. It also carried 27 trucks, 5,000 Lee-Enfield rifles, 5 million rounds of ammunition and 250 Bren guns.[15] Four days later, the platform of the Herut movement was published.[16] After its first journey to Israel, the *Altalena* was expected to return to France to pick up more arms for the Irgun.

In March 1948 Kook and other members of the Hebrew Committee had met the French foreign minister, Georges Bidault, who willingly supplied arms to the Irgun, free of charge. Following the Communist take-over in Czechoslovakia, there was a fear in Paris that pro-Soviet parties such as Mapam would do the same in Israel. This was also part of a British campaign, equating Zionism with Communism, to scare the White House into questioning its support for a Jewish state. In addition to the worry of Soviet penetration in the Middle East, there was also the fear in the Quai d'Orsay that King Abdullah still had designs on Damascus, from which his brother had been ousted in 1920.[17]

Begin, however, had already signed an agreement with the Haganah's Israel Galili which facilitated the wholesale transfer of the Irgun and its weapons to the Israeli Defence Forces (IDF). Begin, however, insisted on retaining an independent Irgun in Jerusalem. Irgun officials both in Europe and in Palestine were seemingly unaware of this arrangement beforehand.

Begin believed that the weapons would fortify the Irgun in Jerusalem, while Ben-Gurion feared that this was the prelude to a coup d'état in classic European style. Begin was originally ready to agree to 20 percent of

---

[15] Shmuel Katz, *Days of Fire* (London, 1968), p. 236.
[16] 'The Principles of the Hebrew Freedom Movement (Founded by the Irgun Zvai Leumi)', *Herut*, 15 June 1948.
[17] Meir Zamir, '"Bid" for Altalena: France's Covert Action in the 1948 War in Palestine', *Middle Eastern Studies*, vol. 46, no. 1 (January 2010), pp. 17–58.

the arms going to the Irgun in Jerusalem, but then was persuaded by the more radical views of Paglin not to accept this. Begin now insisted that the Irgun should unload the weapons, while Israel Galili insisted that it should be the IDF. Trust had broken down and suspicion reigned.

The *Altalena* thus set sail with high hopes amidst the imagery of a Jewish army coming to fight in a war of national liberation. It ended when Ben-Gurion ordered Yitzhak Rabin to fire at the grounded ship near the Tel Aviv shoreline. Shmuel Katz, an Irgun commander, believed that the reason for the attack was to kill Begin, who was on board.[18] An uncompromising Ben-Gurion blessed 'the holy cannon' which had set fire to the *Altalena* in an address to the Provisional National Council on 23 June.

The *Altalena* affair followed in the train of the bombing of the King David Hotel and the killings at Deir Yassin, where a treacherous mixture of incompetence, inexperience, misinterpretation, suspicion and bad luck had led to a terrible outcome. The newly formed Israel Defence Forces even fired at men swimming ashore to Tel Aviv's Frishman Beach. Sixteen people on board the *Altalena* were killed and many more injured. Many who had escaped from the *Altalena* were arrested. Begin scrambled ashore. Dishevelled and disoriented, he was led to the Revisionist headquarters, Metzudet Ze'ev, where he broadcast an emotional and disjointed response. His opponents, he claimed, were 'real Nazis'.

The Irgun itself was distinctly unhappy and wished to retaliate militarily. Israel Eldad similarly attempted to persuade Begin to flee to Jerusalem and to raise the standard of revolt against Ben-Gurion's provisional government. Another suggestion was to hide in a nearby forest; an astonished Begin replied, 'I am not Lenin'.[19] Moreover, Begin remembered the internecine warfare that had befallen the Jews during the siege of Jerusalem by the Romans 2,000 years before and was adamantly opposed to any notion of civil war. Begin wished any opposition to Ben-Gurion to be confined to the parameters of parliamentary discourse. In addition, he was able to persuade a recalcitrant, angry Irgun to follow his approach. Although Ben-Gurion cancelled the recent agreement on the transfer of Irgun arms and men to the ranks of the IDF, he did not outlaw the organisation or order the arrest of Begin. While all this was incredibly damaging to the birth of his new movement, Herut, it did mark the emergence

---

[18] Katz, *Days of Fire*, p. 248.
[19] Shilon, *Menachem Begin*, p. 129.

of Menahem Begin the politician. Begin realised that he could not be both revolutionary and parliamentarian.

Jabotinsky had predicted that after the establishment of the state, a plethora of parties would compete in the marketplace of ideas to advocate the way forward. However, this did not happen overnight with Begin's Herut. It was a national party above class and not one which would serve sectional interests. Without projecting a political programme, Herut came up with simplicities. It would tax the rich and feed the poor.

Even so, Herut did broadcast a message for the electorate. Although it was established as a populist anti-capitalist party of the masses, echoing the radical right of inter-war Europe, it also operated with democratic appendages such as a central committee and a council. It proposed laws to protect civil liberties and advocated a national health service. It proposed non-alignment in the international arena. This was profoundly different from right-wing European analogues which had not feared utilising their military machines to take power.

Begin expected that Herut would receive 30–40 percent of the vote in the first election and would be on a par with Mapai. At the very minimum he hoped that Herut would hold the balance of power. When he visited Jerusalem, he went to its most impoverished areas, Mea Shearim and Mahane Yehudah, to speak to the faithful. Begin depicted Herut as the underclass's champion, rather than Ben-Gurion's Mapai, which he termed 'a bourgeois class of propagandists'[20] which was not promoting the real interests of the workers.

He made an impassioned speech to the gathered crowds from a balcony in Zion Square and demanded the annexation of Jerusalem.[21] There was even an honour motorcycle escort, as had been the case with Jabotinsky before the war in Diaspora cities. Many people came to hear Menahem Begin because they were also curious to see the mysterious leader of the Irgun who had spent long years in the underground. He also visited the prison at Acre which had held Irgun prisoners and where Dov Gruner had been hanged.

Yet once again his plans for Herut were thrown off track. Despite its main forces having joined the IDF at the end of May 1948, Lehi was

[20] Ibid., p. 134.
[21] *Hamashkif*, 10 August 1948.

FIGURE 12. Menahem Begin making his first speech – from a balcony in Zion Square, Jerusalem – since emerging from the Irgun (August 1948).
Courtesy of the Central Zionist Archives, Jerusalem.

deeply opposed to the ethos of the Mapai-led provisional government and 'the dictatorship of the party machine'. Its publications contained virulent attacks on Ben-Gurion and demonstrated a fear of political betrayal. On 16 September 1948, Count Folke Bernadotte, the UN mediator, produced new proposals for a solution to the conflict. Ben-Gurion and his colleagues in government, as well as Begin, had been critical of his previous ideas, which seemingly reversed Israeli gains on the battlefield.[22] The new proposals included international rule in Jerusalem, the Negev under Arab rule and the right of return of the Arab refugees. The following day Bernadotte was assassinated by Hazit Hamoledet, a name suggested by Natan Yellin-Mor[23] and a Lehi front.[24] Lehi believed that Bernadotte was no more than a lackey

[22] *Herut*, 29 July 1948.
[23] Joseph Heller, *The Stern Gang: Ideology, Politics and Terror, 1940–1949* (London, 1995), p. 342 n. 53.
[24] *Yediot Aharanot*, 11 November 1993.

of imperialism and that U.S. oil interests had been behind his latest attempt at a solution.

This last act of political violence did not synchronise with Begin's transition from the Irgun to Herut. He condemned the assassination and disbanded the Irgun's Jerusalem Brigade. He also feared a repetition of the oppression which had followed Lehi's killing of Lord Moyne in 1944. Ben-Gurion, who had originally wished to pursue a hard line against Lehi for its uncompromising hostility to Bernadotte,[25] now brought back the Mandate laws for the prevention of terrorism – administrative detention without trial. On 20 September, Lehi was declared to be a terrorist organisation, outlawed and two hundred of its members arrested. Begin opposed this. Both Natan Yellin-Mor and Matityahu Shmuelevitch[26] were placed on trial, which proved to be more a forensic dissection of Lehi's ideology and policies than an indictment for Bernadotte's murder, which Lehi never condemned. Yellin-Mor received eight years' imprisonment and Shmuelevitch five. Both defendants agreed to abandon the underground and to urge Lehi members to do so. The sentences were then set aside, and Yellin-Mor and Shmuelevitch subsequently pardoned. In the first election, the Fighters' party, headed by Yellin-Mor and Shmuelevitch, submitted a list of candidates but received slightly more than 1 percent of the total vote. Yellin-Mor became its sole representative in the first Knesset.

While the Irgun felt a kindred sense of persecution as a group of dissidents, Lehi had moved towards a pro-Soviet orientation. It avoided any espousal of democracy and supported the prospect of a population exchange between the Jews of Arab lands and the Palestinian Arabs.[27] This was fundamentally different from Menahem Begin's new parliamentary direction, in which he wished to honour the revolutionary past but not to continue it.

In September 1948, formal negotiations between Herut and the official Revisionists broke down. There had been an agreement on a seven-point plan between the two organisations. But Herut raised amendments on almost a daily basis. As a leading Revisionist commented:

Each time they implied a new concession on our part and eventually the original seven points were narrowed down to something that does not fall short of a

---

[25] Heller, *The Stern Gang*, p. 247.

[26] Matityahu Shmuelevitch, *Be-yamim adumim: zikhronot ish Leḥi* (Tel Aviv, 1949).

[27] Heller, *The Stern Gang*, p. 237.

simple instrument of unconditional surrender. It was evident that the whole affair was not serious.[28]

Begin would neither meet the representatives of the Revisionists to discuss the impasse nor repudiate the original agreement. It became clear that he would not brook any compromise and that the only solution was a political umbrella under his leadership. On 3 October the daily *Herut* was published for the first time under the editorship of Yohanan Bader. The list of subscribers to the Revisionist *Hamashkif* was 'poached' and newspaper vendors instructed to sell *Herut* instead.

On 19 October the founding conference of the Herut movement took place in the Ohel Shem Hall in Tel Aviv. Begin had crucially gained the support of Jabotinsky's sister, who was present, and there were photographs of Jabotinsky, Herzl and Raziel. Begin recited the memorial prayer, Yizkor, which included a mention of Avraham Stern and all the fallen fighters of all dissident groups. With all his potential rivals dead, Begin praised them profusely, evoked the memory of their contribution and projected himself as their natural heir. As the conflict seemed to be drawing to a close, he implied that Herut would not compromise over the historic borders. 'The government of [the state of] Israel is the government of the Land of Israel.'[29]

Begin badly needed funding for Herut's election campaign and therefore travelled to New York. He projected himself in the imagery of the founding fathers of the United States, who had fought the same enemy. 'We learned from Jefferson that resistance to tyranny is obedience to God.' The Irgun was depicted as the sole liberator of the Jews of Israel. 'Thus was western Eretz Israel cleared from the British occupation and the Republic of Israel rose to independence.' Herut, he told his audience at Carnegie Hall, was the first party to proclaim 'the inviolability of the rights of man ... based on your own Bill of Rights'.[30]

Yet not all shared this imagery. Hannah Arendt and Albert Einstein, both German refugees, painted Herut in Nazi colours in an advertisement in the *New York Times*.[31] Begin responded by declaring that Herut was the true anti-fascist party and that the British regime in Palestine had been the most fascist and indeed Nazi regime in the entire Middle East.

---

[28] J. I. Kohn, Internal Information letter to the Revisionist Executive and European Bureau, 11 November 1948, Begin Heritage Center Archives, Jerusalem.

[29] *Herut*, 20 October 1948.

[30] Menahem Begin, Statement on arrival in New York, Begin Heritage Center Archives, Jerusalem.

[31] *New York Times*, 4 December 1948.

The Revisionist intelligentsia, as well as the Hebrew Committee for National Liberation, joined Herut in the hope of forging a party in their own image. Most found it difficult to come to terms with Begin's style of leadership. Unlike Jabotinsky's time, now they had no share in the decision-making process. Indeed, Begin had drawn up the electoral list of candidates for Herut by himself.[32] In this fashion, he could pre-empt potential rivals for leadership such as the Revisionists' Altman and the Hebrew Committee's Kook. While Uri Zvi Greenberg was high on the list of candidates, Irgun commanders who found the transition to politics difficult, such as Gidi Paglin, were not. Abba Ahimeir was also sceptical about the move from 'revolutionary heroism' to the humdrum of politics.[33] The intelligentsia also reacted negatively to Begin's persona and to his melodramatic rhetoric. Begin's inner circle were Irgun loyalists who followed him unquestioningly on his political path. Moreover, Betar, the Irgun and the Revisionists had all held different views during Jabotinsky's time, but through force of personality, he was able to hold them together. These differences remained after 1948, but Begin was unable to maintain this coalition, albeit in very different circumstances.

The official Revisionist party, led by Altman and Grossman, was in a dire state. Many of its members had defected to Herut, and the rump could not bring itself to be led by Begin. Both the Revisionists and Herut therefore presented lists of candidates for the first election. Even after the electoral lists were published, the Revisionists proposed a joint list of candidates, but this was turned down by Begin. The Revisionists discussed the nationalisation of all Jewish National Fund land and the compulsory acquisition of cultivatable land. They also suggested the nationalisation of transport, harbours and ports. They argued for the abolition of the system of party settlements as well as their jurisdiction over education, health services and welfare. It urged a strict control over essential commodities such as bread and milk. There was even a proposal to accord Israeli citizenship to any Diaspora Jew who desired it, as well as the right of such extraterritorial citizens to vote in elections.[34]

All this was to no avail, and it became apparent that the Revisionists were entering the election in the most unfavourable of conditions with

---

[32] Yohanan Bader, *ha-Keneset va-ani* (Jerusalem, 1979), p. 21.
[33] Yehiam Weitz, *Mi-mahteret lehemet le-miflagah politit: hakamatah shel tenu'at ha-Herut, 1947–1949* (Jerusalem, 2002), p. 147.
[34] Memorandum of the Revisionist party, undated 1948, Begin Heritage Center Archives, Jerusalem.

meagre resources. They even prepared for a world conference after the election to discuss the prospect of self-liquidation.[35]

Begin in part began to believe his own rhetoric about the struggle of the Irgun, peppered with notions of romantic nationalism. For Begin, the Irgun was the classic national liberation movement, analogous to independence movements in other nations. It therefore followed, given historical precedence, that Herut should have become the natural party of government. However, this determinist sequence of events was derailed because Ben-Gurion and Mapai had actually led the national war against the Arabs.

Begin expected Herut to win around forty seats, but the actual result had brought only fourteen. Some 49,782 (11.5 percent), including a large number of Mizrahim, voted for Herut. In particular the Yemenite Quarter and Hatikvah neighbourhoods in Tel Aviv voted in great numbers for Herut. In Jerusalem, 14.4 percent voted for Herut.

The election took place in January 1949 amidst discussions about a ceasefire and an end to hostilities. More than 6,000 Israelis had been killed and another 15,000 wounded; the public was in no mood to entertain the prospect of a new front against Abdullah's Jordan. Begin remained committed to his belief in a state on both banks of the river Jordan and objected to the ceasefire. He had similarly opposed Ben-Gurion's ceasefire in July 1948 and believed that the IDF would have conquered the West Bank.

THE FRAGMENTATION OF THE RIGHT

In May 1949 Begin was elected chairman of Herut. He based Herut's legitimacy on the Irgun as fighters for the state. He was also the first member of the Knesset to submit a motion of no confidence in an Israeli government. Ben-Gurion ridiculed and often outwitted Begin in the Knesset. Begin regularly exploded with outlandish comments, and this distanced him further from the public.

The attainment of only fourteen seats did not bode well either for Begin or for the Israeli Right. Herut emerged not as the main opposition but as the fourth-largest party. Begin tried to build Herut in the image of the Irgun in the sense that fighting the British promoted unity amongst the disparate elements of the Right. The meagre results of the

[35] Imanuel Kohn, Letter to the Revisionist Executive Committee, 20 January 1949, Jabotinsky Institute Archives, Tel Aviv.

first election was undoubtedly a setback. While both the religious and the Left had fought the election as coalitions of parties and done well, the Right unified as Herut had been marginalised and was in a much more fragile position.

The official Revisionists had been unable to secure the election of even a single candidate. They received 0.7 percent of the total vote. Although the party expected to do badly, it did not expect complete annihilation. The only choice for its members was either to leave politics or to join Herut.

In contrast Jabotinsky's one-time second in command, the veteran Meir Grossman, believed that the crisis would pass and that the Revisionists still had a future. The majority, including Altman, Yunitchman and Eliezer Shostak, disagreed, joined Herut and became its representatives in subsequent Knessets.

Grossman instead established Gush ha-ne'emane ha-Tsohar veha-Betar and referred to the 'foreign dictatorship' of Begin. Two hundred people attended the founding conference on 23 May 1950,[36] yet it eventually disappeared into political oblivion. Lehi too split into factions. Natan Yellin-Mor, leading the Fighters' party in a pro-Soviet direction, became a one-term Knesset member, while Israel Eldad held fast to his ideological convictions as an intellectual engagé and founded *Sulam*, a journal of the Far Right. On the Herut Executive, there were now seven members of Herut and five Revisionists. The Revisionist daily, *Hamashkif*, which had first been published in December 1938, was closed down in May 1949. Itzik Remba, the editor of *Hamashkif*, now became one of the editors of *Herut*.

Ben-Gurion well understood Begin's approach to establishing himself as 'the leader of the opposition' with a clear-cut political philosophy, different from that of Mapai and all the other parties. The politics of political polarisation was played out both by Begin and by Ben-Gurion. Jabotinsky was reinvented by Begin to fit his political agenda, while Ben-Gurion repeatedly demonised the man he had constructively negotiated with in 1934 and now refused to allow his remains to be interred in the reborn Jewish state. The real Jabotinsky was lost in the fog of inter-party strife.

Joseph Klausner, who never joined the Revisionists, now stood as the candidate of Herut for president against Weizmann, who was spoken of as the candidate of 'retreat and submission'.[37] When the list of

[36] Yehiam Weitz, *ha'Tsa'ad ha-rishon le-khes ha-shilton: Tenu'at ha-Herut, 1949–1955* (Jerusalem, 2007), p. 40.
[37] *Herut*, 17 February 1949.

the good and the great who had worked for the creation of the state of Israel was read out in the Knesset, Jabotinsky's name was not mentioned. Ben-Gurion airbrushed out of existence the contribution of the Irgun and Lehi in order to maintain the political hegemony of Mapai. The Irgun and Lehi were hardly commemorated in books or monuments during Ben-Gurion's time in power.

More crucially Ben-Gurion also placed Mapai at the centre of a national consensus in its remembrance of the fight for independence. His defining slogan 'from class to nation' now applied to all – it was beyond class. Mapai was depicted as a respected leading party, while Herut and the Communists were beyond the pale, not worthy of any representation. Ben-Gurion labelled members of Herut 'undeserving participants in government'[38] and wanted Herut rendered invisible in the public perception. The Provisional State Council originally recommended three speakers for the Knesset which would be allocated by the second-, third- and fourth-largest parties. Ben-Gurion demanded that this number be reduced to two, since the last post would have to go to Herut.[39]

Ben-Gurion depicted Begin as a civilian demagogue, an outsider who had taken no part in the founding of the state. He was 'that bespectacled petty Polish solicitor'.[40] In the Knesset he often goaded Begin to the point of exasperation. Ben-Gurion was adept at pinpointing Begin's vulnerabilities in the public perception:

There is nothing he cannot do; there is no country he cannot conquer; there is no enemy he cannot destroy; there are no desires of the public that he cannot satisfy; there are no interests of the masses that he cannot gratify – because all his power lies in the words he utters. He is a talker – and there is no impediment to his tongue.[41]

If Begin was unable to contain himself, his virulent rhetoric assisted Mapai in further depicting the Herut leader as an unworthy extremist. On the Israeli Left and often in the Diaspora, Begin was painted in 'fascist' colours. In July 1950 the Knesset debated a law to commemorate the fallen in the war of 1948. Ben-Gurion argued that this applied only to the Haganah and the period of commemoration commenced following the passing of the UN resolution on 29 November 1947. All military action

---

[38] Udi Lebel, '"Beyond the Pantheon": Bereavement, Memory and the Strategy of Delegitimisation against Herut', *Israel Studies*, vol. 10, no. 3 (Fall 2005), pp. 104–26.

[39] Giora Goldberg, *Ben-Gurion against the Knesset* (London, 2003), p. 46.

[40] Amos Perlmutter, *The Life and Times of Menachem Begin* (New York, 1987), p. 261.

[41] David Ben-Gurion, Speech to the Knesset, 19 June 1956, in Goldberg, *Ben-Gurion against the Knesset*, p. 255.

before that date simply did not count. Natan Yellin-Mor wanted the date put back to 17 May 1939, the beginning of Avraham Stern's campaign. It also meant that those members of the Irgun and Lehi who were hanged by the British were not commemorated. This policy of exclusion was aimed at succeeding generations and at the new immigrants who did not participate in the war. Truly, the writing of history belonged to the electoral victors.

In addition to Ben-Gurion's broadsides was internal criticism of Begin from within Herut. There were comments that Begin was 'a caricature of Jabotinsky' and 'a small man'.[42] There were condemnatory letters from long-time Revisionists such as Yirmayahu Halpern and calls for Begin to step down.[43] There were also calls to Herut to join the government and fight for its views from within.[44]

Another veteran of the Revisionist movement, Eri Jabotinsky, the son of 'the father of the Revolt', had already written to Begin as early as May 1949 to complain that Herut was jaded and only reacted to events.[45] Moreover, the intelligentsia, Greenberg, Kook and Merlin, felt that they had been shunted aside. They were unable to give any input and increasingly concluded that Herut's leadership was both indifferent and inflexible.[46]

Uri Zvi Greenberg soon became fed up with the cut and thrust of politics. He did not like the idea of 'bourgeois compromise' in the political arena, while Eri Jabotinsky, who was never happy with the divisions within the Revisionist camp,[47] declared himself 'an independent Revisionist' in January 1951.[48] Begin was seen as a controlling leader who was concerned solely with the minutiae of party matters.

In December 1950 the Lamerhav faction under Shmuel Merlin and Shmuel Tamir was formed prior to Herut's second conference a few weeks later. About 20 percent of Herut supported Lamerhav.[49] It called for a united front of the Right and a total opposition to the Left.

Hillel Kook and the other former members of the Hebrew Committee grew disillusioned with both Begin and Ben-Gurion. Kook in particular felt that Begin was gradually becoming distant from Jabotinsky's

---

[42] Weitz, *ha'Tsa'ad ha-rishon*, p. 52.
[43] Ibid., pp. 62–63.
[44] *Herut*, 23 June 1950.
[45] *Hayarden*, 30 September 1936.
[46] Weitz, *ha'Tsa'ad ha-rishon*, p. 52.
[47] Eri Jabotinsky, 'The Factions and the Feuds', *Hamashkif*, 12 November 1948.
[48] Ibid.
[49] *Haboker*, 1 March 1951.

understanding of the raison d'être of Zionism. He argued that Jabotinsky had embraced Zionism because he wanted a revolutionary change in the status of the Jewish people – and not out of a fear of anti-Semitism. Jabotinsky's cosmopolitanism was the foundation of his interpretation of Zionism as 'part of a greater international movement that allowed societies to realise that nationalism was the highest manifestation of the human experience'. Jabotinsky's legacy, Kook believed, was that Zionism would normalise the Jewish people and transform its relationship with the non-Jewish world. He wished to disconnect the Jews of Israel from the Jews of the Diaspora despite their common origin. The State of Israel belonged to the people who lived in it – and not to the entire Jewish people. Diaspora Jews would acculturate and eventually assimilate and become part and parcel of the nations in which they dwelled. Their Jewishness would be expressed as a religious Jewish identity. Kook believed that 'the nation of Israel is a political heir of the Jewish people'. He therefore did not see any point in Herut joining the World Zionist Organisation. He told Ben-Gurion that the organisation was 'an absurdity'.

Kook believed that the Law of Return should be radically altered so that people could immigrate on an individual basis, regardless of religious or ethnic origin. Begin's experience had been profoundly different, and his Diaspora background in inter-war Poland profoundly influenced his perspective and his own experience. Moreover, Kook was an ideas man who had resisted the collective pressure of the Jewish leadership in the United States through pageants and plays – his was a world much closer to Jabotinsky's than to Begin's.

Eri Jabotinsky had worked closely with Kook in the United States and shared many of his views.[50] He too wanted a more cosmopolitan approach; he wished to liberate the Kurds, Maronites and Alawites from Sunni Arab domination and wanted them to form an alliance with the Jews of Israel. Eri Jabotinsky in particular was irritated by Begin's continual evoking of his late father's name to support present-day policies. In his mind, Begin's Herut was becoming a populist party that was not averse to aligning itself with the religious parties. This reflected Begin's own selective religious practice and his affinity for those who continued in the traditions of the past. Even so, Begin under pressure from within Herut reluctantly agreed to press for a bill which would permit civil marriage and ease the status of illegitimate children. The religious parties were totally opposed to this.

---

[50] Eri Jabotinsky, *Yediot Aharanot*, 22 December 1950.

Moreover, Kook was profoundly opposed to the absence of a constitution. It had been promised, but Ben-Gurion had made an historic compromise to avoid a religious-secular clash in 1947.

Kook accused Ben-Gurion of engineering the transformation of a constituent assembly into the first Knesset. The political agenda had become the prerogative of government, not parliament. In contrast Kook upheld the sovereignty of the Knesset as opposed to the dictate of government.

Begin attempted to reverse the tide in a speech to the second Herut conference, which set forth his vision for the movement. It highlighted freedom of the individual, the rule of law and free enterprise. Lamerhav also presented its own programme at the second conference: civil rights, a planned economy, the status of non-Jews in the state, a reduction of the powers of the Histadrut and the nationalisation of public transport. It also projected a predilection for radicalism, and this persuaded many critics of Begin to reject Lamerhav and stay with Begin. He thus survived and eventually his critics either conformed or dispersed.

Following the second conference of Herut, Hillel Kook and Eri Jabotinsky left Herut and eventually departed from the political arena. Tamir and Merlin remained within as leaders of the Lamerhav faction. Both Begin and Lamerhav courted Altman and the former Revisionists to support them.[51]

One issue, however, which united Begin's supporters and Herut's dissenters was the ideological question of the borders of Israel. Begin stuck hard and fast to the historic borders of the original British Mandate. He condemned the first partition of Palestine of March 1921 as well as the second one of November 1947.

Begin's broadcast on emerging from the underground on 15 May 1948 predicted that 'the soldiers of Israel will yet hoist our banner on the Tower of David and our ploughs will yet plough the fields of the Gilead'. Moreover, the two banks of the Jordan were clearly depicted on the Herut flag. In the first Knesset, Herut continued to refer to the lost land and cities of the East Bank, now the state of Jordan. The second conference of Herut in February 1951 repeated this line. Following the assassination of King Abdullah a few months later, Begin accused the government of not taking advantage of this opportunity to avail itself of expanding the borders of the state through the conquest of the East Bank.

The Israeli public, however, was less interested in borders than in the dire economic situation. Those disaffected with both Ben-Gurion and

---

[51] Bader, *ha-Keneset va-ani*, pp. 50–51.

Begin now tended to vote for the General Zionists, who were deemed more competent in the economic sphere.

In the campaign for the second general election in 1951, Begin's list of candidates comprised more homogeneously Irgun loyalists and Revisionists who had seen which way the political wind was blowing. He also began to cultivate the new impoverished Mizrahi immigrants, mainly from the Arab world. Begin reflected the new immigrants' sense of tradition, respect and formality. They were uninterested in the delights of socialism and the collectivism of the kibbutz, but preferred small business and private enterprise. Begin attacked Mapai's lack of understanding of these new immigrants whose world outlook was decidedly different from that of the Ashkenazim of Eastern Europe. Even so, the memory of the past was always in the background. Begin told his audiences that if it had not been for Herut, there would have been secret police and concentration camps in the Land of Israel.[52]

Although Begin blamed Mapai for the economic situation, the new Israelis remained in awe of Ben-Gurion, 'the father of the nation', who had led the Jews to victory and independence. In 1951 Herut lost nearly half its seats, the number dropping to eight, while the General Zionists won twenty-three. Only 6 percent of the electorate voted for Herut, while Mapai obtained forty-five seats. Faced with this rejection, Menahem Begin resigned as the leader of his movement.

[52] *Herut*, 29 July 1951.

13

The Survival of the Fittest

In August 1951, Begin went on holiday to Italy. Despite repeated appeals, he refused to return to the leadership and was considering setting up a private law firm. Arieh Ben-Eliezer took over as acting head while Begin was on 'extended leave'. Begin hired a room at a guest house, where he wrote *White Nights* about his experiences in the Gulag and studied for the bar exams. Yet a restless Begin could not distance himself from the political realm for very long. Indeed, his political career in one sense was just beginning.

On 12 March 1951 Israel had made a claim for reparations for Nazi crimes from the Federal Republic of Germany. This was driven in part by Israel's dire economic situation. Like many who had survived, Begin exhibited a deep antagonism towards the new Germany. For Begin, there was no such thing as 'a good German'. Even anti-Nazis were Nazis in disguise. Begin adhered to Mirabeau's celebrated comment that 'some countries possess armies, but Prussia is an army that happens to possess a country.' Only Germany surpassed Britain in Begin's ranking of loathing.

Since his arrival in Palestine in 1942, Begin had made accusations against the failure of the Jewish Agency and the Zionist movement to help Jews in Nazi-occupied Europe.[1] He also cast aspersions on the motives of the Allies and later tarred the British with the Nazi brush. The escalation of violence against returning Jews in post-war Poland reminded Begin of what he had escaped from. Jews were killed near Czorsztyn in April

---

[1] Menahem Begin, 'We Believe', 1944, in *Bamahteret*, vol. 1 (Tel Aviv, 1959), pp. 39–55; 'How to Rescue', *Herut*, 6 February 1944.

1946, near Korscienko in May 1946 and forty-two died in the Kielce pogrom in July 1946. Jewish patients were murdered in a Lublin hospital. Bishop Stefan Wyszynski of Lublin and Cardinal Hlond, archbishop of Warsaw, explained that this had happened because there were so many atheist Jews in the new Communist regime.[2] All this brought an angry response from Begin.[3]

Moreover, there was a concerted difference in the manner in which Begin and Ben-Gurion viewed the Shoah from the heights of the 1950s: 'Begin thought about the victims while Ben-Gurion thought about the survivors.'[4] Begin, by temperament and through experience, looked to the past and tradition – and not 'the new Jew' promoted by Ben-Gurion. In the early 1950s Ben-Gurion spoke little about the Holocaust and was even doubtful about the construction of Yad Vashem as a memorial to those who perished. His view was that the state in itself was the monument. He rarely spoke about his own personal loss in the Shoah. He advised Israelis who were already in Palestine 'to grieve in silence. My niece and her two children were burned alive. Can such a thing be spoken of?'[5]

At the second Herut conference in 1951, Begin suggested that German rearmament would lead to the next world war.[6] While Begin was clearly against any negotiations with Adenauer's Germany, he was not against the notion of reparations themselves. In December 1951 Ben-Eliezer, Begin's replacement, suffered a heart attack and Begin took over once more. Egged on by Yohanan Bader,[7] he raised the emotionally charged issue of reparations publicly. He was in good company, since both Ya'akov Hazan of the Marxist Mapam and Elimeleh Rimalt of the bourgeois General Zionists also strongly opposed reparations from the federal government.

In Begin's eyes, West Germany was 'the abomination of abominations'. At this time, he penned powerful, vitriolic articles in *Herut*.[8] No doubt Begin's motivation was genuine, but there were other considerations. As with the Irgun, the members of Betar who had fought in the Warsaw Ghetto had been airbrushed out of existence by Ben-Gurion and Mapai.

[2] Joanna Michlic-Coren, 'Anti-Jewish Violence in Poland, 1918–1939 and 1945–1947', *Polin* vol. 13 (London, 2000), pp. 34–64.

[3] Menahem Begin, 'In the Aftermath of the Kielce Pogrom and the Words of the Zionist Leaders', Broadcast on the *Voice of Fighting Zion*, 10 July 1946.

[4] Avi Shilon, *Menachem Begin: A Life* (London, 2012), p. 167.

[5] David Ben-Gurion, Letter to A. S. Stein, 17 August 1955, in Roni Stauber, *The Holocaust in Israeli Public Debate in the 1950s* (London, 2007), pp. 52–54.

[6] *Herut*, 27 February 1951.

[7] Yohanan Bader, *ha-Keneset va-ani* (Jerusalem, 1979), p. 191.

[8] Menahem Begin, *Herut* 1 January and 6 January 1952.

Betar had organised itself separately from other Zionist youth in occupied Poland as the Żydowski Ziązek Wojskowy (ŻZW) – the Jewish Military Organisation. It had fought the Germans in Warsaw's Muranowski Square, but most of its commanders and fighters had been killed. There were extremely few public references to the Jewish Military Organisation in communiqués both during the fighting and after the war in Israel. In part this was due to the influence of Mapam, which had led the fighting and had also adulated Stalin at that point in its history.[9] This sore point dovetailed with a desire to undermine Mapai. It was a short step to imply that members of Mapai were no better than collaborators: 'an end to the rule of yesterday's British agents who are now becoming agents of Nazi Germany'.[10] Begin wished to project another narrative, a counter-history.

At the beginning of January 1952, thousands gathered to hear Begin speak in Tel Aviv's Mugrabi Square. Begin invited them to also visit Jerusalem's Zion Square to hear his views prior to the debate in the Knesset. Alongside Professor Yosef Klausner, he excited and incited the crowd. Post-war Germany was no different from its Nazi predecessor and Ben-Gurion was no more than a quisling. He hoisted the imagery of Mapai's storm troopers assaulting them, killing some and imprisoning others in camps. All, he inferred, should wear the yellow star and be ready for any sacrifice. Whereas Begin had been quite clear in instructing his followers not to retaliate during the *Altalena* affair – 'there will be no civil war' – this was significantly not the case with the reparations issue.

Following Begin's speech in Zion Square, with the event officially pronounced to be over, several hundred demonstrators unexpectedly followed Begin to the Knesset. There the policemen who were guarding the Knesset were attacked and stoned. Scores were injured. The police responded by using tear gas. The demonstrators, encouraged by the organisers of the rally, made the connection between the use of tear gas against Jews and the use of Zyklon B by the Nazis.[11]

Begin regarded the agreement of the Ben-Gurion government to negotiate as a turning point in Israel's history. He threatened mass disobedience in the form of non-payment of taxes and requested a national referendum on the issue. He described his contribution to the debate in the Knesset as 'a personal speech' and asked its Arab members not to vote, as only the Jews, he believed, had the moral right to decide this question. He argued

---

[9] Tuvia Frilling, 'A Blatant Oversight? The Right Wing in Israeli Holocaust Historiography', *Israel Studies*, vol. 14 no. 1 (Spring 2009), pp. 123–69.

[10] Menahem Begin, *Herut*, 7 January 1952.

[11] Bader, *ha-Keneset va-ani*, pp. 62–64.

that the government's action would allow Germany to buy 'absolution'.[12] Moreover, he reminded the members of the religious parties that it was the tenth day of the Hebrew month of Tevet, a minor fast day – the day when the Babylonians had commenced their siege of Jerusalem, an event which ended with the destruction of the First Temple.

Begin recalled the Pinsk massacre of thirty-four Jews in April 1919 during the Polish-Soviet War.[13] Major Aleksander Norbut-Luczynski had accused community leaders of being clandestine Bolsheviks. Without any investigation, he had placed them in front of a firing squad. The major's conduct was defended by high-ranking officers in the Polish army. He was never brought to trial, but instead promoted to the rank of general. The Polish government, however, not wishing to antagonise the Western public, which was sympathetic to the Polish cause, offered to pay compensation to the victims' families. Begin compared this to the offer of compensation by 'the new Germany'.

Begin told his fellow parliamentarians that his followers would surround the Knesset 'as in the days of Rome when a Roman governor wanted to put a statue in the Temple. The Jews were alerted from all over the country. They surrounded the Temple and said "Over our dead bodies, shall you pass"'.[14]

Begin also recalled the firing on the *Altalena* by 'the Holy Cannon' and invoked the killing of Jews. In turn, Ben-Gurion deliberately provoked Begin with cutting comments until he exploded. Begin then refused to apologise, which led to a three-hour recess. A stoic and stubborn Ben-Gurion justified his approach by arguing that Begin's behaviour and actions constituted a threat to democracy and proposed a resolution to suspend him from the Knesset.[15]

In a radio broadcast, Ben-Gurion referred to the demonstrators as 'a wild mob of Irgunists and Communists'. Begin said that 'Israel would not be turned into a Spain or Syria.' Presumably he was referring to Franco and Vichy. The vote in the Knesset was split: 61–50 with 9 abstentions.

Although Herut cancelled another demonstration, Begin felt that the authoritarian hand of Mapai was heavy on the country. He was loath to accept the vote in the Knesset and told Yohanan Bader that he was

[12] Shilon, *Menachem Begin*, p. 170.
[13] Jósef Lewandowski, 'History and Myths: Pinsk, April 1919', *Polin* vol. 2 (London 1987).
[14] *Major Knesset Debates*, vol. 3 ed. Netanel Lorch (London 1992) pp. 730–31.
[15] Ned Temko, *To Win or Die: A Personal Portrait of Menachem Begin* (New York, 1987), p. 138.

considering reverting to the underground. Bader persuaded him that this was a futile gesture, and no more was said.

Begin's suspension undoubtedly strengthened his standing as someone who was willing to pay the price for his principles within Herut and could now forge an identity with the marginalised of society. In one sense, his actions over the reparations issue were a watershed which marked the final gasps of Ha-mefaked, the legendary commander of the Irgun before assuming the mantle of responsibility and respectability as the leader of the opposition. In September 1952 Sharett and Adenauer signed an agreement to pay 3,450 million marks to Israel over the next twelve years.

THE KASTNER AFFAIR

The Kastner affair of the mid-1950s became a cause célèbre for those opposed to Mapai. Rudolf Kastner, a leading Hungarian Zionist, who had been involved in the rescue of Jews in wartime Budapest, found himself accused of implicit collaboration with the Nazis, remaining silent about the impending fate of hundreds of thousands of Hungarian Jews in 1944 and his personal selection of 1,685 Jews to board a train to freedom in Switzerland. Such charges originated in the accusations of an obscure pamphleteer, Malkiel Gruenwald, in Israel. Haim Cohn, the minister of justice and attorney general, decided to prosecute Gruenwald for libel. Gruenwald, it later transpired, had a long criminal career in Hungary and Austria. He had also been an informant for the CID.[16]

The trial commenced at the beginning of 1954 in the Jerusalem District Court. At that time, Kastner was the head of the Public Relations Department of the Ministry of Trade and Industry. He had tried to become a Mapai candidate during both the 1949 and 1951 elections and failed. Gruenwald was defended by Shmuel Tamir, a leading figure in Herut and an opponent of Begin. Tamir's astute strategy effectively placed Kastner in the dock, and he had to explain his involvement with Adolf Eichmann, the Blut fuer Ware (Blood for Goods) agreement. The idea of goods for Jews was not new and had been raised even before the German occupation of Hungary in March 1944.[17]

The proposition was that Rudolf Kastner and Joel Brand would facilitate the delivery of supplies to the hard-pressed Germans in 1944 with the aid of international Jewish organisations. In return the Nazis would

---

[16] Shlomo Aronson, *Hitler, the Allies, and the Jews* (Cambridge, 2007), p. 334.
[17] Ibid., p. 227.

ensure the survival of Jewish communities and their transfer to places of safety.

The passengers on the Kastner train contained the intelligentsia and communal workers, millionaires and orphans, as well as Kastner's close family. The list was drawn up as a result of a compromise between all the Jewish parties in Hungary rather than as a result of Kastner's direct intervention. It therefore included supporters of Jabotinsky as well as the anti-Zionist Satmar Rebbe, Joel Teitelbaum. While Kastner ensured that members of his own family were included, others were not and were subsequently killed by the Nazis. This was also the case regarding his home community in Cluj.[18]

Kastner's belief was that this was a rare opportunity to be grasped because it could well be the beginning of a wholesale rescue of Hungarian Jews. Not wishing to jeopardise his scheme, Kastner never revealed to other Hungarian Jews the fate that awaited them. By the autumn of 1944 nearly half a million had been deported 'for resettlement in the east'.

Those who understood the situation urged the bombing of the railway lines leading to Auschwitz-Birkenau. A long report by two escapees from Auschwitz, Alfred Wetzler and Rudolf Vrba, known as the Auschwitz Protocol, reached Switzerland only in June 1944. Its essence was broadcast on the BBC three days later, followed by worldwide pressure on the Hungarian regent, Admiral Horthy, to stop the deportations of Jews.[19]

At the Gruenwald trial, Vrba accused Kastner of sitting on the protocol and not publicising its chilling details to Hungarian Jews. In addition, the mother of Hannah Senesh – the Jewish woman who had returned from Palestine to Hungary, been captured and put to death – accused Kastner of deceit and deception. Yoel Palgi, another parachutist from Palestine similarly accused Kastner of betrayal. He had spent several months with Senesh in Yugoslavia before crossing into Hungary, but unlike Senesh, he had managed to survive the war and returned to Palestine.

Tamir further revealed that after the war Kastner had given supportive testimony on behalf of an SS officer, Kurt Becher. Tamir elevated Becher in the courtroom to Eichmann's importance. Kastner, who had deposited some funds with Becher – to be returned after the war – had testified, it was implied, in the SS officer's favour in order to retrieve the deposit to fill Mapai's coffers. Kastner's omission, its reinterpretation by Tamir, coupled with the literary exploitation of this episode by Uri Avneri and Ben

---

[18] Ibid., p. 261.
[19] Alfred Wetzler, *Escape from Hell: The True Story of the Auschwitz Protocol* (Oxford, 2007), pp. 223–76.

Hecht, easily fed the imagination of an Israel which was still looking for answers to an unimaginable tragedy of a decade before.

Kastner's silence in Hungary was based on the premise that he could save some – including his own family – but not all. Those who sacrificed and were sacrificed did not appreciate this sentiment. Kastner operated in the grey, morally dubious area between good and evil in the hope of saving multitudes as the Nazi empire shrank.

This was not how Shmuel Tamir and the Israeli Right understood it. It was clear-cut. Kastner had not raised the alarm and was implicitly a collaborator. Instead of undertaking a second Warsaw Ghetto uprising, this time in Budapest, the Jews quietly queued in orderly fashion to board the trains for Auschwitz. Kastner had saved only a few Jews at the war's end to provide himself with an explanation should an accusatory finger be pointed at him.

Was Eichmann's proposal a serious proposition? Tamir tried to persuade the court that it was nothing more than a Nazi trick and therefore Kastner was a willing collaborator. Alternatively it may have been an attempt by Himmler to save himself at the end of the war through the possibility of clandestine negotiations with the Allies.

Joel Brand, who was Kastner's colleague in Ha-va'adah le-ezra ve-Hatzalah (Committee for Assistance and Rescue), also negotiated with Eichmann. The Nazis would stop the deportation of Hungarian Jews and release up to 1 million people in return for 10,000 trucks, which would be sent to the eastern front. Brand was permitted to go to Istanbul in order to negotiate with the Allies and to meet Moshe Sharett. On arrival, he was told that Sharett had not been granted a visa by the British and therefore he should proceed to Aleppo. Although he was given assurances by the Jewish Agency that the British would not arrest him, this is exactly what happened. Under British supervision, Brand eventually met Sharett, but he was then taken to Cairo. The British government had apparently been informed about the 'Blood for Goods' proposal and was vehemently against it. The Jewish Agency was powerless to intervene and seemingly acquiesced. For thousands of Hungarian Jews, Eichmann's offer was never explored and the slender possibility of rescue and salvation was lost.

Moreover, was the responsibility for aborting the attempt essentially that of Kollek and Sharett? Was Kastner trapped between his loyalty to Mapai on one side and Tamir on the other?

Tamir, a former member of the Irgun who had been exiled to Africa, stated that Joel Brand had been handed over to the British by Jewish

Agency operatives. This 'collaboration' happened shortly before Begin initiated the Revolt. If Eichmann's offer and Brand's plight had been publicised, it was inferred, then the Jews of the Yishuv would have supported Begin into forcing the British to save Hungarian Jewry. Mapai 'collaborated' with the British in suppressing Eichmann's offer to prevent empowering Begin.[20] It was nothing less, Tamir implied, than a precursor to Ben-Gurion's 'collaboration' during the saison.

Judge Binyamin Halevi, later a Herut member of Knesset, remarked that Kastner had sacrificed the unknowing masses for a chosen few. Halevi quoted Virgil's *Aeneid*, 'timeo Danaos et dona ferentes' (beware of Greeks bearing gifts), in that the success of his agreement with the Nazis was predicated on the view that Eichmann would eventually deliver on his promise. What Kastner did not bargain for was that 'eventually' was a long time in coming – an eternity in which many provincial Hungarian Jewish communities were liquidated. Halevi famously proclaimed the Faustian implication that Kastner had sold his soul to the devil. Ten years after the revelations of the Shoah, many agreed with Judge Halevi.

Mapai lodged an appeal against Halevi's verdict. Instead both Menahem Begin's Herut and Moshe Sneh's Communists brought a no-confidence motion before the Knesset. The General Zionists, members of the government coalition, refused to abstain from the vote, resulting in the fall of Moshe Sharett's government.

The verdict was eventually overturned by the Supreme Court in January 1958, but not before Kastner had been assassinated by a Far Right fringe group, Malkhut Yisrael, which had conducted attacks against the Czechoslovak and Soviet Embassies because of the Slansky trial and the Doctors' Plot as well as the West German legation over the reparations agreement.

Kastner was shot by Ze'ev Eckstein and two associates. Eckstein had been planted by the Shin Bet into Israel Eldad's *Sulam* group and seemingly fell under Eldad's influence instead. Eckstein was sentenced to life imprisonment, but was pardoned and released in 1963.[21] The Shin Bet involvement in the Kastner affair remained unclear and an unresolved matter of controversy extending into the twenty-first century.[22]

Kastner was exonerated of all charges except that he had testified on behalf of an SS officer. The majority judgement by Judge Shimon Agranat

[20] Aronson, *Hitler, the Allies, and the Jews*, p. 229.
[21] *Ha'aretz*, 11 December 2014. See also Ze'ev Eckstein, *Smihat Tla'im* (Tel Aviv, 2014).
[22] *Ha'aretz*, 9 January 2015.

argued that Kastner had been motivated to save as many Jews as possible and was no collaborator. His behaviour stood 'the test of plausibility and reasonableness', and he loyally pursued what he considered to be 'the only chance of rescue'. Judge Moshe Silberg did not concur and produced a minority argument. He argued that Kastner wilfully did not operate in good faith, but actually expedited the task of extermination.

The Supreme Court overturned most of the verdict in the Kastner trial. It rejected Tamir's argument that Kastner and Eichmann were equal negotiating partners. Kastner's conduct could not be explained within normal parameters. A plaque was eventually erected in his memory at Yad Vashem, the Holocaust memorial site, which stated that Kastner had saved the lives of 20,000 people.

Herut, however, was still convinced of Kastner's guilt regardless of the decision of the Supreme Court. The acceptance of powerlessness and inaction fitted into Begin's view of Mapai as indolent and bureaucratic. It dovetailed with the basic raison d'être of Herut, a different mode of Jewish behaviour, a different future for the Jewish people.

Lehi also believed that Lord Moyne had refused to save Holocaust victims and played a major role in adopting a negative attitude to any deal to save the Jews of Hungary. This was a central reason for his assassination in 1944.

Judge Halevi's verdict was given just a few weeks before the 1955 election. Begin characterised members of Mapai as quislings who had already shown their true colours in handing over fellow Jews to the British during the saison. This built on Revisionist criticism of the Yishuv's leadership when the first details of the mass extermination of the Jews were revealed at the end of 1942.[23] Sharett willingly, without qualms, it was argued, similarly handed over Joel Brand to the British in Aleppo.[24] The Jewish Agency was depicted as a Zionist Yevsektsia – the Jewish section of the early Soviet Communist Party. Only Hungarian Betar had demanded an uprising on the Polish model, and the Jewish Agency had prevented it. Begin argued in an election speech that the Jewish Agency refused to relay news of the fate of Hungarian Jews in the summer of 1944. The Jewish Agency was Chamberlainesque, the party of appeasement. Mapai stood behind Kastner, Begin commented, because it feared that he would reveal further 'secrets' about the party's involvement. Moreover, Kastner's train

---

[23] Yehiam Weitz, 'Revisionist Criticism of the Yishuv leadership During the Holocaust', *Yad Vashem Studies* vol. 23 (1993), pp. 369–95.

[24] Menahem Begin, *Herut*, 24 July 1955.

of the privileged few was reminiscent of the selective immigration from countries such as Morocco and Iran in the 1950s. Those without a voice were left behind.[25]

Herut's technique was to simplify situations and polarise opinions into choices of black and white, right and wrong. Some facts proved inconvenient. Brand's own testimony suggested that Sharett and the Jewish Agency representatives had 'argued passionately with the Englishmen' who proved unmoveable.[26] Brand had warned that if he was not allowed to return to Budapest, Eichmann would order the slaughter of his family as well as countless thousands of Jews. Brand was taken to Cairo and imprisoned. During the period from 15 May until 8 July 1944, 434,000 Hungarian Jews were deported to Auschwitz.[27]

Sharett raised the 'Blood for Goods' possibility and the bombing of concentration camps with Eden in London in July 1944. Both Eden and Churchill were opposed, but prevaricated in providing an answer to Sharett and to Weizmann. British duplicity ensured that Joel Brand's message was ignored despite Sharett's continuous efforts over two months, 'all of which drove us to the brink of despair'.[28]

The dilemmas of dealing with the Nazis in order to save Jewish lives – just as Jabotinsky had negotiated with Ukrainian nationalists in 1921 – were not considered. The object of the exercise was to demonise Mapai and to raise questions about its moral integrity and political honesty.

The 1955 election promoted parties which preached an overt nationalism – Herut and Ahdut Ha'avodah – and punished those which did not, such as Mapai and the General Zionists. A Herut poster read: 'He [Kastner] votes for Mapai, you vote for Herut.'[29]

Following Kastner's assassination, Herut, unlike other parties, which were critical of Kastner, was unforgiving with little remorse. Its periodical, *Herut*, promoted the minority opinion of Judge Moshe Silberg. In Herut's eyes, the verdict of the Supreme Court made no difference to Kastner's guilt. Begin even surmised that the assassins might well be located in the security services.[30]

[25] Yehiam Weitz, 'The Herut Movement and the Kasztner Trial', *Holocaust and Genocide Studies*, vol. 8, no. 3 (Winter 1994), pp. 349–71.
[26] Alex Weissberg, *Advocate for the Dead: The Story of Joel Brand* (London, 1958), p. 142.
[27] Ibid., p. 218.
[28] Gabriel Sheffer, *Moshe Sharett: Biography of a Political Moderate* (Oxford, 1996), pp. 154–55.
[29] Shilon, *Menachem Begin*, p. 180.
[30] Weitz, 'The Herut Movement and the Kasztner Trial'.

The verdict in the Kastner affair, published a few weeks before the 1955 election – and Herut's decision to exploit it – were undoubtedly factors in the movement's return to prominence. It virtually doubled its representation in the Knesset and leapfrogged over the General Zionists as the acceptable face of the Israeli Right. Herut was now the second-largest party at fifteen seats but still a long way behind Mapai's forty mandates. Herut's decline was reversed and the scene was set for increasing its Knesset representation.

The question of establishing diplomatic relations with West Germany was a highly sensitive one. In the 1950s many civil servants and political figures had been members of the Nazi Party or simply acquiesced in accepting it. Begin asked what had happened to the millions who had voted against Hitler. The transition from the past to the future, it could be argued, needed those with experience who could run the new Germany. Not all, however, had followed the example of Willy Brandt during the Hitler years and left the country.

At the third conference of Herut in April 1954, Begin demanded a referendum on establishing diplomatic relations with Germany.[31] At the fifth Herut conference in November 1958, Begin repeated his demand. In part, Adenauer's Germany was also reticent about establishing diplomatic relations with Israel. It feared that the Arab states would retaliate by establishing diplomatic relations with its nemesis, Communist East Germany.

Moreover, with the revelation that German scientists were working for Nasser's regime in Egypt, even though army intelligence did not regard it as significant,[32] Herut mounted a campaign at the end of 1962. In a Knesset debate in March 1963, Begin took Mapai to task:

For ten years since Germany began to pay a fraction of what it stole, you have endeavoured to endear yourselves to it and abase yourself before it. It is a paradox. You invite German experts on German education and Germany sends Nasser experts on death. You sew uniforms for the German army and Germany sends knowhow about gases to be used against the Jewish people. You send our 'uzis' to Germany and the Germans gave our enemies bacteria. Please at least now, weigh matters up. How long will you continue to grovel, abase yourself and seek their friendship?[33]

---

[31] *Herut*, 21 April 1954.
[32] Eitan Haber, *Menachem Begin: The Legend and the Man* (New York, 1978), p. 254.
[33] Menahem Begin, Speech to the Knesset, 20 March 1963, in N. Lorch, *Major Knesset Debates*, vol. 4 (Jerusalem, 1992), p. 1349.

Begin compared Ben-Gurion to Vidkun Quisling for his attempts to seek a relationship with West Germany. At the beginning of 1965, Walter Ulbricht, the leader of the German Democratic Republic, visited Egypt at Nasser's invitation. This visit essentially removed the obstacles to establishing diplomatic relations between the Federal Republic and Israel. It also reignited Herut's appeal to the emotions some twenty years after the end of the war.

During the Knesset debate, Begin pointed out that the new German ambassador would also represent those who had voted National Socialist in 1933, including those who had supplied the Auschwitz authorities with coal for the furnaces and metal forks for moving the bodies into the ovens. He reminded Israelis that West Germany's foreign minister, Gerhard Schröder, had joined the Nazi Party in April 1933 and was awarded the Iron Cross second class in 1942.[34] He also omitted to mention that Schröder had resigned from the NSDAP in 1941 and married his half-Jewish girlfriend during the war.

COALITION CONSTRUCTION

During the 1950s Menahem Begin concluded that Herut alone could never overtake Mapai and therefore could not become the leading party in any Israeli election. Herut won fourteen seats in 1949 and only twenty in 1977 when Begin became prime minister. However, in 1977 Herut had become the inner core of the Likud, which emerged as the largest party and therefore had the task of forming the next government. The second election in 1951 had seen Herut lose half its seats. Begin's style of leadership had led to a host of resignations by former Maximalist Revisionists from the Jabotinsky era – Ahimeir, Greenberg, Avraham Weinshal – but also by his Irgun comrades such as Paglin and Livni. Herut was riven by discord.

Many of those who sympathised with the Maximalists followed Stern rather than Raziel. In the 1950s, they gathered around Israel Eldad's journal, *Sulam*. It also provided a focus for opposition to Begin. Shmuel Tamir, Kastner's courtroom interrogator, who had been influenced by Berit Ha-Biryonim in the 1930s, also contributed to *Sulam*. He referred to Begin as 'the oppressor from the Diaspora'.[35]

---

[34] Menahem Begin, Speech to the Knesset, 16 March 1965, in N. Lorch, *Major Knesset Debates*, vol. 4, pp. 1432–33.
[35] *Haolam Hazeh*, 14 September 1955, in Amos Perlmutter, *The Life and Times of Menachem Begin* (New York, 1987), p. 266.

The reparations episode had also persuaded some around *Sulam* such as the Malkhut Yisrael group to campaign by means of letter bombs to Adenauer and his ministers. Dov Shilansky, who had arrived on the *Altalena*, was sentenced to three years' imprisonment. Shilansky was also defended in court by Shmuel Tamir and publicly supported by Begin even though he disagreed with such radical tactics. While this latter-day conflict between the disciples of Stern and Raziel was being carried out privately, Ben-Gurion made no distinction and used the incident to pour more vitriol onto Begin's head.

Sections of the religious Right also began to operate as an underground in protest against the secularism of the Mapai-led government. In May 1951 members of the Berit Hakana'im were arrested for planning to torch IDF recruitment offices and thus prevent the conscription of women. Acts of arson were also planned against butcher shops that sold non-kosher meat.

Following the 1951 election, the General Zionists emerged as the largest non-socialist party, displacing Herut. When Herzl established the Zionist Organisation in Basel in 1897, all Zionists were 'general Zionists'. Factionalism reared its head a year later at the Second Zionist Congress. During the inter-war years, even these non-party general Zionists became a party. It was soon divided between social liberals who were close to the labour movement and a more conservative wing which espoused private enterprise and tradition and which detested any whiff of socialism. The General Zionists 'A' and the General Zionists 'B' coalesced and split periodically. The General Zionists believed that they could emerge as a centrist third force between the labour movement and the Revisionists. They divided once more on the eve of the establishment of the state, but emerged strongly in the 1951 election, with the General Zionists holding twenty seats and its estranged faction, the Progressives, with four seats. Together they accounted for three times the parliamentary strength of Herut.

Begin realised that an alliance with the General Zionists was the path to power, but he would not countenance any approach before Herut was in a dominant position. He therefore banned an article in *Herut* which advocated negotiations and a merger.[36] The General Zionists, the party of private enterprise and small business, was thus pulled by its former liberal faction, the Progressives, in one direction and by Herut in the other. The bourgeois General Zionists were also frightened by the image

[36] Shilon, *Menachem Begin*, p. 175.

FIGURE 13. A cartoon of the General Zionists during an election campaign in the 1950s. It attacks Menahem Begin, who is sporting a 'fascist' armband denoting Herut, seated on a rocking horse, labelled 'demagoguery'. The caption reads 'Swift as an arrow – on a rocking horse' (*Ma'ariv*, 24 July 1955).
Courtesy of the Central Zionist Archives, Jerusalem.

of Begin as 'the demagogue and extremist'. Moreover, they had accepted partition and did not embrace Begin's belief in 'the completeness of the homeland'. Significantly they decided at the General Zionist conference in 1952 to establish a faction within the Histadrut to project a more populist image.

At the third Herut conference in April 1954, Begin emphasised economic and domestic issues and started the process of distancing himself from the Irgun years. He promised to oppose monopolies and trusts from the Left and from the Right. He advocated the elimination of foreign currency control and an end to unfair tax advantages for kibbutz enterprises tied to the Histadrut and 'an end to cartels – [whether] bourgeois (General Zionists) [or] proletarian (Mapai)'.[37]

Begin's approach was to promote Herut as a clear alternative to Mapai – with a different historical narrative and a different political philosophy. In creating a choice, there was a need to enact a political

[37] Menahem Begin, *Herut*, 21 April 1954.

polarisation. Mapai approached Herut in 1952, 1955 and 1961 to join a coalition government, but in every case Begin rejected such approaches. Herut's election strategy in 1955 was to attack the General Zionists at every level.[38]

It was only with the return of Herut's fortunes in the 1955 election and the parallel decline in that of the General Zionists that Begin began to cultivate his future political partner. Indeed, Begin told a meeting of the Herut central committee in December 1955 that he had pre-empted an invitation from General Zionists to discuss their confluence of interests. As Herut was now the larger party, Begin instead invited the General Zionists in order to speak from a position of parliamentary strength.[39] Yet these initial contacts foundered, more on the rocks of internal power struggles within the General Zionists than because of differences with Herut.

Begin had set out to cultivate the Mizrahim as early as 1948. The immigration from Morocco started in 1954, and therefore one of Herut's objectives was to secure their vote in the 1955 election. Many new immigrants, especially those who felt that they had been treated poorly by Mapai apparatchiks, sought out Herut. The movement won 30–40 percent of the vote in locations such as Ramla and Bnei Brak.[40] Begin also played up to the sense of traditionalism which many newcomers from Arab countries exuded. Indeed, one election leaflet distributed during the 1959 election suggested that Begin had in fact been born in Morocco and went to yeshivah (a religious seminary) in Poland.[41] Begin also publicly took up the cause of those Jews who remained in Arab countries.

In 1959 there were riots in Wadi Salib in Haifa by disaffected Mizrahim who demanded a voice in Israeli society. Begin attacked Mapai politicians for their wealth – saying they were secret millionaires, owners of villas – to imply that in reality it was Herut, and not the socialists, which represented the underclass. Herut's election proposals in 1959 were geared towards attracting the vote of the marginalised and to emphasise the widening gap between the haves and the have-nots.

Menahem Begin also started to rebrand himself in the late 1950s and make himself more acceptable to a broader Israeli constituency. He even

---

[38] Yehiam Weitz, *ha'Tsa'ad ha-rishon le-khes ha-shilton: Tenu'at ha-Herut 1949–1955* (Jerusalem, 2007), pp. 176–80.

[39] Jonathan Mendilow, *Ideology, Party Change and Electoral Campaigns in Israel, 1965–2001* (New York, 2003), p. 39.

[40] Weitz, *ha'Tsa'ad ha-rishon*, pp. 215–18.

[41] Interview with Shulamit Hareven, 23 October 1994.

attempted to control his outbursts in the Knesset despite Ben-Gurion's provocations. He positioned Herut as the inheritor of Jabotinsky's liberal values. Thus Herut's 1959 election manifesto was entitled 'Programme for a National Liberal Government' with the subtitle 'Headed by Herut'.

Begin played to different audiences. To the members of Herut, he invoked the saison and accused Mapai of collaboration with the British CID. They were no better than the followers of Marshal Petain in Vichy France. To the General Zionists, he stressed Ben-Gurion's policy of *mamlahtiyut* – the dominance of the state – and Mapai's lack of tolerance for different views. He promoted his criticism of an 'authoritarian socialism' which covered the entire spectrum of political thought from social democracy to Stalinism.

He also attacked the universalism of Mapai's doctrine when he believed that it clashed with Israel's national interests. Thus although he denounced apartheid, he opposed any breaking off of diplomatic relations with Verwoerd's South Africa. While on the one hand he promoted the Irgun as the archetypal model for other national liberation movements during the period of decolonisation in the 1960s, on the other he opposed the Front de Libération Nationale (FLN) in Algeria because he believed that it would increase Nasser's standing in the Arab world and increase the possibility of an Egyptian attack on Israel.

Begin remained deeply antagonistic towards Soviet Communism, which he regarded as no more than Russian imperialism in progressive clothing. He ridiculed any attempt of Mapai to develop better relations with the USSR and attacked any pro-Soviet attitudes of the Israeli Left.

By 1959 not only had the General Zionists declined, but the internal split in the broad movement had become accentuated. In the election of that year, the General Zionists gained eight seats, while the Progressives attained six. Herut, however, gained only two more seats, while Mapai seemed as impregnable as ever with an extra seven mandates.

In May 1961 the General Zionists and the Progressives united for the last time as the Liberals. Any opposition to the merger was diminished by the possibility of an alternative merger between the General Zionists and Herut. The Progressives were vehemently opposed to any alignment with Begin's party because of Herut's aspirations for a Greater Israel and its refusal to join the Histadrut: 'Demagoguery and liberalism are a contradiction.'[42]

---

[42] Letter from Moshe Kol to Nahum Goldmann, 26 February 1962, in Amir Goldstein, '"We have a Rendezvous with Destiny": The Rise and Fall of the Liberal Alternative', *Israel Studies*, vol. 16, no. 1 (Spring 2011), pp. 26–52.

The election took place in August 1961. The new Liberal party improved the combined standing of its constituent parts by only three seats. Herut remained static at seventeen – the same number as the Liberals. It was certainly not a breakthrough for the Liberals. Begin made overtures to them even after the election, but they rejected any pact with Herut. In response Begin wrote an aptly titled article, 'We Have Patience'.[43] Together Herut and the Liberals possessed thirty-four seats and were now within striking distance of Mapai's forty-two. For this reason, Ben-Gurion wanted to include the Liberals in any coalition because he feared that the alternative would be an alliance with Herut. Levi Eshkol had even signed an agreement with the Liberals. The central committee of Mapai, however, was much more attracted to a wider socialist coalition with Ahdut Ha'avodah. Within a short time, the rejected Liberals came to believe that their chances of ever being included in a Mapai-led government were very slim.

The Mapai-led government had fallen after only two years because of the Lavon affair once more raising its head. A ministerial committee concluded that Pinhas Lavon had not in fact instructed Binyamin Givli, the head of military intelligence, to order the planting of explosives in Egypt in 1954. Herut and the General Zionists supported Lavon and brought down the government by a no-confidence motion. Ben-Gurion refused to accept the ministerial committee's decision, called for a judicial review and adamantly refused to back down. The split over the Lavon affair eventually fragmented Mapai, and Begin was astute enough to pick up the electoral pieces.

Ben-Gurion resigned for the last time as prime minister in 1963 and was succeeded by Levi Eshkol. Nearing eighty, Ben-Gurion believed that he could still exert control from his kibbutz at Sde Boqer as he had done during Sharett's short tenure in the 1950s. The mild-mannered Eshkol, however, started to strike out on his own. In 1964, he authorised the return of Jabotinsky's body from New York and approved its burial on Mount Herzl in Jerusalem. Although this was not paid for by the government, but by Herut members, Ben-Gurion retaliated by writing a series of articles in which he attacked the long-dead Jabotinsky and his views. Begin significantly restrained himself and countered Ben-Gurion by writing articles in praise of Jabotinsky. Begin recognised the symbolism of Eshkol's gesture because it conferred legitimacy upon himself and his movement for the first time.

43 *Herut*, 8 September 1961.

FIGURE 14. Cartoon comparing Ben-Gurion's refusal to allow Jabotinsky's remains to be buried in Israel to the British refusal to allow him back into Mandatory Palestine in 1930 (8 August 1958): illustration by Yoseph Ross, courtesy of Gideon Ross.
Courtesy of the Israeli Cartoon Museum Collection.

Moreover, Begin knew that he could widen the fissure lines within the labour movement by joining the Histadrut. It was also one of the conditions for a merger which a now desperate Liberal party would never give up. Despite Jabotinsky's opposition to the Histadrut in the 1930s, Begin realised that he would never take power without the support of sections of the working class – many of whom sympathised with Herut. In January 1963 at the seventh movement conference, it was explained that Herut had to look anew at membership of the Histadrut because that organisation had in fact changed profoundly. Socialism was on the wane. Eliezer Shostak, head of the National Workers' Federation (NWF), which had been established by Jabotinsky, was distinctly unhappy. He felt that this was also a move on the part of Begin to circumvent the NWF, which possessed political muscle within Herut. The conference was split such that Begin intervened to speak on the issue, with the result that there was a wafer-thin majority for joining the Histadrut. Herut established the Blue-White faction in the Histadrut and attracted thousands of adherents.

Even so, the Liberals still rejected Begin's approach. Its central committee voted 42–8 against negotiations with Herut.[44] Begin, however, believed that he could also split the Liberals into their component parts – the General Zionists, which would merge with Herut, and the Independent Liberals, which would secede. Moreover, Begin knew that if he wanted to head the new alliance, the Liberals would certainly exact a price. Begin finally struck a deal which would enact 'a compromise between parity and exact proportionality'.[45] Even though each party possessed seventeen seats, Begin offered the Liberals disproportionately more advantageous places on a joint 1965 election list to the detriment of Herut. Begin, however, would remain in first position on the list.[46]

Even so, there were profound differences between the Liberals and Herut. Begin exuded a sympathetic approach towards Judaism and Jewish tradition, which endeared him to the religious parties. The Liberals were less enamoured and wanted a reform of the religious establishment, which presided over an array of rotten boroughs. While Begin's populism and rhetoric appealed to an Israeli underclass, the middle-class Liberals embraced private enterprise and the world of the small businessman. Begin's long-time vitriolic sentiment against the establishment of diplomatic relations with West Germany[47] was not shared by the Liberals. All of this required a measure of compromise.

Begin's pragmatism was also evident when he agreed to a joint platform with the Liberals – with the exception that Herut could still advocate 'the indisputable right to the Land of Israel'. While Begin accepted the reality of the partition of November 1947, he never accepted the partition borders. Begin always opposed 'the dismemberment of the homeland' and regarded any attempt to do so as illegal. In parallel, he believed that any opportunity to expand Israel to its rightful dimensions should be seized.

[44] Yehiam Weitz, 'The Road to the "Upheaval": A Capsule History of the Herut Movement, 1948–1977', *Israel Studies*, vol. 10, no. 3 (Fall 2005), pp. 54–86.
[45] Mendilow, *Ideology, Party Change and Electoral Campaigns*, p. 49.
[46] Bader, *ha-Keneset va-ani*, pp. 170–73.
[47] Menahem Begin, *Herut*, 12 July 1952.

On the eve of the Suez campaign in 1956, he looked more to Jordan than to Egypt in the hope of reclaiming the East Bank. After having criticised the government for its prevarication, he strongly supported it during the war, only to propose a motion of no confidence in the government in the Knesset when Israel was forced to withdraw from conquered territory under American pressure.[48] In April 1957 he called on Ben-Gurion not to accept that the armistice lines of 1949 were now the actual borders of Israel.[49]

By the early 1960s, Begin had toned down his demands for seeking 'the completeness of the Land'. Moreover, there was no mention of exploiting a crisis to reclaim the East Bank in the agreement with the Liberals. Even so, Begin was not totally able to distance himself from his innermost beliefs. In June 1966, he commented that it was 'wholly inconceivable that any bit of the soil of the Land of Israel will be handed over to foreign rule'.[50]

Begin telescoped Judaic history and Jewish history – without distinction. The continuum between Abraham the patriarch and Herzl the founder of modern Zionism was, in Begin's eyes, uninterrupted. This was a political theology, 'a supra-temporal approach to history'.[51] Begin's belief in the veracity of the biblical narrative as the basis for the aspiration to occupy the entire, non-partitioned Land of Israel differed profoundly from that of the cosmopolitan Jabotinsky, who lauded the virtues of nineteenth-century national movements. Begin was described as 'drawing on religious concepts and modalities of thought that have undergone a process of secularisation'.[52]

The parliamentary bloc, Gahal (Gush Herut Liberalim), which emerged in 1965, actually lost seats. It attained twenty-six compared with a combined thirty-four for the Liberals and Herut in 1961. Even if the five seats of the breakaway Independent Liberals were taken into account, this was still several seats less than the 1961 total. Neither Herut nor the Liberals had benefitted. Even so, Begin's push for Herut to join the Histadrut paid political dividends. Some 100,000 voted for Gahal in the 1965 Histadrut election.

---

[48] Bader, *ha-Keneset va-ani*, pp. 102–03.
[49] Sasson Sofer, *Begin: An Anatomy of a Leadership* (London, 1988), p. 117.
[50] Menahem Begin, 'Address to the Herut and Liberal Centers', *HaYom*, 28 June 1966, in Sofer, *An Anatomy of Leadership*, p. 126.
[51] Arye Naor, 'Hawks' Beaks, Doves' Feathers: Likud Prime Ministers between Ideology and Reality', *Israel Studies*, vol. 19, no. 3 (Fall 2005), pp. 154–91.
[52] Ibid.

MAP 4. The Boundaries of Israel between 1949 and 1967.

Mapai also had embarked on internal coalition-building and had formed the Alignment (Ma'arakh) with Ahdut Ha'avodah. But it too had lost five seats. Even so the Alignment together with its allies in Mapam could account for fifty-three seats compared with Gahal's twenty-six.

Moreover, Ben-Gurion's younger followers were beginning to suggest that the time-honoured socialist methods of the pioneers did not fit the realities of the 1960s. Moshe Dayan was already advocating the privatisation of state land and a cessation of state funding to the traditional labour-controlled sector of Israeli society.

The election slogan in 1959 had been 'Say Yes to the Old Man!' By the summer of 1965, few in Mapai were willing to nod in the affirmative. A vote at the Mapai conference in June 1965 and a withering speech by the ailing Moshe Sharett placed Ben-Gurion in the minority. He told Ben-Gurion:

The leader must not subjugate the movement, paralyse its mind, or impose his personal position on it by a show of his own authority. It is my hope that Mapai will now unite and rid itself of this nightmare, that it will free itself from this malaise so that it can breathe freely and attend to the problems of the future.[53]

The steady hand of Levi Eshkol, the epitome of dullness, was preferred to the towering figure of Ben-Gurion. Indeed, Ben-Gurion had failed to displace Eshkol as he had done with Sharett. The princes of the party – Peres, Dayan, Kollek, Herzog – all dutifully followed Ben-Gurion out of Mapai and established Rafi, the Israeli Workers' List. In part it comprised those on the right of the party and those who were defined by Israel's security interests. Rafi stood in the 1965 election and attained a pitiful ten seats. The Mapai–Ahdut Ha'avodah alignment, which Ben-Gurion wished to displace by Rafi, secured forty-five seats compared with a combined fifty in 1961.

Rafi's exit left Mapai a more dovish party even if it was allied with Yitzhak Tabenkin's Ahdut Ha'avodah, which was not averse to colonising the West Bank with socialist kibbutzim. The lack of ideological symmetry pointed towards an inherent instability within the labour alignment while Rafi solidified as a right-wing party, and this provided new opportunities for Begin to expand his coalition.

The members of Rafi, the fragmented right wing of Mapai, were now cultivated by Begin's Gahal to expand the coalition of Herut and the Liberals. Indeed, in February 1966 Ben-Gurion surmised that there could

---

[53] Central Zionist Archives, A245/139, Jerusalem; Sheffer; *Moshe Sharett*, pp. 1017–18.

now be cooperation on a number of issues with Begin's Gahal.[54] Even the old hostility between Begin and Ben-Gurion seemed to diminish once Ben-Gurion had left Mapai, the party he had founded in 1930.

But Begin too had his party difficulties. The defeat of 1965 was Begin's sixth as party leader. Even with the Liberals in tow, only twenty-six seats had been won – far short of Mapai's total and even further removed from the blocking majority of sixty-one needed to actually form a government coalition.

Begin believed that he had 'opened a new page' with his critics within Herut. Although he appeared to be a serial election loser, he was also viewed as an evergreen fixture of the Israel Right. The Far Right, from Lehi to Eldad's *Sulam* circle, made a lot of political noise, but was unable to develop politically. Attempts at forming new groups of the anti-Begin Right had similarly foundered in the late 1950s.[55] Even so, Begin's opponents, from the Revisionists, the Irgun and Lamerhav, were gathering to preach change and to unseat him. Begin, like Ben-Gurion, seemed part of the jaded old guard. At the next movement congress in June 1966, Ehud Olmert of the Herut students overtly asked Begin to step down, rather than indirectly imply that he should. Olmert was supported by Shmuel Tamir and Gidi Paglin, who ironically told the delegates that they had surrounded Begin with 'an iron wall'.[56] Begin's long, emotional response dwelled on the past. It evoked a public display of his profound hurt and personal betrayal. He also remarked that an alliance of Rafi and Gahal could become an alternative government. Begin resigned as chairman and intimated that he was also prepared to resign from the Knesset.[57]

Many of Begin's supporters regarded him as an infallible father figure. Despite his announcement that he would retire, he continued as a Herut member and, outside the confines of the Knesset, began to lobby hitherto loyal followers. Many were unable to confront Begin in one-to-one meetings.

By February 1967 Begin was reinstated as chairman after a hiatus of several months. Tamir was suspended from Herut after seemingly instigating a critical letter in *Ha'aretz*.[58] Begin's opponents, his Irgun comrades, Tamir and Paglin, his Revisionist rivals, Shostak and Altman, all left Herut with Ehud Olmert to establish the Free Centre. It boasted three

---

[54] *Yediot Aharanot*, 25 February 1966.
[55] Perlmutter, *The Life and Times of Menachem Begin*, pp. 270–71.
[56] Temko, *To Win or Die*, p. 167.
[57] Bader, *ha-Keneset va-ani*, p. 188.
[58] *Ha'aretz*, 26 July 1966.

members of Knesset. They had wished for a more flexible ideological approach than Begin was willing to permit and certainly did not wish to be hemmed in by a belief in an Israel encompassing both banks of the Jordan. They were also open to the prospect of 'a small Israel' and partition. Even Eri Jabotinsky joined the Free Centre on the basis that Menahem Begin had renounced his father's legacy. These defections and a desire by the Liberals to dismember the unsuccessful Gahal placed Begin in a weak and vulnerable position on the eve of the Six-Day War.

14

Expanding the Political Circle

THE SIX-DAY WAR

Menahem Begin was not only an astute politician with a long view of the game, but also someone who was remarkably lucky with regard to the turn of events. In the early months of 1967 it seemed that the Herut-Liberal alliance was on the verge of collapse. The sceptics within the Liberals were in the ascendency. Gahal had stagnated in the 1965 elections, and the Liberals seem to have gained little from the partnership with Herut. The public persona of Menahem Begin remained the same – a dogmatic expounder of extreme views for whom the Liberals provided respectable cover and access to the Israeli middle class. In labour folklore, Begin represented the nationalist anti-Christ.

On 15 May 1967 Egyptian troops advanced towards Sinai. Some eight days later President Nasser blocked the Straits of Tiran. While the IDF pushed for military action, Eshkol attempted to avert war by exploring all diplomatic channels. The lack of immediate action, however, was perceived in the public arena as dithering and a loss of the element of surprise. The uninspiring Eshkol did little to calm an increasingly anxious Israeli public. This situation permitted Mapai's political opponents to call for a national unity coalition to weather the coming storm.

Following the 1965 election, there had been exploratory discussions between Rafi's Shimon Peres and the Liberals within Gahal to examine areas of possible cooperation.[1] Such a discourse bore fruit in May 1967 when Peres proposed a coalition based on Mapai, Rafi and Gahal.

---

[1] Interview with Zalman Shoval, 28 October 1994.

Ben-Gurion would return as prime minister in place of Levi Eshkol.[2] Menahem Begin similarly desired national unity and understood that the entry of Gahal into government would not only boost the alliance's public standing but also create cohesion internally.

Despite the rejection of many past private initiatives to co-opt Herut into government, Begin on this occasion was suddenly ready to agree to Peres's proposal. The prospect of a national catastrophe could be offered as a rationale for reversing Herut's previous policy of standing alone as the central opposition. Some within Herut opposed Begin's expediency,[3] but he smoothly played the role of an assiduous mediator between his political opponent, Levi Eshkol, and his old nemesis, David Ben-Gurion.

Yet not all were happy with the possibility of a return of 'the old man'. Many in Mapai had not forgiven Ben-Gurion for his obstinacy over the Lavon affair and his splitting of the party in 1965. Both Prime Minister Eshkol and Foreign Minister Golda Meir were strongly opposed to the return of Ben-Gurion. In turn Ben-Gurion had not forgiven the unassuming Eshkol for not playing the part of a second Sharett and resigning during the inner-party convulsions of the early 1960s. Ben-Gurion wanted Eshkol's resignation.

With this impasse, Peres instead proposed that Rafi's Moshe Dayan be appointed minister of defence. Gahal together with the National Religious Party (NRP) supported this move.[4] The Independent Liberals surprisingly also wanted Dayan. Eshkol moved to extinguish this attempt by inviting Gahal and Rafi to join the Knesset Foreign Affairs and Defence Committee. He was supported by both Mapam and Golda Meir, who opposed Gahal and Rafi joining the coalition. The Left's preference for minister of defence was Ahdut Ha'avodah's Yigal Allon.

Begin and Dayan had first met in 1943, but their relationship blossomed only when Dayan became chief of staff and Begin was a member of the Foreign Affairs and Defence Committee.[5] Dayan's views were individualistic and not set in stone. While he was an admirer of Ben-Gurion, he had reservations about the saison and turning over Irgun fighters to the British in 1944.[6] Moreover, he opposed Ben-Gurion's about-turn in

[2] Avi Shilon, *Menachem Begin: A Life* (London, 2012), p. 202.
[3] Ned Temko, *To Win or Die: A Personal Portrait of Menachem Begin* (New York, 1987), p. 170.
[4] Amos Perlmutter, *The Life and Times of Menachem Begin* (New York, 1987), pp. 283–87.
[5] Arye Naor, *Begin ba-shilton: edut ishit* (Tel Aviv, 1993), p. 43.
[6] Moshe Dayan, *Story of My Life* (New York, 1976), p. 78.

withdrawing from the newly conquered Gaza in 1957. In March 1967, before the military crisis with Egypt, Dayan said that he was prepared to work with Begin.

At the Herut Conference in 1966, Shmuel Tamir had implied that Begin's caution and reticence were impeding any cooperation with Rafi and Dayan. Begin vehemently disputed this at the time and strongly pushed for Dayan's appointment despite Eshkol's opposition. All this set in place the possibility of a future Gahal-Rafi-NRP cooperation as a rival bloc to Mapai. The young Turks of Rafi had thus returned to the seat of power, but in doing so they had also brought Menahem Begin with them. Begin was appointed a minister without portfolio. A triumphant Begin then visited Jabotinsky's grave to inform him that one of his followers had become a minister in Israel's government.

Israel's victory in the Six-Day War was viewed in Israel as nothing short of miraculous. Fears of a second Holocaust dissipated as Israel's enemies were vanquished. The territory controlled by the state had almost quadrupled. The centrepiece of the war was Israel's defeat of its powerful Egyptian neighbour. All sorts of plans emerged to effectively rearrange the map of the Middle East – it was even suggested that a Druze state be established.[7] However, the long-term political ramifications lay with Israel's conquest of the West Bank – an unintended consequence of Jordan's determination to participate in the war.

Rehavam Ze'evi called for the establishment of a Palestinian state, 'the State of Ishmael', with Nablus as its capital. Jerusalem, the Mount Hebron area, the Latrun enclave, the Jordan rift valley would all be annexed by Israel. Ze'evi also explored the idea of attaching most of the Arab villages in the Israeli triangle to the State of Ishmael, including Baka al-Garbiyeh, Tira and Umm al-Fahm.[8]

Menahem Begin and Gahal were viewed in Israel as part of the leadership responsible for this victory. Begin's public image began to change – not quite the Begin of old, the breather of fiery slogans and unnerving proclamations, but a responsible political leader who like Ben-Gurion had been one of the founders of the state. As a minister without a portfolio, Begin uncharacteristically withdrew from the minutiae of party politics and rarely made a speech in the Knesset. His relative silence and elevated status fortified the aura of an elder statesman.

---

[7] *Ha'aretz*, 26 June 1967.
[8] *Ha'aretz*, 15 October 2010.

MAP 5. The Territorial conquests of the Six-Day War (1967).

FIGURE 15. Menahem Begin in conversation with David Ben-Gurion, late 1960s. Courtesy of the Central Zionist Archives, Jerusalem.

For Begin, the war was 'a war of redemption', a step on the path towards expanding the borders of Israel and reversing the partition of 1947. The political status quo was now the retention of the territories. Begin's labour opponents, however, wanted to retain them for the sole purpose of using them as a bargaining counter – territories for peace. Others across the political spectrum wanted to retain them permanently for ideological, theological and security reasons.

Some members of Mapai simply viewed the victory of 1967 as a continuation of the War of Independence and advocated the colonisation of the conquered territories. Ahdut Ha'avodah viewed the conquest of the West Bank as another step in the onward advance of Marxism Zionism and a further defeat for Arab feudalism and reaction. Its aged leader, Yitzhak Tabenkin, advocated the building of a plethora of kibbutzim to bring socialism to the West Bank.

Young religious radicals within the NRP, however, understood the conquest as literally a sign from God, who had provided the Jewish people with this unique opportunity to reclaim another part of their religious heritage through the conquest of locations of biblical resonance: Hebron, Jericho, Nablus and centrally the Western Wall and Temple Mount in Jerusalem.

Security hawks viewed the West Bank as a territorial buffer, providing strategic depth, against a future invading Arab army. Begin was therefore seen as an advocate of the political consensus after June 1967. Even his

Liberal partners in Gahal were more amenable to the idea of settlements on the West Bank, and any suggestion of the collapse of their alliance with Herut had vanished.

In August 1967, the Arab states, meeting at Khartoum, responded to their defeat with three resounding 'nos' – no to recognition, no to negotiations, no to peace. This strengthened Begin's position. In one sense, the declaration at Khartoum closed the gap between the major parties. Although Mapai was willing to make territorial concessions, the Arabs were not willing to negotiate. Those who believed in the colonisation of the conquered territories rapidly filled the vacuum.

NEW VOICES ON THE RIGHT

Begin perceived the right of the Jews to the Land of Israel as a historic right. No distinction was made by Begin between the biblical narrative eons ago and the factual events of the previous seventy years. It was one continuum of events where the ahistorical merged with the historical.

Begin's raison d'être for remaining in the cabinet as one of its constructive, diligent members was to ensure that there would not be any withdrawal from the West Bank – no implementation of land for peace. Sinai was a different proposition. In Begin's eyes, it was neither part of the Land nor included in the British Mandate and therefore it could be returned in the context of meaningful negotiations. But there were others who also promoted the idea of a Greater Israel, but disagreed with Begin, citing biblical references to justify the retention of Sinai. Thus Gahal actually subscribed to the 'territories for peace' formula as long as the territory in question was not the West Bank.

During the duration and in the immediate aftermath of the war, Begin clearly supported the conquest of territory, regardless of whether it was included within his understanding of the borders of the Land of Israel. Thus the acquisition of the territory in southern Lebanon up to the river Litani was an acceptable possibility.[9]

Begin also agreed with the security hawks who wished to retain the West Bank for reasons of strategic depth. He further believed in Jabotinsky's principle of arguing from a position of strength, outlined in his articles in November 1923, extolling the virtues of the erection of an 'Iron Wall'. Although he differed from Jabotinsky with respect to defensive action as opposed to offensive advance, he concurred that an

[9] Temko, *To Win or Die*, p. 172.

impenetrable 'Iron Wall' would one day bring Israel's adversaries to the negotiating table. Begin also promoted a policy of retaliation rather than havlagah, self-restraint.

In November 1967 the UN Security Council formulated UN Resolution 242, which advocated 'withdrawal from territories occupied in the recent conflict' – not all the territories, only some. The vagueness of interpretation allowed Begin to remain in the cabinet and to pursue a policy of gradualism in a Mapai-dominated government which had no intention of annexing the West Bank. He argued tactically only for the annexation of Jerusalem.

It was clear that the unexpected occupation of the West Bank had produced deeps rifts within all the parties: Mapai, Ahdut Ha'avodah, Rafi – and to a lesser extent within Gahal and the NRP. Was Jewish sovereignty necessary over all the Land? Should Israel settle for sovereignty over part of the Land? What was the effect of controlling part of the Land? Did it marginalise the claim to the whole of the Land or simply delay it?

Begin perceived such schisms within the parties as literally a heaven-sent opportunity. He could lay the basis for an alliance of all those united in opposition to Mapai's belief in a smaller Israel and its unanswered proclamation of 'land for peace'. Herut would be at the centre of a series of concentric circles incorporating the many different opponents of Mapai, including Ben-Gurion's disaffected followers.

However, the expansion of Herut was perceived by many on the right as a betrayal of fundamental principle through unworthy compromise. Begin saw compromise on selected issues such as joining the Histadrut as well worth the price of advancement. On other issues such as the return of the West Bank or a freeze on building settlements, these propositions were clearly non-negotiable, a violation of core principles. Begin believed that with him at the helm and Herut at the centre, he could manoeuvre to compromise on some questions with his political partners but remain firm on central ideological ones. He believed that other parties, attracted by the lure of power in government, would be satisfied with what Begin was prepared to offer them.

Menahem Begin's post-Jabotinskian adversaries in Lehi had become marginalised politically. Its leadership had been fragmented. Lehi's Fighters' party existed only for the duration of the first Knesset. Natan Yellin-Mor moved to the left and would stand for a peace list in the 1969 election. Yitzhak Shamir would join Herut in 1970 and recognise Begin as his leader. The third member of Lehi's triumvirate and its main ideologist, Israel Eldad, remained loyal to the Far Right. He had maintained a barrage of criticism of Begin in his periodical, *Sulam*. Its map of malkhut Yisrael, the Commonwealth of Israel, stretched from the Euphrates to the Nile and incorporated Damascus, Aleppo, Amman and Port Said within its borders. It reached as far as the Nur Mountains on the Turkish border with Syria.

A few weeks after the end of hostilities, the Land of Israel movement (LIM) published its manifesto, which began:

> The whole of Eretz Israel is now in the hands of the Jewish people, and just as we are not allowed to give up the State of Israel so we are ordered to keep what we received there from Eretz Israel.[10]

Zvi Yehudah Kook, the spiritual mentor of the embryonic religious settlers, refused to sign because he argued that only part of the Land of Israel – not the whole – was now in the hands of the Jewish people. But its signatories comprised an array of luminaries from the Right and the Left – from Lehi and the Revisionists, from Mapai and Ahdut Ha'avodah, from Rafi and Hashomer Hatzair. The LIM provided a socialising mechanism which helped detested opponents to actually sit down with each other.

Its adherents included Lehi's Uri Zvi Greenberg and the Revisionists' Eri Jabotinsky. While it was natural that Avraham Weinshall, who had been instrumental in establishing the Revisionist movement in 1925, signed, the list of signatories also included Rachel Yanait-Ben-Zvi, a veteran Poale Zion activist of the second aliyah, as well as Berl Katznelson's daughter. Isser Harel, founder of the Shin Bet, head of the Mossad and capturer of Eichmann, signed, as did Haim Yachil, a former director general of the Foreign Ministry and head of the Israel Broadcasting Authority. Yitzhak Zuckerman (Antek) and his wife, Zivia Lubetkin, leaders of the Warsaw Ghetto Uprising with a background in the labour Zionist movement, also signed.

The literary intelligentsia were represented – the poet Natan Alterman, the Nobel Prize winner Shai Agnon, the Israel Prize winners Yehudah Burla and Haim Hazaz, as well as Ya'akov Orland, who translated Wilde, Shaw and Byron into Hebrew. Several noted academics signed, including Yosef Rivlin, who translated the Koran into Hebrew, and Avraham Kariv, a winner of the Bialik Prize.

There were also leading IDF commanders, such as Dan Tolkowsky, Ya'akov Dori and Avraham Yoffe, as well as a plethora of ambassadors and diplomats.

---

[10] Rael Jean Isaac, *Israel Divided: Ideological Politics in the Jewish State* (Baltimore, 1976), p. 165.

Many from the Left were rebels against the political conformity of their ideological milieu. Moshe Shamir of the dovish Mapam suggested that his former comrades lacked an understanding of the political reality and were mired in idealistic dreams. How could binationalism appeal when there was an Arab refusal to even consider partition? Moreover, the notion that Arab societies were progressive was a figment of the political imagination. Finally Shamir noted that despite the last years of Stalin and the subsequent revelations of the Gulag, there persisted a feeling of unrequited love for the Soviet Union. Shamir believed that it was both blinkered and grotesque.

The members of Ahdut Ha'avodah, on the other hand, were not converts. Yitzhak Tabenkin believed that partition would not lead to peace and in 1947 had opposed UN Resolution 181, which advocated a two-state solution. Tabenkin believed in the colonisation of all the Land of Israel, and the kibbutz wing of Ahdut Ha'avodah, Hakibbutz ha'meuhad, called for the settlement of the conquered territories at the end of the Six-Day War. Tabenkin's two sons signed the LIM manifesto, as did the Palmah Leaders Haim Guri and Benny Marshak.

The manifesto thus brought together a wide range of people. Rabbi Zvi Neriah, who had established the first Bnei Akiva yeshivah, was one of the few religious figures who signed. Yet the wording was framed in quasi-religious language, and devout secularists signed. 'We are ordered' – yet the identity of the instructor in issuing such orders was never revealed.

Menahem Begin and Gahal wisely kept their distance from the LIM. They allowed extra-parliamentary groups to make the running in creating a public voice in Israeli society for the retention of the territories. Such reticence was due to the fact that they did not wish LIM to be perceived as no more than a Gahal front even if a lot of funding came from Reuven Hecht and other right-wing sources. The tremendous preponderance of figures from the labour Zionist movement and from the Marxist Left was remarkable, yet they exuded a loyalty to the principles of their ideological camp and remembered the old Begin. If the LIM was a transitional phase from the old Left to the new Right, it was reasoned, then it required a decent gestation period.

When Gahal eventually resigned from the government in 1970, there was a proposal to join the LIM. Several Labour members were unhappy with this suggestion and eventually formed the 'Labour Movement for a Whole Land of Israel'.

On the other hand, Mapai's Pinhas Sapir and Abba Eban opposed the LIM from the outset within the labour movement. They both strongly rejected the settlement drive on the basis that the presence of settlers and settlements was an obstacle to any negotiations with the Palestinian Arabs. Eban was regarded with particular disdain as a liberal intellectual, somewhat un-Israeli and a clever practitioner of rhetoric, good for public relations externally, but not for public reality internally.

Eban and Sapir also raised the demographic problem in that the birth rate of the Arabs of both the West Bank and of Israel was higher than that of the Jews. If the tenets of democratic behaviour were to be scrupulously observed, then the Jews would become a minority in a Greater Israel and the struggle of Zionism would have been to no avail. A Greater Israel could be Jewish without democracy or democratic without being Jewish. Eban and Sapir argued that it could not be both. The only solution was a smaller Israel with a Jewish majority without West Bank settlements. The demographic problem was relegated by the adherents of LIM to a lower rung. The higher birth rate of the Palestinian Arabs was glossed over. Hope was instead placed in the certainty of a large emigration of Jews from the USSR and the belief that simultaneously many Arabs would voluntarily leave.

LABOUR AND THE RELIGIOUS RIGHT

In 1968 the formation of an Israeli Labour party was mooted. This resonated with the members of Knesset (MKs) of Rafi – the former prominent members of Mapai who felt robbed of their political inheritance through Rafi's poor showing in the 1965 elections. Rafi had not displaced Mapai. Moreover, Rafi as a party was split as to whether to join the Mapai–Ahdut Ha'avodah alignment to form Labour. Sixty percent voted to do so, and nine out of the ten MKs wanted to join Labour. Only Ben-Gurion, stubborn in his old age, refuted the very idea of a return to the party whose predecessor he had also founded. The majority returned and the sizeable rump established the State List with Ben-Gurion at its head.

Within a year, Labour had formed the Ma'arakh – the Labour Alignment – with the Marxist Mapam. This alliance of four social democratic and socialist parties looked like an impregnable coalition. In reality it was a two-headed horse that had no clear policy on the future status of the conquered territories. Ahdut Ha'avodah wanted to plant kibbutzim on the West Bank, while Mapam wanted to return the territory in exchange for peace with the Palestinians.

Yet Labour was not alone. There were tensions within many other political movements – between those who wished to make the most of the newly acquired territories and extend Israel's borders to new boundaries as the early Zionists had intended and those who wished to compromise, accept partition and return territory in the belief that the Arab states and the Palestinians also desired peace and prosperity.

Within Labour, Dayan and Peres, formerly of Rafi, were pitted against Mapai's Sapir and Eban. Ahdut Ha'avodah, led by its aged sage, Yitzhak Tabenkin, preached colonisation, yet Yigal Allon, who had been responsible for several expulsions of Palestinian Arabs during the War of Independence, now began to move away from his mentor's ideological rigidity. In the NRP Hanan Porat and Moshe Levinger challenged the more pragmatic leadership. Moreover, people changed their minds. In 1967 Ben-Gurion said that he wanted to return the territories in general. But on 8 June 1967 he argued that Jews should settle in the Jewish Quarter of the Old City of Jerusalem and to return to Hebron.

The Rafi programme, written by Shimon Peres and published on 13 September, argued for a ring of Jewish settlements around Jerusalem, along the river Jordan and in the Hebron and Nablus hills. Those settlements that had been abandoned in 1948 would be repopulated.[11]

By 1970 Ben-Gurion was interested in retaining the Golan, Jerusalem and Hebron. He referred to Hebron as the sister of Jerusalem and stressed its biblical importance as King David had been anointed there and resided there for seven years.[12] In the year before his death in 1973, Ben-Gurion now said that the territories should be settled.[13]

Dayan's pronouncements were often unpredictable. At the end of the Six-Day War, Dayan stated that he was against returning all the territories.[14] In December 1970, he said that he preferred a smaller Israel for demographic reasons. In November 1968 Dayan argued for the linking of the territories economically to Israel. In 1969 he called for the introduction of Israeli law into the territories and the construction of four settlements next to Ramallah, Jenin, Nablus and Hebron. He then argued for a change in the standard Labour formulation of 'secure and agreed borders'. Instead he wanted in its place the wording 'secure and strategic borders'. Dayan argued that annexation was unnecessary, but the reality on the ground was far more important. In 1973 he argued that the government should not restrict Israeli land purchases from Arabs on the

[11] Ze'ev Ben-Shlomo, Letter to the Editor, *Guardian*, 11 March 1988.
[12] Avi Shilon, *Ben-Gurion: Epilogue* (Tel Aviv, 2013), pp. 77–79.
[13] Isaac, *Israel Divided*, p. 194 n. 73.
[14] Ibid., p. 108.

West Bank. He also argued for the building of Yamit, a seaport in Sinai just outside Gaza, which would block any invading army from Egypt. Yet he believed that there could be territorial concessions on Sinai. The encirclement of Gaza was also applied to Jerusalem.

Dayan opposed the idea of a separate Palestinian state on the West Bank and Gaza in addition to Jordan. West Bank Arabs could possess Jordanian citizenship, he argued, while Israel would have sovereignty over the Land. He also proposed an economic federation between Israel, Jordan and the Palestinians. Like Dayan, Shimon Peres was an advocate of 'functional compromise' and the 'open bridges' policy rather than territorial partition. He therefore supported Dayan on these major questions, as did Israel Galili of Ahdut Ha'avodah on specific issues. While the State List supported Dayan from outside, within Labour there was growing support for Dayan's views on the right of the party.[15]

All this brought Dayan closer to Gahal. It revived Begin's dreams of an alliance between Rafi and Gahal. The threat that the ex-members of Rafi might break away once more and form an alliance with Menahem Begin's Gahal strengthened Dayan's bargaining hand in the Labour party. Golda Meir's attempts to keep the party together were predicated on an empty solidarity and a lack of vision of the future for the West Bank and its Arab inhabitants.

Sapir and Eban repeatedly clashed with Dayan. Eban predicted that the settlement drive would usher in a form of apartheid. He believed that Dayan's outlook assisted creeping annexation and ignored the demographic problem. Dayan's main rival for the leadership of the Labour party, Yigal Allon, also became increasingly critical of his views.

Some nine days after the war, the Israeli cabinet, including the representative of Gahal, publicly expressed its willingness to return the Golan Heights to Syria and Sinai to Egypt.[16] At the beginning of July 1967, Eshkol publicly stated that a Palestinian state could come into existence with the river Jordan as its eastern border and encompassing all Arab population centres.[17] However, the Khartoum rejection of any negotiations, the strength of pro-Jordanian feeling in the West Bank and the first attacks of Yasser Arafat's Fatah induced a reconsideration.

The new Allon Plan was launched in February 1968. It envisaged a partition of the West Bank with Israel holding the Jordan Valley and the

---

[15] Ibid., pp. 117–20.
[16] Reuven Pedatzur, 'Coming Back Full Circle: The Palestinian Option in 1967', *Middle East Journal*, vol. 49, no. 2 (Spring 1995), pp. 269–91.
[17] *Le Monde*, 8 July 1967.

Judean desert adjacent to the river Jordan. The major population centres would be returned to King Hussein with a land corridor including Jericho linking with Jordan to the east. It was opposed by Moshe Dayan and Shimon Peres.

While the Allon Plan proposed the annexation of a third of the West Bank, resolved the demographic problem and proposed autonomy for the Palestinian Arabs, it also invoked partition. Allon's mentor, Yitzhak Tabenkin, on the left opposed this and so did his long-time adversary on the right, Menahem Begin. Yet Begin, who adopted a maximalist approach to settlement, was himself opposed within Gahal by the Liberals, who supported it. There was division within division.

Soon there were settlements along the Golan, in the West Bank and in northern Sinai. Dayan's belief in economic integration did proceed apace. While Dayan was in fact in a distinct minority in the cabinet, he was, according to opinion polls, popular in the country.

Dayan and Peres, however, faced opposition from Pinhas Sapir, who feared that a growing dependence on Palestinian Arab workers from the West Bank and Gaza, now some 60,000 people, would undermine Israel's socialist work ethic. If Israel suffered an economic crisis, then such imported Arab workers would be the first to lose their jobs, which would create an even greater estrangement between the two peoples. Sapir therefore wanted to separate the two peoples economically as much as Dayan wanted to integrate them.[18]

The settlement drive on the West Bank after 1967 was not initiated by the nationalist Right, but by the labour movement and the national religious. Mapai wished to establish security settlements at strategic points to inhibit any invading armies which would cross the river Jordan. The motivation of the religious settlers was to reclaim former settlements from which the Jews had been driven in the earlier part of the twentieth century. The Jewish community of Hebron had abandoned its quarter during the killings in 1929, and Gush Etzion had been evacuated during the war of 1948. Both were settled in 1968 against the wishes of the Mapai-led government.

The ideological motivation of the religious settlers was to expand the borders of Israel to its biblical dimensions. One of the very first settlements, Mehola, was established by the religious youth of Bnei Akiva in the northern West Bank and Jordan Valley as a security settlement. But it also captured

---

[18] Don Peretz, 'The War Election and Israel's Eight Knesset', *Middle East Journal*, vol. 28, no. 2 (Spring 1974), pp. 111–25.

MAP 6. The Allon plan (1967).

the symbolism of returning to the Land of Israel, since the new settlement was named after the biblical city of Abel-Mehola, where Elijah the prophet designated Elisha ben-Shaphat his successor.[19] Within the biblical framework, it was seen as a location where Israel's enemies – the Midianites – were defeated[20] and where the prophetic tradition was continued. It also marked a change in course for religious Zionism, since Mehola was affiliated to Hapoel Hamizrahi, the pioneering religious movement which had actually voted in favour of the partition of Palestine in 1947.

The Hebron settlement was initiated by Rabbis Moshe Levinger and Eliezer Waldman, followers of Zvi Yehudah Kook, in 1968 – both would become stalwarts of the settler movement. Levinger hired rooms at the Park Hotel in Hebron for the Passover festival – and refused to leave even at the request of the city's military governor. A month later Levinger's group opened a yeshivah, a class for primary school children and a kindergarten. By 1970, the construction of a Jewish quarter in Hebron was proceeding together with the urban settlement of Kiriat Arba on its outskirts.

In 1949 two hundred rabbis had signed a declaration that Israel was now at the beginning of the redemptive process. Many religious Zionists may have sympathised with the sentiment, but did not act upon it. Moshe Levinger in his youth had been influenced by a Bnei Akiva group, Gahelet,[21] which promoted Zionism and Torah in the 1950s. Gahelet gradually grew closer to the world of ultra-orthodoxy and more distant from Bnei Akiva. Eventually there was a split and many adherents of Gahelet found a new home in Merkaz Harav, the yeshivah of Zvi Yehudah Kook, who became their *admor* (an acronym for 'our master, our teacher, our rabbi').

By the 1960s, they were working with the NRP's newly established Young Guard to put forward more radical policies, cloaked in messianic language which invoked a redemptionist Zionism. It was the beginning of the change from 'religious Zionism' to 'Zionist religion'.[22] The dream of salvation, it was argued, belonged to all peoples, and thereby preventing the settlement drive meant inhibiting the drive towards redemption. This would cause problems for non-Jews as well as for Jews.[23]

[19] 1 Kings 19:16.
[20] Judges 7:22.
[21] Gahelet – Garin Halutzim Lomdei Torah (Cadre of Torah-Learning Pioneers).
[22] Gideon Aran, 'From Religious Zionism to Zionist Religion: The Roots of Gush Emunim', in Peter Y. Medding, ed., *Studies in Contemporary Jewry*, vol. 2 (Bloomington, IN, 1986), pp. 116–43.
[23] See Gideon Aran, *Kookism: Shorshe Gush Emunim tarbut ha-mitnahalim, te'ologyah, Tsiyonit, meshihiyut bi-zemanenu* (Jerusalem, 2013).

The minister of labour, Yigal Allon, whose Ahdut Ha'avodah movement supported the colonisation of the West Bank, was prevailed upon
to visit Moshe Levinger and his followers – some of whom were far
from religious practice, such as the left-wing writer Moshe Shamir. Allon
arrived in Hebron with Natan Alterman, the poet and Rafi adherent,
to greet the first of the West Bank settlers. On their way back, Allon
and Alterman visited an emerging leader of the national religious youth,
Hanan Porat, in Gush Etzion. Allon and Dayan authorised the army to
provide security for the Hebron settlers. The government later voted to
establish Kiriat Arba as a settlement on the outskirts of Hebron.[24] A road
was built connecting Kiriat Arba to Israel – this was the beginning of
transportation contiguity.

At the same time, in Kuneitra on the Golan Heights, Ahdut Ha'avodah's
Yitzhak Tabenkin attended a Passover reading of the exodus from Egypt.
This site would become the first of several kibbutzim founded in the area.

The NRP had forged a good working relationship with Mapai after
1948 under the leadership of Moshe Chaim Shapira. The blossoming of
Zvi Yehudah Kook's messianic and redemptionist school of thought after
June 1967 changed all this. The imperative of religious Zionists now was
not simply to demand religious rights from a secular government, but to
settle the conquered territories. Any delay would derail redemption. The
victory in the Six-Day War was perceived as divine revelation.

Moreover, the history of religious Zionism was being reinterpreted.
The NRP's Young Guard disparaged the belief that Zionism had emerged
from European nationalism and asserted that this was no more than
rationalist dogma. The Jews were, in fact, different. They were not a
people that should be subject to normalisation. They were not a nation
like any other, but a people that literally dwelled alone. They had been
selected for special tasks by God, who had promised the Land to them,
and there could be no watering down of this core responsibility. The 'land
for peace' formula was false. Real peace would come only with redemption. Such passion for participation in the messianic process attracted
the youth. Zvi Yehudah Kook preached that any Israeli politician who
compromised and returned territory would have contravened a dictate
of the Torah.

When the party's congress took place in October 1968, Kook's adherents argued that the party should embrace the spirit of the times and

---

[24] Gershon Gorenberg, *The Accidental Empire: Israel and the Birth of the Settlements,
1967–1977* (New York, 2006), pp. 147–48.

move beyond purely religious affairs. The NRP Young Guard quietly supported Dayan's attack on their own party leader, Moses Chaim Shapira, who advocated dovish policies. They strongly opposed the notion of returning any territory to 'foreign rule'.

Begin was most adept at cultivating the national religious and in particular the NRP's Young Guard. In January 1970, the Supreme Court had ruled that a Jew was someone who defined himself as a Jew. In a speech to the Knesset during the 'who is a Jew?' debate in February 1970, Begin argued that there had never been a distinction between nation and religion in Jewish history. Progressives, he said, seek 'to humiliate and insult religious law'. If a person wished to join the Jewish people, he must first of all be converted, but, he argued, conversion should be made easier by the rabbinical authorities.[25]

Following the Yom Kippur War in 1973, he argued in the Knesset that any discussions at the subsequent Geneva conference should not take place on the Jewish Sabbath. Shabbat was not merely a religious occasion; it characterised 'our national and eternal historical status.'[26]

He increasingly appealed in this vein for the retention of the West Bank. During the same speech, which occurred during the Jewish festival of Hanukah, he quoted the response of Simon Maccabeus, the first Hasmonean ruler of Israel and high priest, to the complaints and threats of Antiochus, the Hellenising Graeco-Syrian ruler who had lost territory to the Jewish revolutionaries:

We have neither taken other men's land nor held that which appertains to others, but only the inheritance of our fathers which our enemies had wrongfully possessed for a period. Wherefore we, taking this opportunity, retain the inheritance of our fathers.[27]

Moreover, Begin stated that this event had taken place precisely 2,116 years previously.

Begin's view was that 'Judaism and Jewish nationality are two sides of the same coin'. Herut therefore supported Sabbath observance and the observance of Jewish holidays. It praised Jewish religious tradition and related it to Jewish nationalism. Begin would not have dissented from the NRP's claim about 'the religious and historical right of the Jewish people to the Land promised by the God of Israel'.

---

[25] Menahem Begin, Speech to the Knesset, 9 February 1970, in N. Lorch, ed., *Major Knesset Debates, 1948–1977*, vol. 5 (London, 1993), pp. 1700–03.

[26] Menahem Begin, Speech to the Knesset, 20 December 1973, in N. Lorch, ed., *Major Knesset Debates*, vol. 5, pp. 1848–53.

[27] 1 Maccabees 15:33–34.

Begin's Liberal partners in Gahal saw things very differently and demanded reforms of the politics of religion and a restructuring of the architecture erected by the religious authorities. There was also Liberal sympathy for religious pluralism within Judaism.[28]

THE ELECTION OF 1969

The election of 1969 provided an opportunity for the profound changes catalysed by the Six-Day War to be displayed before the Israeli public. Both Rafi's Dayan and Ahdut Ha'avodah's Yigal Allon had been passed over in favour of the veteran Mapainik Golda Meir for the premiership in place of Levi Eshkol.

During the 1969 election Begin, now in his mid-fifties, projected the respectable image of an elder statesman. Gahal entered the election, not as a vociferous opponent, but wearing the mantle of collective responsibility of the previous government.

The Gahal election platform proclaimed that it had taken the initiative in forming the government of national unity in May 1967 as 'the stance of passive waiting ... could only end in disaster'. Gahal, it suggested, generously did not allow memories or political differences to stand in the way of national unity at such a time.[29] The election of 1969 was also the first that featured television broadcasts. All this made no difference; Gahal achieved only 21.7 percent of the vote – less than half the Ma'arakh figure. Gahal repeated its 1965 performance with twenty-six seats. In fact, neither the Ma'arakh nor Gahal had progressed. However, it was the fundamental change that Ben-Gurion's State List had moved from the Centre Left to the Centre Right which was important. Gahal, the NRP, the Free Centre and the State List now totalled forty-four seats, whereas the Ma'arakh accounted for fifty-six. The coalescence of an alternative bloc was now a distinct if distant possibility.

In addition, the Centre Right had increasingly picked up the Mizrahi vote over the years and therefore advanced, whereas the Centre Left and the Religious blocs had essentially stood still. The Gahal economic policy in 1969 preached full employment, the right to strike, national health insurance and grants to families with numerous children. Even so, from the mid-1950s, although a majority of Herut members were Mizrahim,

[28] Jonathan Mendilow, *Ideology, Party Change and Electoral Campaigns in Israel, 1965–2001* (New York, 2003), pp. 47–48.
[29] 'Principles and Programme: The Platform of Gahal for the Seventh Knesset', 1969, Jabotinsky Institute Archives, Tel Aviv.

a majority of the Mizrahi voters in total still supported Mapai.[30] The Mizrahi voters, which now accounted for 28 percent of the Israeli population, were under-represented in terms of Gahal MKs.

Herut itself advanced, albeit at a slow pace. In 1949 it picked up 11.5 percent and the best estimate in 1969 was 14 or 15 percent.[31] Gahal was strongest in the poorer areas of cities. Yet the influence of the Liberals also attracted middle-class voters in the cities. Thirty-one percent voted for Gahal in well-to-do areas of Tel Aviv.

In local elections in 1969, power passed to Gahal from the Ma'arakh in eight local authorities, including Ashdod, Rehovot and Rishon L'Zion.[32] There was a 20 percent increase in the Mizrahi vote for Gahal in local government elections between 1965 and 1969.[33]

Young men voted in much greater numbers for Gahal than did older men in their fifties. Women tended to favour the Ma'arakh. In the age bracket of eighteen to twenty-four, 33 percent of young men supported Gahal, whereas only a slighter larger proportion – some 38 percent – voted for Golda Meir and the Ma'arakh. Gahal significantly did best amongst Israeli-born who had not studied beyond the elementary level.[34]

By 1969 the Liberals and the country at large were more amenable to retaining the newly conquered territories. The Gahal manifesto stated that 'the national sovereignty of the state must be extended to the liberated areas of the country'. It proposed large-scale settlement in Judea, Samaria, Gaza, the Golan and Sinai. Priority, it argued, should be given to the development plans of the state. Significantly there was no trumpeted statement that 'not one inch would be returned' in deference to the Liberals.

The NRP promised to strive for 'large scale, speedy urban and rural settlements in the liberated areas'. The Ma'arakh also said that there should be additional security settlements in border areas. There would never be a return to the 1967 borders.

Menahem Begin remained at the centre of this expanding universe. Significantly Israel Eldad had stood for election for the first time in 1969

[30] Mendilow, *Ideology, Party Change and Electoral Campaigns*, p. 84.
[31] Herbert Smith, 'Analysis of Voting', in Alan Arian, ed., *The Elections in Israel (1969)* (Jerusalem, 1972), pp. 65–66.
[32] Shevah Weiss, 'Results of Local Elections', in Arian ed., *The Elections in Israel*, p. 103.
[33] Moshe Lissak, 'Community and Change in the Voting Patterns of Oriental Jews', in Arian, ed., *The Elections in Israel*, p. 270.
[34] Alan Arian, 'Electoral Choice in a Dominant Party System', in Arian, ed., *The Elections in Israel*, p. 109.

as 'the Land of Israel' party and failed abysmally. It was an indirect measure of Begin's growing status.

Begin was reticent about joining Golda Meir's new government, but was pressured by the Liberals. Moreover, perhaps for the first time since 1948, leading figures in the military were attracted to a non-socialist party. It appeared that the old labour Zionist vehicle for advancement was breaking down. Ezer Weizmann suddenly resigned from the army and was immediately appointed the nominee for the Gahal minister of transport.

The reason for Weizmann's sudden move into the political arena was his being passed over for promotion. Ariel Sharon, on the other hand, wanted to remain in the IDF, but was being forced out by his many enemies within. He flirted with the possibility of a safe position on the Gahal electoral list. Such a possibility unnerved the Ma'arakh. Sharon's difficulties in the army suddenly dissipated, and he thereby postponed his entry into politics. Begin significantly excluded Yohanan Bader from government. A colleague from his Betar days in Poland, a member of the Irgun and founder of Herut, Bader expected to be rewarded for his long service and personal loyalty, but Begin once again demonstrated his willingness to bypass close supporters in the interests of expanding the party and attaining power.

Begin had few responsibilities as a minister without portfolio and could therefore dedicate himself to foreign affairs and act as a watchdog against any move to withdraw from the territories. His self-appointed task became apparent when the United States proposed the Rogers Plan in 1970. Its purpose was to bring about a ceasefire in Sinai and to stop the War of Attrition. Hundreds of Israelis had been killed since 1967 – the victory in the Six-Day War was beginning to assume a pyrrhic nature. Begin said that he would resign over the matter because the Rogers Plan suggested 'the inadmissibility of the acquisition of territory by war'. The Americans had effectively endorsed the prospect of 'land for peace', which Begin rejected as far as the West Bank was concerned. Begin understood this as the first step towards the return of the territories and a new consideration of the status of Jerusalem.

Begin argued that the Ma'arakh had changed its position, since the implementation of the Rogers Plan would mean a return to the borders of 4 June 1967.[35] In a debate in the Knesset, Begin accused Golda Meir of giving 'an explicit undertaking to repartition the western Land of Israel

[35] Menahem Begin, *Ma'ariv*, 28 August 1970.

and give most of Judea and Samaria to Hussein'.[36] Begin also used the security argument for retaining the West Bank, as hostile forces could now easily fire into Israel. Begin linked the historic right and the right to security.[37]

While Nasser agreed with the Rogers Plan, Begin invoked a comparison with the statement of Theobald Bethmann-Holweg, the Kaiser's chancellor, when contemplating the British commitment to Belgium in 1914 that 'agreements are nothing but pieces of paper'.[38] Begin also opposed an American initiative to reopen the Suez Canal in 1970. All this antagonised his Liberal partners in Gahal, who wanted to continue in government, as did Ezer Weizmann. Begin argued that Jabotinsky had had the courage to lead a disputatious Revisionist movement out of the Zionist Organisation and this was a similar situation. Gahal, however, was evenly split, but Begin succeeded in attaining only a sliver of a majority, in a vote of 117–112.[39]

The Rogers Plan eventually collapsed, and no territory was returned. However, it proved fortuitous in the aftermath of the Yom Kippur War. While Begin, the government minister, could bathe in the sweetness of the Six-Day War victory in 1967, Begin, the leader of the opposition, could absolve himself of all responsibility for the debacle of the Yom Kippur War in 1973.

---

[36] Menahem Begin, Speech to the Knesset, 12 August 1970, in N. Lorch, ed., *Major Knesset Debates*, vol. 5, pp. 1727–32.
[37] Eitan Haber, *Menachem Begin: The Legend and the Man* (New York, 1978), p. 287.
[38] Amos Perlmutter, *The Life and Times of Menachem Begin* (New York, 1987), p. 295.
[39] Haber, *Menachem Begin*, pp. 284–85.

15

The Road to Power

By early 1973 Gahal appeared to be stagnating. Like so many before him, Ezer Weizmann had attempted to change the situation in an amateurish manoeuvre to marginalise Begin. After a public chastisement by Begin, a chastened Weizmann left politics for a business career. Even so there was a growing opposition within Gahal, fuelled by the coming of age of a new generation. The commander of the Irgun at sixty was seen as intransigent and jaded. Gahal projected the image of a party which was closed to new ideas. There were even rumours that Weizmann would actually leave Herut and join the Free Centre. At the Free Centre conference, Shmuel Tamir called for a bloc of the Free Centre, the State List and the opposition within Herut. On the eve of the 1973 election, the precarious state of the party resembled the instability of early 1967. Yet Begin's luck held once more.

Ariel, Sharon had been passed over in the IDF and formally decided to join the Liberals. His presence indicated also that the Israeli Right was now beginning to secure the allegiance of a growing number of generals in the IDF – once the prerogative of the Labour party.

Unlike Weizmann, Sharon had found himself increasingly isolated within the military, with an accompanying reputation of disloyalty and insubordination. He had a supreme belief in his abilities and an infinite resilience to counter criticism from any quarter. This ability to never be diverted from a goal propelled him into the orbit of Menahem Begin. In addition, Sharon had drifted away from Labour. His idols in the 1950s were David Ben-Gurion and Moshe Dayan – and like them he had moved to the right.

Within hours of his departure from the army, Sharon attempted to forge a coalition of anti-Labour forces around Gahal. Unlike previous initiatives, it was a move ripe for its time. But Begin was torn between pragmatically expanding Gahal and emotionally listening to the deep concerns of his long-time supporters in Herut, who believed that it would simply lead to ideological compromises. Begin was also worried personally, since any move in the wrong direction could lead to a dilution of his authority and influence.

Even so, the political mood in early 1973 favoured a coalescence of the Right through the fragmentation of labour Zionism. Yitzhak Tabenkin's sons had established a Labour committee for the Land of Israel which attracted former members of Ahdut Ha'avodah. Zalman Shoval, who succeeded to Ben-Gurion's Knesset seat, advocated an alliance between the State List, Gahal, the Free Centre and former members of Rafi who remained within the Labour party. Shoval asked Ben-Gurion for his views on a merger with the historical enemy under the guidance of his nemesis, Menahem Begin. Although Ben-Gurion had written warmly to Begin in 1969 and recalled his agreement with Jabotinsky in 1934,[1] he now responded enigmatically, commenting that he neither supported nor opposed the formation of an alliance of parties.[2] Begin recognised the historic irony of the disciples of Jabotinsky sitting with the followers of Ben-Gurion.[3] Begin also courted former members of Rafi, such as Yigal Horovitz and Zvi Shiloah. He even considered Meir Kahane for membership of this new cluster of anti-Labour parties – an umbrella alliance offering sanctuary to all from the Far Right to the Far Left.

Begin balked at this attempt to homogenise the anti-Labour forces such that Sharon threatened to form the Likud without Herut. Even so, Begin held a pivotal position. He was required as the leader, the archetypal symbolic opponent of Labour. The Likud statement of principles emphasised that 'they were working together for the integrity of the Land of Israel'.

Despite this inauspicious beginning, there was a real anticipation that a genuine opposition party could be created. Yet the Likud vote in the Histadrut election of 1973 was approximately the same as the combined

[1] David Ben-Gurion, Letter to Menahem Begin, 6 February 1969, Jabotinsky Institute Archives, Tel Aviv.
[2] Colin Shindler, *Israel, Likud and the Zionist Dream* (London, 1995), p. 72.
[3] Arye Naor, *Begin ba-shilton: edut ishit* (Tel Aviv, 1993), p. 23.

vote of Gahal, the State List and the Free Centre in the 1969 Histadrut election. The advent of the Likud therefore did not bode well for the advance of this anti-Labour alliance. Once again, Menahem Begin was saved by the arrival of an unexpected war.

The outbreak of war in 1973 caught Begin and the Likud leadership by surprise. There had been a severe lack of awareness on the part of the Israeli military forces as well as by the political elite. The conflict had effectively commenced in early October 1973 when Soviet advisors began to leave Egypt. With the audacious crossing of the Suez Canal on Yom Kippur by Egyptian forces, Golda Meir's rejection of a pre-emptive attack and a late mobilisation, the war resulted in 2,693 dead, 7,000 injured and more than 300 captured and missing. This was approximately four times the casualty rate during the Six-Day War six years previously. The existence of Israel, which had seemed so firm, was now viewed as precarious. Israeli confidence in its abilities had been severely shaken. The post-1967 sense of triumphalism had evaporated.

Eight hundred tanks had been destroyed and 100 aircraft shot down. President Nixon's support had proved crucial in resupplying Israel with arms. The IDF's similarly audacious recrossing of the Canal into Egypt and its encirclement of the Egyptian Third Army brought Israeli forces within touching distance of Cairo. There the Israelis halted – or were requested to halt. The war was more a draw than a clear-cut victory. Indeed, Moshe Dayan had considered abandoning the Canal.

While the iconic Sharon, clad in a bandana-bandage, was one of the inspirations for this about-turn in military fortune, the actual plans had been formulated long before by the IDF. While the other generals fumed quietly at Sharon's self-promotion, many ordinary soldiers viewed him differently:

Sharon radiated presence, charisma, leadership. Men followed him willingly. They heard his voice on the radio, his assurance, his encouragement, his motivation. They saw him, he was with us. He was always there.[4]

Begin was kept abreast of developments at the front by Sharon himself, who was able to circumvent the military hierarchy. The election was now moved to the end of December 1973. With hostilities at an end, Begin returned to the attack on the government – concentrating on the refusal to call up reserves and the inadequate number of troops at the Canal. His words reached a receptive audience and an electorate looking for someone to assign blame.

[4] David Landau, *Arik: The Life of Ariel Sharon* (New York, 2013), p. 96.

If Golda Meir's government was responsible, then did any responsibility attach to the Likud opposition? While loyal and supportive during the conflict, with the benefit of hindsight Begin publicly raised the questions which a bewildered Israeli electorate asked.

Begin's forceful, acerbic rhetoric seemed to meet the psychological need of the times and appealed to the Israeli citizen in the 1970s. Out of power, Begin had returned to the verbal intensity of the 1950s in a period of resurgent Palestinian nationalism, often defined by acts of terror. Yasser Arafat, head of the Palestine Liberation Organisation (PLO), was a demonic figure for Begin – a new Hitler to be extinguished rather than an old-new nationalist adversary with whom Israel would eventually negotiate. The killing of passengers at Lod Airport in May 1972 and of the Israeli athletes at the Munich Olympics further demoralised Israeli citizens. During the Yom Kippur War, Begin described Israel as 'the surviving remnant' which was fighting for its existence. Begin had captured the verbal zeitgeist of the Israeli man in the street.

The Palestinian assailants at the Munich Olympics were labelled 'two-legged ravenous beasts'. The perpetrators of the killing of children in Kiriat Shemona in April 1974 became 'Arab Nazis'[5] – the local school had been named after the Polish Jewish educator Janusz Korczak, who had perished during the Holocaust. The killing of twenty-two schoolchildren at Ma'alot a month later was termed 'renewed Nazism'.[6] Begin's anti-German feelings echoed the sentiment of many Israelis when an Air France aircraft was hijacked and taken to Entebbe in 1976. Members of the German Revolutionary Cells who assisted the Palestinians separated Jewish passengers on arrival. The non-Jewish passengers were allowed to leave. Begin drew the analogy with 'the selection' in the concentration camps.

Begin's rhetoric seemed to embody the Jewish tragedy during the twentieth century – perhaps to impress the experience of the past upon a new generation. He spoke as the representative of 'the generation of destruction and revival'. For Begin, the war had lasted between 1914 and 1945 'with a short armistice in between'.[7]

Moreover, Begin agreed with Golda Meir that there was no such thing as a Palestinian, only an Arab of the Land of Israel. If Arabs living

[5] Menahem Begin, Speech to the Knesset, 11 April 1974, in N. Lorch, ed., *Major Knesset Debates*, 1948–1977 vol. 5 (London, 1993), pp. 1891–97.
[6] *Ma'ariv*, 24 May 1974.
[7] *Jerusalem Post*, 4 February 1975.

on the West Bank were indeed Palestinians, then was this also true of Arabs who lived in Israel? Both Golda and Begin regarded themselves as 'Palestinians', since they were labelled as 'Palestinian Jews' before 1948. He also berated those who recognised the rights of an emerging Palestinian people.[8]

Begin told the Knesset that Yasser Arafat was not a Palestinian nationalist, but in fact a Marxist-Leninist, a Soviet agent and that a Palestinian state would serve Soviet penetration in the Middle East.[9] Begin's enemies began to merge into one another with neither distinction nor differentiation.

Begin's sense of outrage became a political tool in the Israeli election of 1973. In addition to attacking Palestinians involved in acts of terror and highlighting the public perception of a failed Labour government after the Yom Kippur war, Begin still proclaimed his fidelity to a Greater Israel and the colonisation of the West Bank.

The Ma'arakh instead spoke of defensible borders and the need to maintain the Jewish character of the state. Yet like the Likud, it had to praise its own security settlements in the Jordan Valley. One Ma'arakh election advertisement proclaimed:

Mr Begin speaks of settling the territories; we do it! We have 26 settlements; Herut has only 4![10]

Significantly this advertisement was accompanied by photographs of the Ma'arakh leadership representing all the factions: Golda Meir, Yigal Allon and Moshe Dayan, but also Mapai's Pinhas Sapir and Mapam's Ya'akov Hazan – both of whom opposed the settlement drive.

In September 1973 before the war, the Labour party endorsed the Galili Plan, which promoted Israeli investment in the territories. It provided loans and tax relief to businessmen who would establish industrial plants. A special cabinet committee was formed to approve Israel acquisition of land and property on the West Bank. This four-year plan seemed to cement Dayan's desire for economic integration. The Yom Kippur War and its cost – some 7 billion U.S. dollars – encouraged Sapir to once again move against the Galili Plan with his own document proclaiming the necessity for territorial compromise.

---

[8] *Ma'ariv*, 14 December 1973.
[9] Menahem Begin, Speech to the Knesset, 14 January 1976, in N. Lorch, ed., *Major Knesset Debates*, vol. 5, pp. 2016–19.
[10] Efraim Torgovnik, 'The Election Campaign: Party Needs and Voter Concerns', in Asher Arian ed., *The Elections in Israel, 1973* (Jerusalem, 1975), pp. 81–82.

The Likud campaign therefore targeted the dovish Sapir. It opposed the Geneva talks after the war since it was based on UN Resolution 242. Begin was also adept at drawing the increasingly hawkish NRP away from its traditional allies in the Ma'arakh towards a more ideologically comfortable partner by calling for a coalition government, comprising the Likud and the National Religious.

The Likud asked the voters, 'Which is the peace party?' It further suggested that a return of territory would not actually bring peace, but only more terror. 'For peace, not surrender, vote Likud!' The Ma'arakh after the debacle of the Yom Kippur War had no answers. Its fatalistic slogan was 'Nevertheless – the Alignment!'

Begin himself articulated the concerns of the electorate through his articles and speeches. After Ahdut Ha'avodah's Yigal Allon, opinion polls suggested that he was considered the best qualified to assume the office of prime minister.[11]

The Likud's achievement in the 1973 election was remarkable. It attained thirty-nine seats compared with Gahal's twenty-six in 1969. The combined total of Gahal, the Free Centre and the State List in 1969 was thirty-two. Taking into account the Labour defectors, the Likud gained in the region of six or seven seats in 1973. The Ma'arakh polled 39.2 percent, while the Likud attained 30.2 percent. The Likud vote increased by 4 percent, while the Ma'arakh decreased by 6 percent.[12]

The Likud did particularly well in the cities. It won a majority of votes in Jerusalem and equalled the Ma'arakh in Tel Aviv. Younger people were attracted to the Likud, whilst older voters tended towards the Ma'arakh. Many soldiers voted for the Likud because of Sharon's standing and his prominent role in the Yom Kippur War. Another reason was that Golda Meir and the Ma'arakh seemed, in contrast, politically faded and paralysed compared with the sixty–year-old Menahem Begin and the Likud. In addition to the young, a large number of Mizrahim finally deserted Labour and voted Likud in 1973. The Likud also picked up a lot of hitherto undecided voters.

LABOUR'S NEW LEADERS

In the immediate aftermath of the conflict, Golda Meir and Moshe Dayan were responsible for the debacle of the Yom Kippur War in the eyes of

[11] *Ha'aretz*, 23 November 1973.
[12] Asher Arian, 'Introduction', in Arian, ed., *The Elections in Israel 1973*, pp. 15–16.

the public. Begin presented himself as the voice of the people and called upon Golda Meir to resign. While this was shrugged off, the Agranat Commission on the conduct of the war issued its preliminary findings in April 1974 and called for wholesale dismissals in the IDF. Such unprecedented criticism produced a political fallout, with the resignations of Golda Meir and Moshe Dayan. Pinhas Sapir was the obvious successor but declined to serve. In June 1974 Yitzhak Rabin was recalled from his post as Israeli ambassador in Washington to become prime minister. He was the first Israeli prime minister who was not a member of Mapai even though his ideological links with Ahdut Ha'avodah had somewhat lapsed. Although he was perceived as a clean pair of hands, Begin called the change in Labour leadership 'cosmetic' and inferred that Rabin was not up to the job because of his alleged breakdown on the eve of the Six-Day War.

Rabin, on the other hand, was a secular Jew who was distant from the world of religious Judaism. His life had been the army and the labour movement. He had little liking for the zealotry of the religious idealists who wished to colonise the West Bank, labeling them 'propeller heads'. Rabin initially formed a government from the Ma'arakh, the Independent Liberals and the Civil Rights movement (CRM), which was led by Shulamit Aloni, a devout secularist. It was supported by a bare majority in a Knesset of 120 seats. Initially this was the first Israeli government not to have included the religious parties. The NRP, which had ten MKs, then thought better of its initial decision to remain outside and eventually joined the coalition.

Although Begin was generally restrained in his public statements because he now had to answer to an amalgamation of parties, he perceived that the weak link in the new Rabin administration was the NRP, which had reluctantly decided to join the government. Unlike previous Mapai and Ma'arakh governments, the new NRP, which enthusiastically promoted Jewish settlement within the West Bank and Gaza, did not sit comfortably in Rabin's government.

The Young Guard in the NRP was busy cleverly outmanoeuvring the party's aging leadership, which had been well-disposed towards the labour Zionist movement for generations. Its path to power was not to press the obvious issue of West Bank settlement, which all agreed with – at least in theory – or more controversially the leadership's willingness to negotiate with Jordan, but to attack it on a religious issue rather than a political one – the vexed question of 'Who is a Jew?'

Jewish religious law defined a Jew as someone born of a Jewish mother. However, the Knesset had not included the phrase 'according to halakhah' (Jewish religious law), despite numerous attempts by Agudat Yisrael to amend it. In January 1970, the Supreme Court ruled that a Jew was someone who defined himself or herself as a Jew. The question of Jewish status, however, was related to matters of marriage and divorce. It was needed for the population registry, but most important it was linked to the Law of Return, which determined who could claim the benefits of citizenship in Israel. The leadership of the NRP originally agreed to the vague formulation of 'one who is born to a Jewess or is converted' as a means of avoiding a *Kulturkampf* with the secularists.

Golda Meir strongly opposed the policy of the *haredi* political parties to amend the Law of Return because she believed that the orthodox monopoly over religion in Israel should not be extended to the Diaspora. In 1970 the Lubavitcher Rebbe had written to her during the War of Attrition, suggesting that God was punishing Israel for failing to correct the flaws in the Law of Return.[13]

The Young Guard in the NRP soon understood that it could undermine the party's leadership by passionately raising this issue to a new prominence. It could seek allies with other sections of the religious community which were outside the NRP. The opinions of rabbis were important, since there were political ramifications which emanated from their rulings. Respected spiritual leaders such as former Chief Rabbi Unterman, the Lubavitcher Rebbe and Rabbi Joseph B. Soloveitchik thus all attacked the leadership of the NRP for its weak-willed approach to this fundamental question of Jewish status.

At the fourth NRP conference in March 1973, a resolution demanded that there be an amendment of the Law of Return as a condition of participating in the next cabinet. A convert to Judaism, it was argued, was someone who was converted according to Jewish religious law and under orthodox supervision.

The party leadership under siege unwisely decided to consult Chief Rabbi Shlomo Goren on a compromise formulation of words and thereby on whether the NRP should join the government. It had expected a positive response from Goren, who had previously demonstrated leniency towards questions of conversion. Shlomo Goren, however, replied critically. There were those in the NRP who had argued from the outset that Goren should never have been consulted, as the party had refrained from involving rabbis in the past and that this was an internal party matter.

---

[13] Stanley Rabinowitz, 'Who Is a Jew? Prime Minister Begin and the Jewish Question', *Judaism*, June 1997.

On the other hand, the veteran leader, Zerah Warhaftig, took note of the chief rabbi's view and aligned his faction with the Young Guard. The NRP centre was split in a vote to join the coalition: for 296; against 198; abstentions 71.

The NRP leadership eventually joined Rabin's coalition in order to balance the secular influences of the CRM, Mapam and the Independent Liberals. While the leadership hoped that such a fait accompli would lead to a calmer situation, this decision was strongly opposed from within the party by the Young Guard and its allies, which had gained in authority. Moreover, the opposition within the NRP wanted a much closer relationship with the Likud.[14] There were even threats that the Young Guard would break away from the NRP.

Begin cultivated this drift towards the right and began to include religious motifs in his public statements and speeches. He noted, for example, that the Lubavitcher Rebbe had argued that the Land of Israel belonged to the Jewish people and that such a right would never be revoked.[15] During the shuttle diplomacy to bring about a disengagement of forces, Begin characterised Henry Kissinger as an assimilated Jew who would bend over backwards to prove his loyalty to others. On another occasion, Begin argued in a Knesset debate that it was sheer folly 'to repartition the western land of Israel'. He recalled Ben-Gurion's abrupt withdrawal from Gaza under American pressure in 1957 and pledged that there would be no withdrawal this time.[16]

Following Rabin's appointment as prime minister, Begin led demonstrators to a hill outside Nablus – Elon Moreh – where God had promised 'the Promised Land' to Abraham. The settlers had attempted to establish Elon Moreh on several occasions but were thwarted by Rabin's refusal to tolerate unauthorised settlement.

The Labour party similarly had its troubles with internal power struggles. Dayan was forced to resign and was brooding about his fate – and his future. The fight to succeed Golda Meir was initially between Allon, Peres and Rabin – none of whom were from Mapai. The eventual vote for the leadership was between Rabin and Peres, and this was split almost evenly 298–254. This was the genesis of a bitter rivalry between the two

[14] Eliezer Don-Yehiya, 'Religion and Coalition: The NRP and Coalition Formation in Israel', in Arian, ed., *The Elections in Israel*, pp. 264–80.
[15] Menahem Begin, Speech to the Knesset, 14 January 1976, in N. Lorch, ed., *Major Knesset Debates*, vol. 5, pp. 2018–19.
[16] Menahem Begin, Speech to the Knesset, 21 September 1976, in N. Lorch, ed., *Major Knesset Debates*, vol. 5, pp. 2014–44.

candidates, with Peres effectively refusing to accept this verdict. Such disunity played into Begin's hands.

Moreover, as part of this ongoing tussle over a disputed leadership, both men looked for allies to bolster their position. Peres tended to align himself with the religious settlers of Gush Emunim, while Rabin wished to keep them at arm's length. The religious settlers became very adept at harnessing this rivalry to aid the settlement drive in the mid-1970s.

In August 1974 the Knesset voted to remove those settlers who had attempted to establish a settlement at Sebastia on the West Bank. Rabin argued in his speech that the debate was not over the right of the Jews to the Land of Israel, but over the foundations of the democratic system. He stated that he regarded the clash at Sebastia as a test of the inner strength of Israeli society. The establishment of any future settlements could be determined only by the decisions of the government of Israel. Yet the Sebastia settlers were supported by members of the Likud, the NRP and Agudat Yisrael, the main haredi party.

Rabin was supported by Dayan, who argued the case for settlement on the West Bank, but said that its opponents should be challenged at the ballot box and not physically on the ground. Menahem Begin commented that Judea and Samaria without Jews was the height of irresponsibility.

The Labour party was divided in its approach to the permanence of the settlements. Rabin's foreign minister, Yigal Allon, did not rule out the possibility of removing settlements if an Israel government so desired it. Israel Galili, chairman of the ministerial committee for settlement affairs, believed that settlements were established in strategic areas on the basis that they would not be abandoned.

Hundreds of Gush Emunim settlers returned to resurrect the settlement at Sebastia in December 1975. Shimon Peres, minister of defence in Rabin's administration, told the Knesset that the controversy was not over 'the vision, but the timing'. He signalled to the settlers and to the Israeli Right that he was more accommodating than his rival, Yitzhak Rabin. In part Peres was positioning himself for a future challenge to Rabin. In part it was a reaction to the passing of the 'Zionism Is Racism' resolution at the United Nations a few weeks earlier.

Yet Peres's visit to the Sebastia settlement had been anything but friendly, and he reported to the cabinet that if the IDF was sent in then violence would not be averted. The cabinet decision combined the elements of a political compromise with a willingness to send in the troops. Peres's proposal was to move the settlers to a nearby military camp at

Kadum rather than to expel them. Rabin concurred – much to the anger of other Ma'arakh cabinet members, who were calmed down by assurances that this was merely a temporary measure.

Five months later the difference in approach between Peres and Rabin became apparent at a meeting of the Ma'arakh in Tel Aviv. Rabin had told Labour's moshavim section that it would have been better to have invested time and effort into the Gush Etzion bloc rather than Kiriat Arba, where there had been few settlers. He said that this was a prime example of the mistake in establishing 'Jewish appendages to major Arab population centres'. Peres responded by suggesting that Israel should permanently retain the entire Samaria region. Rabin, he pointed out, had no mandate to speak about Israel's readiness for large scale withdrawals from the West Bank. He further disputed Rabin's contention that his government followed exactly the same settlement policies as the Meir government previously.[17] Rabin argued that retaining large parts of the West Bank would deprive Israel of its credibility as a negotiating partner in future negotiations with the Arabs. While both Peres and Rabin still opposed any Jewish settlement in Arab populated areas, the revelations of this sharp exchange in the public arena did little to enthuse a depressed electorate.

The twelfth Herut conference symbolically opened in Kiriat Arba in January 1975. Begin welcomed the delegates to 'the city of Caleb Ben-Yefuneh' – one of the two spies who had surveilled the Promised Land and reported his positive impressions.[18] According to the biblical account, Ben-Yefuneh willed himself to be strong and determined and was given Hebron/Kiriat Arba as an inheritance by Joshua.[19] In this speech Begin called for a three-year truce between Arabs and Jews in order to secure a peace treaty and to define borders. Neither Jew nor Arab, he reminded his audience, desired a situation which resembled the Hundred Years' War between England and France. He offered the Palestinians 'cultural autonomy' and a free choice of citizenship, including Israeli citizenship. Begin paid tribute to 'the fighting Jew' with both Dayan and Sharon in the audience. They were linked to others in Revisionist folklore: Jabotinsky and Trumpeldor; Raziel and Stern. Dayan remained a member of the Labour party, but following his reluctant resignation after the Yom Kippur War, he frequently distanced himself from official Labour views.[20]

[17] *Jewish Telegraphic Agency*, 17 May 1976.
[18] Numbers 26:65.
[19] Joshua 14:13–15.
[20] Ned Temko, *To Win or Die: A Personal Portrait of Menachem Begin* (New York, 1987), pp. 189–90.

Begin also defined the right to the Land of Israel as inseparable from the right to security. He then described those who called for a return of the territories for demographic reasons as using 'the voice of Chamberlain'.[21] Begin believed that the demographic issue would be averted because Israeli Arabs would – like the Druze – vote for Zionist parties.[22]

President Katzir, who attended all major party conferences, commented that it was good for Jews to return to a part of the country which had been taken by force of Jordanian arms in 1948.[23]

Rabin had been elected as a new broom, a representative of a fresh generation. However, it soon became apparent that he was unable to cleanse the Augean stables because of the accumulation of problems, framed by a staid political culture. He had come to power during a time of change – not only within Israel, but in the world at large. The emergence of a Palestinian people was in tune with the anti-colonial struggle of the 1970s. The developing world, the Soviet bloc and the European New Left identified more with the Palestinians than with the Israelis, who were now seen as occupiers of Palestinian land through the settlement drive. The election of Jimmy Carter in 1976 as U.S. president brought an emphasis on human rights, a recognition of Palestinian national rights and an impetus to locate a solution to the Israel-Palestine question.

The increase in the price of oil in the aftermath of the Yom Kippur War brought about an isolation of Israel as one country after another succumbed to Arab economic pressure and broke off diplomatic relations with Israel. In addition, there was an intolerable financial burden on the shoulders of the Israeli public. Defence spending had escalated dramatically after the Yom Kippur War. There were increased oil prices and huge inflation – the cost of living index had trebled between 1969 and 1975.

Such developments pushed Israel almost symbolically into the arms of apartheid South Africa. Peres visited South Africa clandestinely in November 1974 and offered to sell 'Chalet' missiles to the regime, which were capable of carrying nuclear loads. Their cooperation, Peres told his hosts, was based on 'the unshakeable foundations of our common hatred of injustice and our refusal to submit to it'.[24] In the 1970s the government of Rabin and Peres began to sell arms to unsavoury regimes such

---

[21] Menahem Begin, Speech to the 12th Herut Conference, 12 January 1975, Begin Heritage Center Archives, Jerusalem.

[22] *Ha'aretz*, 6 June 1975.

[23] *Jewish Telegraphic Agency*, 14 January 1975.

[24] Sasha Polakow-Suransky, *The Unspoken Alliance: Israel's Secret Relationship with Apartheid South Africa* (New York, 2010), p. 80.

as Mobutu's Zaire and to hand over tritium, an isotope of hydrogen, to apartheid South Africa – a necessary ingredient for increasing the power of thermonuclear weapons. To ensure its own survival, it was argued, Israel needed to confront the reality of its isolation and to cross hitherto impermeable red lines. Like Lenin, Israel embraced expediency in desperate times. Whereas Labour reluctantly compromised for reasons of necessity to the detriment of socialist norms, the Likud deemed the national interest paramount, above such concerns, and suffered no qualms of conscience. To the international community such subtleties did not matter.

THE TRIUMPH OF THE MARGINALISED

Despite all these difficulties, Rabin believed that he could still hold off the advance of the Likud and the broad swing to the right. Rabin could not foretell that an unlucky sequence of events would lead to his downfall. In contrast Begin maintained his remarkable run of political fortune.

In December 1976, the first delivery of U.S. F-15 fighters was scheduled to arrive in Israel, an hour before the onset of the Jewish Sabbath. For the representatives of religious Jewry in the Israeli cabinet, there was therefore insufficient time to return home. In a more general sense, this was interpreted as crass insensitivity towards the religious public. This led to a no-confidence motion in the government in the Knesset. An NRP cabinet minister, Yosef Burg, voted in support of the government, while all the other NRP MKs abstained. Rabin took advantage of this move and resigned in order to bring the election forward. This was initially regarded within the Ma'arakh as an astute move – and one which unnerved both the NRP and the Likud.

However, a few days after the arrival of the F-15s, an investigation by Uri Avneri's *Haolam Hazeh* revealed that Asher Yadlin, a leading figure in the Histadrut, had been taking bribes as head of the Kupat Holim, the health service of the Histadrut. He had also just been appointed governor of the Bank of Israel. Yadlin was arrested, admitted his guilt and was sentenced to five years' imprisonment. Peres used this as further evidence of Rabin's inability to rule.

A few weeks later, Avraham Ofer, minister of housing, committed suicide, out of allegations arising from the Yadlin affair. He left a suicide note, protesting his innocence. Nothing was proved and the charges were eventually dropped. Rabin's wife was then charged with the technical offence of breaking foreign currency regulations because she kept a bank account in Washington. Similar charges were levelled against Abba Eban and later dropped. The annual report of the State Comptroller noted that there was a lack of crucial supplies in army emergency warehouses. In mid-May 1977 a military helicopter carrying fifty-four soldiers crashed.

But most important, the former chief of staff of the IDF in the early years of the state, Yigal Yadin, had established the Democratic Movement for Change (DMC), which reflected the crisis of leadership within the labour movement.

Rabin's tactic of bringing forward the election had backfired. A cataclysmic sequence of events had brought him down. In April 1977 a conference of the Labour central committee once more voted for Rabin (1,445) rather than Peres (1,404), with 16 abstentions. On the eve of a difficult election, there was still no unity but a symmetrical split. Although Rabin was once more the victor, following his wife's misdemeanour the weight of one disaster after another was just too great and he decided to step down – to be succeeded by his great rival, Shimon Peres.[25]

Yet the die was cast. The Ma'arakh was viewed as tired and untrustworthy. Both Peres and Rabin were viewed as political pigmies compared with their predecessors. At the end of 1976, fully 60 percent of voters were still undecided as to whom to vote for.[26] An ongoing *Ma'ariv* poll of election issues revealed that public concern about corruption had increased from 25 percent to 35 percent between March and May 1977. Nearly half those polled on the eve of the election viewed the rising rate of inflation as a permanent worry.[27]

While Labour was imploding, the Likud was consolidating. In addition to Herut and the Liberals, other groups took shelter under the umbrella of the Likud. The internal composition of the Likud had truly changed, indeed solidified, since 1973. The third faction within the Likud was La'am, which consisted of the State List plus Labour supporters of a Greater Israel. Ahdut was a faction of the Independent Liberal faction within the Likud. It was led by Hillel Zeidel, who had been head of the Independent Liberal faction in the Histadrut.

Just before the 1977 election, the Free Centre split, with two members going to Yigal Yadin's DMC and two transferring to La'am. This produced a conflict within the Likud between those who espoused free enterprise and those from the labour movement who favoured collectivism. Despite Liberal opposition, Moshe Dayan was prevailed upon by

[25] Arian, 'Introduction', pp. 9–19.

[26] Judith Elizar and Elihu Katz, 'The Media in the Israeli Election of 1977', in Arian, ed., *The Elections in Israel 1977*, p. 208.

[27] Ibid., p. 203.

Begin to join the Likud on the eve of the 1977 election, but he eventually refused to do so. Within the Labour party, he argued that Jews should be permitted to settle in a demilitarised West Bank. 'Judea and Samaria', he commented, '[are] Israel and we are not there as foreign conquerors but as returners to Zion.'[28]

Arik Sharon wanted to join, but he was blocked by his former party, the Liberals. Sharon established his own list, Shlomzion, and chose his own candidates. The list won two seats and then promptly dissolved itself to join the victorious Likud.[29]

The Likud platform had hardly changed from the 1973 manifesto. Begin was entering his ninth election campaign. He had remained at the helm for an unprecedented twenty-nine years. Begin was uncertain about his chances and had dropped hints that he would retire if this proved to be as unsuccessful as past campaigns. Yet Herut had made strides in loosening Begin's hold on the party. A raft of younger candidates were selected by secret ballot even though Begin was elected unopposed. Ezer Weizmann returned from a career in business to run the campaign with Begin's approval. Israeli and American advisors were hired. But ironically, a blessing in disguise proved to be Begin's long hospitalisation following a heart attack. It kept him off the campaign trail for three months and allowed Weizmann to project the image of a homely elder statesman, a founding father of the state as a trustworthy and worthy candidate. The Dahaf Agency was hired for a makeover of Begin's image.[30] An informal Begin was revealed to the Israeli public without his statuary white shirt and tie. Moreover, the Israeli public was sympathetic to an ailing Begin and did not have to react to an active, strident one. As Weizmann commented afterwards: 'We sold the Likud like Coca-Cola'.[31]

Begin came out of hospital eleven days before the election. He took part in a televised debate with Peres, performed well and projected a receptive image. The television exit polls unexpectedly indicated a Likud victory. When the first prediction of the result was made on Israeli television, it was aptly described as ha-Mahapah – 'the earthquake'. Likud had emerged as the leading party with forty-three seats. The DMC had scythed off a sizeable proportion of votes, leaving the Ma'arakh with

[28] *Jerusalem Post*, 15 July 1976.
[29] Benjamin Akzin, 'The Likud', in Arian ed., *The Elections in Israel 1977*, pp. 43–55.
[30] Avi Shilon, *Menachem Begin: A Life* (London, 2012), p. 252.
[31] Jonathan Mendilow, *Ideology, Party Change and Electoral Campaigns in Israel, 1965–2001* (New York, 2003), p. 77.

thirty-two mandates. In 1977, a majority of Mizrahim finally came over to the Likud – as did the under-twenty-fours and the Israeli underclass.

A long campaign to draw moshavniks away from traditionally voting Labour also paid off. Private farmers, outside the Labour consensus, were often members of the Farmers' Federation, which maintained close ties to the Liberals. Labour public support for the agricultural sector was a tenet of socialist faith and it exhibited favouritism towards the kibbutzim. The Likud called for an equalisation between kibbutzim and moshavim. In 1977 many moshavniks switched to the DMC such that a majority of them did not vote Labour – the first time since 1948.[32]

The NRP achieved its best result since its formation in attaining twelve seats. But more important, the Young Guard had succeeded in marginalising the old leadership and taking control of the party. One by one, the NRP factions allied themselves with those who preached colonisation of the West Bank and an uncompromising ideological approach. Even Yosef Burg, traditionally close to the labour movement, bowed to the inevitable and forged ties with Zevulun Hammer, now the leader of the party. The number two on the party list for the election was Haim Druckman, a leader of Gush Emunim. Moreover, Begin had promised the religious parties before the election that he would try to amend the Law of Return, to include the words 'according to the halakhah'.[33]

The DMC wanted to project itself as widely based despite its elitist and Ashkenazi composition. Its leadership, however, comprised both Labour and Likud defectors: Amnon Rubinstein (Shinui), Yigal Yadin (Democratic Movement), Shmuel Tamir (Free Centre), Meir Amit (Labour).[34] The DMC's position on the territories was very similar to that of the Ma'arakh, which made it easier for Labour voters to defect. The Ma'arakh lost a third of its 1973 support. Moreover, the rise of the DMC also affected support for the Independent Liberals and the CRM.

Labour's civil war – a legacy of the conquest of the West Bank – had allowed Menahem Begin in his ninth election campaign, at the age of sixty-four, to emerge triumphant through the debris of the warring parties. Begin's victory speech[35] at the Likud headquarters suggested not only change but also continuity. Yet Begin was viewed as a figure from

[32] Neil Sherman, 'The Agricultural Sector and the 1977 Knesset Elections', in Arian, ed., *The Elections in Israel 1977*, pp. 157–68.
[33] Rabinowitz, 'Who Is a Jew?'.
[34] Ephraim Torgovnik, 'A Movement for Change in a Stable System', in Arian, ed., *The Elections in Israel 1977*, p. 81.
[35] *Yediot Aharanot*, 18 May 1977.

another age and time – which he undoubtedly was – though he simultaneously projected a sense of continuity of the founding generation, which Rabin and Peres could not do. His comment about Jabotinsky at the Seventeenth Zionist Congress in 1931 probably passed over most Likud heads. His statement, however, that the Likud would not be 'slaves to the Ma'arakh' certainly struck a chord with the anti-Labour coalition of parties which he had painstakingly constructed since 1949. He quoted Abraham Lincoln following his election victory in 1864 and the subsequent victory over the Confederacy at the end of a civil war which pitted brother against brother. Like Lincoln, Begin revealed himself to a weary public as the great unifier, the soother of the furrowed brow, the healer of the nation's wounds. Menahem Begin had slain the socialist dragon and Israel had moved to the right.

16

A Coming of Age

THE PROPHET ARMED

Menahem Begin was a student and lover of history. It could provide insights into the future and lessons from the past. Yet it was contemporary history that weighed down upon him. The territorial appetite of the Nazis and the Stalinists in 1939 had temporarily been satisfied by the devouring of Poland – and in its train the destruction of the Jewish civilisation that had rooted itself in Eastern Europe. The poets and the businessmen, the Bundists and the capitalists, the assimilated Germanophiles and the devout ultra-orthodox had all disappeared into the ovens of Auschwitz. Despite his desire to inhabit the world of modern Israel, Menahem Begin remained very much a Polish Jew, permeated by the demons unleashed by the Shoah.

Begin had always summoned up the ghosts of the past to justify the policies of the present. In mid-1971 he compared the defence pact between the USSR and Egypt to the Molotov-Ribbentrop Pact. As he got older and in particular as he embraced the premiership, the equating of Palestinians with Nazis became more common. Arafat in besieged Beirut became Hitler in his Berlin bunker. During the Lebanon War in 1982, Begin's use of historical examples was even more accentuated. He spoke of the PLO's Maginot Line and reminded the cabinet that there would be 'no more Treblinkas'.[1] As one writer observed, 'Israel was an idea [to Begin] not a place or an environment in which he lived.'[2]

---

[1] Arye Naor, *Begin ba-shilton: edut ishit* (Tel Aviv, 1993), p. 282.
[2] Amos Perlmutter, *The Life and Times of Menachem Begin* (New York, 1987), p. 392.

Yet his continual evoking of the Shoah to justify controversial events deepened the rift between Left and Right in Israel. Amos Oz told him:

The urge to revive Hitler, only to kill him again and again, is the result of pain that poets can permit themselves to use, but not statesmen . . . even at great emotional cost personally, you must remind yourself and the public that elected you its leader that Hitler is dead and burned to ashes.[3]

Begin's throwaway remarks about 'a blood libel levelled at Israel',[4] which seemingly belittled the massacre of Palestinians in the camps of Sabra and Shatilla, was described as 'moral autism' by the playwright Yehoshua Sobol.[5] His psychological separation from the killing of Muslim Palestinians by Christian Phalangists – while Israeli troops stood unaware outside – was a reflection of Begin's broad fatalism, a recognition of a world where the Jews could never do any good in the eyes of non-Jews. Even foreign leaders such as the German chancellor, Helmut Schmidt, and the French president, Giscard D'Estaing, became targets for a tongue-lashing.

Menahem Begin had commenced his term of office in 1977 by granting refuge to the Vietnamese boat people. He finished it in 1983 with the condemnation of the Kahan report, which blamed him for being 'unaware of such a danger' when the Phalangists were allowed into the camps and slaughtered civilians.

Begin was accused of 'indirect responsibility' for the killings, recording 'the obligations applying to every civilised nation and the ethical rules accepted by civilised peoples'. The Kahane report invoked the treatment of Jews down the centuries and the pogroms enacted against them. It quoted from Deuteronomy:

And the elders of that city who are nearest to the slain man, shall wash their hands over the heifer whose neck was broken in the valley.

And they shall speak and say: 'Our hands have not shed this blood neither have our eyes seen it.'[6]

Begin's desire for Jewish power to push back the tides of history had had exactly the opposite effect.

As prime minister, Begin had looked to Jabotinsky, but also to fighters for national independence such as Garibaldi. He admired Churchill

---

[3] Amos Oz, *Yediot Aharanot*, 21 June 1982.
[4] Menahem Begin, Speech to the Knesset, 22 September 1982, Israel Ministry of Foreign Affairs, Tel Aviv.
[5] Yehoshua Sobol, *Al Hamishmar*, 21 September 1982.
[6] Deuteronomy 21:6–7.

for his leadership of Britain during World War II. And like Ben-Gurion and Ahimeir, he acknowledged Lenin's political acumen as a leader who brought about revolutionary change. Even before the de-Stalinisation of the 1950s, he recognised Lenin as 'a far greater man than Stalin'.[7] On his election in 1977 there is no doubt that Begin saw himself as a historical figure, a Diaspora Jew who had made a difference in the struggle for independence, someone who had directed the flow of Jewish history into new channels. He represented neither Ben-Gurion's 'new Jews' who constituted the fighting force of the IDF nor the socialist pioneers of the kibbutz who had made the desert bloom. He understood himself primarily as a survivor and an outsider, a battler against all the odds who had climbed to the top of the tree, someone who profoundly believed that political wisdom did not necessarily reside in the hands of the majority.

Above all, he regarded himself as 'a Jewish prime minister' rather than as an Israeli leader. Although he was not strictly observant, he regarded religious tradition as the highest expression of Jewishness. Unlike Jabotinsky and Ben-Gurion, Begin believed that the upholders of Jewishness in the new Israel would be the same people as in the old Poland. In stark contradistinction to Jabotinsky at the beginning of the twentieth century, Begin believed that it was both Judaism and the Jewish national will which had kept Jewishness alive for two millennia. The Jewish Sabbath was therefore an all-important occasion which had to be maintained. On Saturday afternoons Begin maintained an open house for all visitors.

As early as 1958, much to the chagrin of the old comrades of Jabotinsky, Begin began to describe religion and nationality as instrinsically related. In one tense exchange, he rebuked President Reagan, exclaiming that 'Jews do not kneel except to God'. Following his election in 1977, Begin strengthened the ramparts of Jewish observance. When he presented his first government to the Knesset, he quoted from the book of Micah:

> For let all the peoples walk, each one in the name of its god
> But we will walk in the name of the Lord our God forever and ever[8]

In his first television broadcast, Begin quoted from the book of Psalms. He then visited Zvi Yehudah Kook, the head of the Mercaz HaRav yeshivah and spiritual mentor of the West Bank settlers to receive his blessing,

[7] Menachem Begin, *White Nights: The Story of a Prisoner in Russia* (London, 1957), p. 236.
[8] Micah 4:5.

as well as that of the non-Zionist Lubavitcher Rebbe, who similarly promoted the biblical dimensions of the Land of Israel. Kook sent him a letter stating that Begin's victory was 'a divine enlightenment'.[9]

Under Begin's government, the demands of orthodoxy met little resistance. Issues such as the exemption of women from army service were now placed on the political agenda. In 1977 the education portfolio was placed in the hands of a religious party for the first time. Moreover, this was also the first occasion that the NRP had received a ministry which did not deal directly with matters of religious practice. Begin gave the Ministries of Education and the Interior as well as Religious Affairs to the NRP. This marked a clear break with the secularism of socialist Zionism.

Begin instructed the national airline, El Al, not to fly on the Jewish Sabbath. Yeshivot were promised an expansion of their budgets and a loosening of the limit on the number of exemptions from military service. Begin also argued that only rabbis had the right to authorise a conversion to Judaism – a conversion only according to Jewish religious law, the Halakhah. This was profoundly different from the ruling of the minister of the interior, Israel Bar-Yehudah, in 1958 that a Jew was someone who regarded himself or herself as a Jew. Bar-Yehudah's ruling which had deeply antagonised the NRP, explicitly upset the status quo between the religious and the secular. While Begin argued in the 1950s that only the rabbis had the right to determine who was a Jew, the Revisionist intelligentsia and some Irgun commanders were strongly opposed.

Begin was also forced to consider NRP demands due the constraints of coalition politics. The Democratic Movement for Change split into three factions in September 1978 and this strengthened the position of the NRP. Begin therefore needed the NRP to remain in government, since the coalition would otherwise dip below the blocking majority of sixty-one seats. The NRP voted to boycott the cabinet vote on Camp David, but there was a free vote in the Knesset due to divisions within the party. The NRP threatened to leave the government unless its adherents were allowed to continue to settle in Judea and Samaria. Begin agreed.

After forming his second, more radical administration, Begin commented in September 1981 that Israel was not only a state of law but also a state of Halakhah.[10]

In the first decade of the state, the NRP, like Mapai, did not want a Kulturkampf. In 1963, however, Levi Eshkol and Golda Meir moved

---

[9] Naor, *Begin ba-shilton*, pp. 53–54.
[10] *Ma'ariv*, 28 September 1981.

away from Ben-Gurion's policy of including different ideological trends within Mapai-led coalitions as a means of preventing rival blocs from coalescing.

CAMP DAVID AND THE DISINTEGRATION OF THE COALITION OF THE RIGHT

With the Likud finally in government, decisions had to be made. The responsibility of power did not resemble the freedom of opposition. The grand alliance with Herut at its core began to fragment. This had several causes.

Firstly, the process of building a cluster party such as the Likud meant that the leadership of other parties such as the Liberals had to be given positions in government at the expense of Herut loyalists. Secondly, although Begin ruled with an iron rod, the presence of other parties meant an inevitable ideological dilution of hitherto sacred principles. Thirdly, Begin through his persona and rhetoric had created a home for both the Centre Right and the Far Right. Both sheltered under the Likud umbrella. Fourthly, the different factions of the Right were united by their anti-Labour animus. They knew what they were against, but what they were for often divided them.

Begin had demonstrated a pragmatism in building a coalition of disparate anti-Labour parties with a determination that often relegated personal loyalties and long-time friendships to a secondary position. His appointment of Labour's Moshe Dayan as foreign minister in 1977 caused disbelief in Herut. Dayan was held responsible by the Israeli public for the catastrophe of the Yom Kippur War. Begin shared this view, but was careful to cultivate Dayan privately and not to criticise him publicly.

In the Rabin administration, some regarded Dayan as a liability despite the fact that his ally in Rafi, Shimon Peres, was minister of defence. Dayan felt that he had been treated badly by the Agranat Commission on the conduct of the Yom Kippur War and was unable to relate to the political mood prevailing in Labour. He was particularly irked by the protests in 1974 which demanded some political accountability for the losses in the Yom Kippur War:

In nothing [the protest leader] Motti Ashkenazi said, did I find a spark of trust, of faith, of anything constructive. All was nihilistic. It was not because of Motti Ashkenazi and people like him that Israel had been built, and not through them that Israel would grow and prosper. On the face of it, we had been sitting in the same room dealing with different things and living in two different worlds, separated by something far wider than the generation gap.[11]

By October 1974, Dayan had already signed a Likud motion calling for the retention of Judea and Samaria. The resignation of Yitzhak Rabin in 1977 and his replacement by Shimon Peres, however, did not produce the expected rehabilitation of Dayan. The three men whose names were first on the Labour candidates' list, Peres, Allon and Eban, all favoured territorial compromise. Dayan had become so politically distant from Labour politics that Arik Sharon suggested they should establish a 'Front for Eretz Israel Loyalists'.

Begin had originally wanted to establish a national unity government including Labour but excluding the Communists. The Labour party refused. Dayan's inclusion in the government was therefore yet another exercise in expanding the Likud cluster – without Dayan actually joining the party. Begin believed that Dayan's appointment would lend the new government gravitas. The internationally recognised general with the eye-patch would provide a veneer of respectability to neutralise the anxiety generated by Begin's election.

Begin trusted Dayan's 'hawkish pragmatism',[12] and the relationship between the two men proved to be the bedrock of the administration. Begin held together a government of diverse parts, at the cost of very few Herut loyalists becoming members of the cabinet.

Begin had always held to the view of a state on both sides of the river Jordan. The desire to expand Israel's borders resembled the aspiration of the Poles to a form a Greater Poland. Yet as the Poles had understood in the inter-war years, politics for countries surrounded by larger, unfriendly neighbours was governed by the art of the possible.

Begin understood the term 'West Bank' as encompassing both Israel and the contemporary geographical area known conventionally as the West Bank – the land between the Mediterranean and the river Jordan. Together with the leadership of the NRP, Begin now referred to the West Bank as Judea and Samaria. At the beginning of his tenure as prime minister, Begin visited the settlers at Kadum who wished to establish the settlement of Elon Moreh and famously promised them that 'there would be many more Elon Morehs'.

While Begin was an ideological politician through and through, he was able to differentiate between theory and practice. He was flexible enough

[11] Moshe Dayan, *Story of My Life: An Autobiography* (New York, 1976), p. 599.
[12] Perlmutter, *Life and Times of Menachem Begin*, p. 320.

to interpret ideology differently if it conflicted with his understanding of the political reality. During the Six-Day War, Begin had refrained from proposing an invasion of Jordan even though he continued to recognise the historic right to the East Bank.

The 1977 Likud manifesto stated that the Land of Israel from the sea to the river would never be partitioned. Israeli law would operate on the West Bank. Yet Dayan opposed the extension of Israeli law to the territories. Begin ultimately accepted Dayan's approach to the West Bank – sovereignty and military authority would remain in Israel's hands, but the Palestinians would exercise autonomy. Begin looked to the Helsingfors Programme concerning minority rights in Tsarist Russia, which Jabotinsky had formulated in December 1906 as the template for Palestinian autonomy. The Palestinians would have rights on the land; the Israelis would have rights to the land.[13] They could choose between Israeli and Jordanian citizenship. Those who chose Israeli citizenship could settle within Israel's borders and purchase land.

Begin's desire to obtain power inevitably led to a obfuscation of former positions. He now supported UN Resolution 242, whereas he had opposed it during Golda Meir's premiership and eventually resigned from the government. In 1973 the Likud rejected any ceasefire terms that would imply an acceptance of UNR 242.

Begin saw the Israeli-Egyptian negotiations of 1977–1979 as a vindication of Jabotinsky's 'Iron Wall' philosophy, in which he predicted that concessions would be made once it was recognised that Israel could not be defeated by military force.

Begin differentiated ideologically between the West Bank, which was part of the Land of Israel, and Sinai, which in his eyes was not. Many Herut loyalists interpreted Begin's actions in forging the Camp David Accord, which handed back Sinai to Egypt, as the prelude to the return of Judea and Samaria to the Palestinians. A former member of Lehi and a Likud MK, Geula Cohen, said that the Camp David agreement was designed 'to wipe out Judea and Samaria'.[14] Anwar Sadat and Jimmy Carter paradoxically also expected Begin to be as pragmatic over the West Bank as he had been over Sinai.

Begin agreed to remove the settlements in Sinai after Sharon stated that their removal did not pose a security threat. Begin seemingly also

---

[13] Ibid., p. 290.
[14] G. R. Kieval, *Party Politics in Israel and the Occupied Territories* (New Haven, CT, 1983), p. 149.

FIGURE 16. Anwar Sadat in conversation with Jimmy Carter during the Camp David negotiations (September 1978). Reproduced by permission of Ken Stein; courtesy of the Central Zionist Archives, Jerusalem.

agreed to freeze settlement construction during the autonomy negotiations. Begin, however, understood 'a freezing of settlements' as lasting solely for a three-month period – from the end of the negotiations until the actual signing of the agreement. Carter, on the other hand, believed that it covered the entire five-year period for the autonomy negotiations. Such confusion worked in Begin's favour. Begin clearly wanted a separate peace treaty with Egypt, and he strongly opposed any notion of Arab sovereignty over the West Bank.

Begin had to balance the views of those opponents who had unquestioningly supported him throughout his career with the realpolitik of securing peace with Israel's largest and most powerful neighbour. This was symbolised in the text of the 'Framework for Peace in the Middle East'. Whilst the English version referred to 'the Palestinians', the Hebrew one referred to 'the Arabs of the Land of Israel'. Significantly it was the English-language version which was the working version, accepted by Begin, Sadat and Carter.

Begin was the first Israeli prime minister to recognise the rights of the Palestinians, but when the future of Jerusalem was raised, Begin responded by telling the story related on Yom Kippur of the medieval figure of Amnon of Mainz, who refused to convert to Christianity. Amnon

FIGURE 17. Menahem Begin in conversation with Jimmy Carter during the Camp David negotiations (September 1978).
Reproduced by permission of Ken Stein; courtesy of the Central Zionist Archives, Jerusalem.

paid for his defiance of the local bishop with a lingering death, caused by the amputation of his limbs. For Begin, the retention of Jerusalem was projected as a matter of faith.[15]

Such philosophical subtleties and verbal acrobatics did not impress a growing number of the faithful within Herut. Many long-time members of the movement were no longer willing to put up with what they perceived to be a betrayal of their core principles. Unlike the younger generation, they had actually known Jabotinsky and were well versed in his writings. They were well aware of the contradictions in Begin's approach. Others could not contemplate that this had been the case. The chairman of the Herut faction in the Knesset, Chaim Kaufman, commented:

It came down to one's faith in the Prime Minister and our party chairman. He is, after all, my mentor. It is a question of having confidence in his team.[16]

While the Israeli public was overwhelmingly in support of the Camp David proposals, Begin's opponents demonstrated with Chamberlainesque

---

[15] Avi Shilon, *Menachem Begin: A Life* (London, 2012), p. 302.
[16] *Jerusalem Post*, 6 October 1978.

umbrellas. His long-time nemesis of the Far Right, Israel Eldad, accused Begin of facilitating a new partition of western Eretz Israel[17] and diluting his ideological principles.[18] In response to comparisons with Ernest Bevin, Begin expressed his great appreciation of Gush Emunim, 'the finest of pioneers, the builders of the Land', but he also accused them of exhibiting a messiah complex.[19]

Ironically the wheel of time had turned a full cycle and Begin thus began to have a difficult relationship with his own radicals just as Jabotinsky had had with the young Begin in the 1930s.

Apart from Sharon and Weizmann, Herut veterans generally opposed the autonomy plans. He had argued earlier that a peace agreement with Jordan did not automatically mean surrendering the historic right to the East Bank.[20] Yet when he made the same argument regarding Judea and Samaria, such a merging of theory and practice did not impress. Even a promise at the end of October 1978 to expand the population of the existing settlements failed to appease them.

Rebuffed by his loyal supporters in Herut, he significantly did not seek their support, but only the government's and the Knesset's approval for the Camp David accord. Sharon was one of the few Herut members to support it. In addition to the NRP's opposition, members of the Marxist Ahdut Ha'avodah also opposed the negotiations and Yigal Allon abstained during the Knesset vote. While nearly 70 percent of the government coalition voted for the Camp David framework, only 57 percent of the Herut faction supported it. Seven out of eight of the La'am MKs did not vote in favour.

Those who opposed any withdrawal from Sinai included Ehud Olmert, Moshe Arens and Yitzhak Shamir. Many who opposed Begin initially founded 'a circle of Herut loyalists', but Begin's triumph at the Herut conference in November 1978 persuaded some of his adversaries to leave the Likud.[21] Those who rejected the return of territory either on security grounds or for reasons of ideology eventually left the Likud to establish a new party of the Far Right, Tehiyah. It included former members of Herut, Gush Emunim and Ahdut Ha'avodah. Former adherents of Rafi and the State List in La'am also broke away to form Telem in order to support Moshe Dayan's return to political life.

---

[17] *Jerusalem Post*, 9 January 1978.
[18] *Yediot Aharanot*, 30 December 1977.
[19] Naor, *Begin ba-shilton*, p. 163.
[20] Ibid., p. 104.
[21] *Jerusalem Post*, 23 November 1978.

Zvi Yehudah Kook, who had given his blessing to Begin on taking office in 1977, now bitterly condemned him for surrendering part of the Land of Israel.[22] Where Kook and Begin drew the borders was rooted in their different definitions of the Land of Israel, one according to biblical boundaries, the other according to the parameters of the Mandate of the 1920s. Begin never made any mention in his speeches of either the Nile or the Euphrates as the borders of the Land of Israel.[23]

Begin said that the choice was either an agreement with Egypt or retaining the settlements in Sinai. It could not be both.[24] Begin therefore relied on his Labour opponents to ensure Knesset approval. Peres highlighted Begin's discomfort by calling it 'the Palestinians' Balfour Declaration'.

As soon as the ink was dry on the separate agreement with Egypt, Begin stonewalled on the autonomy deliberations with the Palestinians. Both Dayan and Weizmann considered this a political about-turn. They grew weary of Begin's attitude and suspicious of his motives. Both soon resigned from Begin's government. Another moderating force, Yigal Yadin's Democratic Movement for Change, once the hope of reformists in 1977, had disintegrated.

Dayan was replaced in the autonomy negotiations by Yosef Burg, a long-time NRP leader, who endorsed such procrastination in the cause of retaining Judea and Samaria. Yitzhak Shamir, a Lehi leader, was appointed Dayan's hard-line replacement as foreign minister. All of this signalled a move towards a more radical policy.

Menahem Begin had achieved peace with Egypt and was honoured with the Nobel Peace Prize. Yet his enduring failure at Camp David was that he was unable to avert a split in the national camp. It allowed the Far Right to form its own parties outside the Likud.

This was the pattern which subsequent Likud prime ministers would come to know well. A decision regarded as pragmatic by the leadership would be deemed ideological heresy by factions within the Likud. Populist accusations of betrayal also served the ambitions of those within the Likud who sought high office. The Oslo Accord (1993), the Hebron agreement (1997), the Wye Plantation agreement (1998) and the unilateral withdrawal from Gaza (2005) all produced fragmentation in a party which Menahem Begin had built and held together until 1979.

---

[22] Naor, *Begin ba-shilton*, pp. 183–84.
[23] Arye Naor, 'Hawks' Beaks, Doves' Feathers: Likud Prime Ministers between Ideology and Reality', *Israel Studies*, vol. 19, no. 3 (Fall 2005), pp. 154–91.
[24] Ned Temko, *To Win or Die: A Personal Portrait of Menachem Begin* (New York, 1987), p. 234.

The NRP similarly experienced repeated schisms, reducing its Knesset representation from its heyday in 1977. Its fragmentation was perhaps even more profound than that of the Likud. Haim Druckman, who was high on the NRP electoral list in 1977, opposed Camp David and specifically the withdrawal from Sinai. In 1983 he formed Matzad because he rejected any form of evacuation from the settlements. The NRP also lost Gush Emunim members who teamed up with secular opponents of Camp David to establish Tehiyah.

There was yet another fragmentation initiating the formation of ethno-national parties. Even though many Mizrahim remained faithful to Begin and the Likud was becoming less a party of Ashkenazim, many felt the need to create a party which would cater to their needs and promote issues such as the demand for an increase in the children's allowance. In 1981 the Mizrahi party, Tami, was formed mainly from the NRP.

Even in the haredi world, there was a sense that the Mizrahim were always being discriminated against, always on a lower rung to the Ashkenazim. Ovadiah Yosef broke away from Agudat Yisrael and created Shas, a party with its own Council of Sages.[25] Shas developed into a major party in Israel to broadly represent the interests of the Mizrahim. It consisted of an inner core of young haredim which attracted traditional, yet not strictly observant Mizrahim to their standard. Those who exuded pride in ethnic traditions and others who felt aggrieved at the Ashkenazi elite also joined. Moreover, unlike the Ashkenazi haredim, the Mizrahim did not carry the historical baggage created by all the internal conflicts ignited by the Haskalah in Eastern Europe. There were different attitudes towards the less observant, towards the state per se and towards service in the IDF.[26] In accounting on average for 10 percent of the vote in Israeli elections, the emergence of Shas damaged both the Likud and the NRP.

With the exit of Dayan, Weizmann and Yadin from the cabinet and with a separate agreement signed with Egypt, pragmatic moderating influences on Begin no longer existed. The assassination of Sadat and the electoral defeat of Jimmy Carter freed Begin of his partners in forging the Camp David agreement. Begin was now able to rally his lukewarm supporters in Herut to prevent any compromise on the issue of the West Bank. Carter in particular had viewed 'autonomy' as a means to thwart self-determination for the Palestinians.

[25] Ilan Greilsammer, 'Campaign Strategies of the Israeli Religious Parties', in Asher Arian and Michal Shamir, eds., *The Elections in Israel, 1984* (Oxford, 1986), pp. 79–96.
[26] Etta Bick, 'The Shas Phenomenon and Religious Parties in the 1999 Elections', in Daniel J. Elazar and M. Ben Mollov, eds., *Israel at the Polls, 1999* (London, 2001), pp. 55–100.

Yet the Liberals in the Likud were moderate nationalists who could accept the idea of a territorial compromise. They also disagreed with Begin's pronouncements on 'who is a Jew?' While both the Liberals and Herut had retained their party structures within the Likud, the Liberals gradually came to the conclusion that it would be impossible to leave because Begin brought in the votes in any election. Existence outside the Likud would invite political extinction. The Liberals by 1981 therefore had become totally dependent on Herut. This subservience within the Likud allowed Begin to return to his ideological roots and to enact a more radical policy in 1981.

THE LONG ROAD TO BEIRUT

Begin's return to a more aggressive approach chimed with the views of the Israeli public in endorsing a more hard-line perspective on the territories.[27] During the first Begin administration, there were fifty-five new settlements on the West Bank and its population had quadrupled. By 1981 half the Israeli public believed that no territory should be returned to the Palestinians. One slogan brandished by the Likud in its election campaign was 'Save Eretz Israel from Labour'.

To those who questioned the non-existent pace of negotiations and the lack of self-determination of the Palestinians after the euphoria of Camp David, Begin pointed to the past. France's granting of autonomy to the Corsicans and the autonomy of the southern Tyrol were given as working examples where a state had not been created.[28]

Begin's second administration was more a Herut government than a Likud one. It virtually reversed the coalescence of the past thirty years for the radicalism of the 1950s. As with military affairs, Begin handed over the economy to those he believed had expertise in such matters. It was part of the long-standing arrangement that Herut had with the Liberals that the latter would put into effect their own ideas of private enterprise and develop an efficient economy, based on the supremacy of the individual entrepreneur over the collective, privatisation over nationalisation. In this, the Likud reflected the advent of Thatcherism and Reaganomics, the coming of age of deregulation and globalisation. The Liberals, whose antecedents had been the Polish middle class of the fourth aliyah, were keen to finally put their cherished ideas into practice.

---

[27] *Jerusalem Post*, 6 May 1981.
[28] Zvi Harry Hurwitz, *Begin: His Life, Words and Deeds* (Jerusalem, 2004), p. 202.

However, such aspirations sharply clashed with the economic interests of many of Herut's working-class supporters.

Under the Liberals' Simha Ehrlich, the cost of subsidised goods went up 15 percent, while electricity and water rose by 25 percent. Cigarettes increased by 21 percent and coffee by 26 percent. VAT increased from 8 percent to 12 percent . The cost of health care rocketed. Subsidies on basic goods were cancelled, and the cost of apartments rose astronomically. Everything was determined by market forces. This led to hyperinflation nearing Weimar proportions and a very large balance-of-payments deficit. Ehrlich eventually resigned, but even more hard-line policies were implemented by his successor, La'am's Yigal Horovitz.

In November 1980 there was a vote of confidence in the Likud government's economic policy. Begin won narrowly by 57–54. When Hurwitz resigned in January 1981, the rate of inflation was 140 percent.

With an election looming and an electoral disaster facing the Likud, Begin turned to his followers in Herut. He appointed Yoram Aridor, a member of Herut, who straightaway put previous policies into reverse. The austerity measures were lifted and consumer goods were now made accessible. The people of Israel bought as if there was no tomorrow. Yet tomorrow came and it brought the Likud a dramatic victory. Begin's return to Herut's aggressive dynamism of the 1950s brought electoral success in 1981. Despite opinion polls a few months earlier suggesting that the Likud might do well to achieve twenty seats, the Likud pipped Labour by securing forty-eight. This was the best result achieved by an Israeli political party before or since 1981.

Labour was seen as appealing to the world of yesteryear's pioneering values, the collectivism of the kibbutz and an Ashkenazi elite. Labour's anti-religious ethos and patronising attitude were not appreciated. Israel, however, had changed. Many treated Likud's admonition that four years of Likud rule were not sufficient to reverse thirty years of Labour misrule with the utmost credibility. Labour's slogan, 'Anyone but the Likud', had completely backfired. Most Mizrahi voters remained with the Likud in 1981. The Likud victory in 1977 was no flash in the pan, and Begin was not a dyed-in-the-wool fascist as Labour had asserted.

Instead Begin was admired for his honesty, traditionalism and hard-line, but pragmatic policies. He had submitted an addition to Israel's basic laws which proclaimed a united Jerusalem as the capital of Israel. A few days before the election, Begin was supported by a vote of 10–6 in the bombing of the Osirak nuclear reactor in Iraq, but Dayan, Weizmann and Yadin were opposed.

Yet there were many within Herut who still were unhappy with the after-effects of Begin's pragmatism. The agreement to evacuate Yamit and leave Sinai was unacceptable to both Moshe Arens and Yitzhak Shamir. They therefore rejected the office of minister of defence when it was offered to them because this was one ideological bridge that they would not be able to cross. Despite many warnings against the appointment and his own reservations, Menahem Begin offered the post to Arik Sharon.

Sharon quickly developed a new military doctrine. He forced out many senior officers and began to neutralise the IDF's traditional strategy of defence – a question of self-restraint, havlagah – and to replace it with an offensive approach. This mirrored Begin's own belief in military Zionism from the 1930s onwards and his own interpretation of the meaning of Jabotinsky's 'Iron Wall'.

In essence, Begin believed in taking the military initiative before it was too late. He had advocated an attack after the formation of a joint military command by Egypt, Jordan and Syria in October 1956. He had argued for an attack in 1967 following the assaults on the Jordanian and Syrian borders. He also believed in pressing for military advantage when Arab states were in a vulnerable position, such as following the assassination of King Abdullah in 1951. In an address to the Herut Centre in March 1967, he said, 'It is your right not merely to repulse the aggressor but also to attack him.' The Herut leadership baulked at authorising the release of this statement.[29] Many Israelis, however, believed that war was essentially a last resort and not a means to change the political order when the state's existence was not in danger. Herut favoured deadly campaigns to eliminate an enemy rather than a tit-for-tat reprisal to deter terrorists. Reprisals, it was argued, were often ineffective in the long run.

In an address to the National Security College in August 1982, Begin said that his security strategy had not changed since the Irgun campaign to capture Jaffa in 1948. It was better to attack than to await attack – a modern-day enactment of the much quoted Talmudic adage 'If someone comes to kill you, rise up so as to kill him'.[30] Begin argued that World War II could have been averted if France had attacked Germany in March 1936 when Hitler entered the Rhineland.

In the case of Lebanon, the growing danger of the PLO on the northern border of Israel, he stated, had necessitated the invasion. There were

[29] Menahem Begin, Address to the Herut Movement Centre, 23 March 1967, in Gad Barzilai, *Wars, Internal Conflict and Political Order: A Jewish Democracy in the Middle East* (New York, 1996), p. 64.

[30] Babylonian Talmud Sanhedrin 72a.

wars of no choice, such as those in 1948, 1970 (the War of Attrition) and 1973. There were also wars of choice, such as those in 1956 and 1967. The current war in Fatahland in Lebanon and against the PLO in Beirut was such a war of choice.

Begin had reiterated this point to Reagan that the war was essentially one of self-defence. It was also, however, a war for regime change in Lebanon and a new order in which the Christian Bashir Gemayel would rule as president as an ally of Jewish Israel. This desire for empowered Jews to help beleaguered Christians also related to Begin's tortuous odyssey through recent history. This in part also forged an alliance with Christian Evangelicals in the United States. The Moral Majority's Jerry Falwell was presented with 'the Order of Jabotinsky' by Begin.[31]

In June 1981 a perplexed Yitzhak Rabin questioned Begin about a commitment that he had given to the Phalange that the Israel Air Force would be placed on alert if the Phalangists were attacked by the Syrian Air Force.

Begin's return to the populism of the 1950s also indicated a diminishing degree of tolerance for his opponents. Critics were deemed unpatriotic. This lack of respect for different views found its echo in the election campaign of 1981 when Shimon Peres's speeches were regularly disrupted. Peres was depicted as a wheeler-dealer and made responsible for Mapai's past misdemeanours. The Likud slogan was 'Don't trust Shimon Peres'. The 'back to basics' approach was pointedly demonstrated during the controversial invasion of Lebanon in 1982.

At the beginning of the hostilities, the public and the opposition Labour party supported the war, but the government diverged from its stated aims and its official pronouncements did not match the reality on the ground. The sense of duplicity and disarray polarised views such that any consensus began to evaporate. Soon there was no middle ground.

The Likud responded to criticism with vitriol and passion. As Labour's Abba Eban, a defender of liberal values and practitioner of language, wrote:

There is a new vocabulary with special verbs 'to pound', 'to crush', 'to liquidate', 'to eradicate all to the last man', 'to cleanse', 'to fumigate', 'to solve by other means', 'not to put up with', 'to mean business', 'to wipe out'.

It is hard to say what the effects of this lexicon will be as it resounds in an endless and squalid rhythm from one day to the next. Not one word of humility, compassion or restraint has come from the Israel government in many weeks,

---

[31] *Hadashot*, 8 March 1985.

nothing but the rhetoric of self-assertion, the hubris that the Greeks saw as the gravest danger to a man's fate.[32]

The Peace Now movement, which had organised opposition to the war, was regarded as a fifth column, with hints that it was funded by foreign agencies. Begin compared its activities in stimulating discussion within the IDF to that of Bolshevik agitation within the Tsarist army in 1917 in order to undermine the war effort.

Begin's repeated use of the past and in particular the Shoah served to fortify opposition:

If in World War II, Adolf Hitler had taken shelter in some apartments along with a score of innocent civilians, nobody would have had any compunction about shelling the apartment even if it had endangered the lives of the innocent as well.[33]

Begin viewed the Lebanese Christians as reliable partners with a shared religious tradition who challenged the dominance of an all-Arab Middle East. He envisaged that once Sharon had finally defeated the PLO in Beirut and forced Arafat to leave, they would bring stability to Lebanon. A formal peace treaty with Lebanon would be followed by 'a free confederation between western Eretz Israel and eastern TransJordan'. Begin therefore did not authorise the IDF to leave Lebanon immediately. Instead the IDF was pulled down further into the Lebanese quicksand.

The Christian Phalangist leader and newly appointed president of Lebanon, Bashir Gemayel, however, was assassinated. The Phalangists were therefore in no mood to exude Christian virtues. Instead they went into the camps of Sabra and Shatilla, which housed several thousand Palestinians, to exact revenge. Operation Iron Mind was supposed to be the Phalangist sweep for terrorists. It resulted instead in the killing of hundreds of Palestinian civilians, while Israeli soldiers stood guard outside unaware of what was happening within.

This became Begin's Holocaust nightmare. Sharon had allowed the Phalangists to go into the camps under IDF supervision. The IDF bore indirect responsibility. In his testimony to the Kahan Commission, Begin said that he did not believe that an atrocity would be committed even though David Levy had warned him beforehand.

With the death of his wife, a growing realisation of the folly of the war and a deepening perception that he had been deceived by Sharon, Menahem Begin resigned and faded away. The achievement of Camp

---

[32] *Jerusalem Post*, 8 August 1982.
[33] *Jerusalem Post*, 15 June 1982.

David was juxtaposed with the debacle in Lebanon. While members of the Right deeply loved him and were grateful to him for having brought them to power, the Left in the early 1980s truly detested him. A kibbutznik whose family had also emigrated from Poland and who had lost his son in the ill-fated war in Lebanon wrote to Begin:

Remember: the history of our ancient people will judge you with whips and scorpions and your deeds will be a warning and a verdict for generations to come.

And if you have a spark of conscience and humanity within you, may my great pain – the suffering of a father in Israel whose entire world has been destroyed – pursue you forever, during your sleeping hours and when you are awake. May it be a mark of Cain upon you for all time.[34]

---

[34] *Ha'aretz*, 5 July 1982.

17

The Permanent Revolution

Under his successor, Yitzhak Shamir, the former head of operations of Lehi, Israel took forward the legacy of Menahem Begin. Shamir's public image was characterised as a safe pair of hands, emerging from Begin's giant shadow. In the 1984 election he was depicted as tough and silent:

Israel's friends respect him, Israel's enemies fear him ... his pleasant smile hides an iron will. Pressures won't bend him. He has a heart to feel with, a mind to judge with and a hand to act with.[1]

Shamir himself commented that he had been chosen 'not to succeed [Begin] but to follow him'.[2] Yet the colourless Shamir had none of the charisma, political sensitivity or sense of drama which his predecessor had evoked. He exhibited a profound disdain for the intelligentsia and was reticent about initiating any move towards peace. He had abstained in the vote in support of the Camp David Accord. Indeed, he said that he would have resisted pressure during the Camp David negotiations for a much longer period than Menahem Begin. He clearly believed that Begin had compromised in agreeing to evacuate Sinai. There was no sense of innovation in his political approach and he preferred to stonewall.

Even though Shamir was seemingly even more dogmatic than Begin and impervious to the allure of compromise, a plethora of Far Right parties emerged as an ideological response to the Camp David Accord. The

[1] Nurit Gertz, 'Propaganda Style of Election Ads from 1977 to 1984', in Asher Arian and Michal Shamir, eds., *The Elections in Israel, 1984* (Oxford, 1986), p. 217.
[2] Yitzhak Shamir, *Summing Up* (London, 1994), p. 144.

combined number of seats for Labour and Likud decreased in elections in the 1980s – ninety-five (1981), eighty-five (1984), seventy-nine (1988) and seventy-six (1992).

The Far Right Tehiyah believed that Begin's proposal for individual autonomy would result in Palestinian sovereignty and not Israeli sovereignty over the West Bank. It also wanted a revision of the peace treaty with Egypt and a halt called to the proposed dismantling of the settlement of Yamit in Sinai. The NRP demanded legislation preventing the evacuation of settlements on the West Bank and on the Golan Heights.

The election of Meir Kahane's Kach in 1984 was perhaps symbolic of the dramatic changes that were taking place on the wilder fringes of the religious Right. Kahane had labelled Begin 'a traitor' after Camp David.[3] During the evacuation of the settlers at Yamit in Sinai, Kahane's followers threatened a mass suicide in imitation of the legendary suicides at Masada some 2,000 years before when Jewish Zealots were surrounded by the legions of Rome. Kach advocated a show trial of the mayor of Hebron and organised demonstrations to urge the Arabs to emigrate. Kach appealed to the poorest and most disaffected elements in Israeli society, mirroring the European Far Right. Kahane regarded democracy as a distinctly un-Jewish concept. Even so, he was elected to the Knesset by more than 26,000 votes in 1984. During the previous election his party had barely mustered 5,000 votes. Many had suffered from the cutbacks and unemployment which resulted from Aridor's economic policies.[4] Kahane's Kach attracted votes not only from the alienated and disenfranchised, but also from a considerable number of youth in the army who had had to deal with the aftermath of the war in Lebanon. They indicated their disillusionment with organised politics by voting for Kahane. A poll for the Van Leer Institute in 1985 indicated that Kahane's ideas were attractive to more than 40 percent of Israeli youth.[5]

Some sections of the religious Right did not shrink from using violent methods to attain their spiritual aim. The attempt to destroy the Dome of the Rock mosque on the Temple Mount by two members of Gush Emunim was also a reaction to the Camp David Accord. The Jewish underground in the early 1980s, which committed acts of terror against Palestinian mayors as well as killing students at the Islamic College in Hebron, was

[3] *Yediot Aharanot*, 21 January 1981.
[4] *Davar*, 2 June 1985.
[5] *Ha'aretz*, 6 June 1985.

FIGURE 18. Meir Kahane making a speech in the Knesset (1980s).
Photo: Ya'akov Sa'ar; courtesy of the Israel Government Press Office, Tel Aviv.

composed of young people who were close to the leadership of Gush Emunim or had studied at the Merkaz HaRav yeshivah. Yehudah Etzion was the guiding light of many of these attempts which further radicalised religious attitudes towards the state per se.[6] Unlike Zvi Yehudah Kook, he did not accept the sanctity of the state.[7] Etzion significantly had been influenced by the writings of a former Lehi member, Shabtai Ben-Dov, who in turn had been inspired by the poetry of Uri Zvi Greenberg.[8]

Moreover, these actions were given halakhic approval by Moshe Levinger.[9] Like Meir Kahane, Etzion argued that after the Camp David agreement, the State of Israel was not moving towards redemption. It even allowed the Dome of the Rock mosque to continue to exist on the Temple Mount, and it should therefore be removed.

[6] Ehud Sprinzak, *The Ascendance of Israel's Radical Right* (Oxford, 1991), pp. 94–99.
[7] Eliezer Don-Yehiya, 'The Book and the Sword: The Nationalist Yeshivot and Political Radicalism', in Martin E. Marty and R. Scott Appleby, eds., *Accounting for Fundamentalism*, vol. 4 (Chicago, 1993), pp. 280–81.
[8] Colin Shindler, *Israel, Likud and the Zionist Dream: Power, Politics and Ideology from Begin to Netanyahu* (London, 1995), pp. 194–200.
[9] Ibid., p. 156.

The advocacy of the voluntary – and involuntary – transfer of the Arab population of Israel was mooted in the 1930s. Shamir's Lehi and its political successor in the first Knesset, the Fighters' party, had advocated population exchange between Arabs in Palestine and Jews in the Arab states. Kahane resurrected it in the 1980s as a religious obligation in order to bring about redemption more speedily. Rehavam Ze'evi's party, Moledet, advocated it in the 1988 election and thereby secured two seats. Opinion polls suggested that a large number of Israelis thought that it would resolve the intractable Israel-Palestine conflict. But when asked if they also believed that it was feasible, a huge majority responded in the negative.

In the 1980s the parties of the Far Right, such as Tehiyah, Tsomet and Moledet, emerged out of both the Likud and Labour. The parties of the religious Right, such as Morashah, similarly emerged from the NRP. Its electoral list in 1984 was drawn from the Zionist Matzad – a breakaway from the NRP – and the non-Zionist haredi party, Poalei Agudat Yisrael, which possessed several kibbutzim. Mixed religious-secular parties such as Tehiyah attracted votes from both the Likud and the NRP. They were also joined by an ethno-nationalist party, the Mizrahi Shas, which had split from the Ashkenazi-dominated Agudat Yisrael. In the next election in 1988 there was a further split due to the secession of Degel ha-Torah, the mitnagdic opposition to hassidic Judaism within Agudat Yisrael.

The clear ideological boundaries clarifying Left from Right, secular from religious, Zionist from non-Zionist had partially dissolved in the post-Begin era. The gradual atomisation of what had been essentially a two-party system – 95 out of 120 seats were held by the Likud and Labour in 1981 – brought a growing identification of these new parties with the Right, and not with the Left. This was demonstrated clearly when the centrist Kadima gained the most seats in the election of 2009, yet was unable to form a government despite weeks of trying. The religious, ethno-nationalists and Far Right parties felt far more comfortable with Netanyahu's Likud. Shas certainly was unhappy with the idea that a woman, Tsipi Livni, might become prime minister and instruct the party. Even the fallback position of forming a rotational government with the Likud fell on deaf ears.

In part voting intention now began to express itself through the politics of identity rather than the politics of ideology as understood previously. The Israeli sociologist Baruch Kimmerling explained this development in the 1980s, not with the labels of the conventional Right and Left, but in terms of a 'primordial' identity constituting religious and nationalist orientations and a 'civil' identity which invoked universalism and the rights of the citizen.[10] This developed into an alliance of interests between the religious, ethno-nationalists and Far Right which looked to the Likud for leadership against a secular liberal discourse of the broad Left. The old idea of a melting-pot philosophy which characterised the early years of the state was laid to rest.

The reaction to the armed struggle of the Palestinians fortified the Right in its expansion and its aspirations. Arafat's leadership of Fatah in the 1980s veered between the path of diplomacy and the use of the Kalashnikov. When acts of terror were committed in the later part of the 1980s – usually by other Palestinian groups – the Right blamed Fatah. Any outbreak of violence moved the Israeli electorate in the direction of the Likud and parties further to the right to act as uncompromising protectors of the Jews. Thus the onset of the First Intifada produced a clear-cut Likud victory in the election of 1988. The bus bombings by Hamas in 1996 overturned Labour's huge lead and secured the election of the Likud's Binyamin Netanyahu. The introduction of suicide bombers by the Islamists into the al-Aqsa Intifada similarly cemented the election in 2001 of the Likud's Ariel Sharon, who shortly before had been regarded as yesterday's man.

In the wake of a series of Likud-led governments of the Right, the number of settlements on the West Bank increased apace. By 2015 almost 400,000 Jews lived on the West Bank. Yet opinion polls regularly indicated that a majority of Israelis did not ideologically agree with the settlers and wished for a way out of the quagmire – a withdrawal that would both preserve Israel's security and bring their sons and daughters home. Yet this wish became secondary to the need for protection by a succession of governments which regarded the struggle against Palestinian nationalism as not having ended in 1948. Thus a plethora of Israeli parties which deeply believed in the ongoing Jewish settlement of the West Bank were elected by an electorate which did not, but regarded it as the price to pay for security and protection. These parties in turn constituted a coalition, led by the Likud, which displaced Labour as the natural leading party of government.

By 1988 Herut and the Liberals finally gave up their individual structures. The Likud became one party rather than a political alliance

---

[10] Baruch Kimmerling, 'Between the Primordial and the Civil Definitions of the Collective Identity: Eretz Israel or the State of Israel', in Eric Cohen, Moshe Lissak and Uri Almagor, eds., *Comparative Social Dynamics* (Boulder, CO, 1986), pp. 262–83.

between two parties. Leading members of what had been the State List and Tami all became members of the new Likud. Despite this, its number of seats continued to diminish with each election, and it therefore became dependent on the Far Right to form a coalition to govern.

For the first time, the non-Zionist religious parties in the 1980s actually gained more seats than the religious Zionists. Moreover, together the religious parties held the balance of power in the new Knesset. Significantly Shimon Peres now approached Shas's Ovadiah Yosef and other rabbis in the hope of mitigating Labour's secular image.

Following the results of the 1984 election, an unholy alliance of Labour and the Likud constituted the nucleus of government. Such a coalition would have been unacceptable in Labour ranks before 1977. Yet ten years later it had become the mainstay of government in Israel. In part it reflected Labour's diminishing status and a public fatalism that the conflict with the Palestinians was seemingly eternal.

The First Intifada, an eruption of Palestinian civil resistance without bullets and bombs, at the end of 1987 certainly communicated a political message to the Israeli public. The Likud considered the Intifada more a military problem than a political one. It opposed an international peace conference and suggested further negotiations on autonomy. Labour, on the other hand, began to understand that military force did not solely solve a political question. Moreover, King Hussein's announcement that he was abandoning any responsibility for the West Bank meant the death knell for Labour's cherished Allon Plan. This coupled with Arafat's ambiguous embrace of UN Resolution 181, proclaiming the existence of two states in Palestine, propelled the PLO into the political arena as a credible player.

These developments moved Labour towards accepting the possibility of negotiations with the PLO and consideration of the very idea of a Palestinian state. On Labour's left, those who dissented from Labour's policies in working with the Likud in government coalesced as Meretz.

The Far Right, on the other hand, opposed all such developments and just wanted more settlements. Moledet, which emanated from a Labour background, preached the voluntary transfer of Arabs from Palestine. Moledet had taken over from the now-banned Kach in promoting this policy, although Kahane was never squeamish about advocating involuntary transfer. While Kach, Moledet and Tehiyah were clearly on the political fringe, they all eventually won election to the Knesset.

Meir Kahane's killing in New York in 1990 did not lead to the extinction of his philosophy of catastrophic Zionism. Baruch Goldstein, who had been a member of Kahane's Jewish Defense League in the United States, killed worshippers at the Hebron mosque in February 1994 – before being beaten to death. Kahane's son and a younger group of followers established Kahane Hai, which in turn inspired the Hilltop Youth of the twenty-first century to erect makeshift unauthorised outposts on the West Bank. Some of Kahane's closest followers, such as Baruch Marzel and Michael Ben-Ari, followed the parliamentary road. Ben-Ari was elected to the Knesset for the National Union in 2009.

In 1990 the differing interpretations of the evolving political situation led to a breakdown of the Likud-Labour coalition. The Shamir government fell due to the absence of several haredi MKs absenting themselves from the Knesset vote. The haredi MKs were not a homogeneous political group. They consisted of the territorially expansionist Lubavich and the 'dovish' Degel ha-Torah. The Lubavicher Rebbe ordered two MKs to withdraw from supporting Peres. Degel ha-Torah did not believe that the Land of Israel was intrinsically holy. It did not matter where you lived. Their spiritual mentor, Rabbi Eliezer Schach, moreover, opposed the concentration of Jews in any one location. Schach, however, was critical of the secularism of the Labour party. Shas's Rabbi Ovadiah Yosef broadly followed Schach's line. Yosef believed that in the final analysis, Israel would acquire the territory it had been promised, even if in the interim compromises had to be made. Shas, having ousted Shamir, was now about to restore him to power in place of the expectant Labour party.

Shimon Peres's negotiations ended in the dead-end street of byzantine haredi politics. It did not lead to a Labour government, as predicted by most observers, but to a repetition, in a sense, of the scenario of 1981 when a pragmatic administration was replaced by a more radical one.

In 1990 the Likud-Labour coalition was replaced by a Centre Right–Far Right coalition.[11] The three Far Right parties, Tehiyah, Tsomet and Moledet, together held seven seats. In February 1991 Moledet was co-opted into government. It was no longer regarded as being outside the parameters of political respectability.

Yitzhak Shamir had to balance prime ministerial responsibility and pragmatism with his own ideological beliefs in retaining all of the West Bank and Gaza while expanding the settlements. Within the Likud, he was continually harassed by a resurrected Ariel Sharon, who became the

---

[11] Allan Metz, 'Israel, the Religious Parties, the Coalition Negotiations of March–June 1990 and Beyond', *New Political Science*, vol. 11, no. 1–2 (1992), pp. 117–35.

standard bearer for the party's right wing. During the 1988–1990 government, Shamir was torn between working with Labour and the demands
of his own party activists. During the 1990–1992 government, Shamir
was seen as a virtual centrist. Indeed, he described Tehiyah, Tsomet and
Moledet as 'blinded by their own extremism'.[12] Shamir was simultaneously confronted by the demands of Sharon within the Likud and the Far
Right parties outside it which opposed any meaningful negotiations with
the Palestinians; in addition, he had to cope with the frustrations of the
Americans who were strongly pressing for negotiations.

In 1991 Shamir grudgingly attended the Madrid peace conference.
Tehiyah and Moledet left the coalition in January 1992 because they
believed that too many concessions had been conceded to the Palestinians.

The tired electorate in 1992 was looking for a problem solver in the
wake of the First Intifada and Shamir's stationary policies. Shamir fell
back on the traditional ideology of the Likud and the territorial integrity
of the Land of Israel. The Israeli public, however, was not in a responsive
mood. Moreover, many Likud voters were discouraged from supporting Shamir once again by allegations of corruption, high unemployment
and the nihilistic odour of contemporary politics. There were also a large
number of new voters as well as some 260,000 immigrants from the
former Soviet Union. On election day, the voters found their saviour in
Yitzhak Rabin, who had finally overcome Shimon Peres to reclaim the
leadership of the Labour party in February 1992.

This was conveyed on a national level by the slogan 'Israel is waiting
for Rabin' – a subtle reference to Rabin's military leadership during the
Six-Day War. There were five generals on the Labour list to underline the
party's commitment to security, while the party doves were instructed to
remain in the shadows. There were even respectful references to Menahem
Begin. Labour portrayed itself as the embryonic 'New Labour' without
any reference to socialism. The red flag had been jettisoned, and all election material was portrayed in national blue and white colours. This
attracted 47 percent of the vote of the newly arrived Russians, whose rec-
ollections of socialism in the former USSR were less than memorable.[13]
The party propaganda requested a vote for the Labour party 'headed
by Yitzhak Rabin'. While there was no mention of territorial compromise in the election material, Rabin promised territorial compromise and

---

[12] Shamir, *Summing Up*, p. 249.
[13] Etta Bick, 'Sectarian Party Politics in Israel: The Case of Yisrael B'Aliyah, the Russian Immigrant Party', *Israel Affairs*, vol. 4, no. 1 (1997): pp. 121–45.

elections on the West Bank nine months after the election. He also promised to end 'political settlements' in the territories.

In 1992 the threshold for representation in the Knesset had been raised to 1.5 percent, and only ten lists were able to meet it. The fragmentation of the right-wing vote meant that on this occasion several lists were actually wasted votes since they could not reach the required threshold. This allowed Labour to emerge as the leading party. Despite the fact that an alliance of the Far Right, Mizrahim, haredim and NRP supported Shamir's candidacy, together they could not assemble a blocking majority of sixty-one in the Knesset. This permitted Rabin to take power in a coalition with the enthusiastic Meretz and the reticent Shas – with the silent extra-governmental support of the Arab parties in any Knesset vote.

NETANYAHU AND THE TRANSFORMATION OF THE LIKUD

The signing of the Oslo Accord on the White House lawn in September 1993 was lauded in the United States and in the West in general as a tremendous breakthrough. In Israel and in Palestine, both Rabin and Arafat faced divided houses and angry accusations of betrayal. The Knesset vote was 61 for, 50 against, 8 abstentions.

Oslo forced a split within the Likud. There were ideological purists who opposed any sort of compromise, while others entertained the hitherto heretical idea of negotiating with the PLO. The new leader of the Likud, Binyamin Netanyahu, took a middle path. Netanyahu and Sharon argued that the Likud now had to adapt to the reality in the post-Oslo era. Netanyahu's task was to prevent the wide coalition, forged by Menahem Begin, from further unravelling.

He was aided by widespread popular opposition, led mainly by Labour hawks, to any return of the Golan Heights to Syria. Unlike Sadat and King Hussein, Israelis were highly suspicious of Arafat and were perturbed by the ambivalence of his comments. Likud therefore stressed the unreliability of the PLO and the need for security.

The religious parties were irrevocably opposed to the Oslo process. Shas, which wished to remain in government, abstained on the Oslo vote. It was torn between the dovish inclinations of its spiritual mentor, Ovadiah Yosef, and its hawkish constituency. There were Shas demonstrations outside Yosef's home.

The opposition to the Oslo Accord by Palestinian Islamists mirrored the rejectionism of the Israeli Far Right and its allies. This Palestinian opposition led to acts of terror by Hamas and Islamic Jihad which polarised Israeli and Palestinian opinion. With each atrocity, Rabin's standing in the opinion polls plummeted and Netanyahu's ascended.

Rabin's answer to the introduction of suicide bombers into the Israel-Palestine conflict was to endorse the idea of separation through a security fence. The Likud opposed this because it did not want hard and fast borders delineated by any barrier. It would separate not only Palestinians from Israel, but also the West Bank settlers to the east. They would be outside the 'borders' of Israel. Netanyahu wanted a continuation of the blurring of the pre-1967 lines.

The Likud now began to coordinate and cooperate with the Far Right. The deepening fears over the Oslo Accord led to a demonisation of Rabin, especially through a poster campaign, depicting him sometimes as a Nazi in Gestapo uniform and at other times as an Arabophile dressed with a keffiyeh. Rabin's wife was compared to Clara Petrucci, Mussolini's mistress, who had met the same fate as the Italian dictator. The 'fascist' label was applied to Rabin himself, as the Israeli answer to Marshal Pétain, who had presided over the French capitulation to the Nazis. Netanyahu himself simply equated Rabin with the Romanian Stalinist Ceausescu.[14]

A few months after the signing of the Oslo Accord, many notable rabbis in the territories publicly opposed the agreement with a Declaration of the Rabbis of Judea, Samaria and Gaza. It argued that no part of the Land of Israel could be given over to either non-Jews or to Diaspora Jews. It implicitly challenged the legitimacy of Rabin's government to do so and evoked the necessity to move from halakhic theory to contemporary practice. The logic of *din rodef* – the 'law of the pursuer' – was raised within the realm of discussion and debate. This argued that any assailant who was ready to strike down a Jew should himself be struck down beforehand. At the same time, the Rabin government had agreed to arm the police force of the Palestine Authority. For many the prospect of a 'mortal danger' directed at Jews living on the West Bank was an emerging issue. It initiated a debate in which many rabbis did not intervene and unambiguously rule on the issue. In this fashion, a blurred context emerged which allowed an individual to translate theory into practice.[15]

The Far Right further propagated the idea that any government that handed back territory was illegitimate. Rabin and Peres, it was argued,

---

[14] *Ha'aretz*, 19 October 1995.
[15] Arye Naor, 'The Security Argument in the Territorial Debate in Israel: Rhetoric and Policy', *Israel Studies*, vol. 4, no. 2 (Autumn 1999), pp. 150–77.

had saved an already weakened Arafat due to his support for Saddam Hussein during the first Gulf War. The Likud's cooperation with the Far Right allowed such ideas and images to flow into the mainstream of Israeli political life. The Likud portrayed itself as the saviour of the nation. Yet following Rabin's assassination, the public perception was that the Likud had played a major role in whipping up the Far Right into a frenzy. Leah Rabin pointedly refused to greet Netanyahu at the funeral or to accept his condolences.

The Left unequivocally blamed the Right for forging the path that had led to the assassination. The writer Amos Elon, invoking the direction of Hebrew writing, commented that 'the bullets in Israel are always fired from right to left'.[16]

The Likud internal debate following the assassination was centred on the need to be pragmatic and not to be hemmed in by ideology. Dan Meridor, who had challenged Netanyahu's leadership in 1994, now defined the Likud as 'a liberal centrist movement'.[17]

In the run-up to the 1996 election – with the actions of Hamas's suicide bombings whittling away Peres's tremendous lead – Netanyahu announced that the Likud would neither reconquer Gaza nor abolish Palestinian autonomy. The sound bite in the past had been that Oslo was the Israeli equivalent of the 'peace in our time' pledge made at Munich in 1938. Netanyahu had originally wanted to establish a commission of enquiry into the entire Oslo process. Now the election slogan became 'Peace will prevail under Netanyahu'. This move towards the centre ground produced a recognition of the Oslo process in April 1996. Netanyahu remarked that concessions would inevitably have to be made. If necessary, he would even meet Arafat.[18]

There was less emphasis on ideology and a blurring of the differences between Labour and the Likud to secure the floating voters. It was 'Coca Cola versus Pepsi Cola'.[19] Moreover, Peres now announced that any final agreement with the Palestinians would be put to a national referendum by Labour.

---

[16] Ami Pedahzur and Arie Perliger, *Jewish Terrorism in Israel* (New York, 2011), pp. 98–110.

[17] Jonathan Mendilow, *Ideology, Party Change and Electoral Campaigns in Israel, 1965–2001* (New York, 2003), p. 176.

[18] *Ma'ariv*, 22 April 1996.

[19] Jonathan Mendilow, 'The Likud's Double Campaign: Between the Devil and the Deep Blue Sea', in Asher Arian and Michal Shamir, eds., *The Elections in Israel, 1996* (New York, 1999), p. 172.

However, Netanyahu's apparent volte-face was conditional and underpinned by an ideological reassurance. There was also an emphasis on the importance of a military presence in the West Bank rather than an endorsement of separation by a fence. The Likud also advocated the expansion of settlements to encircle Palestinian centres of population. Moreover, party leaders were decidedly hawkish when speaking to the party faithful, but 'pragmatic' when speaking publicly or to the media. The Likud platform for the 1996 election clearly stated that 'the right of the Jewish people to Eretz Israel is an eternal right that cannot be questioned'.

Unlike Begin and Shamir, Netanyahu promised allegiance to retaining 'the Land of Israel' – but not in its entirety. Any mention of 'wholeness' was omitted. The guiding principle for Netanyahu was not totally a matter of ideology, but one of reciprocity. Israel would respond to a Palestinian negative action by a punitive action against Palestinian interests – more often than not, the announcement of an expansion of an existing settlement. In one sense this had originated under Shamir in the 1980s when the 'peace for peace' slogan was initiated to rival the Left's 'land for peace' mantra. This tit-for-tat approach led to a general stagnation in meaningful political negotiations and too few Israeli initiatives to break the logjam.

The emphasis moved from opposition to any withdrawal from territory to a focus on security. The idea that settlements provided strategic depth was much more amenable to the Israeli public than ideological fidelity to the borders of either the British Mandate or the Bible. Thus while Netanyahu proclaimed the consensual 'no division of Jerusalem' and 'no retreat to the 1967 borders', he was willing to hand back a large part of the West Bank in the Wye Plantation negotiations. Moreover, he did not seemingly negate the possibility of Palestinian sovereignty in the West Bank.

Netanyahu had achieved great success during his tenure in the United States in the 1980s. He became a favoured and eloquent exponent of Israel's case in the American media. He was lauded as 'the Abba Eban of the CNN era'. The emphasis on *hasbarah* (explanation), however, merged with *ta'amulah* (propaganda). Netanyahu believed deeply in public relations as a means of combatting the exposition of the pro-Palestinian position in the media. Public relations, however, was not public reality. Salesmanship was not the same as ideology. While this approach was successful in appealing to the Israeli public and to the Jewish Diaspora, it irritated the proponents of ideology on the right.

Netanyahu now attempted to overcome the Likud's diminishing number of seats by repeating Menahem Begin's tactic of forming a joint list with other parties, purely for electoral purposes. Thus in 1996 the Likud went into the election partnered with David Levy's Mizrahi grouping, Gesher, and Raful Eitan's Tsomet, whose members were often former members of the Labour party. In 1996 the socio-economic, ethnic and religious cleavages in Israeli society and their political representation became more important.

This was also the first election in which the electorate had two votes – one for the prime minister and one for the party. Thus Shas sympathisers could vote for the party as well as for Netanyahu. The Shas vote doubled in 1996. Whereas Labour (thirty-four) achieved more seats than the Likud (thirty-two), Netanyahu (50.5 percent) beat Peres (49.5 percent) by a sliver of 30,000 votes. Yet 150,000 voters refused to vote for either Netanyahu or Peres. The national religious and haredi parties both supported Netanyahu, as did the growing number of West Bank settlers. The Russians, who did not appreciate even the slightest whiff of socialism, given their experience in the Soviet Union, voted in excess of 70 percent for Netanyahu – well above the national average.[20]

The new electoral system further fragmented the vote for the large parties since voting for the Likud and voting for Netanyahu were not synonymous. Under this quasi-presidential system of electing the prime minister, ideology was more readily shed for celebrity status and management ability. Moreover, smaller and often peripheral parties could put up candidates for the premiership and then wait to be bought off by either Labour or Likud to prevent any splitting of the vote for their own candidate. Thus both Gesher and Tsomet were offered safe positions on a joint list with the Likud in return for withdrawing their prime ministerial candidates.[21]

Netanyahu had to balance the demands of the ideologists, often the older generation, with the demands of those who wished to accept the post-Oslo reality. The Likud in power was obliged to undertake three withdrawals as phases towards a final status agreement.

The Likud's negotiating tactics were generally to continue Shamir's approach and stonewall. This was accentuated by Sharon's belief that no negotiations should take place while acts of violence – no matter the size

---

[20] Tamar Horowitz, 'Determining Factors of the Vote among Immigrants from the Former Soviet Union', in Arian and Shamir, eds., *The Elections in Israel, 1996*, p. 118.
[21] Mendilow, *Ideology, Party Change and Electoral Campaigns*, p. 166.

and significance of them – were taking place. In addition, the planning and implementation of the expansion of settlements – a central point of opposition for the Palestinians – proceeded apace. American demands for a settlement freeze to pave the way for negotiations were often resisted. U.S. statements concerning the need to preserve the territorial contiguity of any Palestinian entity were not treated seriously. All this led to a political stagnation in the negotiating process. Despite the eventual recognition of the Palestinian right to a state by both Sharon and Netanyahu, its authority would be geographically limited to an archipelago of population enclaves.

The Hebron agreement in 1997 and the Wye Plantation agreement in 1998, based on the second Israeli redeployment of troops, led to defections from the Likud. Seven government ministers absented themselves from the Knesset vote on the Wye Plantation agreement and only twenty-nine MKs from a coalition of sixty-six actually voted in favour. Netanyahu was denounced by Shamir, the settlers and the Far Right for agreeing to hand back territory. These defections led to a realignment within the Israeli Right.

Netanyahu's approach was 'Allon Plus', a redeployment within Hebron – an approach midway between ideology and pragmatism. Netanyahu's defeat by Ehud Barak in 1999 was also due in part to the defection of part of the Likud leadership because of personal antagonism towards Netanyahu – Benny Begin, Dan Meridor and David Levy all left the party. This produced further factionalism. Netanyahu was personally blamed for the defeat. A book published at the time carried the title *The Man Who Defeated Himself.*[22]

---

[22] Orly Azulay-Katz, *The Man Who Defeated Himself* (Tel Aviv, 1999).

18

The Resurrection of Sharon

Ariel Sharon's dramatic defeat of Ehud Barak in the election for prime minister in 2001 was a remarkable turnaround for the bête noir of Israeli politics. Sharon's military career and political odyssey had been characterised by controversy since the early 1950s.

Ben-Gurion, who had protected Sharon from his critics, asked him in November 1958, 'Have you weaned yourself of your off-putting proclivities for not telling the truth?' A sheepish Sharon assured Ben-Gurion that he had been cured of his addiction.[1] When Rabin took over as head of the IDF in 1964, at the behest of Ben-Gurion, he brought Sharon in from the cold. Rabin told him:

Your trouble is, though, that people tend to believe you're not a decent human being. I don't know you well enough to say, I want to promote you, but I've got to be sure that your accusers aren't right.[2]

Many recognised Sharon's abundant talents, but were perturbed by his deviousness. He had at various times been accused of insubordination, recklessness, manipulation, and disobedience, yet he was also a courageous commander on the battlefield who led by example. He was credited with having turned the tide during the Yom Kippur War. On the other hand, despite instructions not to enter the Mitla Pass during the Suez campaign in 1956, he did so, resulting in a quarter of all Israeli casualties taking place there. An official account of the 1973 Yom Kippur War

[1] David Landau, *Arik: The Life of Ariel Sharon* (New York, 2013), p. 49.
[2] Ibid., p. 53.

by the IDF's History Department in 2002 pointed to Sharon's violation of orders as the commander of the 143rd Division, and discussions were held to remove him.

His tarnished reputation in the 1960s emanated from a raid which took place on the village of Qibya on the night of 14–15 October 1953 and resulted in the deaths of scores of men, women and children.[3] The acting prime minister, Moshe Sharett, was given a version of Sharon's orders from which a sentence had apparently been deleted.[4] Upon discovering this, Sharett committed to the intimacy of his diary the words 'The forgery of the Qibya order: To kill and destroy – all know that he deceives the prime minister'. It was surmised that Sharon had been instructed to kill as many Arabs as possible without distinction between combatants and non-combatants.[5] There were even stories that when he was working for Haganah intelligence in the 1940s, he had no qualms about beating up members of the Irgun.[6]

He was hated by the Left and feared by the Right. Shamir spoke of his 'wilfulness and a disregard of accuracy'.[7] A one-time member of Mapai, he had moved to the right during the 1960s. He first joined the Liberals, then left to form his own party, Shlomzion, then dissolved it and joined Herut as the prelude to entering Begin's first government. The journalist Uzi Benziman entitled his biography of Ariel Sharon *He Doesn't Stop at Red Lights*.[8]

Following Ezer Weizmann's departure, both Shamir and Arens were reticent about taking the position of minister of defence for fear that they would become involved in the removal of settlers and settlements in Sinai. Sharon's remonstrations to Begin overcame the latter's reluctance to select him. Sharon was finally appointed to the post that he coveted despite warnings from Moshe Dayan and other members of the defence establishment. Dayan predicted that Sharon would entangle Israel in Lebanon.[9]

The PLO had ensconced itself militarily in 'Fatahland' on the Lebanese border with Israel. Cross-border attacks from a Lebanon still in disarray

[3] Benny Morris, *Israel's Border Wars, 1949–1956* (Oxford, 1993), pp. 244–48.

[4] Ibid., pp. 245–46 no. 84.

[5] Moshe Sharett, 'Diary Entry', 29 July 1954 *Yoman Ishi*, vol. 2 (Tel Aviv, 1978); 'The 1953 Qibya Raid Revisited: Excerpts from Moshe Sharett's Diaries', *Journal of Palestine Studies*, vol. 31, no. 4 (Summer 2002), pp. 77–98.

[6] Landau, *Arik*, pp. 8–9.

[7] Yitzhak Shamir, *Summing Up* (London, 1994), p. 135.

[8] Uzi Benziman, Ariel Sharon: He Doesn't Stop at Red Lights (Tel Aviv 1985).

[9] Avi Shilon, *Menachem Begin: A Life* (London, 2012), p. 357.

from a brutal civil war clearly worried Israel. Two plans for responding were envisaged:

Little Pines – a limited advance such that there would be no contact with the Syrians.

Big Pines – a cutting of the Damascus-Beirut Highway and collaboration with the Maronite Christians.

While Begin was sympathetic to the Big Pines plan, he could not implement it because of a concerted opposition within the cabinet as well as by the U.S. administration. Sharon, however, was determined to press ahead with a maximalist version of the plan and to rid Lebanon of the PLO.

Despite warnings from military intelligence that a clash with the Syrians could not be ruled out, Sharon believed that it could certainly be averted. The Syrians, he argued, would doubtlessly withdraw after being outflanked through the Shouf Mountains.

The entire Operation for Peace in Galilee was scheduled to last forty-eight hours, and the IDF would sweep an area no more than 40 kilometres north of the Israeli border. From the very beginning, this limit was violated, and it became clear that Operation Big Pines was being implemented instead. As the Israelis pushed deeper into Lebanon, they did indeed clash with the Syrians, who responded vociferously. Sharon's desire to defeat the PLO in Lebanon led to more and more deviations from the stated intentions of a forty-eight-hour 40-kilometre incursion.

The USSR threatened to intervene, and President Reagan demanded a ceasefire. Sharon, however, pressed on. Beirut airport was attacked, and the IDF advanced on the presidential palace. Many of these moves were made without cabinet approval and without Begin's knowledge.[10]

Begin's long-time belief in and unquestioning reliance on his military advisors had run their course. In this case he had allowed Sharon a full arena in which to manoeuvre, but the political fallout from a lack of firm control was seen as a mixture of incompetence and duplicity. Sharon wanted a quick, clear-cut victory without interference – and therefore the end justified the means.

The greater the public and international criticism of Sharon, the more Begin defended him. Begin told the Knesset session on 29 June 1982, 'Blessed is the state that has Arik Sharon as its Defence Minister'.[11] An increasing number of Israelis did not see it that way.

---

[10]   Arye Naor, *Begin ba-shilton: edut ishit* (Tel Aviv, 1993), pp. 286–87.
[11]   Ofer Grosbard, *Menahem Begin: deyokano shel manhig: biografyah* (Tel Aviv, 2006), p. 278.

Following American pressure on Begin, Sharon was told that he was no longer empowered to bombard Beirut. After months of fighting, most of the PLO finally left Beirut for Tunis while the Syrians redeployed to the Beqaa Valley.

Much to Begin's surprise, the Christian Maronites kept Israel at arm's-length and rejected any formal alliance. They preferred covert contacts instead. The Lebanon War effectively destroyed the idea of alliances between minorities in the Middle East. Above all, the massacre of civilians in the Sabra and Shatilla camps at the end of the war by the Phalangists caused outrage in Israel and internationally. President Navon demanded a commission of inquiry and threatened to resign if there was not.

The Kahan Commission duly reported in 1983. It found Sharon to have been 'negligent' and recommended that he not serve as minister of defence. Sharon accused Begin of 'handing him over' just as members of the Irgun had been handed over to the British by the Haganah during the saison.[12] Begin, however, did not dismiss Sharon from government but instead appointed him a minister without portfolio. Moshe Arens became minister of defence and ordered the IDF to prepare for a withdrawal. Even the Israel ambassador to the UK, Shlomo Argov, whose attempted assassination had sparked this ill-conceived invasion, criticised the war in Lebanon from his hospital bed.

At the beginning of the war, almost 80 percent of MKs supported the operation. As it unfolded, there was first silence and then outright opposition from the Left. An angry protest spread from the Far Left towards the political centre. Even soldiers in uniform were present at the ever-growing demonstrations. They appeared on television singing:

> Airplane, airplane, come on down
> Take us off to Lebanon
> There we'll fight for Arik Sharon
> And return home in a coffin.[13]

'Raful' Eitan, head of the IDF, was disparagingly referred to as the 'Professor of Truth Sciences'.

After the killings in the Sabra and Shatilla camps, even Labour finally abandoned the consensus position of support which was usual in times of war. It gradually dawned on the Israeli public in general that the war a mistake and a disaster. No songs were written about that war. The Lebanon War was increasingly seen as Israel's 'Vietnam' and the killings

---

[12] Landau, *Arik*, p. 218.
[13] *Yediot Aharanot*, 6 June 1985.

at Sabra and Shatilla as its 'My Lai massacre'. Although the scenarios were considerably different, the public reaction to such events was similar.

Begin eventually resigned and withdrew almost totally from public life. For those who had opposed the war, Sharon truly became a figure of hate:

Born of the ambition of one wilful, reckless man, Israel's 1982 invasion of Lebanon was anchored in delusion, propelled by deceit and bound to end in calamity. It was a war for whose meagre gains Israel has paid an enormous price that has yet to be altogether reckoned.[14]

Moreover, the cost of the war was estimated at $5 billion by a leading Israeli economist.[15] Yet within twenty years all this was forgotten. Sharon had become the wise elder statesman, the decisive leader who would protect Israelis from the suicide bombers of Hamas and take the war to the very doors of Arafat's palace.

Throughout the tenures of both Shamir and Netanyahu, Sharon resurrected himself as the standard bearer of the Israeli Right from within the Likud. Indeed, if Sharon had won another fifty-four votes in the internal party voting, he would have become the Likud candidate in the general election of 1984.

In 1985 as minister of commerce and industry, he recommended bombing 'terrorist bases in Jordan'.[16] Moreover, any moves that even remotely hinted of compromise, such as attending the Madrid conference in 1991 or signing the Hebron agreement of 1997, were vigorously opposed by Sharon. He resigned publicly at a meeting of the Likud central committee over the question of a Palestinian state in February 1990.

During the first Gulf War, Sharon opposed Shamir's policy of self-restraint. Some thirty-nine Skud missiles hit Tel Aviv, Haifa and other cities. Sharon wanted the IDF to retaliate and to fly over Iraq – albeit without U.S. consent. He had antagonised the Bush White House and Secretary of State Baker refused to meet Sharon in Washington.

Following Begin's death in 1992, Sharon began to revise his past actions. He commented that he had regretted evacuating the Sinai settlements in 1981.[17] He remarked that Begin's idea of autonomy had been no more than a subterfuge to sign the peace treaty with Egypt.[18]

---

[14] Ze'ev Schiff and Ehud Ya'ari, *Israel's Lebanon War* (New York, 1984), p. 301.
[15] *Al Hamishmar*, 10 March 1986.
[16] *Hadashot*, 30 July 1985.
[17] *Ma'ariv*, 8 July 1994; 7 December 1997.
[18] Landau, *Arik*, p. 280.

On 5 October 1995, Sharon participated in the demonstration of the Far Right in which Rabin had been depicted as an SS officer. Sharon introduced the term 'collaborators' – he compared Rabin and Peres to Petain.[19] He said that the threats to assassinate Rabin were 'deliberate provocations', similar to those which Stalin had fabricated in order to eliminate his enemies.

For many Israeli politicians, positioning oneself on the right and attacking the leadership for indecision and weakness was often the path to ministerial office. Attaining office, however, brought responsibility, and more often than not, it led to political failure. Sharon, however, was no ordinary politician on his way up. It was not for nothing that he was labelled 'the bulldozer' – a man who seemingly had no doubts. Despite all the criticism and bitterness directed at him after the Lebanon War, Sharon was not the retiring type.

After the bus bombings in 1996, Sharon called for a government of national unity. He hoped that Netanyahu's victory in the 1996 election would return him to high office and effectively rehabilitate him. While he followed the party line and professed loyalty to Netanyahu, he was initially kept out of government. Netanyahu was eventually forced to appoint him minister for national infrastructure.

During this period, Sharon appeared to turn over a new leaf. His voice became more authoritative in the aftermath of the Rabin assassination, and he was consulted by both the Americans and the Jordanians. Sharon dined with King Hussein, entertained Mahmoud Abbas at his ranch and met President Clinton's envoy, Dennis Ross. This gradual transformation during Netanyahu's first administration was rewarded by his appointment as foreign minister in 1998.

As far as the Right was concerned, Sharon had an impeccable ideological background. He was credited with having translated the Right's desire to colonise the West Bank and Gaza into an ongoing enterprise during Begin's first administration. As early as September 1977, he stated:

If we want a strong independent state, we must give up settling just on the coastal strip and move elsewhere. Otherwise Israel would consist of a mass of concrete from Ashkelon to Nahariya, all within the range of Arab guns and having to rely on friendly powers for protection.[20]

In 1979 Sharon proposed the establishment of settlements along the mountain ridge on the West Bank to safeguard the coastal plain where most

[19] Ibid., p. 287; *Ha'aretz*, 6 October 1995.
[20] *Jerusalem Post*, 4 September 1977.

Jews lived. He argued for settlements to encircle Arab areas of Jerusalem and in the Jordan Valley to impede any invading army. Whichever post he held in government, it was always turned to accelerating the growth of the Jewish population in the West Bank. Sharon believed that Israel's victory in 1949 had not ended the conflict with the Palestinian Arabs. While tied neither to the ideology of the religious Zionists of the NRP nor to the nationalist zeal of Herut, Sharon fundamentally believed that territory would provide strategic depth and that settlements were a means of enhancing Israel's security. One explanation of the Yom Kippur War was that Israel had been saved from catastrophe because it possessed strategic depth due to the post-1967 borders. Indeed, he believed that if the IDF had been able to expel the PLO from Lebanon in 1982, its members would have gone to Jordan and re-created a Palestinian state there. At that time, Sharon propagated the belief that 'Jordan is Palestine'. Even so, if he uttered quasi-ideological comments occasionally to impress the faithful, he remained at heart a security hawk for whom Begin's ideological pronouncements were vacuous and unreal.

Sharon eventually became leader of the Likud in 1999 when he was in his early seventies, following Netanyahu's troubled tenure as prime minister. He was regarded as yesterday's man and a tainted hero who would never win a contest against the incumbent prime minister, Ehud Barak.

Netanyahu had stepped out of the political arena due to a bribery allegation. He was cleared in September 2000 and the path was open for his return to public life. Ehud Barak suddenly resigned to stand in a new election for prime minister. Only sitting MKs were eligible to run, but Netanyahu was not an MK. Even though a law was passed which would have permitted him to run, Netanyahu decided to stay out of the race.

The advent of the al-Aqsa Intifada changed the approach of the Israeli public towards Sharon, regardless of whether they believed that he had truly changed. The electors understood that only the menacing Sharon could put the fear of God into the hearts of the Palestinian suicide bombers. It was only Sharon who could confront the Islamists and protect the Jews.

Significantly during the election campaign, Sharon promised not to build any new settlements and even sent a goodwill message to Arafat on the id-al-Fiter holiday.[21]

Sharon's coming to power in 2001 had been due to deep disillusionment with the peace process. The Israeli public held Arafat responsible

---

[21] *Ma'ariv*, 5 January 2001.

for the outbreak of violence in 2000. Even before Barak met Arafat at Camp David, Shas, Yisrael B'Aliyah and the NRP all withdrew from his government. The rejections of Barak's offer at Camp David, the long list of reservations about the Clinton parameters and the stalemate during the Taba negotiations induced a lack of credibility in Arafat's policies. For many Israelis, the dream of Oslo was dead and buried – and replaced by the death and destruction wreaked by the Islamist suicide bombers. Sharon sealed the elimination of the Oslo peace process by disposing of other similar proposals. The Geneva initiative, the Ayalon-Nusseibeh discussions and the Saudi peace plan were later either ignored or circumvented by Sharon.

Sharon did not accept the idea of two territorially contiguous states, 'side by side'. His approach in the 1970s was that a Palestinian state was unnecessary because Jordan was in fact Palestine. This was replaced in the early 1990s by attempts to disrupt Palestinian territorial contiguity while urging the settlers to do the opposite in the West Bank.[22] Palestinian autonomy was to be reduced to a series of enclaves of population concentrations. In September 2001, now as prime minister, he moved to offer the Palestinians the possibility of establishing its own state – a segmented one and not a territorially contiguous one.

Initially Sharon believed that he could negotiate with Arafat. He sent his son, Omri, to meet Arafat and spoke to him by telephone. However, Arafat was caught in a vice between Sharon and his Islamist opponents. He prevaricated over a draft agreement on a proposed ceasefire and was suspected of giving a green light to suicide bombings within the Green Line.[23] Arafat further refused to arrest the assassins of Rehavam Ze'evi, and the Palestinian Authority had seemingly financed an arms ship, the *Karine A*. Despite the objections of Foreign Minister Shimon Peres, who believed that Arafat held the key to securing peace, this marked the beginning of eliminating Arafat from the political equation.

Sharon had already unleashed the full force of the IDF against the Palestinians. Following a suicide bombing in a Netanya shopping mall in May 2001, F-16s attacked security headquarters in Nablus and Ramallah. Islamist leaders were picked off, one after another, through targeted killings. This culminated in the assassination of Sheikh Yassin, the founder and spiritual mentor of Hamas, as well as his successor, Abdel Aziz al-Rantisi, shortly afterwards. Supported by George W. Bush in the White House,

---

[22] *Yediot Aharanot*, 7 August 1992.
[23] Landau, *Arik*, pp. 367–70.

Sharon isolated Arafat both militarily and politically. When Arafat died in 2004, the signing of the Oslo Accord on the White House lawn was a forgotten memory. All this was a far cry from Shimon Peres's promotion of 'a new Middle East'. Sharon was seen as forceful and decisive – someone who would not negotiate under duress. His standing amongst the Israeli public thereby allowed him to act in the political arena.

The surge of support for Sharon mirrored the decades-long decline of the Labour party. From forty-four seats in 1992 under Rabin, it had sunk to nineteen under Mitzna in 2003. Labour had become identified with the failed peace process and a perceived political naïveté – albeit in hindsight – in believing that peace could be attained. Labour had been led by generals since 1992 – Rabin, Barak, Ben-Eliezer, Mitzna. It did not matter; the Israeli electorate preferred Sharon in 2003.

Restoring the Likud to its pre-Netanyahu representation in the Knesset in the election of 2003, Sharon persuaded the Israeli cabinet to endorse the Quartet's Road Map albeit with a host of reservations. It was clear from the cabinet vote that the Likud was split.

At that time Sharon mentioned the term 'occupation' for the first time. He had already accepted the idea of a Palestinian state, fashioned on a series of enclaves of Palestinian population. Moreover, in June 2002, the cabinet had decided to build a security fence to impede the passage of suicide bombers into Israel. It also separated 24 percent of the West Bank settlers from Israel. This was Sharon's first break with the settlers.

He had begun to accept the demographic argument that Israel's democracy would be undermined by retaining the territories, given the higher birth rate of the Palestinians. Moreover, he was being outmanoeuvred by the detailed Geneva Initiative of Yossi Beilin and Mahmoud Abbas – a plan which had seemingly won favour in Washington. Sharon was also under increasing pressure from the Bush White House to move forward with the Quartet's Road Map.

His ally, Ehud Olmert, projected specific views on withdrawal from Gaza and the northern part of the West Bank in the Israeli press, which astonished readers.[24] A few weeks later, in December 2003, Sharon announced a unilateral withdrawal from Gaza and part of the West Bank. Sharon reasoned that this would divert American support into a channel which he would be able to control and direct. It would also buy Israel time by keeping any negotiating process in deep freeze.

---

[24] Ehud Olmert, Interview with David Landau, *Ha'aretz*, 14 November 2003; Interview with Nahum Barnea *Yediot Aharanot*, 5 December 2003.

In April 2004, there was an exchange of letters between Bush and Sharon. Bush refused to support the wholesale return of the Palestinian refugees and argued that the large settlement blocs close to the Green Line should remain part of Israel. A side letter between Sharon's lawyer and aide, Dov Weissglas, and Condoleezza Rice effectively legitimised settlement building within the construction line of the fence. It also agreed to the removal of unauthorised outposts 'within thirty days'. Sharon was even willing to initiate a freeze on settlement building.[25]

The prospect of evacuating the Gaza settlements was strongly opposed by the Far Right and by sections of Sharon's own party. Sharon was defeated in a vote on disengagement by Likud party members by a large margin. Sharon dismissed Yisrael Beinteinu's Avigdor Lieberman and the National Union's Benny Elon in order to secure a majority in the cabinet for his plan.

Netanyahu initially threatened a referendum; otherwise he would resign from government. Yet when he and his supporters realised that there was a majority in support of evacuation, they also voted in favour. Netanyahu eventually stayed in the cabinet on the basis that Arafat was dying and that this would create major changes in the Middle East.

Throughout his career, Sharon had always utilised ideology for his own purposes. He therefore turned to the comments and writings of Begin and Jabotinsky in support of his policy. He repeated Begin's characterisation of members of Gush Emunim after their opposition to the Camp David Accord as suffering from 'a messianic complex'. He also quoted from an article that Jabotinsky had written in 1915:

We have never seen a settlement as an end in and of itself. We have seen it as one of the most powerful means of state-oriented Zionism for achieving our sovereignty over the land of Israel. To us, a settlement has been precious as one of our finest cards in the statesmanship game of the future. But should this settlement suddenly become an impediment in the crucial statesmanship game – to this we shall not agree. A settlement is a means and no more than that.[26]

On 21 November 2005, Sharon sought the dissolution of the Knesset and then astonished the Israeli public by announcing that he was leaving the Likud to establish a new party to fight the forthcoming election. The Likud had always declared itself to be 'a national-liberal movement'. But Sharon now spoke about 'a new national liberal party'. The disengagement

[25] Yael S. Aronoff, 'From Warfare to Withdrawal: The Legacy of Ariel Sharon', *Israel Studies*, vol. 15, no. 2 (Summer 2010), pp. 14–172.

[26] Vladimir Jabotinsky, 'Tsurik Tsum Tsharter', *Di Tribune*, 15 October 1915.

from Gaza and the prospect of the evacuation of the settlements there separated the pragmatists from the ideologues in the Likud. Half the Likud
MKs left to join Sharon's new party, Kadima. Its election platform stated
that the 'Jewish people have a national and historic right to the Land
of Israel in its entirety', but that the demographic and security questions
necessitated compromise. While it attracted figures such as Ehud Olmert,
who had opposed Begin's ideological rigidity as far back as 1966 and had
been a member of the Free Centre, Shimon Peres left the labour movement for Kadima after nearly half a century. Both Peres and Sharon had a
common background in Mapai and in following Ben-Gurion's flexibility
in political choices.

It was, however, a risky move for Sharon. Centre parties in Israel had
historically failed unless there was a charismatic leader to rally around.
On this occasion, the gamble paid off. Despite Sharon's stroke, incapacitation and subsequent absence from the election campaign, Kadima
became the largest party, with twenty-nine seats. The Likud, however,
now once more under Netanyahu's leadership, was reduced to a mere
twelve seats – a far worse result than even Begin had realised for Herut
in 1949 during the first election in Israel. This appeared to be the final
unravelling of the grand coalition that Menahem Begin had established
over a thirty-year period.

Begin had always fought against the power of the Histadrut and ridiculed his Mapai opponents as posing as tribunes of the workers. This
resonated strongly with the Israeli underclass. Just before his election in
1977, he had commented that 'hegemony in Israel is not the hegemony of
the workers but hegemony over the workers.'[27]

This defence of the workers had all but disappeared with the development of a neo-liberal economy in Israel. The Histadrut was a shadow
of its former self. Israeli Labour had tried to move with the times and
tinkered around the edges, but it was Netanyahu's belief in a free market that characterised economic policy in Sharon's second government.
As minister of finance Netanyahu pushed ahead with developing a
trickle-down economy, a shrinking of the public sector and lower taxes
for the private sector. With Avigdor Lieberman as minister of transport,
Netanyahu privatised El Al and other forms of national transportation.
Such moves disillusioned traditional Likud voters and persuaded them to
vote for Arik Sharon.

---

[27] *Ma'ariv*, 20 June 1977, in Dani Filc, *The Political Right in Israel: Different Faces of Jewish Populism* (London, 2010), p. 27.

THE RETURN FROM THE MARGINS

The Far Right had made significant advances as the old century ended.[28] Tekumah was founded by the settlers in 1998, and such NRP leaders as Hanan Porat and Zvi Hendel defected to join it. Benny Begin resigned from the government and left the Likud. He founded the Herut party, which called for a total cessation of all discussions with Arafat and the PLO. Yitzhak Shamir also resigned from the party that he had led for almost a decade to join the new Herut. These Far Right parties, Moledet, Tekumah and Herut, then coalesced as the National Union. In the 1999 election, the National Union did well in the territories. It obtained more than 60 percent of the vote in locations such as Elon Moreh and Beit-El on the West Bank and Netzarim in Gaza.[29] Yet like Tehiyah in the 1980s, it appealed only to the faithful and fared poorly in Israel itself, winning only four seats.

The Ashkenazi haredim were also able to unite their warring factions, Agudat Yisrael and Degel ha-Torah into the United Torah Judaism (UTJ) party. In contrast Ovadiah Yosef could not be tempted to return to the UTJ due to the tremendous success of Shas in representing the Mizrahi constituency. In 1996 Netanyahu had called for the expansion of religious education. He also argued that yeshivah students should receive similar privileges to university students. He had been endorsed by the influential sage, the Lubavitcher Rebbe, who had coined the slogan 'Netanyahu is good for the Jews'. At the next election in 1999 the rebbe significantly refused to endorse Netanyahu since the Likud leader had negotiated away parts of the Land of Israel.

Yet UTJ still had its practical concerns. The high birth rate and lack of willingness to join the labour market meant impoverishment and limited living conditions for the haredim. In 2002, the haredim constituted 6 percent of Israel's Jews, but 18 percent of the births.[30]

In 1999 UTJ accepted a deputy ministry for the first time. This implied that it had not only entered a government but thereby also afforded some recognition of the authority of the state. Meir Porush became deputy minister for housing and proceeded to build homes for the haredim on

---

[28] Ami Pedahzur, 'Supporting Conditions for the Survival of Extreme Right-Wing Parties in Israel', *Mediterranean Politics*, vol. 5, no. 3 (Autumn 2000), pp. 1–30.

[29] *Ha'aretz*, 23 June 1999.

[30] Asher Cohen, 'The Religious Parties in the 2006 Election', in Shmuel Sandler, Manfred Gerstenfeld, and Jonathan Rynhold, eds., *Israel at the Polls, 2006* (London, 2008), p. 102.

the West Bank in locations such as Kiriat Sefer, even though ideologically they were not enthusiastic about settling in the territories.

Shas had undergone a similar process and drifted towards a more favourable policy on settlement even though Ovadiah Yosef had been perceived as a dove twenty years before when he argued that a withdrawal from territory was permissible if it saved lives. Shas had been part of Rabin's government, which signed the Oslo Accord and had even voted in favour of both the Hebron agreement and the Wye Plantation agreement. Yet most Shas voters possessed decidedly more hawkish views than its leadership. Only 18 percent supported the Oslo Accord, while 71 percent were opposed to the establishment of a Palestinian state.[31]

Shas further encouraged an anti-immigrant ethos which was directed at foreign workers in Israel. This xenophobic approach was particularly accentuated during the 1999 election campaign and was also directed at the influx of Jews from the former Soviet Union who were accused of importing criminality, alcoholism, prostitution and drug dealing into the country.[32]

In 1996 Avigdor Lieberman became director general of the Prime Minister's Office. In 1999 he established Yisrael Beiteinu as a hybrid party for both the Far Right and the hundreds of thousands of Russians who had emigrated to Israel in the 1990s. Yisrael Beiteinu developed into a party with a Russian-speaking constituency, but it went far beyond this to embrace veteran Israelis, newly arrived Ethiopians and many others who were attracted to its combination of anti-religious sectarianism and Far Right beliefs.

Yisrael Beiteinu also benefitted from opposition to the unilateral withdrawal from Gaza in the summer of 2005. Israelis opposed to Sharon's withdrawal found Yisrael Beiteinu a more congenial receptacle for their beliefs than the Likud, once more under Netanyahu's aegis. During the election of 2006 many Russians in the Likud and within the right wing generally transferred their political allegiance to Yisrael Beiteinu. The Russians – large numbers of whom had non-Jewish partners – were attracted by Yisrael Beiteinu's proposals for civil marriage and viewed the party as a bulwark against the political influence of the rabbis in Israeli society.

One innovation which found favour was a proposal to exchange Jewish territorial blocs on the West Bank for Arab-populated areas of Israel.

[31] Etta Bick, 'A Party in Decline: Shas in Israel's 2003 Elections', in Shmuel Sandler, M. Ben Mollow, and Jonathan Rynhold, eds., *Israel at the Polls, 2003* (London, 2005), p. 115.
[32] *Yediot Aharanot*, 6 May 1999.

FIGURE 19. Ariel Sharon in conversation with Avigdor Lieberman (early 2000s).
Photo: Moshe Milner; courtesy of the Israel Government Press Office, Tel Aviv.

Lieberman's proposal of redrawing the boundaries of both Israel and the Palestinian territories was popular with Israeli Jews, but strongly antagonised Israeli Arabs who had no desire to become part of the future state of Palestine.

The public demands of Israel's Arabs during the al-Aqsa Intifada eventually brought a backlash from the Israeli Right. The alienation of Israeli Arab intellectuals had produced 'The Future Vision of the Palestinian Arabs in Israel' in December 2006. This report had been sponsored by the National Committee for the Heads of the Arab Local Authorities in Israel and called for a consociational system/binational state.[33] Yisrael Beiteinu responded with a 'no loyalty, no citizenship' campaign. Israeli citizenship, the party argued, should be conditional on identification with democratic norms and service in the armed forces. This was aimed at both the Arabs and the haredim.

Lieberman undertook the role of populist leader while moving his party closer to the Centre Right. As the Likud had once labelled leaders of the Labour party 'kibbutz millionaires', the Kishinev-born Lieberman now termed the political establishment 'oligarchs'.

[33] *New York Times*, 8 February 2007.

Yisrael Beiteinu also benefitted from Hamas's ousting of Fatah from Gaza in 2007. In Gaza, long a stronghold of the Muslim Brotherhood, workshops were now established to develop more sophisticated missiles which could be fired at Israeli civilians. During Operation Cast Lead at the end of 2008, Lieberman argued that Israel had bowed under pressure and did not finish the task of destroying Hamas in Gaza. The vote for Yisrael Beiteinu increased by 40 percent in 2009. It had emerged as a major player in Israel politics – even centrist Kadima voters changed to Yisrael Beiteinu in the 2009 election.

Another feature of twenty-first-century politics was an emphasis on the coalescence of smaller parties for the purpose of elections. In addition, the Likud and Labour projected themselves as neo-centrist parties during election periods, stressing national unity. Thus Labour in 1999 stood as 'One Israel' as part of a list with the Mizrahi Gesher and the religious Meimad lists. In 2013, Netanyahu headed the joint Likud–Yisrael Beiteinu list. Although the two-vote system – for prime minister and for party – had been abandoned by Sharon, the electorate still refused to support Labour and the Likud. The days in which Labour and the Likud accounted for two-thirds of the Knesset seats were long past.

The growth of the Far Right, ethno-nationalist and religious parties made joint lists a necessity for the Likud so that it could become the largest group and then be called upon by the president to form a government. In 2009 the Likud won twenty-seven seats by itself, but as part of the joint list with Yisrael Beiteinu in 2013, it attained only twenty seats. The need to accommodate so many different interest groups produced a lack of direction and a blurred ideology. Menahem Begin projected himself as a strong leader with a strong ideological direction who could win elections. Netanyahu did not exude such a public persona and was seen as a manager of squabbling factions. This situation also mitigated against taking difficult decisions and initiating any meaningful processes affecting the peace process. The status quo, however, was safe and would ensure that any government coalition stayed intact. Moreover, it was argued that government stability – even at the expense of political immobility – was exactly what was needed while the storm of Islamism was blowing through the Middle East.

Yisrael Beiteinu emerged from an array of Far Right parties which were united by a refusal to give back territory but divided by a plethora of other issues. Even so, such parties often overcame their differences and formed joint electoral lists. Thus the National Union stood with Yisrael

Beiteinu in 2003 and with the NRP in 2006. In all, the new Russian electorate, which supported Yisrael Beiteinu in great numbers, could account for seventeen seats.

The election of 2009, which took place after Operation Cast Lead, starkly indicated the decline of the Israeli Left and the Labour party in particular. The centrist Kadima, Labour, Meretz and the Arab parties could muster a total of only fifty-five seats – short of the blocking majority of sixty-one. Labour under Ehud Barak had led to disillusionment and defection. It attained a mere fifteen mandates in 2009. It had been displaced by Kadima and was only the fourth-largest party in 2009. Ever since the formation of its predecessors – Poale Zion, Ahdut Ha'avodah, Mapai – during the early part of the twentieth century, Labour had been the central party of government or opposition, but no longer.

Likud, however, could count upon Yisrael Beiteinu, the National Union, NRP, Shas and the haredi United Torah Judaism to make up a total of sixty-five seats. So it did not matter whether Kadima emerged as the largest party – it did not have allies in sufficient numbers to produce a blocking majority.

Labour was seen as yesterday's party, rooted in the romanticism of the pioneering past and the idealism of Oslo. Yisrael Beiteinu was seen as the pragmatic face of tomorrow and Lieberman as a possible successor to Netanyahu.

THE NEW RIGHT

As Yisrael Beiteinu moved towards the Likud, the Far Right attempted to coalesce its forces, which accounted for up to twelve seats in the Knesset. In November 2008 the NRP, Moledet and Tekumah formed HaBayit Hayehudi (the Jewish Home). This cluster disintegrated virtually as soon as it was formed because various factions were dissatisfied with their places on the list of candidates for the 2009 election. HaBayit Hayehudi became little more than a revamped NRP.

Despite this, under the dynamic leadership of Naftali Bennett in the 2013 election, the party attained twelve seats – a return to the NRP's best days. Yet it did not reflect the NRP's position in the pre-Begin era before 1977, but continued to espouse a Far Right position, albeit with a modern face. Bennett, a high-tech entrepreneur, had been director general of Yesha, the settler's representative organisation before being elected by

HaBayit Hayehudi in 2012. The party continued to espouse the view of
Nahmanides, the medieval Talmudic commentator, that the Jews were
commanded to settle the Land of Israel and not to leave it in the hands of
others. The party's manifesto for the 2013 election stated:

We oppose the over-judicialisation of Israel ie the excessive intervention of the
Israeli Supreme Court and the State Attorney in the policymaking and spirit of
Israel. Furthermore it is our opinion that the Supreme Court has historically
been dominated for generations by a liberal-left and does not fairly represent the
Israeli public.

HaBayit Hayehudi wanted new legislation in the appointment of judges.

Despite a pact with the newly emergent centrist party, Yesh Atid, led
by Yair Lapid, to force the haredim to join both the labour force and
the army, HaBayit Hayehudi did not move towards the centre on the
issue of the West Bank settlements. It recognised the Palestinians only in
the sense that they had illegally lived on the Land in the absence of the
rightful owners – the Jewish people in exile. This sense of Palestinian ille-
gality mitigated against Netanyahu's government conducting meaningful
negotiations. By 2015, Naftali Bennett clearly believed that the process of
peacemaking had become meaningless and that direct annexation of the
West Bank was the only viable solution.

The Far Right also made some headway by operating within the Likud
itself. Those who had come from a traditional Irgun background and
revered the memory of Menahem Begin found themselves marginalised.
Benny Begin was unable to secure a reasonable position on the Likud
candidates' list for the election of 2013.

At the beginning of 2011, Avigdor Lieberman attacked numerous civil
liberties NGOs. He called for the establishment of a parliamentary commission of enquiry to investigate 'terror-aiding organisations'. This was
strongly opposed by members of the Likud, such as Dan Meridor and
Reuven Rivlin, who continued to support Menahem Begin's traditional
approach to the rule of law and freedom of debate. Lieberman attacked
them as 'traitors to the national camp'.[34] This episode symbolised the
growing division between those who had grown up in the shadow of
Jabotinsky's liberal nationalism and those who had not.

Moshe Feiglin, a founder of Zo Artzeinu, an extra-parliamentary
group of the Far Right, challenged Netanyahu for the Likud leadership in 2007. Like others on the right, he looked back to a time when

---

[34] *Jerusalem Post*, 11 January 2011.

ideological issues were clearer, free from the national claims of the Palestinians:

Back then, when we were sure of the justice of our cause, we demanded a Jewish state from the Jordan River to the sea.[35]

In Feiglin's view, appealing to the political centre was a mistake, since the only area of expansion was on the right. He argued for the annexation of the entire West Bank and Gaza while encouraging the Palestinians to emigrate through the provision of funds. Even so, he failed to gain a realistic position on the candidates' list in the Likud primaries in December 2014 and left the party.

Another Far Right group, Im Tirzu, which purported to reinvigorate 'Zionist values', directed its energies against the liberal Left in Israel and organisations such as the New Israel Fund and university departments. Ronen Shoval, a former chairman, was reputedly inspired by Johann Gottlieb Fichte, a German romanticist whose writings influenced the emergence of fascism in the twentieth century.[36] Shoval stood for HaBayit Hayehudi in the 2015 election.

There has been a drifting away from a belief in the moral norms of liberal states – a decline in the belief in democracy and an increase in the sense of particularist Jewishness. This has been prevalent in religious circles. Yeshivah students burned *Be-shem ha-tevunah* (In the name of reason: conversations with Rabbi Chaim Amsellem) by Ari Eitan.[37] Amsellem had fallen out with the leaders of Shas and had voiced his criticism of Shas in this book. For example, he called its members 'Sephardo-Lithuanians' because of their tendency to adopt the stringency and culture of the Lithuanian Ashkenazim. The students seemed oblivious of the significance of book burning in the annals of Jewish history.

Netanyahu has been under attack from both those within the Likud and others in Far Right parties. Even though it returned the Likud to government in 2013, the pact with Yisrael Beiteinu was unpopular in Likud circles. This growing criticism of Netanyahu was most prevalent amongst the Likud rank and file. Following his criticism of Netanyahu during Operation Protective Edge in the summer of 2014, Danny Danon was dropped as deputy minister of defence. On a platform of opposing a two-state solution, he was then elected chairman of the Likud central committee.

[35] *Ha'aretz*, 10 December 2014.
[36] *Ha'aretz*, 7 September 2013.
[37] Ari Eitan, *Be-shem ha-tevunah* (Tel Aviv, 2013).

For the New Right the two-state solution has become a pipe dream because the two sides, it is argued, are too far apart. The right-wing alternative is to annex the West Bank and grant Israeli citizenship to the Palestinians as well as the right to vote. Without Gaza, there would be six Jews for every four Arabs. Israel would police Palestinian cities and oversee education. They would be taught Hebrew and asked to take a loyalty oath. There would be a five-year transition period and no right of return for the refugees. Switching to a constituency model rather than proportional representation would henceforth ensure a Jewish majority.

Danon regarded the idea of 'land for peace' as flawed and 'an ideological mistake'.[38] He argued that the current conflict was not simply a question of territorial demands, but also one of cultural difference. Israel could therefore manage the conflict only from a position of strength, and all current talks with the Palestinians should cease. Israel should refuse to transfer tax revenues to the Palestinians until incitement and terrorism cease. Danon regarded the decision of Netanyahu to initiate a ten-month settlement freeze as 'against the DNA of the Likud'.[39]

In 2011 Danon proposed in the Knesset that Israel should annex all territory in the West Bank where Jewish communities reside. He advocated annexing Area C of the West Bank – which is under full Israeli control – while giving Gaza to Egypt and the remainder to Jordan – a three-state solution.

Naftali Bennett also advocated annexing Area C, which contains most Jewish settlers plus 100,000 Palestinians. The remaining Palestinians on 40 percent of the West Bank would receive autonomy. Gideon Sa'ar, a former Likud minister, argued that Israel's eastern border should be the river Jordan. Netanyahu's government spent $360 million on the settlements in 2012. This worked out at approximately $1,000 per settler. While this sum was subtracted from the U.S. loan guarantees to Israel, the Israeli Ministry of Finance did not produce any breakdown of such expenditure.[40]

Yet despite financial inducements, only 5 percent of Israelis live in the settlements. Eighty-five percent of all settlers live in blocs which constitute less than 6 percent of the West Bank. In eighty-nine settlements, there are fewer than 2,000 inhabitants. The number of families that would be

[38] Danny Danon, *Israel: The Will to Prevail* (New York, 2012), p. 57.
[39] Ibid., pp. 53–54.
[40] *Ha'aretz*, 1 July 2014.

called upon to leave their homes in the event of a land swap would be in the region of 30,000.[41]

Avigdor Lieberman revived his ideas of territorial exchange during the 2015 election campaign. He suggested a demilitarised Palestinian state on most of the West Bank, even ceding his own home in the settlement of Nokdim. In exchange for the settlement blocs, Lieberman suggested that regions such as Wadi Ara and the Triangle in the north of Israel and its Israeli Arab citizens become part of the new Palestinian state. He also advocated economic incentives to facilitate the immigration of Israeli Arabs from mixed cities such as Jaffa and Acre to the Palestinian state.[42]

The appointment of right-wing military officers since the late 1990s has indicated the profound changes that have taken place since Weizmann and Sharon entered the political arena in the early 1970s. Since Eli Geva's dissent during the Lebanon War of 1982, there has been an ongoing debate about the limits of public criticism within the IDF.[43] Prior to his appointment as chief of staff of the IDF in 2002, Moshe Ya'alon argued that the political echelon should not be permitted to obstruct the progress of the military to ensure victory in the al-Aqsa Intifada.[44] Like Sharon, he regarded the Intifada as a continuation of the war of 1948.

The election of 2015, however, was caused by Netanyahu's siding with the New Right to develop the recognition of 'Israel as a Jewish state' as an addition to the Basic Law. The delicate balance between the Jewishness of Israel and its democratic nature that had been maintained since the emergence of Zionism, it was argued, was now being upset. Ambiguity and obfuscation had hitherto maintained this precarious balance. Diaspora leaders said that any innovation was unnecessary, while others viewed it as a precondition for preventing negotiations with the Palestinians. The proposal not only aroused the ire of the Left, which complained that the word 'equality' had been deliberately omitted in order to promote the seniority of the Jews, but also provoked the opposition of the traditional Right, which had come of political age under Menahem Begin. The newly elected president, Reuven Rivlin, as well as the Likud veteran Moshe Arens, strongly argued that the rule of law and democratic norms defined the state. Many writers rediscovered Jabotinsky and quoted freely from his writings against Netanyahu's proposals.

---

[41] *Ha'aretz*, 15 October 2012.

[42] *Al-Monitor*, 1 December 2014.

[43] Gershon Hacohen, 'The Officer's Right to Dissent: A Military Perspective', *Jerusalem Quarterly*, no. 43 (Summer 1987), pp. 122–34.

[44] *Yediot Aharanot*, 22 December 2000.

FIGURE 20. Binyamin Netanyahu.
Photo: Avi Ohayon; courtesy of the Israel Government
Press Office, Tel Aviv.

Due to the proposed increase in the electoral threshold to 3.25 percent for the 2015 election, many smaller right-wing parties would not
gain representation in the Knesset. In addition, Shas was split into warring camps following the death of Ovadiah Yosef in 2013, while Avigdor
Lieberman's Yisrael Beiteinu was beset by arrests of senior members and
party officials on corruption charges. Moreover, there was a broad dissatisfaction with Netanyahu, now in his sixties, and a sense that a jaded
Likud had lost its way.

HaBayit Hayehudi therefore became more attractive to many voters.
It became the nucleus for a coalescence of different right-wing groups. It
united traditional religious Zionists, nationalist haredim, the Far Right
and secularists who were unimpressed by the old politics. Together Naftali

Bennett's party and the Likud constituted a bloc of approximately forty seats. This appeared more attractive to a plethora of centrist parties than a prospective alliance of Labour, Tenuah and Meretz, which could muster fewer than thirty seats.

Yet the March 2015 Israeli election confounded the predictions of experienced pollsters that a lacklustre Likud would do badly. There appeared to be a last minute switch of up to ten seats from the Far Right to the Likud. An astonished Netanyahu retained 30 seats while his rivals on the Far Right, Lieberman and Bennett, saw their respective parties reduced to single figure representation in the Knesset. This effectively reversed the political fragmentation of the Right that had commenced after the signing of the Camp David agreement in 1979.

Netanyahu's election-eve address to the US Congress and his open alignment with the Republican party antagonised the Obama White House and brought criticism from even conservative Jewish organisations. His action was perceived as weakening Israel-US relations, alienating the Democratic party and practising the politics of partisanship – especially as three quarters of American Jewish voters were not Republicans. Moreover, the leading Democrat contender for the presidency, Hillary Clinton, had signalled her dismay at the erosion of liberal values in Israel at the Saban Forum in December 2011

Since Netanyahu's taking office in 2009, the West Bank population has grown at twice the rate of Israel's population. On average, $950 was spent in 2014 on each West Bank resident – twice the sum expended on an inhabitant of Tel Aviv.[45] Even so, any resentment was marginalised by a fear for the future. In a period of religious passion in the Islamic world and an ongoing instability in the Arab Middle East, Netanyahu was perceived by Israeli voters as the best and most experienced guarantor of Israel's security in dark times. His fourth administration in 2015 was thus a repeat of past Likud-Far Right coalitions.

If Labour had been viewed as the natural party of government for much of Israel's early history, the Likud had now taken its place during the opening decades of the twenty-first century.

[45] *New York Times*, 13 March 2015.

Bibliography

Ahad Ha'am, *Kol Kitve Ahad Ha-'am* (Jerusalem, 1956).

Ahimeir, Aba, *Yuda'ikah* (Tel Aviv, 1960).

Revolutionary Zionism (Tel Aviv, 1965).

ha-Mishpat (Tel Aviv, 1968).

Moto shel Yosef Katsnelson (Tel Aviv, 1974).

Atlantidah: 'Olam she-shaka': sipurim ve-zikhronot (Tel Aviv, 1996).

Ahimeir, Aba, and Yehudah Margolin, *ha-Shenayim: kovets ma'amarim aktu'aliyim* (Tel Aviv, 1981).

Ahimeir, Yossi, ed., *The Black Prince: Yosef Katznelson and the National Movement in the 1930s* (Tel Aviv, 1983).

Ahimeir, Yossi, and Shmuel Shatzky, *Hinenu sikarikim* (Tel Aviv, 1978).

eds., *Aba Ahimeir veha-tsiyonut ha-mahpekhanit* (Tel Aviv, 2012).

Akzin, Benjamin, *Mi-Riga li-Yerushalayim* (Jerusalem, 1989).

Alfassi, I., ed., *Ha-Irgun ha-Tseva'i ha-Le'umi be-Erets Yisra'el*, vol. 6 (Jerusalem, 2002).

Aran, Gideon, *Kukizm: shorshe Gush Emunim tarbut ha-mitnahalim, te'ologyah Tsiyonit, meshihiyut bi-zemanenu* (Jerusalem, 2013).

Arian, Asher (Alan), ed., *The Elections in Israel, 1969* (Jerusalem, 1972).

The Elections in Israel, 1973 (Jerusalem, 1975).

The Elections in Israel, 1977 (Jerusalem, 1980).

Arian, Asher(Alan), and Michal Shamir, eds., *The Elections in Israel, 1984* (Tel Aviv, 1986).

The Elections in Israel, 1992 (New York, 1995).

The Elections in Israel, 1996 (New York, 1999).

Aronson, Shlomo, *Hitler, the Allies, and the Jews* (Cambridge, 2007).

Avineri, Shlomo, *The Making of Modern Zionism* (London, 1981).

Bader, Yohanan, *ha-Keneset va-ani* (Jerusalem, 1979).

Banai, Ya'akov, *Hayalim Almonim* (Tel Aviv, 1958).

Barzilai, Gad, *Wars, Internal Conflict and Political Order: A Jewish Democracy in the Middle East* (New York, 1996).

Barzilay-Yegar, Dvorah, *Bayit le'umi la-'am ha-Yehudi: ha-musag ba-hashivah uva-'asiyah ha-medinit ha-Britit, 1917–1923* (Jerusalem, 2004).

Begin, Menachem, *White Nights: The Story of a Prisoner in Russia* (London, 1957).
The Revolt (London, 1980).
Mori, Ze'ev Z'abotinski (Jerusalem, 2001).

Beilin, Yossi, *Mehiro shel ihud: Mifleget Ha-'avodah 'ad Milhemet Yom ha-Kipurim* (Tel Aviv, 1985).
The Path to Geneva: The Quest for a Permanent Agreement, 1996–2004 (New York, 2004).

Bela, Moshe, *'Olamo shel Z'abotinski* (Tel Aviv, 1972).

Bellamy, Richard, *Modern Italian Social Theory: Ideology and Politics from Pareto to the Present* (Cambridge, 1987).

Ben-Ami, Shlomo, *Scars of War: Wounds of Peace: The Israeli-Arab Tragedy* (London, 2006).

Ben-Gurion, David, *Anahnu u-shekhenenu* (Tel Aviv, 1931).
Medinat Yisra'el Ha-mehudeshet (Tel Aviv, 1969).

Benjamin, Rodney, and David Cebon, *The Forgotten Zionist: The Life of Solomon (Sioma) Yankelevitch Jacobi* (Jerusalem, 2012).

Bentwich, Norman, *England in Palestine* (London, 1932).
My Seventy Seven Years: An Account of My Life and Times, 1883–1960 (London, 1962).

Ben-Yehuda, Nachman, *Political Assassinations by Jews: A Rhetorical Device for Justice* (New York, 1993).

Ben-Yerucham, Chaim, ed., *Sefer Betar: Korot u-mekorot*, vol. 1, 'From the People' (Tel Aviv, 1964).

Bernstein, Eduard, *Ferdinand Lassalle as a Social Reformer* (London, 1893).

Bilski Ben-Hur, Raphaella, *Every Individual a King* (Washington, DC, 1993).

Bodenheimer, Max, ed., Henriette Hannah Bodenheimer, *Prelude to Israel: The Memoirs of M. I. Bodenheimer* (London, 1963).

Boswell, Alexander Bruce, *Poland and the Poles* (London, 1919).

Bowyer Bell, J., *Terror Out of Zion: The Fight for Israeli Independence* (London, 1996).

Briscoe, Robert (with Alden Hatch), *For the Life of Me* (London, 1958).

Cohen, Eric, Moshe Lissak and Uri Almagor, eds. *Comparative Social Dynamics* (Boulder, CO, 1986).

Croce, Benedetto, *History of Europe in the Nineteenth Century* (London, 1934).

Crossman, Richard, *Palestine Mission: A Personal Record* (London, 1947).
A Nation Reborn (London, 1960).

Dayan, Moshe, *Story of My Life* (New York, 1976).

Dieckhoff, Alain, *The Invention of a Nation: Zionist Thought and the Making of Modern Israel* (London, 2003).

Di Motoli, Paolo, *I mastrini della terra: la destra israeliana dalle origini all'egemonia* (Lecce, 2009).

Don-Yehiya, Eliezer, ed., *Israel and Diaspora Jewry: Ideological and Political Perspectives* (Jerusalem, 1991).

Dubnov, Simon, *Nationalism and History* (New York, 1970).

Dubnov-Erlich, Sophie, *The Life and Work of S. M. Dubnov: Diaspora Nationalism and Jewish History* (Bloomington, IN, 1991).

Elazar, Daniel J., and M. Ben Mollov, *Israel at the Polls, 1999* (London, 2001).

Eliav, Binyamin, ed., Danny Rubinstein, *Zikhronot min ha-yamin* (Tel Aviv, 1990).

Even, Ephraim, *The Schism in the Zionist Movement: Why Jabotinsky Established the New Zionist Organisation* (Jerusalem, 1992).

Evron, Boaz, *Jewish State or Israeli Nation* (Bloomington, IN, 1995).

de Felice, Renzo, *The Jews in Fascist Italy* (New York, 2001).

Filc, Dani, *The Political Right in Israel: Different Faces of Jewish Populism* (London, 2010).

Fishman, Judah L., *The History of the Mizrachi Movement* (New York, 1928).

Frankel, Jonathan, *Prophecy and Politics: Socialism, Nationalism, and the Russian Jews, 1862–1917* (Cambridge, 1982).

Friedman, Saul S., *Pogromchik: The Assassination of Simon Petlura* (New York, 1976).

Galili, Ziva, and Boris Morozov, *Exiled to Palestine: The Emigration of Zionist Convicts from the Soviet Union, 1924–1934* (New York, 2013).

Galnoor, Itzhak, *The Partition of Palestine: Decision Crossroads in the Zionist Movement* (New York, 1995).

Garlicki, Andrej, *Jósef Pilsudski* (Aldershot, 1995).

Ginossar, Yaira, *Lo bi-shevilenu shar ha-saksofon: al shire Ya'ir, Avraham Shtern* (Tel Aviv, 1998).

Glynn, Jennifer, ed., *Helen Bentwich: Tidings from Zion: Letters from Jerusalem, 1919–1931* (London, 2000).

Golani, Motti, *Palestine between Politics and Terror, 1945–1947* (Waltham, MA, 2013).

Goldberg, Giora, *Ben-Gurion against the Knesset* (London, 2003).

Goldstein, Yaacov N., *From Fighters to Soldiers: How the Israeli Defense Forces Began* (Sussex, 1998).

Goren, Ya'akov, *ha-'Imut ha-kove'a: ben tenu'at ha'-avodah la–tenu'ah ha-revizyonistit be-Erets Yisra'el, 1925–1931* (Tel Aviv, 1986).

Gorenberg, Gershon, *The Accidental Empire: Israel and the Birth of the Settlements, 1967–1977* (New York, 2006).

Graetz, Michael, *The Jews in Nineteenth Century France: From the French Revolution to the Alliance Israélite Universelle* (Stanford, CA, 1996).

Graur, Mina, *ha-'Itonut shel ha-tenu'ah ha-revizyonistit ba-shanim, 1925–1948* (Tel Aviv, 2000).

Yeme ha-Ts.ha-r: kronologiyah shel ha-tenu'ah ha-revizyonistit (Tel Aviv, 2013).

Greenberg, Uri Zvi, *Rehovot Ha-nahar* (Jerusalem, 1951).

Sefer ha-kitrug veha-emunah, Collected Works, vol. 3 (Jerusalem, 1991).

Gregor, James, *Young Mussolini and the Intellectual Origins of Fascism* (Berkeley, CA, 1979).

Grosbard, Ofer, *Menahem Begin: deyokano shel manhig: biyografyah* (Tel Aviv, 2006).

Haber, Eitan, *Menachem Begin: The Legend and the Man* (New York, 1978).

Haberer, Erich E., *Jews and Revolution in Nineteenth Century Russia* (Cambridge, 2004).

Halkin, Hillel, *Jabotinsky: A Life* (London, 2014).

Hecht, Ben, *A Child of the Century* (New York, 1954).

Heller, Joseph, *The Stern Gang: Ideology, Politics and Terror, 1940–1949* (London, 1995).

Hetényi, Zsuzsa, *In a Maelstrom: The History of Russian-Jewish Prose, 1860–1940* (Budapest, 2008).

Hurwitz, Harry, *Menachem Begin* (Johannesburg, 1977).

  Begin: His Life, Words and Deeds (Jerusalem, 2004).

Isaac, Rael Jean, *Israel Divided: Ideological Politics in the Jewish State* (Baltimore, 1976).

Jabotinsky, Vladimir, *Feulletons* (St. Petersburg, 1913).

  Introduction to *Chaim Nachman Bialik: Poems from the Hebrew*, ed. L. V. Snowman (London, 1924).

  Pocket Edition of Several Stories – Mostly Reactionary (Paris, 1925).

  The Jewish War Front (London, 1940).

  The Story of the Jewish Legion (New York, 1945).

  Ketavim tsiyoniyim rishonim, Ketavim 8, ed. E. Jabotinsky (Jerusalem, 1949).

  Umah ve-hevrah, Ketavim 9, ed. E. Jabotinsky (Jerusalem, 1949–1950).

  Ba-derekh la-medinah, Ketavim 11, ed. E. Jabotinsky (Jerusalem 1952–1953).

  Felyetonim, Ketavim 13, ed. E. Jabotinsky (Tel Aviv, 1953–1954).

  'Al sifrut ve-omanut, Ketavim 6, ed. Eri Jabotinsky (Jerusalem, 1958).

  Zikhronot ben-dori, Ketavim 15, ed. Eri Jabotinsky (Jerusalem, 1958)

  Reshimot, Ketavim 16, ed. Eri Jabotinsky (Tel Aviv, 1958).

  Mikhtavim, Ketavim 18, ed. Eri Jabotinsky (Jerusalem, 1958).

  Avtobiyografyah: Sipur Yamai, Ketavim 1, ed. E. Jabotinsky (Jerusalem, 1958).

  Shirim, Ketavim 2, ed. E. Jabotinsky (Jerusalem, 1958).

  Ne'umim, 1905–1926, Ketavim 4, ed. Eri Jabotinsky (Jerusalem, 1957–1958).

  Ne'umim, 1927–1940, Ketavim 5, ed. Eri Jabotinsky (Jerusalem, 1958).

  Ba-sa'ar, Ketavim 12, ed. Eri Jabotinsky (Jerusalem, 1959).

  'Ekronot manhim li-ve'ayot ha-sha'ah, ed. Yosef Nedava. (Tel Aviv. 1961).

  Samson (New York, 1966).

  ha-Revizyonizm ha-tsiyoni be-hitgubshuto, ed. Yosef Nedava (Tel Aviv, 1985).

  Igrot, May 1898–July 1914, ed. Daniel Carpi and Moshe Halevi (Jerusalem, 1992).

  Igrot, September 1914–November 1918, ed. Daniel Carpi and Moshe Halevi (Jerusalem, 1995).

  Igrot, December 1918–August 1922, ed. Daniel Carpi and Moshe Halevi (Tel Aviv, 1997).

  Igrot, September 1922–December 1925, ed. Daniel Carpi and Moshe Halevi (Jerusalem, 1998).

  The Political and Social Philosophy of Ze'ev Jabotinsky: Selected Writings, ed. Mordechai Sarig (London, 1999).

  Igrot, January 1926–December 1927, ed. Daniel Carpi and Moshe Halevi (Jerusalem, 2000).

  Igrot, January 1926–Dec Igrot, January 1928–December 1929, ed. Daniel Carpi and Moshe Halevi (Jerusalem, 2002).

Igrot, January 1928–December 1929, ed. Daniel Carpi and Moshe Halevi (Jerusalem, 2002).

Igrot, January 1930–December 1931, ed. Daniel Carpi and Moshe Halevi (Jerusalem, 2004).

The Five, trans. from the Russian by Michael R. Katz (New York, 2005).

Igrot, January 1932–December 1933, ed. Daniel Carpi and Moshe Halevi (Jerusalem, 2006).

Igrot, 1934, ed. Daniel Carpi and Moshe Halevi (Jerusalem, 2007).

Igrot, 1935, ed. Moshe Halevi (Jerusalem, 2009).

Igrot, 1936, ed. Moshe Halevi (Jerusalem, 2011).

Igrot, January 1937–February 1938, ed. Moshe Halevi (Jerusalem, 2013).

Igrot, March 1938–December 1938, ed. Moshe Halevi (Jerusalem, 2014).

Jacobs, Jack, *On Socialism and the Jewish Question after Marx* (New York, 1992).

Karsh, Efraim, ed., *From Rabin to Netanyahu: Israel's Troubled Agenda* (London, 1997).

Katsis, Leonid, ed., *Vladimir (Ze'ev) Zhabotinskii, Polnoe sobranie sochinenii v 9 tomakh*, Kniga 1 (Minsk, 2008).

Vladimir (Ze'ev) Jabotinsky and His Recently Discovered Works: Problems of Attribution and Analysis (Leiden, 2012)

Katz, Shmuel, *Days of Fire* (London, 1968).

Lone Wolf (New York, 1996).

Katznelson, Yosef, *ha-Nasikh ha-shahor: Yosef Katsnelson veha-tenu'ah ha-le'umit bi-shenot ha-sheloshim* (Tel Aviv, 1983).

Kieval, G. R., *Party Politics in Israel and the Occupied Territories* (New Haven, CT, 1983).

King, Charles, *Odessa: Genius and Death in a City of Dreams* (New York, 2011).

Kister, Yosef, *Tagar u-magen: Ze'ev Z'abotinski veha-Etsel* (Tel Aviv, 2004).

Klausner, Joseph, *Menachem Ussishkin* (London, 1944).

Kleiner, Israel, *From Nationalism to Universalism: Vladimir Ze'ev Jabotinsky and the Ukrainian Question* (Toronto, 2000).

Klier, John D., and Shlomo Labroza, eds., *Pogroms: Anti-Jewish Violence in Modern Russian History* (Cambridge, 1992).

Kling, Simcha, *Joseph Klausner* (New York, 1970).

Krassow, Samuel D., *Students, Professors and the State in Tsarist Russia* (California, 1989).

Labriola, Antonio, *Socialism and Philosophy*, trans. Ernest Untermann (Chicago, 1934).

Landau, David, *Arik: The Life of Ariel Sharon* (New York, 2013).

Laqueur, Walter, *History of Zionism* (London, 1972).

Lassalle, Ferdinand, *Franz von Sickingen*, trans. from German by Daniel De Leon (New York, 1904).

Levine, David, *David Raziel: The Man and the Legend* (Tel Aviv, 1991).

Litvinoff, Barnet, and Joseph Heller, Nechama A. Chalom, eds., *The Letters and Papers of Chaim Weizmann, May 1945–July 1947*, Series A, Letters vol. 22 (New Jersey 1979).

Lochery, Neill, *The Israeli Labour Party: In the Shadow of the Likud* (London, 1997).
  The View from the Fence: The Arab-Israeli Conflict from the Present to Its Roots (London, 2005).
Lorch, Netanel, ed., *Major Knesset Debates* (London, 1993).
MacDonald, J. Ramsey, *A Socialist in Palestine* (London, 1922).
Marty, Martin E., and R. Scott Appleby, eds., *Accounting for Fundamentalism*, vol. 4 (Chicago, 1993).
Medding, Peter Y., ed., *Studies in Contemporary Jewry*, vol. 2 (Bloomington, IN, 1986).
Mendes-Flohr, Paul R., and Reinharz, Jehuda, *The Jew in the Modern World: A Documentary History* (London, 1995).
Mendilow, Jonathan, *Ideology, Party Change and Electoral Campaigns in Israel, 1965–2001* (New York, 2003).
Michaelis, Meir, *Mussolini and the Jews* (Oxford, 1978).
Michaelson, Menachem, *Yad Yamino* (Tel Aviv, 2013).
Michels, Roberto, *La sociologia del partito politico nella democrazia moderna* (Turin, 1912).
Morris, Benny, *Israel's Border Wars, 1949–1956* (Oxford, 1993).
  1948: The First Arab-Israeli War (London, 2008).
Namir, Mordechai, *Shlikhut be-Moskva* (Tel Aviv, 1971).
Naor, Arieh, *David Raziel: ha-mefaked ha-rashi shel ha-Irgun ha-Tseva'i ha-Le'umi be-Erets Yisra'el; hayav u-tekufato* (Tel Aviv, 1990).
  Begin ba-shilton: 'edut ishit (Tel Aviv, 1993).
  Le'umiyut liberalit, ed. Ze'ev Jabotinsky (Tel Aviv, 2013).
Nedava, Yosef, ed., *Trotsky and the Jews* (Philadelphia, 1971).
  Abba Achimeir: The Man Who Turned the Tide (Tel Aviv, 1987).
Netanyahu, Ben-Zion, Introduction to Leon Pinsker, *Road to Freedom: Writings and Addresses* (New York, 1944).
Nicosia, Francis R., *Zionism and Anti-Semitism in Nazi Germany* (New York, 2008).
Nimni, Ephraim, ed., *National Cultural Autonomy and Its Cultural Critics* (London, 2005).
Niv, David, *ha-irgun ha-Tsevai' ha-Le'umi: ha-haganah ha-le'umit*, vol. 1, *1931–1937* (Tel Aviv, 1965).
  Ma'arakhot ha-Irgun ha-Tseva'i ha-Le'umi: mi-haganah le-hatkafah 1937–1939, vol. 2 (Tel Aviv, 1965).
  A Short History of the Irgun Zvai Leumi (Jerusalem, 1980).
Ofir, Yehoshua, *Rishonei Etzel, 1931–1940* (Tel Aviv, 2002).
O'Hegarty, P. S., *The Victory of Sinn Fein: How It Won It and How it Used It* (Dublin, 1924).
Pedahzur, Ami, *The Triumph of Israel's Radical Right* (New York, 2012).
Pedahzur, Ami, and Arie Perliger, *Jewish Terrorism in Israel* (New York, 2011).
Penueli, S. Y., and A. Ukhmani, eds., *Anthology of Modern Hebrew Poetry*, vol. 2 (Jerusalem, 1966).
Penslar, Derek J., *Jews and the Military: A History* (Princeton 2013).
Peri, Yoram, *The Assassination of Yitzhak Rabin* (Stanford, CA, 2000).

Generals in the Cabinet Room: How the Military Shapes Israeli Policy (Washington, DC, 2006).

Perlmutter, Amos, *The Life and Times of Menachem Begin* (New York, 1987).

Pilsudski, Jósef, *The Memoirs of a Polish Revolutionary and Soldier* (London, 1933).

Pinto, Vincenzo, *Imparare a sparare* (Milan, 2007).

Polakow-Suransky, Sasha, *The Unspoken Alliance: Israel's Secret Relationship with Apartheid South Africa* (New York, 2010).

Rabinovitch, Itamar, *Waging Peace: Israel and the Arabs, 1948–2003* (Princeton, NJ, 2004).

Rabinowicz, Oscar K., *Vladimir Jabotinsky's Conception of a Nation* (New York, 1946).

Raphaeli-Tsentiper, Arieh, *Be-ma'avak li-ge'ulah: sefer ha-Tsiyonut ha-Rusit mi-mahpekhat 1917 'ad yamenu* (Tel Aviv, 1956).

Ravitsky, Aviezer, *Messianism, Zionism, and Jewish Religious Radicalism* (Chicago, 1996).

Reinharz, Jehuda, *Chaim Weizmann: The Making of a Statesman* (Oxford, 1993).

Renner, Karl, *Der Kampf der österreichischen Nationalen um den Staat* (Vienna, 1902).

Rubinstein, Amnon, *From Herzl to Rabin* (New York, 2000).

Ruppin, Arthur, *Arthur Ruppin: Memoirs, Diaries, Letters, ed.* Alex Bein (London, 1971).

Sachar, Howard M., *History of Israel: From the Rise of Zionism to Our Time* (Oxford, 1977).

Dreamland: Europeans and Jews in the Aftermath of the Great War (New York, 2002).

Sacher, Harry, *Zionism and the Jewish Future* (London, 1916).

Sandler, Shmuel, M. Ben Mollov and Jonathan Rynhold, *Israel at the Polls, 2003* (London, 2005).

Sandler, Shmuel, Manfred Gerstenfeld and Jonathan Rynhold, eds., *Israel at the Polls, 2006* (London 2008).

Schattner, Marius, *Histoire de La Droite Israelienne: De Jabotinsky à Shamir* (Paris, 1991).

Schechtman, Joseph B., *The Jabotinsky Story: Rebel and Statesman – The Early Years, 1880–1923* (New York, 1956).

Fighter and Prophet: The Last Years, 1923–1940 (New York, 1961).

Schechtman, Joseph B., and Yehuda Benari, *History of the Revisionist Movement*, vol. 1 (Tel Aviv, 1970).

Scheib, Israel (Eldad), *Ma'aser Rishon* (Tel Aviv, 1950).

The Jewish Revolution (Jerusalem, 2007).

Schiff, Ze'ev, and Ehud Ya'ari, *Israel's Lebanon War* (New York, 1984).

Schwartz, Solomon M., *The Jews in the Soviet Union* (Syracuse, NY, 1951).

Shamir, Yitzhak, *Summing Up* (London, 1994).

Shapira, Anita, *Land and Power: The Zionist Resort to Force, 1881–1948* (Oxford, 1992).

Shapiro, Yonathan, *The Road to Power: The Herut Party in Israel* (New York, 1991).

Sharett, Moshe, *Yoman Ishi* (Tel Aviv, 1978).

Shavit, Yaacov, *The New Hebrew Nation: A Study in Israeli Heresy and Fantasy* (London, 1987).
   Jabotinsky and the Revisionist Movement 1925–1948 (London 1988).
Sheffer, Gabriel, *Moshe Sharett: Biography of a Political Moderate* (Oxford 1996).
Shilon, Avi, *Menachem Begin: A Life* (London 2012).
   Ben-Gurion: Epilogue (Tel Aviv, 2013).
Shimoni, Gideon, *Jews and Zionism: The South African Experience, 1910–1967* (Cape Town, 1980).
Shindler, Colin, *Ploughshares in Swords? Israelis and Jews in the Shadow of the Intifada* (London, 1991).
   Israel, Likud and the Zionist Dream: Power, Politics and the Zionist Dream from Begin to Netanyahu (London, 1995).
   The Triumph of Military Zionism: Nationalism and the Origins of the Israeli Right (London, 2006).
   Israel and the European Left: Between Solidarity and Delegitimisation (New York, 2012).
   History of Modern Israel (London, 2013 [2008]).
Shmuelevitch, Matityahu, *Be-yamim adumim: zikhronot ish Lehi* (Tel Aviv, 1949).
Shrayer, Maxim D., ed., *An Anthology of Jewish-Russian Literature 1801–1953: Two Centuries of Dual Identity in Prose and Poetry* (New York, 2007).
Sicker, Martin, *Pangs of the Messiah: The Troubled Birth of the Jewish State* (Westport, CT, 2000).
Sofer, Sasson, *Begin: An Anatomy of a Leadership* (Oxford, 1988).
Sombart, Werner, *Die Juden und das Wirtschaftsleben* (Berlin, 1911).
Spengler, Oswald, *The Decline of the West* (Oxford, 1991).
Sprinzak, Ehud, *The Ascendance of Israel's Radical Right* (Oxford, 1991).
   Brother against Brother: Violence and Extremism in Israeli Politics from the Altalena to the Rabin Assassination (New York, 1999).
Stanislawski, Michael, *Zionism and the Fin de Siècle: Cosmopolitanism and Nationalism from Nordau to Jabotinsky* (Berkeley, CA, 2001).
Stauber, Roni, *The Holocaust in Israeli Public Debate in the 1950s* (London, 2006).
Stern, Avraham, *Sefer ha-shirim* (Jerusalem, 1964).
Sternhall, Ze'ev, *Neither Right Nor Left: Fascist Ideology in France* (Princeton, NJ, 1986).
Tabenkin, Yitzhak, *Ne'umim* (Tel Aviv, 1976).
Talmon, J. L., *Israel Among the Nations* (London, 1970).
Temko, Ned, *To Win or Die: A Personal Portrait of Menachem Begin* (New York, 1987).
Tirosh, Yosef, *The Essence of Religious Zionism: An Anthology* (Jerusalem, 1975).
Unna, Moshe, *Separate Ways: In the Religious Parties' Confrontation of Renascent Israel* (Jerusalem, 1987).
Vital, David, *A People Apart: The Jews in Europe, 1789–1939* (Oxford, 1999).
Weinberg, David H., *Between Tradition and Modernity* (New York, 1996).
Weinberg, Robert, *The Revolution of 1905 in Odessa* (Bloomington, IN, 1992).
Weinshal, Yaakov, *ha-Dam asher ba-saf: sipur hayav u-moto shel Ya'ir –Avraham Shtern* (Tel Aviv, 1978).
Weissberg, Alex, *Advocate for the Dead: The Story of Joel Brand* (London, 1958).

Weitz, Yehiam, *Mi-mahteret lohemet le-miflagah pulitit· hakamatah shel tenu'at ha-Herut, 1947–1949* (Jerusalem, 2002).

ha-Tsa'ad ha-rishon le-khes ha-shilton: Tenu'at ha-Herut, 1949–1955 (Jerusalem, 2007).

Weizmann, Chaim, *Trial and Error* (London, 1949).

The Letters and Papers of Chaim Weizmann, Series A Letters, vol. 10, *July 1920–December 1921* (Jerusalem, 1977).

The Letters and Papers of Chaim Weizmann, Series A Letters, vol. 13, *March 1926–July 1929* (Jerusalem).

The Letters and Papers of Chaim Weizmann, Series A Letters, vol. 14, *July 1929–October 1930* (Jerusalem).

Wells, H. G., *Joan and Peter: The Story of an Education* (London, 1918).

Wendehorst, Stephan E. C., *British Jewry, Zionism and the Jewish State, 1936–1956* (Oxford, 2012).

West, Benjamin, *Struggles of a Generation: The Jews Under Soviet Rule* (Tel Aviv, 1959).

Be-derekh li-ge'ulah (Tel Aviv, 1971).

Wetzler, Alfred, *Escape from Hell: The True Story of the Auschwitz Protocol* (Oxford, 2007).

Wyman, David S., *The Abandonment of the Jews: America and the Holocaust, 1941–1945* (New York, 1984).

Wyman, David S., and Rafael Medoff, *A Race against Death: Peter Bergson, America and the Holocaust* (New York, 2002).

Yedlin, Tova, *Maxim Gorky: A Biography* (Westport, CT, 1999).

Zamoyski, Adam, *Holy Madness: Romantics, Patriots and Revolutionaries, 1776–1871* (London, 1999).

Zimmerman, Joshua D., ed., *Jews in Italy under Fascist and Nazi Rule, 1922–1945* (Cambridge, 2009).

Zipperstein, Steven J., *Elusive Prophet: Ahad Ha'am and the Origins of Zionism* (London, 1993).

Zohar, David M., *Political Parties in Israel: The Evolution of Israeli Democracy* (New York, 1974).

Index

Note: An *i* following a page number indicated an illustration; an *n* following a page number indicates a note.